D1478380

A Fence
around
the Empire

A Fence around the Empire

Russian Censorship of Western Ideas
under the Tsars

Marianna Tax Choldin

Duke Press Policy Studies

Duke
University
Press
Durham
1985

© 1985 Duke University Press
All rights reserved
Printed in the United States of America
on acid-free paper
Library of Congress Cataloging in Publication Data
Choldin, Marianna T. (Marianna Tax)
A fence around the empire.
Bibliography: p.
Includes index.
1. Censorship—Soviet Union—History—19th century.
2. Soviet Union—Intellectual life—19th century.
3. Foreign language publications—Censorship—Soviet
Union—History—19th century. 4. Soviet Union—
Civilization—Occidental influences. I. Title.
Z658.S65C36   1985   363.3'1'0947   85-4557
ISBN 0-8223-0625-5

To my family,
especially parents:
Gertrude and Sol Tax,
Hannah Choldin, and
the memory of David Choldin

Contents

Appendixes

Tables and Figures

Acknowledgments

So many people helped me in so many ways as I worked on this book. In the early stages I benefited greatly from the advice and support of Professors Jeffrey Brooks and W. Boyd Rayward of the University of Chicago; Professors F. W. Lancaster, David L. Ransel, Benjamin Uroff, and Dr. Barbara Widenor Maggs of the University of Illinois at Urbana-Champaign; Professor Sidney Monas of the University of Texas; and Mr. David H. Kraus of the Library of Congress. Two colleagues at Illinois deserve special mention: Professor Seymour Sudman of the Survey Research Laboratory worked with me on the statistical aspects of the study; and Professor Jack Stillinger of the Department of English, with whom I share a study, provided an example of diligence and a steady beam of encouragement across the bookcase separating us.

Later I turned to Professors W. Bruce Lincoln of Northern Illinois University, Robert A. Maguire of Columbia University, and Alfred E. Senn of the University of Wisconsin at Madison, who gave most generously of their time and to whom I owe a tremendous debt of gratitude. For help in the final stages of revision, thanks go to Professor Martin Miller of Duke University.

From beginning to end I relied on my mentor, friend, and colleague at the University of Illinois, Professor Maurice Friedberg, without whom this book simply would not have been possible.

My colleagues at the Slavic and East European Library and the Russian and East European Center assisted me in a variety of ways and—perhaps most important—made life run smoothly so I might complete the book. I am particularly grateful to Professor June Pachuta Farris, Ms. Helen Sullivan, and Mr. David Arans of the library and to Professor Ralph T. Fisher, Jr., director of the center; Ms. Dianne Merridith, administrative aide; and Ms. Lynne Curry, Ms. Leanna Gotthard, and Ms. Vicki Miller, typists. Professor Lizabeth Wilson, now on the University of Illinois Library faculty, was a splendid assistant in the early stages of the project.

Professor Edgar H. Lehrman of Washington University kindly brought to my attention the article by Isabel Hapgood reproduced in Appendix 3. Karl Reyman of Radio Free Europe/Radio Liberty directed me to an interesting source, and Professor Mark Kulikowsky of the State University of New York at Oswego bombarded me with valuable bibliographic leads.

As for my family, I shall always be grateful for the patience and good humor exhibited by my husband, Professor Harvey M. Choldin, my greatest adviser and supporter. His common sense has kept me on course. My daughters, Kate and Mary, tolerated in the course of several years—without complaint and with many jokes—a "part-time" mother. My sister, Professor Susan Tax Freeman, has set an example for me by the high quality of her scholarship. To my father, Professor Sol Tax of the University of Chicago, and my mother, Gertrude Tax, I owe a lifetime of thanks. In matters professional and personal they are invaluable to me. My parents-in-law, Hannah and David Choldin, have always been interested in my work; I am only sorry that my father-in-law did not live quite long enough to see this book in print.

Introduction

Since the end of the seventeenth century, when Peter the Great opened his famous "window on the West," Russian rulers have displayed a consistently ambivalent attitude toward things foreign. They covet Western technology and know-how, but are uneasy with Western values and ideas, and because the latter always seem to infiltrate along with the former, the government is confronted constantly with the problem of dealing with those troublesome foreign intruders. Ideas of any kind are elusive, but the government has always taken the position that control of at least their written expression must be attempted nonetheless. Consequently, printed works from abroad always have been controlled at the borders, while domestic works have been examined closely for unwelcome foreign concepts.

The continuity of the Russian attitude is especially striking in the case of foreign publications. Consider, for example, this account by a mid-nineteenth-century traveler to Saint Petersburg: "The inspection of my suitcase resulted in one incident: the discovery of a volume of *Parents pauvres* by Balzac and *Ikarische Flügel* by Carl von Bernard, which lay on top of my underwear and were thus easy to see; the books were immediately confiscated."[1] Compare that with my own recent experience in a Soviet train approaching the same city, an experience shared by countless foreign visitors arriving by train or plane. Shortly after crossing the Finnish-Soviet border a Soviet Customs official inspected my belongings and asked me if I were bringing in any foreign books or magazines (being forewarned, I had nothing controversial with me). The regime has changed but the concern remains the same. It is important to recognize this continuity—the Soviet censorship is rooted deeply in prerevolutionary Russia. An examination of these roots enhances our understanding of current conditions.

This book describes Russia's nineteenth-century censorship operation, particularly the ways in which the imperial government attempted to protect Russians from harmful Western influences, and examines the themes that caused official concern. Both method and substance can be seen most clearly in the treatment of works imported into the empire, the most prevalent type of reading material in Russia until well into the nineteenth century. In dealing with foreign works the authorities were responding directly to ideas expressed by Western writers. Published abroad, these books and articles had in most cases not been written for the Russian reader nor had their authors been forced to submit their manuscripts to the Russian censorship prior to publication, as was the case with domestic publications. Because of this requirement Russian writers practiced—and still practice today—an insidious self-censorship dictated by a sense of what was and was not likely to be tolerated by the government. Foreign authors may well have been responsive to conditions in their own countries, but their works certainly had not been tailored to please the Russian authorities. Thus by examining the Russian response to such material we can see precisely what Western ideas were considered unacceptable for Russian readers.

The Russians, of course, did not invent censorship. It has a long history, stretching back at least to classical antiquity and extending forward to the present time. The British classicist M. I. Finley reminds us that in ancient Greece and Rome it was the spoken, not the written, word that was censored and that "in a society which relies on oral communication, the most effective method of censorship, short of the death penalty, is expulsion from the community. Remove a man physically from his audience and the danger he represents is also removed."[2] There is a parallel here with modern Russia. Writers are great cultural figures in the Soviet Union and the spoken word is still important there. A writer whose works cannot be published is surrounded by gossip and rumor, especially in literary centers such as Moscow and Leningrad. Such writers become troublesome presences and are expelled occasionally and forced to live in exile.

If we take Freud's view, censorship goes beyond any single society or age; it is a fundamental human function, constituting "a selective barrier between the unconscious system on the one hand and the preconscious-conscious one on the other." He first used the word in an 1897 letter and his remarks are uncannily appropriate to this discussion. Attempting to account for the apparently absurd character of certain delusions, he asked his correspondent, "Have you ever seen a foreign newspaper which has passed the Russian censorship at the frontier? Words, whole clauses, and sentences are blacked out so that what is left becomes unintelligible."[3]

Whether or not we think in Freudian terms, it is clear that no society is immune to some form of censorship. To quote from a work on censorship in England, "The relevant question at any stage of human history is not 'Does censorship exist?' but rather, 'Under what sort of censorship do we now live?'"[4] If we use the term in a broad sense, as one writer does, to "describe the processes whereby restrictions are imposed upon the collection, dissemination and exchange of information, opinions, and ideas,"[5] then clearly twentieth-century America has censorship too, albeit in a considerably less ominous form than that found elsewhere. Here is just one appalling example, cited by Erik Barnouw in his penetrating study *The Sponsor: Notes on a Modern Potentate*, which ought to jolt us out of our complacency. Barnouw discusses a 1959 Federal Communications Commission study of television program decision making. A vice president of the advertising agency representing the natural gas industry was interviewed about a *Playhouse* 90 drama dealing with the Nuremberg trials that the industry was sponsoring. "The script came through and this is why we get paid, going through the script. In going through the script, we noticed gas referred to in a half dozen places that had to do with the death chambers. This was just an oversight on somebody's part. We deal with a lot of artistic people in the creative end, and sometimes they do not have the commercial judgment or see things as we are paid to see." The advertising agency took up the matter with CBS and an agreement was reached: the word "gas" would be removed. But at air time the sponsor found the word still mentioned in some places and at the last minute the broadcast engineer deleted it. The interview continued:

Q: The objection with respect to the word "gas," did it come from you originally, or was it on the part of your clients?
A: It came from us. This is our job.
Q: That's part of your job?
A: Darn right.[6]

Returning now to writing: as printing techniques spread from Germany into other countries in the fifteenth century, local governmental and ecclesiastical authorities were quick to realize the dangers inherent in this new invention. Because of their potentially wide dissemination, books have always been subject to censorship even more rigorous than that of manuscripts. A review of censorship activities in several countries shows that official attitudes toward printed matter have been strikingly similar, even if the degree of stringency varied considerably from one country to another and from time to time.

One of the most significant of these attitudes, and the one that interests me the most, is the deep and abiding fear of alien ideas. Every country has taken measures to guard its populace against the penetration of foreign ideas—witness the Russian border checks—but in almost every country the authorities eventually have had to concede the utter futility of those measures. The USSR is a twentieth-century exception to the rule; after the Revolution Russia's nineteenth-century operation was expanded by the Soviets into a far more pervasive and effective system.

The great intellectual and religious movements that shook the foundations of medieval European society spread from their countries of origin and were everywhere viewed with the utmost suspicion by the authorities. Humanism, for example, entered Germany from Italy and Holland in the mid-fifteenth century, introduced by the writings of Erasmus and others. With humanism came the problem of translation. It was considered then to be not only *wrong*, but actually *impossible* to translate certain Latin and Greek religious works into the vernacular German; the meaning simply would be lost. Later, translation would pose the opposite problem—the authorities came to fear that the meaning of dangerous works would be all too clear to readers—but in the early years of printing the technique was seen as divine, God-given for the purpose of enlightening humanity, and tampering with a sacred tool was a serious crime indeed.

Even after printing was secularized this attitude must have remained to enhance the great power and authority that were attached to printed works of all kinds, including pictures, mottoes, insignia, and musical scores. Modern Americans may forget that three and four hundred years ago censorship was far more than a cause for mere annoyance, or even for moral outrage; it was, quite literally, a matter of life and death. People were mutilated and executed in the most horrible ways for mere possession of a banned book. In England, one might be hanged and then drawn and quartered for the crime of writing a seditious book; in France authors were often burned together with their books. The twentieth century has its own equally grim examples: in Stalin's Russia or in Nazi Germany one was almost certain to end up in a camp for the possession of a forbidden book. A memorial at Dachau bears Heinrich Heine's prophetic words:

Das war ein Vorspiel nur, dort wo man Bücher
Verbrennt, verbrennt man auch am Ende Menschen.

"That was but a prelude, where books are burned, there in the end will men be burned too."[7]

The German Reformation was viewed by the governments of France and England as an immense threat and it was over this issue that those countries waged their first censorship battles. Protestant dissidents emigrated to Holland where they published pamphlets to be smuggled back into their native lands. Three hundred years later the Russian government had the same problem with Alexander Herzen and other émigrés. It is not surprising, of course, that governments should be especially unhappy about the publications of their own expatriates. This is a most damaging way to introduce dangerous alien ideas—via the former insider who now can speak freely. He sends his unwelcome message home in the familiar language, easily understood by all.

However, works in foreign languages were threatening too. We must remember that, unlike modern Americans, educated Russians and other Europeans were fluent in languages other than their own. Perhaps only the Russians knew Russian, but nearly every educated European could read at least French and German and sometimes English as well. Of course there were also the languages of the minorities: Polish, Ukrainian, and Yiddish plagued the Russians; Hungarian and Czech troubled the Austrians. This is a perennial problem in the maintaining of empires.

It is worth noting that in the first decades of printing and censorship, the universities were not the bastions of radicalism and freedom of expression they were later to become. On the contrary, the Sorbonne, the University of Cologne, and others were part of the "establishment," charged with maintaining the censorship and given special privileges. The same pattern was followed later in Russia. A distinction was made everywhere between educated people and "the masses." The former might not always be trustworthy but they were at least a known quantity. The masses, on the other hand, were seen as a sleeping beast, docile now but capable of who knew what dreadful acts if roused. As literacy spread the authorities feared that trouble makers both inside and outside the country would use this new vehicle to transmit their poisonous ideas to the common people in language they could understand, in the form of scurrilous and illegally produced pamphlets and periodicals inciting rebellion against the status quo: the rulers, the religion, the established social order.

It happened over and over again. In the sixteenth century Martin Luther and other reformers successfully challenged the Catholic church and encouraged the people to read. At the end of the eighteenth century European royalty looked on in horror as the French monarchy fell, accompanied by "La Marseillaise" and quantities of incendiary pamphlets. Fifty years later, in 1848, revolution shook them all. Schiller's poem "Die Gedanken sind frei" (Ideas Are Free) was heard frequently during that struggle, which ended traditional censorship in Austria and the German states. Russia, observing all this, responded by redoubling her efforts to erect a fence around her empire to keep out alien ideas and by attempting to prevent the internal press from expressing those ideas in popular language to the masses.

Chapter 1 traces the historical development of censorship in Russia and places it in its European context. Although the first laws regarding censorship of foreign publications were enacted just after the French Revolution, it was not until 1828 that a formal system was established. From that year on imported works were handled by the Foreign Censorship Committee which continued its operations, with only minor changes, up until the collapse of the empire in 1917. This committee is a fascinating object of study, not the least because of its remarkable staff. Russia was not the only country to employ brilliant writers as censors—Humboldt and Fichte served Prussia in that capacity, and Goethe was a censor in Weimar—but in the course of the nineteenth century the Foreign Censorship Committee surely had more than its share of great minds, along with some notoriously petty ones. Chapters 2, 3, and 4 discuss the committee and its actions in the context of the men who shaped it, from the ridiculous— the bureaucrat-censor Krasovskii— to the sublime—the poet-censors Tiutchev, Maikov, and Polonskii. Krasovskii, the quintessential civil servant of the Russia of Nicholas I, took his job seriously and devoted his life to the task of protecting his countrymen from corrupting Western influences. The poets, on the other hand, conducted a literary seminar in the committee offices and saw themselves as intellectual men of the world; the committee in their time was an altogether different sort of place.

Chapter 5 raises and addresses a number of questions about imported publications. For instance, what was the range of subjects represented?

Were some categories of publications (e.g., encyclopedias and almanacs) banned? Were works treating particular groups, such as Russians or Jews, singled out? Were some subjects more likely to be banned than others and, for a given subject, did the probability of banning change over time? How were the different types of ban imposed, especially the two main types: banning in entirety and permission with excisions? Did the application of these bans vary from subject to subject, and did the practice change over time? In order to deal with these questions one group of publications — works in the German language — was selected for further study. The last two chapters discuss in some detail the four main themes that concerned the Russian censorship: disrespect toward Russian royalty, opposition to the existing social order, the portrayal of Russians as non-European barbarians, and ideas contrary to religion and morals. These themes and their numerous variations are illustrated by examples of banned German-language publications.

There are several reasons why I have chosen German works to study. German had been an important language in Russia since the reign of Peter the Great; the Academy of Sciences and institutions of higher learning had been established on German models and staffed largely with Germans. As a result there was a good market for German publications in Russia. To deal with the demand, German booksellers had established relations with firms in Riga and Saint Petersburg, and trade was lively in the eighteenth and nineteenth centuries. Many Germans lived in the Baltic provinces of Latvia, Lithuania, and Estonia, and a significant German population had settled in colonies in the Volga region. Newspapers and especially cheap books from the homeland were in great demand. One Volga German wrote that "perhaps one must be rather familiar with the living conditions of Germans in foreign countries in order to appreciate fully the cultural importance of Phillip Reclam's *Universalbibliothek*. Thousands of us — indeed, precisely those whose national identity [Volkstum] is in the greatest danger — owe it to the Reclam volumes that we remained Germans, that the country of Goethe and Hebbel, which they never saw with their own eyes, is their spiritual homeland, and that the German language is the language of their hearts."[8]

However, émigré Germans were by no means the only readers of German works. Russian intellectuals kept in close touch with the currents of German thought. In the second quarter of the nineteenth century they were inspired by the philosophy of idealism as expounded by Schelling, Fichte, and Hegel; by midcentury the achievements of science had resulted in the replacement of idealism by materialism in German philosophy, and the works of men such as Büchner and Feuerbach became popular in Russia. Later the names of Marx and Engels were added to the list. And not only German philosophy was of interest; the censors' reports discussed below reveal a deep and lively interest in German historical and scientific literature. Russian students flocked to Germany to study and, according to historian Richard Pipes, Russians were the largest single group of foreign students in Germany from the 1860s through the 1880s.[9] German writers of belles lettres—those now considered minor figures as well as the literary giants—also found an enthusiastic audience in Russia.

In 1869 over six thousand issues of German newspapers and periodicals—more than in any other foreign language—were received on subscription in Russia. The nearly three hundred titles ranged from the popular (*Modenwelt* and *Criminalbibliothek*) to the scientific and technical (*Annalen der Physik und Chemie, Zeitschrift für das Bauwesen*). A 1908 directory of German book dealers in the Russian Empire lists over 2,540 firms in 64 cities and towns, further testifying to a lively interest in German publications.[10] Finally, the Russian royal family was itself heavily German, from the empresses Anna and Catherine the Great in the eighteenth century to the empress-consorts of the nineteenth century, ending with the last empress, Alexandra, the former Princess Alice of Hesse-Darmstadt.

It is not surprising, then, that the Foreign Censorship Committee devoted a great deal of attention to German works. Indeed, the second part of this book focuses on German publications in Russia, rather than on their French or English counterparts—French works constituted the other large group imported from abroad, while English was represented by only a very small number of publications—precisely because of the special danger posed by German works. By the middle of the nineteenth century French was still the favorite language of Russian high society, the nobility, but German was favored by the new "intelligentsia," especially the *raznochintsy*, a group described by Riasanovsky as consisting of "people of mixed background below the gentry, such as sons of priests who did not follow the calling of their fathers, offspring of petty officials, or individuals from the masses who made their way up through education and effort."[11] French often was associated in the public mind with levity and entertainment, German with non-fiction (theoretical and practical works, pure and applied science, historical scholarship, philosophical and theological treatises). The French wrote novels of adultery, which made for good reading. It was the Germans, however, who expressed themselves in the language of ideas.

This characterization of German literature was widespread in nine-teenth-century Russia; readers were quite familiar with the stereotype in both serious and comic settings, thanks to their own writers. For instance, Bazarov, the nihilist hero of Turgenev's novel *Fathers and Sons*, reads Ludwig Büchner's *Kraft und Stoff* (Force and Matter), which rivaled Dar-win's *The Origin of Species* in popularity; and Simeonov-Pishchik, the absent-minded landowner in Chekhov's play *The Cherry Orchard*, an-nounces in the third act to the student, Trofimov, that "Nietzsche, the philosopher, the greatest, most famous of men, that colossal intellect, says in his works, that it is permissible to forge banknotes." When Trofimov, clearly surprised, asks whether he has read Nietzsche, Pishchik replies, "Well, Dashenka told me . . ."[12] As we shall see, the lessons of Pishchik's antecedents were not lost on the imperial Russian censors. Works express-ing dangerous foreign ideas (including *Das Kapital!*) were permitted occa-sionally by the Russian censorship to appear, presumably on the grounds that few people would read them. But popularizations, by contrast, were viewed as potentially threatening.

The themes identified in these chapters are certainly not unique to German publications. Many of the passages judged "reprehensible"—a favorite word in the lexicon of Russian censors—carried ideas and values that were not just German but were, rather, common to much Western thought. As such they embody characteristics common to all "harmful" foreign literature, whatever the country or language of origin.

When one thinks about censors, one tends to picture a certain type: the petty bureaucrat, the hack, the small mind. But information accumulated in the course of this study has resulted in a radical recasting of that picture. The small minds are still there, to be sure—legions of them—but they have been joined by a fascinating and significant number of intellectuals, and above all artists—among them some giants—whose presence adds new depth to the scene.

Appendix 1 contains a brief discussion of my system of classifying and coding banned and permitted German publications. Unless otherwise indi-cated, all translations into English are my own. Appendix 2 lists as many as possible of the censors who were associated at one time or another with the censorship of foreign publications in prerevolutionary Russia. At least a few Westerners knew about Russian censorship of foreign publications from first-hand experience. Appendix 3 reproduces an article by one such ob-server, Isabel F. Hapgood, the well-known American translator of Russian literature, which eloquently illustrates many of the points made in this book.

Part
One

Guard at the Gates:
The Foreign Censorship Committee

1
Building the Fence:
Russian Censorship
in its
European Context

After the events of 1848, many European governments moved from preliminary to punitive censorship, from administrative to legal measures. It did not happen all at once, but by the end of the nineteenth century the generally overt and heavy-handed Russian style of censorship was dead in most countries of Europe. Russia, on the other hand, followed her own timetable. She began censorship two hundred years later than the others and was not yet exhausted by 1848. She seemed to be always a bit behind the rest of Europe. As Mikhail Zetlin observes about Russia in the 1820s:

> While in the West the romantic era was coming into its own, in Russia Pushkin still read Voltaire's *La Pucelle* and the sentimental poems of Parny. Whereas Paris raved about Chateaubriand and de Maistre, St. Petersburg was only just beginning to discover Adam Smith and Montesquieu. At a time when throughout the Western world people were seeking to adjust themselves to post-Napoleonic reaction, in Russia there was growing up a generation kindred in spirit to that which, a score of years earlier, had made the French Revolution.

Reminiscing about the early 1840s, P. V. Annenkov recalls the passionate interest of his Petersburg circle in the works of the French philosophers Proudhon, Fourier, Louis Blanc, and even the rather obscure Cabet; their ideas, he says, were not to be expressed in Russian writing for another fifteen years.[1] Incidentally, most of the works of these philosophers were banned in Russia in the 1840s; Annenkov and his friends undoubtedly had illegal copies.

Even in 1917 the censorship proved to be curiously immune to the disaster that overtook the tsarist government. Although no longer openly admitted, censorship continues in a considerably more effective form, and even the name of the body controlling literature is familiar: Glavnoe upravlenie po delam pechati (Chief Administration for Press Affairs) became Glavlit. The techniques may be modernized, but the substance remains the same. Looking back, Russia can be viewed as a case of "arrested development" vis-à-vis Europe, locked into the pre-1848 stage of censorship. This is certainly true of foreign publications, still subject to regulations established in 1828 and never substantially changed.

Russia had been well aware of other countries' censorship policies as she formulated her own, and she borrowed and adapted as she saw fit. The 1804 statute, Russia's first, drew on some aspects of a recent Danish statute and rejected others. The Danish law, drafted in a liberal period under King Christian VII and Count Struensee, called for punitive rather than preliminary censorship. The Russians recognized the drawbacks of preliminary censorship but were not prepared, then or at any time later, to really give it up. In the 1860s when they finally did institute some measure of punitive censorship, they could not bring themselves to forego the preliminary variety, so, to the horror of intellectuals, they practiced both.

In questions of censorship Russia was influenced especially by two close neighbors, Prussia and Austria. Bound by strong ties of language and culture and by common borders, these two autocracies of Central Europe and the Russian Empire to the east had an understandable affinity for one another. Despite their many differences, these three had more in common with each other than with parliamentary England or with unstable France, rushing from monarchy to republic to empire and back. In the course of the eighteenth and nineteenth centuries Russia borrowed much from France, including several censorship laws—the regulation of the Russian periodical press in 1865 was based on French laws of 1819 and 1852, and the "Temporary Regulations" of 1865, which changed censorship of domestic publications significantly and ended preliminary censorship of many works, were practically copied from French laws of Louis XVIII and Napoleon III[2]—but it was Austria and Prussia, the steady and autocratic enemies of the French Revolution and allies against Napoleon, that provided models for the Russian government as it worked out the patterns of its censorship operation. The *letter* of some Russian laws, particularly in regard to domestic publications, may have been borrowed from France, but the *spirit*, especially the attitude toward foreign publications, came from Austria and Prussia. A brief glance at censorship in those countries in the eighteenth and first half of the nineteenth centuries puts Russian censorship of foreign publications in its European context.

AUSTRIA

In the early years of Empress Maria Theresa's reign the Austrian censorship was run by Jesuits based at the University of Vienna. It was illegal to publish a work or distribute an imported one without their approval. An individual purchasing a publication had to show it to his priest within four weeks or pay a fine. Denunciations were encouraged; travelers' suitcases were searched for publications, which were confiscated and subsequently burned if found to be banned; censors in plain clothes searched bookstores for illegal works. Then in 1745 the Dutch doctor Gerard van Swieten, a Catholic but strongly anti-Jesuit, came to court and to power and took over the censorship a few years later. A strong supporter of science, van Swieten stopped the banning of medical books (the Jesuits had found the nudity depicted in them objectionable), but in other areas he was an active censor, banning works by Rousseau, Voltaire, Hobbes, Fielding, Boccaccio, Lessing, etc.

A story is told of the scholar Meinhard, a well-known expert in the field of Italian literature, whose volumes of Machiavelli and Rousseau were confiscated as he entered Austria on his way to Italy. Meinhard asked van Swieten to seal the books and return them to him at the border. It was too late, he was told, the books had already been burned. On his journey to Italy Meinhard stopped in Klagenfurt and found there another copy of Machiavelli, an inferior edition but better than nothing. He took it with him to Rome, where his books were confiscated again, this time by Dominicans. The Machiavelli was returned the next day; although it contained objectionable passages, he was a scholar and surely would not misuse his privilege. The censor did advise him, however, to get himself a better edition of Machiavelli, and recommended the very one burned in Austria![3]

Maria Theresa's son, Joseph II, reformed his mother's censorship when he became emperor. It has been said that he did it for business reasons, to support Austria's book trade, and that any benefits to literature were purely coincidental. At any rate he did establish an enlightened system of pre-publication censorship in which a writer could choose even a friend to censor his book. Austria had something rather close to freedom of the press for a few years: a program of reviewing forbidden works was undertaken and many bans were lifted; Protestants in this Catholic empire were given access to their literature; Viennese printers were allowed to print many works without prior review. One great accomplishment of Joseph's reign was the cessation of police searches of private property; this is said to be the only aspect of Joseph's reforms that survived the French Revolution.[4]

Joseph II was succeeded in 1790 by Leopold II, Marie Antoinette's brother. Certainly spurred on by events in France, he worked for stricter censorship during his two-year reign. His son, Francis II, who reigned until 1835, put a new censorship law into effect in 1795 that completely undid Joseph's reforms. One could no longer print anything without prior approval. Hundreds of works that had been allowed to circulate freely under Joseph were banned again. An 1810 edict established four categories to which censored works could be assigned: *admittatur*, unlimited printing and circulation; *transeat*, permitted but not to be advertised (in addition such works might be forbidden for lending libraries); *erga schedam*, permitted with limitations, not to be advertised, available only with permission of the censorship; and *damnatur*, forbidden, available only to specialists and then only with permission.[5] From 1815 until its collapse in 1848 the Austrian censorship was administered along these lines by Count Sedlnitzky and overseen by Prince Metternich.

Emperor Francis feared the liberal movements taking shape in neighboring states after the defeat of Napoleon and instructed his censors to deal firmly with any publications using inflammatory words such as "constitution." Indeed, this word was so upsetting to him that, as the story goes, when his doctor once praised his good constitution, he responded angrily, "Say I have a sound nature, or in God's name a good complexion; there is no such thing as a good constitution! I do not have a constitution, and shall never have one!" On the other hand, Francis did seem at least occasionally to have a sense of humor about his own censorship. He is quoted as saying, "I must go to the theater today. Any time now the censorship might find a hair in the milk and forbid the play and I won't get to see it!" And, more bluntly, "Our censorship is really stupid!"[6]

PRUSSIA

Although Frederick the Great of Prussia had issued a censorship edict in 1749, there was for all practical purposes a free press in that country during his reign. (Between 1716 and 1763 only twenty-six books had been banned, a small fraction of total book production in that period.) Frederick apparently chose to ignore his own law, while his successors chose to enforce that and subsequent laws. In any case, Frederick has a reputation for liberalism with regard to the press. There are dozens of anecdotes about him: how he helped a Hungarian priest to smuggle banned books into Vienna, how he delighted a crowd on a Berlin street by laughing at a caricature of himself, etc.[7] (The only such anecdote that comes to mind about a Russian ruler is that of Nicholas I laughing at Gogol's *Inspector General* and noting that everybody got what he deserved, and he, the tsar, most of all.)

Like Emperors Leopold and Francis in Austria, Frederick the Great's successor, Frederick William II, felt the sting of the French Revolution. A new and strict censorship edict was issued in 1788 that remained valid until 1819. Written by the king and his conservative minister von Wöllner, the edict referred to the decline of *Pressfreiheit* (freedom of the press) into *Pressfrechheit* (insolence of the press).[8] Following Austria's example the Prussians began to use corporal and capital punishment for censorship offenses, something unheard of in Frederick the Great's time. In 1791, in accordance with the Austrian Emperor Leopold's wishes and over the protests of the book trade, the king issued a special order requiring examination of every domestic and imported publication before it could be permitted for sale. Prussia, with a large publishing industry, had always concentrated on the censorship of manuscripts prior to publication. Austria, on the other hand, which had only a small publishing industry (although she was a large producer of reprints), had always emphasized the censorship of imported works. The Prussian king, acutely aware of what had happened in France, now insisted that antireligious books must be kept out of the country, but his ministers joined the book trade in opposition to the plan. The government would have to hire an army of censors, they cautioned, and force the booksellers into bankruptcy if all imported publications were to be examined. The king eventually backed down. (If this argument was made in Austria or Russia, it obviously did not convince either emperor.)

As a result of increased strictness in Prussia several leading journal publishers left Berlin and moved to other German states where the situation was more favorable. The fact that each independent German state had its own censorship policy complicated matters immensely. A dissatisfied author or publisher could simply move a few miles away to another jurisdiction and thumb his nose at his former censors. Those governments with strict policies, such as Austria or Prussia during this period, had a difficult job keeping track of who was where and of exactly what German publications were coming across their borders. Sometimes it was not even necessary for a publication to actually enter the country in order to cause trouble. One enterprising Saxon innkeeper in a village across the border from the Prussian city of Halle kept copies of a popular magazine banned in Prussia; Prussians would cross the Saale River and read them while drinking beer at his establishment.[9]

Metternich wanted uniform policies in Austria and the German states regarding the press and related matters. The assassination by a German student of the playwright August von Kotzebue (who had various Russian connections) provided a reason for calling a conference at Karlsbad in 1819. The resulting Karlsbad Decrees included censorship regulations, although the word "censorship" was not used because some states were against it. The more liberal governments had to reinstate old laws; Austria, of course, already had a more stringent censorship than was called for in the new agreement. The Karlsbad Decrees were meant to be temporary but, as observers of Russian censorship well know, such arrangements have a way of becoming permanent. The decrees remained in force until that fateful March of 1848.

RUSSIA

Let us turn now from censorship in general to the treatment of imported works. The first Russian law regulating foreign publications was enacted in September 1796, the year of Catherine the Great's death. Since the beginning of Catherine's reign there had, of course, been official concern about the availability of "harmful" foreign publications in Russia; for instance, the sale of Rousseau's *Emile* and other forbidden books in the store of the Academy of Sciences itself resulted in a 1763 decree by the empress calling for stricter supervision of booksellers, forbidding them to deal in works "against the law, good morals, Our Person, and the Russian nation which are forbidden in the whole world." It was proposed to the Senate that the academy take on the job of overseeing the censors in port cities and making sure that they know the necessary languages. The academy recommended a broad view regarding foreign publications: an author might criticize the Russian form of government and the Eastern church, even make prejudiced statements about Russia, as long as he was expressing his own true opinions and as long as the work was permitted in other European countries. After all, the government would not wish to restrict the freedom to read all kinds of books.[10]

However, by the end of Catherine's reign such liberal views were no longer possible; the Pugachev Rebellion in her own country and the Revolution in France took care of that. The empress died disillusioned with the French culture and philosophy she had embraced so warmly earlier in her life. The literature of the Enlightenment, about which she had been so enthusiastic, now threatened Russia with revolutionary horrors. Two months before she died, the empress ordered all private printing presses—in any case a relatively recent phenomenon in Russia—to be shut down and established censorship offices in the two capitals (Moscow and Saint Petersburg), in the port cities of Riga and Odessa, and at the Customs office at Radziwill (in Lithuania). There were to be three censors in each office, one for ecclesiastical and two for secular works. No book was to be brought into the country without passing inspection; those judged to be "contrary to the laws of God or the Supreme Power, or corruptive of morals" were to be burned. Periodical publications were to be checked at the post office and judged in the same way.[11]

The following month more details were forthcoming. The censorship offices were to be placed under the authority of the Senate. The ecclesiastical censors were to be selected by the Holy Synod, the secular censors by the Senate, and the academic censors by the Academy of Sciences and Moscow University. (There was as yet no university in Saint Petersburg.) Each group was to present its staff and budgetary needs to the Senate.[12]

The 1796 law, reminiscent of the strict Prussian edict of 1788, was the culmination of some years of concern on the part of the empress and her officials. In light of recent revolutionary activities in France Catherine was dismayed to learn that some of her military officers were maintaining in their quarters a collection of the latest foreign books and newspapers; she had them removed immediately. In 1791 the governor-general of Moscow proposed that a special censor be appointed to deal with foreign works, and that censorship operations, then being handled both by university authorities and the police, be combined. This proved to be too much work for the censors, however, and the idea was abandoned. The Senate too was concerned about censorship and devoted several sessions in 1794 to the preparation of a plan for its reorganization. The anonymous writer of these words probably was expressing sentiments shared not only by his fellow Russians, but by other Europeans as well: "If the government of France had been stricter in its censorship of books, its youth would not have been so wild."[13]

After Catherine's death her son, Paul, became emperor, and continued her censorship policy with increasing vigor until his death in 1801. In February 1797 the first group of secular and academic censors was named, but at the suggestion of the Senate, the cities of Odessa and Radziwill were no longer to have censors. Two special censors were appointed in Riga, however; Mozes Gekil' and Ezekil' Davyd Levi were charged with the examination of Hebrew-language works entering the empire through the port. The hiring of Jews to monitor Hebrew (and, to a much lesser extent Yiddish) publications in those parts of the empire with significant Jewish populations was a practice followed up until 1917; censors with knowledge of Polish, Ukrainian, Baltic and Central Asian languages were also in demand.[14]

Salaries were set for the secular and academic censors: eighteen hundred rubles per year in Saint Petersburg and Riga, one thousand rubles per year in Moscow. (The Holy Synod was to name the ecclesiastical censors and fix their salaries.) It is difficult to judge accurately what these figures meant at the time, but they appear to have been fairly good salaries; a Saint Petersburg censor receiving eighteen hundred rubles annually was earning considerably more money than, for example, a staff surgeon at the imperial hospital, with a salary of one thousand rubles.[15] Salaries in Riga may have been higher than in Moscow because the cost of living was probably higher in Riga at the time. As for Saint Petersburg, everything cost more there because everything had to be imported; the city had no hinterland.

One year later, the emperor decided that there should be an office at Radziwill after all, since this port was to be the only point at which publications were permitted to enter that part of the empire.[16] In May, he assumed a sterner tone: since the present French government was attempting to disseminate its atheistic views to law-abiding, God-fearing countries, it would be necessary for Russia to defend herself by placing censors in all ports to monitor publications arriving on ships. Customs authorities would inform the captains and passengers of all incoming vessels of the Russian laws. The post offices in both capitals and in border towns also would be directed to look at all incoming publications. Any individual receiving a foreign newspaper or other periodical from any source who gave it to another person without first submitting it to the censorship authorities would be liable to punishment under the law. The wrath of the government would fall with particular force on any post office official or censor who allowed French or French-influenced material—or, indeed, any offensive material—to enter the country.[17]

Finding censors qualified to deal with foreign-language publications was no easy proposition. The civil governor of Saint Petersburg complained that he was having difficulties; in Odessa port officials were finally seconded to do the job, and no one at all could be found in Astrakhan. In some cases scholars were pressed into service but they did not always wish to serve. Academician Iakov Dmitrievich Zakharov, a professor of chemistry, declined the appointment despite the high salary offered on the grounds that he did not know anything about literature and had no wish to be a censor.[18]

In June 1799 an office was opened in Vilno and the budgets for the offices in Saint Petersburg, Moscow, Riga, Radziwill, and Vilno were published. In addition to the censors themselves, there were secretaries and readers with a knowledge of foreign languages, librarians, clerks, and watchmen. Secretaries earned 600 rubles annually; librarians, 500 rubles; readers, 400 rubles; clerks, 125 rubles; watchmen, 45 rubles. For the Saint Petersburg office 200 rubles per year were set aside for subscriptions to foreign journals containing information about new works in various languages. Budgets for salaries and other expenses ranged from 3,500 rubles annually in Saint Petersburg and Riga to 1,300 rubles in Moscow.[19]

The censorship offices in various cities exchanged information regarding decisions to ban imported works. In arriving at decisions on specific titles the Russians also took into account actions taken by the Austrian censorship in Vienna; a work banned there was likely to meet the same fate in Russia. They also kept a sharp eye on Prussia, where prior to 1788 the press was not as tightly controlled as it was in neighboring autocracies. In general the Prussians had tried to keep Russia happy; in 1724, for example, the king had ordered a Berlin newspaper publisher not to print anything about the Russian Empire except what the Russian ambassador gave him.[20]

By the end of the century, however, it was no longer possible to keep the Russians happy. Emperor Paul's response to the threat of the French Revolution was even more hysterical than that of other European monarchs: in October 1797 he banned all Berlin newspapers and journals, including the official Prussian gazette, an action that astounded the Prussian government. Apparently even the elaborate censorship structure now in place was deemed inadequate by the emperor because in April 1800 he imposed the strongest ban possible. Henceforth no publications or musical scores at all were to be imported from abroad, a move that was disastrous for the German book trade, since Russia had been a major market.[21]

Fortunately for the future of foreign publications in Russia, Paul died in 1801 and was succeeded by his son, Alexander I, who revoked Paul's latest law. Continuing in the spirit of reform, Alexander abolished the censorship offices and returned the importation of foreign works to its pre-1796 condition, which had been based on the Tariff Act of 1782. Booksellers were required to sign statements that they would not sell publications containing material contrary to divine and secular laws, on pain of severe punishment. The burden of censorship thus was placed on the bookseller himself. The new emperor also signed an agreement with Napoleon in 1801 that neither country would permit its subjects to carry on correspondence "with the internal enemies of the existing government of the two states" with the aim of propagating "principles contrary to their respective constitutions or to incite disorders."[22]

In August 1802 Dorpat (today, Tartu) University was permitted to receive works ordered from abroad or brought in by scholars without the usual delay at the Customs office. Dorpat, of course, was really a German university in a German setting that happened to be part of the Russian Empire, but this kind of special treatment accorded universities and other educational institutions became customary in later years.

There is a great deal of evidence, in official documents as well as memoirs and letters, that a considerable number of "harmful" foreign works made their way into the country despite government efforts to block their entry. Official concern over this state of affairs is reflected in a decree of May 1803, which reminded Moscow booksellers in no uncertain terms that they must not deal in foreign banned publications, openly or secretly.[23] To discourage them from succumbing to temptation, the Moscow military governor was directed to call a meeting of all Moscow booksellers and warn them of the dire consequences of breaking the law. The police were also ordered to increase their vigilance.

Before 1804 censorship had been dealt with, as we have seen, by means of single laws. Now, for the first time, a special statute was devoted to the subject. In his introductory report Count Zavadovskii, the minister of education, assured the emperor that "these measures are in no way intended to restrict freedom to think or write, but are only proper measures against abuse of that freedom."[24] This, the mildest of Russian censorship statutes, also has been considered by some observers to be the best because it is the shortest, consisting of only forty-seven articles. All works intended for the public were to be examined, with the aim of "providing the public with those leading to true enlightenment of the mind and formation of morals and removing those books contrary to that aim" (article 2). Not a single work was to be printed in the Russian Empire, or offered for sale, that had not been examined first by censors (art. 3).

Censorship committees, under the administration of the Ministry of Education, were established at the universities; they were responsible for the printers in their vicinity and for works ordered from abroad for university employees (art. 4). Ecclesiastical works were subject to separate censorship administered by the Holy Synod (art. 8), and foreign periodical publications were to be handled by special censors in the post offices (art. 9). Each committee was to meet regularly to discuss decisions of individual censors; each censor filed a written report on each work examined and was held responsible for the decision to approve a work. However, a recommendation to ban a publication required a committee vote (arts. 12, 13). No work was to be approved that contained anything against "religion, the government, morality, or the personal honor of a citizen." A censor approving such a work was subject to punishment (art. 15).

Article 21 is particularly interesting: "in the case of a doubtful passage having a double meaning, it is better to interpret it in the way most advantageous to the author, than to prosecute him." As we shall see, quite a different attitude was to be expressed in 1826, followed by a shift back in this direction in 1828.

Foreign publications were not given special treatment in this statute; they were to be handled the same way as domestic works by the censorship committees (art. 26). Just as before, booksellers were obliged to sign statements that they would not deal in harmful foreign works. They were also required to give the censorship committee all their catalogs of foreign works for inspection several times each year (art. 27). If a bookseller had any doubts about the propriety of a particular publication, he was to get permission from the committee before selling that item (art. 29). Careful records were to be kept by the secretary of each committee, and there was to be regular communication between committees, especially regarding decisions to ban works (arts. 31–33).

Despite the 1804 statute, unsuitable foreign publications must have been making their way into the empire because in 1811 the Ministry of Police took over the surveillance of bookstores and printers.[25] The police were also to watch for harmful passages in approved publications that might have escaped the attention of the censors. When the Ministry of

Police was liquidated in 1819, censorship was moved to the Ministry of Internal Affairs.

During the Napoleonic Wars, when Russia and Prussia were allies, the censorship administrations of the two countries did not always agree. The Russian censorship approved some fiery literature in German aimed at arousing hatred of the French and a proper fighting spirit in Russian subjects in East Prussia and the Baltic region. By that time, however, the Prussians were more interested in sounding peaceful than warlike. Nonetheless, the Prussian censorship was quite ready to protect the Russian ally from perceived ridicule; a Breslau censor struck two adjectives from a statement to be printed in a newspaper describing Cossacks as riding small ugly horses. The resulting statement—that Cossacks ride horses—could hardly have offended anyone.[26]

Prussian sensitivity to Russian feelings continued in peacetime. In 1816 the Prussian king ordered a newspaper to be shut down for calling the Russians unreliable allies and Alexander I a mystic. A few days after Alexander's death late in 1825, the newspaper *Literarisches Wochenblatt*, published in Leipzig by Brockhaus, won official disfavor by noting that Prussian calendars (presumably the new 1826 editions) were naming Nicholas as his successor, since the older brother, Constantine, had renounced the throne. This fact must have been known in Berlin, but the Prussian government considered it a great indiscretion to publish it before an official announcement had been made. After all, Nicholas was the son-in-law of the Prussian king and relations between the two countries were in some sense a family affair. Sometimes, as is often the case with censorship, sensitivity to things Russian approached paranoia. In 1827 a diligent Berlin censor refused to permit a newspaper to print an announcement of a work on Russian baths. Wait until the book has been examined, he cautioned, so we can see what it is *really* about.[27]

As indicated above, educational institutions in Russia were given preferential treatment, granted special customs privileges and a considerable degree of autonomy. In 1820, for example, new procedures were established for Dorpat University's censorship committee. Publications ordered by the university bookseller for the university were to bypass the usual channels and be sent directly to the university from the customs office. The boxes were to be specially marked and accompanied to the university by customs officials; receipts were to be given, and only then could the boxes be opened. All publications ordered for personal use by university employees had to go through the university censorship committee with the exception of those ordered by the highest ranking professors. Works ordered by the university bookseller for private citizens were to be examined by the regular secular censor, so as not to overburden the university.[28]

This pattern of exceptions to the rule recurs frequently in the course of the century. During the Crimean War the government permitted high-ranking officers to receive foreign publications directly so that they might know what was going on abroad. Two 1862 laws exempting the Riga Polytechnical School and the Saint Petersburg Medical-Surgical Academy from the usual censorship restrictions are typical. Earlier that year two groups of high government officials also were granted permission to receive foreign publications for personal use directly from abroad. In 1871 the Ministry of Education, former headquarters of the censorship, also arranged for foreign publications to bypass the committee, the minister having explained that his staff needed to see this material quickly and could not afford the considerable delay engendered by going through channels. The French ambassador stirred up trouble in the Odessa censorship in 1884 with his complaint to the Ministry of Foreign Affairs that the French consul in Odessa was having difficulties receiving newspapers and magazines from abroad.[29]

In 1826 a remarkable document, nicknamed the "cast-iron statute," superseded the earlier censorship law. As in 1804 nothing specific was stated regarding foreign works. A special committee of the Ministry of Education was given the task of writing a complementary statute for foreign publications but since the 1826 statute itself proved to be unworkable, the committee turned instead to reform, and the document it prepared was incorporated into the new statute of 1828.

Nicholas I had become emperor in 1825 upon the death of his brother, Alexander I. His reign was marked by reaction, from the abortive Decembrist uprising of 1825, the Polish rebellion of the early 1830s, the events of 1848 in Europe, and finally the Crimean War at the end of his life. When he died in 1855, the country had been subjected to more or less steady repression for thirty years. It is not surprising, then, that the "cast-iron statute" should be a product of 1826. Although the "reform" statute of 1828 was not liberal by any means, it seemed so in comparison to its predecessor. Admiral Shishkov, Nicholas's archconservative minister of education, was the chief architect of the 1826 statute. He resigned, angered by the turn of events, and the new censorship law went into effect on 22 April 1828.

The 1826 statute was nearly five times as long as its predecessor.[30] It created a new layer of administration at the top: the Supreme Censorship Committee, consisting of the ministers of education, internal affairs, and foreign affairs. The bureaucracy was enlarged and the amount of paperwork required of every individual was increased greatly. This statute placed much greater responsibility on the censors by itemizing every imaginable crime an author might commit and promising punishment to the poor censor who missed a single one. Here is the 1826 version of the article in the 1804 statute regarding double meanings: "Do not permit passages in works and translations to be printed if they have a double meaning and one of the meanings is contrary to the censorship laws" (art. 151). The censor Glinka once said that if one applied the 1826 statute properly, "It would be possible to interpret 'Our Father who art in heaven' as a Jacobin expression."[31] Publishers too were under new pressure; they retained responsibility for what they had printed even after the censors had given their approval. For the first time authors had to submit to editorial control over their work: not only could censors make minor changes and deletions without the authors' consent, but the authorities might insist on substantive changes in a manuscript in the interest of "purity of language."[32]

Russian censorship, especially during the reign of Nicholas I, is known for its pettiness and absurdity. It should be noted that the situation in Austria and Prussia at this time was no better; every Russian anecdote can be matched by at least one from those countries, and no doubt from many other countries as well. A Russian censor once demanded that the artist who made the statue of Venus depicted in a book add a fig leaf for decency, and had to be told that the artist had been dead for a thousand years. But is this any more ridiculous than permitting the exclamation "Oh, God!" for the Viennese stage but requiring the substitution of "Oh, Heavens!" for the suburbs? In Berlin a poem entitled "An meine Nachbarin" (To my lady neighbor) was banned until the censor was told the identity of the lady in question.[33]

The 1828 legislation that replaced the cast-iron statute was the project of Prince Lieven, Shishkov's successor as minister of education. With regard to the treatment of foreign publications this statute was to remain in effect, with only minor changes, until 1917.[34] The aim of censorship under the new law was to examine all works printed in the empire or imported into the empire in order to determine their position with regard to the Orthodox church and Christianity, autocracy and the imperial house, morals, and the honor of individuals. If found to be harmful in any of these areas, a book was to be banned (arts. 1–3). Censorship was to be administered by the Ministry of Education through the Chief Censorship Administration, consisting of the presidents of the Academy of Sciences and the Academy of Arts, the minister of education, an ecclesiastical member, representatives from the ministry of internal affairs and the emperor's "Third Section" (his special gendarmerie), a member of the Saint Petersburg Educational District, and various other special appointments.

On the next administrative level were the committees for internal and foreign censorship. According to the 1828 statute the job of censoring foreign works was to be performed by the Foreign Censorship Committee, located in Saint Petersburg at the Ministry of Education and consisting of the chairman, six censors (three senior and three junior), a librarian, three assistants to the senior censors, and a secretary (art. 105). In addition to the central committee in the capital, there were to be censors for foreign works attached to the censorship committees in Riga, Vilno, Kiev, and Odessa (art. 104). The Warsaw censorship committee was independent until 1851, when the customs borders between Poland and Russia were abolished; thereafter the Warsaw committee was subject to the Foreign Censorship Committee in Saint Petersburg, capital of the empire. In 1894 the committee's name was finally changed to Central Foreign Censorship Committee to conform with the realities.

This statute calls for greater tolerance toward foreign publications and is thus reminiscent of the 1804 law: "In examining foreign books it is even more important than in the judging of books published in Russia to consider their purpose, the authors' spirit and intentions, rather than to interpret all expressions in the narrow sense" (art. 99). Works on religions other than Russian Orthodoxy were permitted if they were respectful (art. 101); works on philosophy were acceptable as long as they did not contain anything contrary to the general censorship laws (art. 102). Novels had to be examined with special attention to the morals expressed (art. 103). The post office would continue to censor periodicals arriving from abroad (art. 110).

As in the Austrian system described above, the Russian censors were to examine each work and decide whether it should be permitted for distribution in its complete form, banned for general public, banned in entirety, or—going beyond the Austrians—permitted for distribution only after certain passages had been excised—lined, cut out, or pasted over (art. 98). Each censor bore the responsibility for his own decisions to permit publications, with the result that the guilty party was clearly identified if a work subsequently should be found objectionable. A censor had to do more than indicate the general characteristics of a work when recommending that it be banned; he was required to cite specific "reprehensible" passages. In the first half of the century such passages were cited in great quantities. Later on fewer quotations were given and censors referred instead to specific pages to support their decisions.

The ban "for the public" meant that circulation of the publication would be limited to a small circle of people known for their trustworthiness. Such people had to apply to the committee for a work in this category, using a special request form. (The procedure is very similar to the one employed in Soviet libraries, where many publications are obtainable by special permission only. Then, as now, news of newly imported and restricted works apparently circulated quickly.) In the first years after the 1828 statute went into effect, the Chief Censorship Administration and the Ministry of Education apparently were deluged by requests, both written and oral, for banned publications. Predominantly members of the aristocracy and high-ranking government officials, most of these petitioners wanted similar kinds of works: those containing minute details about famous people, both Russians and foreigners, active in politics in the last decade. As for the masses, they were reported to be indifferent to serious works with any kind of true scholarly orientation.[35]

The third type of ban—permission only with the excision of specified passages—could be imposed for all readers or for the public only. The passages were to be cut out or covered with black ink. Variations on these ban types and committee procedures at different times are discussed in some detail in the following chapters.

Thirteen articles of the statute (111–23) are devoted to the procedures for handling material. Instructions are given in the minutest detail: for example, how packages were to be stamped at Customs and brought to the offices of the Foreign Censorship Committee; how the packages were to be opened and checked against the inventory lists in the presence of the bookseller who ordered the publications. Before 1850 booksellers were allowed to unwrap the packages at their stores and were required only to bring the invoices to the office, where they were checked against the committee files for publications previously banned. But in 1850, in order to tighten control, all packages had to be sent from Customs directly to the committee office and unwrapped in the presence of the bookseller, a requirement that forced the committee staff to function as Customs and police officers as well as censors.[36] This practice apparently was maintained up until the Revolution. There were procedures for prepublication

checking of the catalogs of local dealers in foreign publications and procedures for return to the country of origin of banned books (except for one
copy of each to be retained in the committee's library for future reference).

The committee was required to present a monthly report of its activities
to the Chief Censorship Administration, as well as a separate report on
every publication banned (art. 123). The individual or institution ordering
a work subsequently banned was to be notified of the decision so that
arrangements for return could be made (art. 161). Publications banned for
the public were marked as such and given to the person who had requested
them (if approved by the Ministry of Education). That person had to sign a
statement that he or she would not circulate the piece (art. 162).

Booksellers and libraries were not permitted to handle any material not
approved by the committee (art. 179). The proprietors were held personally responsible for any infringements of the law unless a previously approved work subsequently was judged harmful, in which case the bookseller or librarian would not be held responsible (art. 181).

These are the main features of the 1828 statute as it applied to foreign
publications. Censorship was now part of the Ministry of Education, where
it was to remain until 1862, when it was moved to the Ministry of Internal
Affairs. Before 1863 the administrative layer between the ministry and the
committees was the Chief Censorship Administration, from 1865 it was
called the Chief Administration for Press Affairs.

Other official agencies also were involved in the censorship of foreign
material. The church and academic institutions had their own arrangements, and there was also a special postal censorship under the Chief
Postal and Telegraph Administration. This agency was responsible only for
the control of periodicals sent to subscribers through the mail, since all
other foreign publications ordered by institutions, booksellers, or individuals or brought into the country by travelers were sent directly from the
Customs office to the Foreign Censorship Committee or one of its regional
branches. Connected with the postal censorship was a secret operation
known as the "black office" (*chernyi kabinet*), responsible for interception
and reading of domestic and foreign mail.[37]

The Foreign Censorship Committee originally was organized by language into four departments: French, German, English, and Russian-
Polish. However, there were evidently some changes in the committee's
internal organization between 1828 and 1917: in 1870 one large department apparently handled French, English, Italian, Spanish, and Portuguese material, and in the 1880s reference is made simply to the "Anglo-

French department." It is not clear why Russian was in the purview of the Foreign Censorship Committee at all, but the explanation obviously had something to do with émigré Russian publications sent to Russia from abroad. The committee received this material along with other imports and the chairman discussed it in his annual reports, but there are indications that Russian-language works were handed over to the internal censorship committee for review.

As mentioned above, every censor was required to write a report on every work examined—a brief one if he were recommending that the work be permitted, a more detailed report if it were to be banned. As the volume of publications increased, however, procedures were streamlined. Works recommended for permission were reported en masse by each censor at the weekly meeting of the committee. Whereas before the final decision on banning had been left to the Chief Censorship Administration, after 1856 this body no longer wanted to be bothered with routine cases and only problems were referred to the higher level.

Beginning in 1848 the committee was authorized to permit or forbid the translation of foreign works into Russian, thus relieving the internal censorship of that task, but in 1871 the committee was accused of incompetence in this regard and its power was curtailed. The case that got the committee into trouble involved the famous poet Iakov Polonskii, then a censor, who had permitted the book in question for translation into Russian (this incident is discussed in chapter 3).

In 1862, in keeping with the spirit of reform of the late 1850s and early 1860s, many foreign works previously banned were reviewed and permitted. Censorship of imported publications was relaxed again after the 1905 Revolution and the events of 1906, when new regulations essentially freed domestic publications from censorship restrictions. In the last years of the old regime the committee tended to permit foreign works if the Russian translations of those works already had been approved. Censors were also lenient toward those foreign publications that seemed to be less dangerous than other works on the subject, in the same language, currently circulating legally in Russia.

This, then, is the legal structure underlying the censorship of foreign publications in imperial Russia. In the eighteenth and early nineteenth centuries the majority of the books and magazines read in the empire were imported but as the domestic publishing industry developed, Russia became a big producer as well. With the examples of Prussia and Austria clearly visible, Russia established in the 1820s elaborate mechanisms for controlling both domestic and imported literature. In the worst tradition of her two neighbors she insisted on examining each work, Russian or foreign, before permitting it to circulate in the empire. Going one step further than Austria, Russia added a category of censored works—"permitted with excisions"—and proceeded to mutilate books and journals by obliterating or cutting out words, lines, pages, and entire chapters from imported works.

It should be noted that Russia already had a tradition of excision; as early as 1750 foreigners living in Saint Petersburg had been ordered to deliver certain publications in German and other languages to the authorities to have objectionable pages cut out and, apparently, people complied.[38] The Soviets have devised more effective techniques, and excision is for the most part no longer necessary. They simply reprint the offending page to their specifications. Occasionally, however, an item in a published work becomes an embarrassment and the old technique is used again. A case in point from the Stalinist period is the article on Lavrentii Pavlovich Beria, chief of Stalin's secret police, in the second (1949) edition of the *Bol'shaia sovetskaia entsiklopediia* (Large Soviet Encyclopedia). After Stalin's death, when Beria fell from power and was executed, the editors of the *BSE* sent a notice to all subscribers, domestic and foreign, instructing them to remove the offending pages (including the full-page portrait of Beria) and to replace them with pictures of the Bering Sea, the contiguous article. This notice is reproduced and translated in figure 1-1.

In the last years of the empire the Russian government was just as worried about alien ideas entering the country via foreign publications as it had been in the mid-eighteenth century. N. M. Druzhinin relates a sad incident at Oxford in the summer of 1899. He asked a Japanese man how people in Japan obtained works of foreign literature. The man replied with pride that Japan had complete freedom of the press and that there was no difficulty in obtaining anything. The Japanese then asked Druzhinin about Russia: "Alas! I had to tell him how the window to Europe that was opened up by Peter the Great is being obstructed with all kinds of rags to insure that no more light penetrates than is absolutely unavoidable."[39] Intellectuals deplored the situation then, as they do now, and longed for the release of the Russian press from what one of them called "those cruel fetters borrowed from gloomy West European torture chambers." He advocated a more relaxed attitude toward foreign writers on the basis of European experience: "There is no danger that public school pupils and barely literate peasants will start reading Nietzsche, Spencer, and others. These

ПОДПИСЧИКУ
БОЛЬШОЙ СОВЕТСКОЙ ЭНЦИКЛОПЕДИИ

Государственное научное издательство «Большая Советская Энциклопедия» рекомендует изъять из 5 тома БСЭ 21, 22, 23 и 24 страницы, а также портрет, вклеенный между 22 и 23 страницами, взамен которых Вам высылаются страницы с новым текстом.

Ножницами или бритвенным лезвием следует отрезать указанные страницы, сохранив близ корешка поля, к которым приклеить новые страницы.

Государственное научное издательство
«Большая Советская Энциклопедия»

To the Subscriber to the *Bol'shaia sovetskaia entsiklopediia*

The State Scientific Publishing House "Bol'shaia sovetskaia entsiklopediia" recommends that you remove from volume 5 of the *BSE* pages 21, 22, 23 and 24, as well as the portrait inserted between pages 22 and 23, in replacement for which you have been sent pages with a new text.

The designated pages can be cut out with scissors or razor blade, preserving the inner edge, to which the new pages can be attached.

Fig. 1-1. Excision Soviet-style. After Stalin's death the editors sent this notice to all domestic and foreign subscribers of the *Bol'shaia sovetskaia entsiklopediia*.

authors are not known to the masses in Europe, despite their complete availability there. They will not penetrate into our wretched villages either."[40]

However, the Russian government never was able to relax and, indeed, viewed from the top, the experience of neighboring countries had been anything but comforting. The French Revolution and the events of 1848 a half-century later had toppled monarchies and destroyed much of the old order in Europe, including traditional censorship operations. In the course of the next fifty years books and articles containing political and social ideas seen by the Russian authorities as distinctly hostile and threatening had been published in the West. Other states might choose to countenance such publications but they certainly would not be welcome in Russia. Seen from this perspective, it is not at all surprising that the Russians were unwilling to take a chance on Nietzsche and Spencer.

Hindsight proves, of course, that the imperial Russian system failed in its mission; single lines in obscure poems had been banned, but Marx had been considered too abstract to be of danger. Perhaps if the government had taken the advice of moderates, things would have turned out differently. As it was, the fence around the empire proved incapable of keeping out the really dangerous ideas. The Soviets have erected a far more formidable fence but even now there are reasons to question its effectiveness.

2
The Committee and the
Bureaucrat-Censor

The period from 1828 to 1855 is framed neatly by wars, opening with the Russo-Turkish War of 1828–29 and closing with the Crimean War of 1853–56. It also is dotted liberally with rebellion and revolution. In July 1830 the Bourbons were overthrown in France and replaced by the liberal monarchy of Louis Philippe; shortly thereafter, in 1830–31, Poland rebelled against her Russian masters; and in 1848–49 revolutions broke out all over Europe. Russia became involved when, upon the request of the Austrian emperor, the Russian army moved to suppress the Hungarian uprising against Austria. It was this step that earned Russia the nickname of "Europe's gendarme." Russian relations with France were disrupted by the French Revolution of 1848. The uprisings in Germany were viewed by the Russians with horror, as was the abolitionist activity in the United States in the pre–Civil War years. In general, the Russian emperor, Nicholas I, responded to these turbulent events by viewing foreign influence with suspicion.

Censorship, both internal and foreign, was particularly strict during this period, and the years 1848–55 often are called the "censorship's reign of terror." Intellectual productivity during this period was exceptionally high. In literature, looking first at Germany, it encompasses the last years of Johann Goethe's activity (he died in 1832) and all but the first years of Heinrich Heine's career. The writers of the "Junge Deutschland" group, including Karl Gutzkow, Ludolf Wienbarg, and August Hoffmann von Fallersleben, were all active in these years, as were the philosophers Friedrich Schelling and Ludwig Feuerbach, as well as Karl Marx. In France, Pierre Jean de Béranger and Alfred de Musset were writing poetry; Stendhal, George Sand, Honoré de Balzac, Alexandre Dumas, and Victor Hugo were producing their novels and plays. The utopian socialists Claude Saint-Simon and François Fourier and the philosopher Auguste Comte were publishing their works. The English writer Lord Byron was particularly popular at home and abroad, as was the American novelist Harriet Beecher Stowe. However diverse otherwise, these writers have at least one common attribute: all had at least some of their works banned by the Russian censorship during this period.

The Foreign Censorship Committee was chaired by two men during the first four years of its existence—M. M. Demchinskii (1828–29) and Prince P. P. Shirinskii-Shikhmatov (1830–32)—but its story really begins with the chairmanship of Aleksandr Ivanovich Krasovskii, who ruled (a most appropriate word) from 1832 until his death in 1857. Son of the archpriest of the Petropavlovsk cathedral, Krasovskii studied at the *gimnaziia* of the Academy of Sciences. In 1796 he was employed as a translator in the academy offices and from 1800 on was associated with the Imperial Public Library in Saint Petersburg, where he worked first as a librarian and then, starting in 1810, as secretary. In 1821 he was appointed censor and in 1826, under the new statute, he was named a member of the Chief Censorship Committee. In May 1832 Krasovskii became chairman of the Foreign Censorship Committee. During his career on the committee Krasovskii was an active member of the Russian Academy and, from 1841 on, an honorary member of the Second Section of the Academy of Sciences.

The primary source of information about Krasovskii and the functioning of the committee at this time is an article by A. I. Ryzhov, a member of the committee staff. In addition, several articles by Soviet scholars include reports by Krasovskii's censors in Saint Petersburg and their colleagues in other cities in the empire; these reports show how they applied the principles of the 1828 statute in their consideration of foreign works.[1] Precisely how the censors expressed their concerns and justified their decisions can be illustrated with examples of the reports themselves.

Ryzhov's reminiscences of Krasovskii appeared in the journal *Russkaia starina* (Russian antiquity) in 1874,[2] along with excerpts from Krasovskii's remarkable diary. The reminiscences, in the best tradition of the genre, are filled with amusing anecdotes and spitefully witty observations about their subject. Ryzhov clearly despised Krasovskii and took malicious pleasure in exposing him to the world sixteen years after his death. Perhaps another colleague might have given a more positive view of Krasovskii's character, but none is available; indeed, at least one other staff member—M. L. Zlatkovskii, the poet Apollon Maikov's biographer—corroborates Ryzhov's view.[3] Even if one moderates Ryzhov's description, Krasovskii still emerges as an extremely strange character. In his diary he speaks for himself, after all, and what he recorded faithfully every day was the way he spent his time during the few hours away from his work. Apparently he dined and prayed with prominent people and then dreamed about them at night. He kept track of those dreams in his diary, along with the temperature, the atmospheric pressure, the quality of his sleep during the preceding night, and the changing state of his bowels. He is a Gogolian character, an Akakii Akakievich with special touches.

Aside from his potential as subject for a work of fiction, Krasovskii is interesting because he left such a mark on the committee. He appears to have been the perfect bureaucrat in the government of Nicholas I, when, as James Billington observes, "The imperial government committed itself to the difficult reactionary position of simply preventing the questions from being asked."[4] Let us learn what we can from Ryzhov's description of Krasovskii and his committee, bearing in mind the contempt that Ryzhov obviously felt for his chief.

> A. I. Krasovskii was a creation of his times, cut from cloth which, as it seemed to him, was in demand; this was a totally bureaucratic [*kazennyi*] man, as bureaucratic man was understood in those times, and he always tracked his official prey with the most acute scent, which never deceived him. Everything in him was for show; his body and soul in full dress coat; piety, Orthodoxy, human feeling, work—all of the same cut. His blind zeal, meek humility, obsequiousness in the presence of superiors, deliberate hypocrisy—all these served him in good stead in the pursuit of his activities in the Foreign Censorship Committee.[5]

Krasovskii apparently played the role of patriarch in the committee "family," a role made easier by the fact that at least some of his subordinates had living quarters in the same building as the committee offices. He concerned himself with all aspects of their lives: religious observance, sex life, drinking habits, leisure activities (what few were permitted), marriage (frowned upon because it kept a man from concentrating on his work). In short, he attempted to stand in loco parentis to his staff, supervising their physical, moral, and spiritual life. Extreme caution in these matters was apparently characteristic of Krasovskii. When Maikov, who had recently joined the committee, wished to marry in 1852 and requested permission from his new superior, Krasovskii insisted on checking with Maikov's former superior, Baron Korf, head of the Rumiantsev Museum, although, as Zlatkovskii maintains, Krasovskii knew full well that Maikov was indeed a bachelor, already having reviewed Maikov's papers at the time of his appointment. Here Zlatkovskii permits himself some sarcasm: Krasovskii was afraid of having to "answer to God and the emperor for committing an act of grave negligence, on the chance that the clerk who copied the papers might have made an error."[6]

The staff's response to Krasovskii appears to have been appropriately juvenile. For example, Ryzhov tells us that they would go to any lengths to avoid having to converse with Krasovskii. One effective means of holding him off was to exhibit pictures of naked women, plentiful in the office because so many were confiscated from foreign shipments. Krasovskii was so appalled by these "temptations of the devil" that he would leave the room. He always communicated with his subordinates by means of lengthy memos, which served as a source of entertainment for their recipients, who "declaimed" them to one another in Homeric style.[7]

Several of Ryzhov's malicious anecdotes yield valuable information about the committee during the twenty-five years of Krasovskii's chairmanship. For instance, we learn a little about the committee personnel situation from Ryzhov's statement that during Krasovskii's entire term as chairman there were only two vacancies—one due to death, the other to retirement—and that both were filled from above, by the minister of education, because Krasovskii was unable to make up his mind. Regardless of this very low turnover, Krasovskii encouraged people to apply for the job of censor, and Ryzhov says the office had a constant flow of candidates, mostly Germans, each of whom was given a book to censor as a sort of entrance exam. The doors of the committee library were apparently always open to would-be censors, thus perhaps permitting, even encouraging, the reading of dubious works by members of the public.

We learn some details about the handling of banned publications within the committee; apparently employees were able to read such works in their own quarters in the building, although it was against the rules. After inspecting one man's room (a man he also accused of sexual relations with a maid), Krasovskii confronted his subordinate: "On your windowsill I found a book with 'permitted with excisions' written in pencil on the cover. Is it possible that you do not know that by law office employees are not permit-

ted to read any books but completely permitted ones?" Ryzhov reports that
the man replied that he was indeed aware of that rule, assuring Krasovskii
that he did not read the banned works at all, and only read those permitted
with excisions after having first cut out the banned passages. Ryzhov notes
that "this bureaucrat had in his keeping about six thousand books of the
first two categories (banned and permitted with excisions) and it is difficult
to imagine that he did not read them."[8]

While a committee staff member might merely be chastised for possessing banned works in his private quarters, the penalty was considerably
harsher for an ordinary citizen. In a letter to his wife written in June 1858
Fedor Tiutchev, the great poet who was to succeed Krasovskii as chairman
of the committee, told of meeting one "Mr. Pavlov, a very well-known
Moscow literary figure." N. F. Pavlov had been arrested in 1852 at the
request of his wife—he had lost her fortune at cards—and imprisoned.
His situation worsened substantially when "banned publications" were
found in his home; he was accused of "free thought" as well as profligacy
and exiled to the city of Perm.[9]

However, banned publications seem to have been fairly easy to obtain;
one simply had to be careful. E. I. Lamanskii tells of his own experience in
the 1840s. He and his brother kept forbidden publications in their rooms
but removed them when they heard the police might come. A few weeks
after one such search, he reports, his old banned books were back on the
shelves, along with some new ones, and he was again receiving visits from
antiquarian dealers specializing in works banned by the Russian censorship. These antiquarian dealers were a perennial annoyance to the authorities. As we have seen, special legislation to control the trade in banned
publications was enacted as early as 1803. Again in the 1840s, with trouble brewing in Europe, the government worried about its failure to stop the
flow of contraband entering the empire through its border cities. A secret
report in 1845 that the Austrians were watching for books published in
Leipzig and Brussels especially for Russian and Austrian distribution
alerted Russian authorities to this new danger.[10]

As might be expected, Krasovskii considered contraband to be a very
serious problem; Ryzhov gives several examples of his vigilance in this
regard. Once, a shipment of official postal paper was suspected by Krasovskii (and, Ryzhov suggests, possibly by his superiors too) of carrying
incendiary Polish slogans written in invisible ink. No one at the committee
offices knew how to perform the necessary chemical analysis so the paper
was sent to an apothecary (who found nothing). The wrapping paper in

which publications were received also came under suspicion, since it was often newsprint, and newspapers might contain harmful material. That too was to be examined, along with other packing debris brought from the Customs offices; great piles of rubbish apparently accumulated in the committee quarters. Krasovskii also insisted that his people inspect every box for a false bottom. Ryzhov makes it clear that no one bothered with this sort of thing except when the chairman came to inspect.

Article 115 of the 1828 statute specified that publications were to be confiscated from travelers arriving in Russia and that only those permitted by the censors were to be returned to their owners. Ryzhov tells of a young man (who later occupied an important position) who came to the committee office in 1838 to complain because one poem had been cut out of the volume of Byron's collected works that he had brought back from abroad. Krasovskii had the book brought to him and examined it on the spot, whereupon he concluded that the censor had been much too lenient and that the entire book was dangerous. The young man had to leave without his Byron. Another committee procedure is illustrated by the following incident: a new edition of a well-known dictionary had been received and upon examination Krasovskii decided that some of the words were "improper" and had to be cut. The entire edition (many thousands of copies) had to be returned to the foreign publisher for reprinting (although, Ryzhov remarks, the same words appeared in earler editions of the dictionary that were not banned). Procedures for the return of banned publications to their foreign sources are outlined in article 102 of the statute, but the actual reprinting of an edition for the Russian market to conform to censorship decisions is a practice brought to our attention by Ryzhov.[11]

These memoirs also provide a vivid picture of the physical appearance of the committee offices. Of Krasovskii's own section Ryzhov writes that he "burrowed in like a mole among newspapers, lists, catalogs of books, registers, and various other objects of the unskilled bureaucrat. All of this office mess he kept under his own direct control and he wallowed in it as in a swamp. There was no end to the writing and recopying, which reached incredible dimensions. The poor clerks got callouses on their hands from this Sisyphean labor day and night."[12] A very similar picture of the Warsaw committee office later in the century emerges from the memoirs of another censor, Kh. Emmausskii. The senior censor in Warsaw at the time was one State Councillor Fekht, a German who barely spoke Russian after nearly forty years in the emperor's service. Emmausskii, clearly no admirer of his superior, describes Fekht's office thus:

In the first and largest room of the Foreign Section were placed the cupboards with books selected by Fekht in the course of examining booksellers' shipments received from abroad. There was also a special kind of small cupboard with catalogs in which were entered all foreign works which passed through the censorship office with notes: "permitted, permitted with excision of such and such passages, banned." In front of these little cupboards sat Herr Staatsrath himself in an armchair, the stuffing of which had long since disappeared, to be replaced by packs of confiscated foreign newspapers. In the middle of this room was a large table designated for sorting mail, under which lay heaps of some sort of old books which, they say, had already been there for seventeen years and which were completely mildewed and rotted. But the pedantic German would permit no one to touch them, assuring all Committee employees and couriers that someone would come and take these books away. Similarly, he permitted no one to touch the great number of old books and magazines heaped in the cupboards. Appearing in the room at precisely nine o'clock every morning, Fekht first of all carefully examined all the corners and cupboards to satisfy himself that no impertinent hand had touched the rubbish and moldy stuff which had lain around for years and was of no use to absolutely anyone. Having assured himself that everything was in its place and that the thick layer of dust which covered all this trash had not been disturbed, he set about his work, beginning with the sorting of foreign mail.[13]

All the committee censors met weekly, on Wednesdays, to discuss their reports and record the decisions taken. Krasovskii paid close attention to these reports and was rarely willing to permit a work. Fortunately, says Ryzhov, "thanks to the censors and the Chief Censorship Administration, who moderated his indiscriminate [verdict], 'it would be less dangerous to ban,' books still passed through to the public, in spite of him, and against his wishes." Ryzhov observes that Krasovskii was seldom sick and never missed a Wednesday meeting. He never took a vacation and left the city only once, to travel to Tsarskoe Selo, the imperial residence outside Saint Petersburg, to receive a medal. A staff member had to ask permission to be absent from the weekly meeting. Ryzhov tells of a secretary in the 1840s who wanted to miss the meeting to go to Kronstadt (the city's port) to visit his brother, a naval officer. The emperor, he explained, would be present. Krasovskii was enraged: "How dare you ask when you know that the emperor will be in Kronstadt? The emperor will see you and he will say: 'Today is Wednesday, Krasovskii is having a meeting, and the secretary is in Kronstadt.'"[14]

Krasovskii was convinced that foreign literature was dangerous in the extreme; in his florid style he called it a stinking, festering wound emitting malodorousness perditious to the soul.[15] He viewed Paris as "the favorite haunt of the devil," refused to read any foreign literature himself, and tried to persuade others against it as well. Ryzhov accuses him of knowing nothing about the history of foreign literature or current trends, and of ignoring everything going on in Europe. Everyone else on the committee read the foreign newspapers that were received, but Krasovskii read only the official Russian *Severnaia pchela* (Northern bee). A book, concludes Ryzhov, meant nothing to him but a ban decision.

Making allowances for Ryzhov's jaundiced view, it still seems safe to conclude that Krasovskii did indeed lead the committee along very conservative, if not reactionary, paths, and that despite some "liberal" victories, the prevailing attitude toward foreign literature was extremely negative. His policies clearly met with approval from above; Minister of Education Uvarov said that "Krasovskii is like my watchdog; I sleep securely knowing he is there."[16] This is the same Uvarov of whom Sidney Monas writes, "On one occasion, bedeviled by pressures from all sides, he [Uvarov] expressed the wish to one of his assistants that literature might be abolished altogether."[17] But Ryzhov downplays Krasovskii's role, describing him as a dog barking at the wind. It was his subordinates, says Ryzhov, who kept things running smoothly: "They, without the knowledge of their boss, fulfilled the demands of the law with accuracy, and although it was a strict law, it was not absurd, as Krasovskii made it seem."[18]

Who were Krasovskii's subordinates? Appendix 2 contains information on those prerevolutionary censors I have been able to identify. The two most prominent men during this period were the poet Apollon Nikolaevich Maikov (discussed in detail below) and Prince Vasilii Fedorovich Odoevskii (1803–96), a well-known figure in Russian intellectual history. Odoevskii had served earlier on the censorship committee that had been formed under the short-lived 1826 statute. In the 1830s he was associated with the Krasovskii committee as librarian and, occasionally, as a censor. The last scion of one of Russia's ancient families, Odoevskii began his public service in 1826 in the Administration of Foreign Faiths (Vedomstvo inostrannykh ispovedanii) and also edited the journal of the Ministry of Internal Affairs. In 1846 he was named assistant to the director of the

Rumiantsev Museum and when the museum moved to Moscow in 1861 he was named a senator in the Moscow departments of the Senate. His biographer in the *Entsiklopedicheskii slovar'*, the great Russian encyclopedia, calls Odoevskii a profound and sensitive thinker, a talented and original writer who was well informed about the scholarly and social life of his time. His biographer also notes that in 1865 Odoevskii worked for reform of the censorship laws, advising against the absolute ban on "harmful" publications imported into Russia. Observations such as this one show his reservations about the Russian system of censorship: "Most books (except for the great ones, which appear very rarely) are in fact merely thermometers of ideas already present in the society. To smash the thermometer does not mean that one changes the weather, but only that one destroys the means of keeping track of its changes."[19]

The law required that works be judged on the basis of their treatment of the Orthodox church and Christianity, autocracy and the imperial house, morals, and the honor of individuals. Examination of approximately one hundred reports (or fragments of reports) written during this period indicates three main areas of concern, corresponding closely to the categories specified by law: God or country, the existing structure of society, and social mores. It would seem, then, that Ryzhov was correct in his assertion that Krasovskii's censors interpreted the 1828 statute strictly.

Sometimes a single report encompassed all three themes. A volume of *Chansons* by Pierre-Jean de Béranger was recommended for banning in 1831 by censor Dukshinskii because "the satires in the first group, directed against the former government of France and the clergy, contain jibes at autocracy and religion; the songs in the second group are filled with pictures of shamelessness and depravity; and the verses in the third group, partly political and partly erotic, are written in the same reprehensible spirit as the others." The committee decided to ban the book unconditionally on grounds of its "revolutionary, profane, and dissolute character,"[20] thus neatly covering the three main areas of concern in one brief clause.

Expediency and precedent were occasionally the grounds for banning particular works. In an 1840 report on Henri Auguste Barbier's *Nouvelles satires* we find the following statement:

The many passages which are reprehensible and offensive to Russia, for example on pages 14, 16, 19, 25, 61, 98, 113, and the various statements of the revolutionary Polish government and the Paris Committee on pages 205 and 225 require that this satire be banned, and together with it the entire book, because although the second satire would be permissible, it takes up only a few pages and cannot be issued in this form separately from the first.

Censor Rode, in his 1852 report on Heinrich Heine's *Romanzero*, concluded his report by noting that "this book is even banned in many states of Germany, in Prussia, for example, and since we consider it impossible to proceed less strictly, we propose placing the book under an absolute ban here." Gutzkow's *Wally die Zweiflerin* was banned for immorality in 1852. Earlier, in 1836, in connection with a report on another book, the censor had noted that *Wally* was a detestable novel and that many German states had banned it. Another example is Heine's pamphlet *Über den Denunzianten* which, incidentally, had been banned by German censors when it appeared as the introduction to the third volume of *Der Salon*. Censor Grave found several unacceptable passages and the committee, "finding one of these passages reprehensible in regard to the Russian government and the other passage ticklish in terms of censorship, and finding it inconvenient to excise the pages mentioned by the censor from a small pamphlet, and because the work is of slight value, decided to ban it for the public."[21]

AGAINST GOD OR COUNTRY

In most cases, the censors point to specific shortcomings of the works under consideration. Censor Dukshta-Dukkshinskii, in his 1829 review of the Grimm-Diderot correspondence, states unequivocally that religion is of paramount importance. "Can any good be expected from the works of one of atheism's leading figures?" he said of Diderot, "Of the fifty-nine pieces contained in the book, most deal with religion; in the others politics and other less important subjects are discussed." He goes on to say that "the most shameless unbelief, disgusting blasphemy, materialism and enmity towards the monarchical form of government are the characteristic qualities of their works, which are displayed in this correspondence." It should be noted that the Soviets admire Diderot and Béranger for these same qualities.[22]

Even the correspondence of the Russian Empress Catherine II and Voltaire was questioned by the censors when an 1850 edition was reviewed. Minister of Education Prince Shirinskii-Shikhmatov gave this report: "The censor who reviewed this correspondence encountered difficulties in including for publication some portions containing either indiscreet praise of

Voltaire and his works, or jokes and witticisms regarding subjects closely
tied to our religious convictions." The Soviet scholar Aizenshtok comments that "the censor's opinion is particularly piquant because the work
in question is letters of the Russian empress, whose actions and writing, it
would seem, should not be subject to any sort of censorship." In any case
Nicholas I, no great admirer of Catherine II, forbade the publication of
this new edition on the simple grounds that "there is no particular need
for one."[23]

The emphasis on religion emerges repeatedly throughout these years of
the committee's activity. In a report on Ludwig Feuerbach's *Vorlesungen
über das Wesen der Religion* in 1852 the censor characterized the philosopher's teachings as "pantheism and the deification of man." The book was
reexamined in 1908, during a period of relative liberalism when a number
of bans were lifted. But in this case the earlier decision was reconfirmed:
"Despite the considerable length of time during which this book has been
banned, it has not lost one bit of the sharpness of its negative treatment of
religion and the existence of God." Nine years later religion was again the
theme of greatest concern, in censor Sots's review of Theophile Gautier's
novel *Fortunio* (1838): "The descriptions of epicureanism, Sybaritism, and
voluptuousness in this book do not make a harmful impression in the
novel, which is fantastic rather than aimed at offending morals." But, he
says, numerous passages are reprehensible for the blasphemy contained in
them and it is because of these passages that the entire book must be
banned.[24]

Heine also came in for a good deal of criticism in this area. Censor Rode,
in his review of *Romanzero* mentioned earlier, observed that "in this collection of poems Heine . . . expresses atheistic opinions which are not only
capable of insulting a believer, but will even fill with disgust those people
who are in general not particularly concerned about religion." The reports
contain numerous illustrations of Heine's disgust-inducing poetry and
prose. Among the passages to be excised from *Atta Troll* censor Vashkevich
(1847) included a line from the poem *Herodias* in which the poet urges
Herodias to "love me and be my lover, and put down that bloody, stupid
head." The head referred to is that of John the Baptist, which Herodias has
been carrying around with her. Of course, Heine was not the only blasphemous and disgusting writer to shock the authorities. Censor Sots
opposed permitting Theophile Gautier's novel *Une larme du diable* in 1839
"because of its indecent contents and because of the many jokes in the
conversation of the Holy Trinity, of Virgin Mary, of the sainted Magdalen,

Desdemona, Othello, etc." In linking the first three names with the last two, Sots was apparently quite unconscious of his own joke.[25]

In 1834–35 Odoevskii reviewed the first two volumes of a French edition of Heine's collected works, comprising the *Reisebilder*: "Although Heine assures everyone that he is a Christian and devoted to the laws of monarchy, I do not believe it would be proper to allow everyone in Russia to read phrases such as these." Here is one example cited by Odoevskii: "'I am the most polite person in the world, I love carp in butter, and sometimes I believe in the resurrection of the dead.'" He also points out a passage in which "a person introduced into the scene by the author calls a picture of the Virgin 'the prima donna with the baby Jesus.'" But Heine could also be subtle in his antireligious and antimonarchical expressions. In the same report Odoevskii discusses Heine's attitude:

> It is difficult to define the intention of this author—this intention is, in fact, to joke; his irony is not the malicious irony of Voltaire, with its hidden or obvious goal of refuting religion and monarchy, but for all that, Heine jokes about everything in the world, and his jokes extend from the German demogague in ancient dress to the most exalted objects of deity and sacred things. The combination of sacred objects with profane ones and the form of expression lead one to conclude that although his jokes cannot be called strictly harmful, they are still improper to the highest degree.[26]

Apollon Maikov deals with the same problem in his 1853 report on a French translation of Heine's *Götter im Exil*:

> There is nothing in the contents of this book contrary to the censorship statute; it is impossible even to pick out especially reprehensible passages; but nonetheless the book, in my opinion, cannot be permitted because of the extremely subtle irony overflowing onto practically every page. . . . To make clear what type of irony this is, let me indicate one character portrayed by the author, a scholar who has written several works but who has not published any of them because, having taken a position and considered the objections which might be raised, he always concluded by abandoning his former position and embracing the opposite opinion. Thus he wrote a monumental work about the Christian religion and then decided to throw it into the fire, because he convinced himself absolutely of the opposite view, concluding that Christianity brought to the world greater evil than good.

Although the author appears to rise up indignantly against the new convictions of this scholar, he cites only those facts which even more strongly challenge refutation. For this reason I considered it better to recommend to the Committee that the work be banned for the public.

Maikov's concern that the wrong kind of opinion not be expressed is reminiscent of a sarcastic plan for introducing uniformity of thought in Russia that was published (under a pseudonym) by three nineteenth-century authors. Everyone wishes to have opinions of his own; the government should, however, issue instructions indicating which opinions are correct![27]

The historical approach to religion taken by some German historians was deeply disturbing to the Russian censorship. A famous example is David Strauss's *Das Leben Jesu*, of which the censor wrote in 1836 that "the author shakes the Christian faith in its very foundations and demolishes not only its dogmatic aspect, but its historical aspect as well, by uniformly treating everything which is miraculous and difficult to explain as poetic fancy and ornamentation."[28]

Anti-Russian sentiments, whether general or specific, oblique or explicit, also caught the censors' attention. In his correspondence with Zelter, Goethe made some observations about Russia that disturbed censor Grave in 1834:

In vol. IV, on p. 267, there is a discussion of the great flood in St. Petersburg, and Goethe says: "Since that great disaster made clear the unfortunate location of the huge city, I cannot help recalling that situation whenever the barometer begins to fall, especially at night, when a storm rages through my pine trees. When people such as the Venetians settle in a swamp out of necessity, or, like the first Romans, accidentally settle in a poorly chosen place, that is understandable; but to bring of one's free will the greatest calamity on one's citizens, as did the great emperor [Peter the Great]—that is too sad a consequence of the principle of absolute monarchy. An old fisherman, according to legend, warned him, saying that this was no place for a city."

The Committee will have to decide whether these lines should be destroyed.

The committee's decision was that "these expressions of Goethe's, as the private opinions of a foreign writer, cannot make a bad impression on readers in Russia."[29]

Heine had been criticized that same year for various passages in his book *Zur Geschichte der neuen schönen Literatur in Deutschland* (later *Die romantische Schule*). Censor Rode singled out the following passage. Although the main thrust is antimonarchical in general, it is surely significant that the passage deals with a Russian emperor: "Once the French ambassador, while conversing with the Russian Emperor Paul, observed that an important person in his country was interested in something or other; and the emperor interrupted him sternly with the following remarkable words: 'In this country there is no important person except the one with whom I am speaking, and he is important only while I am speaking with him.'"[30]

A more immediate example is Heine's introduction to a book entitled *Kahldorf über den Adel*, in which he writes of his fear of Russia. This passage was cited by censor Rode in the report in which he recommended banning the book:

> Oh! The wolf has clothed himself in the whole wardrobe of the old grandmother and is tearing you up, poor little red riding hoods of freedom! It seems to me while I write this as though the blood of Warsaw were splattering even onto my paper, and as if I could hear the joyous cries of the Berlin officers and diplomats. But are they not exulting too soon? I do not know, but the Russian wolf is so frightening to me and to us all, and I am afraid that we too, the German little red riding hoods, will soon feel the clumsy grandmotherly long arms and big jaws.

In 1843 censor Nagel' examined a book entitled *Reiseskizzen*, the anonymous author of which called himself "H. Heine's Nachfolger." According to the Soviet scholar Fedorov, the author was really Otto Kox, but Nagel' was convinced that Heine was responsible, because of the "Russophobia" exhibited in the book: "The author also uses the slightest excuse to fall with rage upon Russia and her institutions, and often returning to this subject, he feels it his duty, so to speak, to present everything about this country in the most unfavorable light." Honoré de Balzac too is guilty of anti-Russian sentiments; in *Les fantaisies de Claudine* censor Gin'e (1853) notes several unkind jibes at Russia, among which is this one: "On p. 89 he portrays his vaudeville performer . . . being rewarded with the Order of St. Vladimir (second class)."[31]

AGAINST THE EXISTING STRUCTURE OF SOCIETY

Antimonarchical expressions, whether general or specific, were almost certain to result in a decision to ban. Hugues Lammenais's *Parole d'un croyant* was forbidden in 1834 because it was "written in the spirit of manifest hatred for monarchical power and the social institutions arising from it," and Alexandre Dumas's novel *Dix ans plus tard, ou le vicomte de Bragelonne* was criticized and banned in 1850 simply because "the author has Athos and D'Artagnan speak with the king in an insufficiently respectful tone." Writings on particular countries and their rulers were examined with special care. Censor Sots recommended banning a French translation of Heine's *Französische Zustände* in 1833 because, he asserted, in his letters on France Heine "paints a picture of that country in 1831 and 1832 filled with critical and satirical observations on the government, politics, parties . . . in his introduction to the book Heine describes in libelous terms the government and politics of the Austrian emperor and the Prussian king." Hugo's *Napoléon le Petit* outraged censor Dukshta-Dukshinskii, who wrote of it in 1852:

> Filled with hatred for Louis Napoleon for his destruction of the plans of the party of disorder, of which the author confesses himself to be an advocate, Victor Hugo has poured into this booklet all his bile against the president of the French Republic, using for this purpose all his eloquence and the inspiration of poetry. This tract—or rather, this piece of libel [*paskvil'*], in which Hugo presents Louis Napoleon not only as a political criminal and breaker of oaths [*kliatvonarushitel'*], but as the lowest scoundrel and cheater, heaps reproaches on the people who took part in the coup of December 2 and on those participating in the government of France, rouses the people to an uprising, and foretells the fall of the new Nero of France.

Another problem with this book was that Hugo spoke ill of Nicholas I; the book was later permitted with the excision of that passage.[32]

Some works were seen as clear threats to the established order. Auguste Comte's *Système de politique positive* also was banned unconditionally because, in the censor's view, it set forth "the most dangerous sort of utopia, perhaps more to be feared than communism and socialism taken together." Ludolf Wienbarg's *Wanderungen durch den Tierkreis* was roundly denounced in 1849:

> Wienbarg, a fanatical communist, presents in this spiritual-political work the most harmful principles regarding government, society, and

religion. Arming himself against class differences, especially against monarchical power, he demands political equality and freedom, approves of revolution, and encourages "Bund," and in his discussions of religion he expresses the most audacious blasphemy.

George Sand, who was unacceptable to the censors for a number of reasons, shocked them by her attacks on the social and legal structure of society. In 1851 censor Gin'e reported to the Warsaw committee that her novel *Indiana* is "against the institution of marriage, which is in her eyes tyranny, while adultery is a return to the inalienable right of women to freedom. . . . vindication of suicide stands side by side with numerous sophisms and grandiloquent statements against society and the laws which govern it."[33]

In some cases a work might appear harmless, but was in fact deemed dangerous. Despite the misleading title of August Hoffmann von Fallersleben's book *Unpolitische Lieder*, the keen-eyed censor observed in 1841 that "there are plenty of political and even liberal ideas, merely disguised by allegorical expressions or puns." Other works were banned because of the danger they represented, no matter how far removed that danger might be. Louis Saint-Just's *Fragments sur les institutions républicains* was banned "because some of the ideas . . . are contrary to the principles of monarchy and could make a dangerous impression on inexperienced readers." An article in the *Revue de Paris* entitled "De la doctrine politique et religieuse de Saint-Simon" was banned in 1830 because the censor found the aim of Saint-Simon's teaching to be "against the Christian faith and the main foundation of the social order." The danger lay in the possibility that this philosophy might "attract and seduce incautious readers, who could be carried away by the dreams of freedom and equality promised by this teaching." Another similar example is Balzac's *Traité de la vie élégante*, banned by the Chief Censorship Administration in 1853 for its implied criticism of the social order, although the censor, Dukshta-Dukshinskii, did not feel banning was necessary: "In the author's opinion, contemporary society is divided into three classes: the working class, the intellectual class, and the idle class. In the last, under the name of *vie élégante*, he deals with people who have neither the need nor the desire to work, and are concerned with only their toilette and the pleasurable passage of time." The Chief Censorship Administration apparently felt sufficiently uncomfortable with this description of the "idle class" to ban the work.[34]

If the author, while not strongly antiestablishment, were not strongly proestablishment either, the work might be harmful. From her reading of the report on Dumas's *Ange Pitou*, the Soviet scholar Polianskaia concluded that the book was not permitted because "in portraying the events of the revolution the author, while not expressing direct sympathy, did not refute those ideas either, so that a harmful impression could be made on the reader."[35]

Some books were considered dangerous because they were too readily available to the masses. Censor Paleolog banned George Sand's *Le Piccinino* in 1848: "Since this work is a novel intended for a large mass of readers, we propose that it be banned for its spirit of liberalism and for the opinions of the author, which inspire one class of the country to turn against another." Two other novels by Sand were banned for the same reason, both by censor Gin'e in Warsaw. Of *Mauprat* he wrote: "This novel, although one of the best and most interesting novels of George Sand, was just reprinted in an illustrated and cheap edition and cannot, in my opinion, be permitted." And of *Indiana* he wrote in 1851 that "although the censorship has up until now permitted this novel with insignificant cuts, it must not be permitted in one of those cheap editions in which, for the most part, the worst works of foreign literature are published."[36]

In some cases books were permissible in their original language, but not in Russian translation; for example, Balzac's *Scènes de la vie de campagne* was examined by censor Gol'mbladt in 1853 with this result: "The author had in mind the condition of the peasantry in France. . . . he portrays that condition, at least in some parts of France, as being in a state of deep moral decline. . . . the volume can be permitted, but not for translation into Russian." Since only the educated classes, already corrupted, could read French, there was no harm in permitting the original. A similar case is Johann Eckermann's *Gespräche mit Goethe in den letzten Jahren seines Lebens*, 1823–1832 (Conversations with Goethe in the Last Years of His Life, 1823–1832). Censor Dukshinskii examined the book in 1836 and recommended two passages for excision because they were counter to the teachings of Orthodoxy. A third passage, however, dealt with French affairs and could, in the censor's opinion, be permitted. There is a clear implication that if Goethe had written the same words about *Russian* affairs, that passage, too, would have been recommended for excision.[37]

In other cases it was not even deemed necessary to ban books, even though they were clearly counter to the established order. The works of Karl Marx often fell into this category; a French edition of his *Das Elend der Philosophie* was permitted in 1848 because "the subject of the work cannot be applied to Russia and presents rather abstract speculations." An edition of the German original was permitted in 1885 and an American edition in 1889, so this work obviously maintained its reputation as too abstract and "foreign" to be harmful. In 1852 censor Rode reported on Heinrich Dunzer's commentary on Goethe's *Faust*. He recommended certain excisions in the chapter in part two entitled "Mummenschanz," in which Faust and Mephistopheles are at the court of a Roman emperor. The censor recommended permitting the chapter without excisions, even though it contained offensive statements, because "we are obviously dealing with the Roman Empire of the Middle Ages, an empire whose institutions are most unsuitable to serve as an example; therefore, the subject is not governments and rulers in general, but merely one ruler who, having devoted himself to pleasure, fails to fulfill his obligations as head of state." Anyway, he added, the second part of *Faust* was not likely to be read much, and the commentary even less. However, the work ultimately was banned.[38]

Sometimes books were considered "safe" because they were beyond the reach of most readers. Schelling's *Bruno, oder über das göttliche und natürliche Princip der Dinge* (Concerning the Divine and Natural Principle of Things) was recommended for circulation in 1843 for these three reasons: the scholarly language and difficult form of exposition; the fact that Schelling had partially disavowed the teaching contained in this book; and the fact that the teaching cannot be viewed as running clearly counter to Christianity. Despite this argument, however, the Chief Censorship Administration still "deemed it advisable" to ban the book.[39]

An interesting case is Maikov's report on an 1852 German edition of the famous Russian writer Mikhail Lermontov's work, translated into German and with an afterword by Friedrich Bodenstedt. Maikov found this two-volume set problematical for several reasons. In his afterword Bodenstedt expressed hostility toward the Russian government for its persecution and exiling of Lermontov. Bodenstedt also mentioned several Russians by name, and not always to their credit. Finally, the translator accused the Russian censorship of hindering the development of talent in Russia and announced that in his translations he had used some unpublished sources to fill in gaps, caused by censorship, in the published Russian text. Maikov identified those gaps for the committee and proposed, albeit reluctantly, that the corresponding passages in the translation be excised. In justifying this recommendation he remarked that it might seem strange for a Russian author to be banned in his native language but permitted in translation. As for Lermontov's exile, Maikov noted that the decision to send the poet to

the Caucasus because of his verses on Pushkin's death had been taken by
the "highest authority." Bodenstedt's comments on Lermontov's mistreat-
ment were thus a criticism of that authority and as such could not be
countenanced.

The committee referred this delicate case to the next higher level, the
Chief Censorship Administration, which decided to ban the entire translation for the public.[40] Maikov, aware of Western attitudes as well as his
obligations as a censor, urged the greatest possible leniency, so as not to
earn the contempt of the translator, and of foreigners in general, by banning this work. The Krasovskii committee and its superiors were not
sympathetic to such arguments, however; Maikov was to fare better under
his next chairman, Fedor Tiutchev.

AGAINST SOCIAL MORES

Not surprisingly, perhaps, French writers appear to be the most frequent offenders against decency. Of Balzac's *La Cousine Bette* censor Nagel'
wrote in 1849:

> It would take too long to itemize here all the abominations contained
> in this book, and we shall limit ourselves to the statement that the
> tenor of the book is deeply immoral: depravity and voluptuousness
> are presented from the most attractive and dangerous angle. To enu-
> merate the passages confirming this conclusion would be superfluous
> and embarrassing, since the novel is overcrowded with perverted
> scenes.

In 1857 Maikov hesitated to permit Flaubert's *Madame Bovary* for translation into Russian because "it portrays the amorous intrigues of a married
woman who abandons herself to love with all the lack of restraint of a de-
praved imagination." Not all cases were clear cut, however; there are several
examples of dissension within the censorship establishment itself. Censor
Sots had proposed banning Balzac's *La Peau de chagrin* in 1831 for the public because the philosophy of the novel was very favorable toward people
"who are concerned only about present pleasure." He found the work to
have "quite a dangerous spirit" as well as "wicked and indecent expressions
and thoughts." But A. N. Olenin, a member of the Chief Censorship Administration, disagreed and protested, writing that there was "nothing revolutionary, atheistic, or too forbidden [*skoromnoe*]" in the novel. The decision
was reversed at the committee's next meeting and the work was permitted.[41]

The censors paid particular attention to the moral lesson inherent in novels. De Musset's novel *La confession d'un enfant du siècle* was banned by the Chief Censorship Administration in 1836 because

> the main subject of the novel . . . is the description of the vile and disgusting life of the hero; the advice and opinions of a skeptic and epicurean which lead to the suppression in the hero of shame and conscience are offered not only without refutation, but without any indication of the harmful consequences of a depraved life. . . . crime or vice remain unpunished.

In his 1853 report on *Rolla* censor Gin'e in Warsaw accused de Musset of portraying decadence and immorality as pitiable rather than reprehensible:

> The poem *Rolla* is not only immoral, in that it attempts to make interesting characters and angels out of two people wallowing in depravity, but it is also imbued with skepticism and anti-religious feeling, portrays Christianity as something dead, and the world as bereft of a guiding religion and the hope of a new Messiah.

Eugène Sue's *La Salamandre* had been banned in 1832 because of "the basic idea of the novel, that vice prospers much more frequently in life than does virtue." But Stendhal's *Le rouge et le noir* was permitted in 1881, albeit with excisions, because Stendhal at least indicated that crime may not pay:

> In making his hero a cold-blooded villain and criminal, under the pretence that the advantages of the upper class and its intrigues did not offer another path to the attainment of excellence by personal merit, he is teaching, of course, a thoroughly false lesson. On the other hand, the method of Julien's death weakens the unpleasant impression produced by his deeds.[42]

If, on the other hand, the work was for some reason sufficiently obscure, even a degree of obscenity might be tolerated. In 1832 censor Sots permitted Balzac's *Contes drolatiques* because, he wrote, "These stories are written in an old-fashioned dialect and for this reason probably will not make a harmful impression on readers."[43] This is similar to the literary custom (common in the English-speaking world in the nineteenth century) of using "dirty" words in Latin, which somehow makes them respectable and puts a distance between the reader and the word.

These, then were the chief danger signals—red flags, as it were—

perceived by the censors of foreign publications during the reign of Nicholas I. They appear to reflect quite accurately the principles laid down in the censorship statutes of 1828. The tone is generally conservative, as one might expect from servants of this particular emperor. It was Fedor Tiutchev who in the first two decades of the reign of Alexander II was to let some fresh air into the stuffy offices of the Foreign Censorship Committee.

3
The Committee
and the Poet-Censors:
The Tiutchev Years

With the appointment of Tiutchev as chairman in April 1858, the committee moved into a new phase. Although a few educated and talented men such as Odoevskii and Maikov had served under Krasovskii, their influence had been negligible. However, with the advent of Tiutchev the atmosphere changed. In 1860 another poet, Iakov Petrovich Polonskii, joined the committee as secretary, becoming a junior censor in 1863. This triumvirate of Tiutchev, Maikov, and Polonskii transformed a paper-pushing operation into a literary establishment, and the friendship that grew out of their association affected the creative work of all three men for the remainder of their careers.

Until the late 1860s, when the liberalism of Alexander II had waned, Tiutchev was able to moderate to some extent the severity of the censorship of foreign publications. By the time of Tiutchev's death in 1873, however, reaction had set in and there was once again strong governmental pressure to place greater restrictions on foreign literature. The next chairman of the committee was another intellectual, Prince P. P. Viazemskii, who presided until April 1881, when he became head of the Chief Administration for Press Affairs. Son of Prince P. A. Viazemskii, the poet and friend of Pushkin, Pavel Petrovich Viazemskii came to the committee with several years of experience as an administrator in various ministries. His scholarly interests lay in the areas of history, literature, and paleography, in which fields he published extensively; at Viazemskii's initiative the Society of Friends of Old Literature (Obshchestvo liubitelei drevnei pis'mennosti) was founded in 1877. Viazemskii was succeeded in 1882 by Maikov (by this time a veteran censor of thirty years), who remained chairman until his death in 1897. The last chairman of the committee was Count Aleksandr Nikolaevich Murav'ev, who presided from 1897 until 1917.

There is little published information on either Viazemskii's or Maikov's chairmanship but fortunately the Tiutchev years are well documented. A number of reports by Maikov and Polonskii on individual books are also available and these, together with some other primary and secondary material, provide valuable, if sparse, evidence of the role played by these two men on the committee.

In general, the areas of concern expressed in the approximately 150 censors' reports examined for the second half of the nineteenth century are quite similar to those of the Krasovskii period.[1] The law, after all, remained unchanged, despite some attempts to modify it, and the Chief Censorship Administration, to which the committee reported, still expected foreign literature to be subjected to rigorous review. An examination of a few reports from this period will reveal some subtle shifts in style and emphasis, to be sure, but considering the steadily worsening political situation, one could hardly expect the official attitude toward foreign literature to be a liberal one. The attempted assassination of Alexander II by Karakozov in 1866 may have been an isolated incident, but from the mid-1870s on terrorism had become a constant threat, culminating in the assassination of the emperor himself in 1881. Foreign literature, often supportive of the violent overthrow of monarchies, was viewed by the government with the utmost suspicion. Books and articles—especially French—dealing with the Paris Commune of 1870–71 were seen as a threat to the Russian way of life, as were German socialist writings and German and English scholarly and popular works on the natural sciences and philosophy. Anti-Russian sentiments in West European literature became more prevalent as Russia grew increasingly isolated and as her internal policies grew more repressive. Not until the Revolution of 1905 would there be a suspension of domestic censorship restrictions and a degree of relaxation regarding foreign publications.

When he came to the Foreign Censorship Committee as chairman, Tiutchev already had accumulated ten years of experience as a senior censor in the Ministry of Foreign Affairs, where he was responsible for examining newspaper articles dealing with external politics. He was known there as a liberal censor; one editor noted in his memoirs that Tiutchev passed everything sent to him for approval. Due to his important connections . . . he permitted much more than an ordinary official of the Ministry. Editors did not know if Tiutchev was reproved for his censorship liberalism because he never appeared at the editorial offices with reproaches that he had been "done in." This was an extremely unusual personality.[2]

On at least one occasion Tiutchev complained bitterly about his colleagues at the ministry, writing to his wife:

> The other day I had some unpleasantness at the Ministry, again because of this wretched censorship. It certainly was not anything very important. . . . On the ruins of the world which will collapse under the weight of their stupidity, they are fatally damned to live and die in the ultimate obduracy of their idiocy. What a breed, heavens! Well, to be completely sincere, I must admit that this unspeakable, this immeasurable mediocrity does not dismay me, in the interest of the cause, as much it might reasonably be expected to do. But when one sees to what degree these people are bereft of any ideas and of any intelligence, and as a result, also of any initiative, it is impossible to attribute to them the least bit of participation in anything, and to see them as anything but passive wheels moved by an invisible hand.[3]

Tiutchev's association with the Ministry of Foreign Affairs actually dates back to 1823 when, as a young man of twenty, he had been sent to Munich with the Russian diplomatic mission. He spent much of his life abroad, especially in Germany (both his wives were German), and was as much at home in German and French as in Russian. His intellectual development was influenced by his close associations with German scholarly and literary figures such as Schelling and Heine. His relationship with the latter is particularly interesting, both from a literary point of view and in terms of censorship, since much of Heine's work came up for review during Tiutchev's term as chairman of the committee.[4] Tiutchev's involvement with the diplomatic service, which he maintained throughout his career in the censorship, kept him politically aware of Russia's relations with Western Europe. At the dawn of a liberal era, with reforms just around the corner, Tiutchev seemed an ideal choice to replace the rigid and insular Krasovskii.

In November 1857 Tiutchev wrote a letter to his superior, Prince

Gorchakov, then minister of foreign affairs, on the subject of censorship. The letter was apparently in response to a proposal under consideration by the government—eventually abandoned—to publish a journal that would counteract the influence of Alexander Herzen's *Bell* (*Kolokol*), published in London beginning in 1857 and smuggled into Russia. Tiutchev's response to this proposal was that such a journal could succeed only if those involved with it could be assured "that they are participating not in a work of the police, but in a work of conscience; and that is why they would believe themselves right to demand the full measure of liberty a really serious and effective discussion implies and necessitates." This is the message of the entire letter: that a society's intellectual life is vital to its survival, and that the intellect can only remain healthy in a state of freedom.

> If there is one truth, among many, which has emerged perfectly plainly from the harsh experience of recent years, it is surely this: it has been sternly proven to us that a restraint, a too absolute, too prolonged repression cannot be imposed on intellects without resulting in serious damage to the whole social organism.

He uses the example of Germany before and after the Revolution of 1848 to show that the government itself can serve as that guide by, in effect, co-opting the opposition. It is essential, he says, that "the authority itself be sufficiently convinced of its own ideas, sufficiently imbued with its own convictions to feel the need to spread their influence abroad, and to make it penetrate, like an element of regeneration, like a new life, into the depths of the national consciousness." If the government is unwilling or unable to collaborate with what he calls the country's "énergies morales et intellectuelles," then the government will be impotent. "For it is necessary to insist for the thousandth time on a fact whose obviousness is as evident as the following: in our days, whenever there is not a sufficient measure of freedom of discussion nothing is possible, but absolutely nothing, morally and intellectually speaking." As for the censorship, Tiutchev dismisses it as essentially inconsequential: "I have not even any marked animus against the censorship, even though it has latterly weighed on Russia like a real public calamity. While admitting its expediency and its relative usefulness, my principal complaint against it is that it is, so far as I can see, profoundly inadequate at the present moment to our true needs and our true interests." At the heart of the matter is the question of the government's attitude toward the press: "It is, when all is said, in the greater or lesser legitimacy it accords to the right of individual thought."[5]

Almost certainly as a result of this letter Tiutchev was appointed chairman of the Foreign Censorship Committee, at an annual salary of 1,193 rubles and 68 kopeks.[6] He also continued to draw a salary from the Ministry of Foreign Affairs. According to an unpublished study by W. Bruce Lincoln, "an income of approximately 1,400 rubles a year . . . seems to have been sufficient for an unmarried *chinovnik* (official) to live comfortably in St. Petersburg in the mid-1850s," but was not sufficient to live the life of a gentleman.[7] With a private fortune and two salaries, however, Tiutchev must have had no problem in this respect. Zlatkovskii claims that Maikov had something to do with Tiutchev's appointment to the post of chairman. Maikov, we recall, had been a censor under Krasovskii since 1852; as soon as the news of Krasovskii's death reached him, Maikov is said to have rushed to Minister of Education A. S. Norov, with whom he had long been on friendly terms, and suggested to him that there was no man more capable than Tiutchev of occupying this new vacancy with dignity. "'You have sound political acumen!' exclaimed Abram Sergeevich, stamping his wooden leg." Norov was a very different man from Uvarov, his predecessor, who had relied so on Krasovskii. Zlatkovskii calls him one of the most cultured men of his time and notes that he was a hero of the Battle of Borodino—hence the wooden leg.[8]

Tiutchev's criticism of censorship policy and his disillusionment with the direction taken by the government continued throughout his life. His letter to Prince Gorchakov on censorship was published for the first time shortly before his death (sixteen years after he wrote it) in the May 1873 issue of the journal *Russkii arkhiv* (Russian archives). In a letter to his daughter Anna in April the poet made his last comments on the subject of censorship:

> First of all, my dear daughter, thank your husband for his excellent Russian translation of my memorandum, published in the *Arkhiv*, which increases its value tenfold. This article has appeared just in time to show clearly the step backwards which we have taken since 1857. I learned yesterday that a new law on the press is being prepared which seriously reproduces, in legal form, Figaro's famous monologue on freedom of speech. This law reserves for the administration the right to determine those questions which may not be addressed in print. In today's circumstances it is braver and more honest to openly reestablish a censorship which would, by replacing

all this fantastic legislation with something clear and positive, be accepted by the press as a real boon. False ideas are inconvenient in that it takes such a long time to get rid of them.

The monologue by Figaro to which Tiutchev referred is in act 5, scene 3, of Pierre Beaumarchais's play *Le mariage de Figaro*. In the monologue Figaro speaks ironically about Spanish censorship:

> There has been established in Madrid a system of freedom for the sale of products which extends even to products of the press and which, as long as I do not speak in my writings about the authorities, or about worship, or about politics, or about morals, or about people of station, or about groups in favor, or about the Opera, or about other entertainments, or about a person who has firm beliefs, leaves me free to publish anything, subject to the inspection of two or three censors.[9]

In his obituary of Tiutchev, A. V. Nikitenko wrote:

> Everyone who took part in the fate of native thought and literature was very familiar with his enlightened ideas about matters relating to the press. His attempts to support and carry out protective measures in this administrative sphere without harm to the development and dissemination of healthy ideas, on which the intellectual and moral progress of society rests, are well known.

Nikitenko, a professor of literature and censor of Russian-language publications, reported in his diary a discussion with Tiutchev in October 1858 about a proposal to adopt the French system of postpublication censorship. The Russian government apparently was inclined to introduce this new system while maintaining preliminary censorship as well, a proposal against which Tiutchev, according to Nikitenko, protested strongly.[10] There is no doubt that the emperor too was aware of Tiutchev's critical attitude; in December 1859, when Minister of Education E. P. Kovalevskii, Tiutchev's superior, proposed him along with other literary figures to be members of a high-level committee to discuss censorship problems, Alexander II is reported to have burst out angrily, "Oh, your writers! One cannot rely on a single one of them!"[11]

Clearly, one always had to deal very carefully with the royal family. For instance, the preceding year Tiutchev had been confronted with the problem of a novel by August Theodor Grimm (1805–78), tutor to the emperor's son, the future Alexander III. On 13 November 1858, Tiutchev's daughter Anna wrote in her diary:

> Concerning Grimm, my father, who has become the head of the censorship committee, told me that he received from one of the censors the following report on his novel: that a German teacher has had the audacity to write a very nasty novel of everyday life in a spirit most hostile to Russia, and that the novel ought to be banned. It would be strange, however, to ban a book for its hostility to Russia when the author of this book is directing the studies of the heir to the Russian throne. My father had to revoke the censorship ban and permit the book.

The novel in question, *Die Fürstin der siebenten Werst*, apparently made quite a stir at court. As one of the empress's ladies-in-waiting Anna was part of the august audience, including the empress and the dowager empress, to whom Grimm read his work aloud. First mentioned on 20 October, the reading concluded on 13 November. Anna obviously shared the censor's opinion of the novel. On 7 November she referred to Grimm's work as "his endless novel," and at the conclusion her expression of disgust echoed the censor's: "This is one of those things which cause me true grief. . . . People everywhere will know and say that in the course of two months both empresses spent three evenings a week, and even mornings, listening to the reading of a very nasty novel by a German teacher who, to the great dissatisfaction of the country, is directing the education of the heir to the throne."[12]

The conflict between Tiutchev's personal views and the official positions he was obliged to take emerges clearly from several samples of his private and public writing. Each year the chairman of the Foreign Censorship Committee was required to submit to his superiors a report on that year's accomplishments. Fortunately, portions of four of Tiutchev's annual reports have been published, which reveal a great deal about the functioning of the committee during his chairmanship and about his official stance.[13] The first two reports, for 1858 and 1860, were written while the censorship was still part of the Ministry of Education. In 1863 an important change took place: censorship was moved to the Ministry of Internal Affairs. Tiutchev's biographer, Pigarev, suggests that Minister of Education A. V. Golovnin wanted to be rid of responsibility for the press now that the revolutionary movement was growing; in any case, Tiutchev's reports for 1863 and 1865 were submitted to his new superiors.[14] Throughout these reports he took pains to reassure his superiors that censorship was being properly carried out, and to justify the apparent liberalization of censorship practices.

Reviewing the year 1858, the new chairman saw his first task to be "to bring the affairs of the foreign censorship into a more rational condition." The Russian reading public needed good material and, although Russian literature was developing to meet the need, Tiutchev attempted to broaden the scope of foreign literature too, "always remaining, of course, within the legal limits and holding to the exact meaning of the censorship statutes."[15] Early in his tenure as chairman Tiutchev was instructed by the government to review works that had been under ban for many years. So not only were more publications to be permitted but some old ones were to be rehabilitated as well.[16] His task was made easier, Tiutchev noted, by the fact that contemporary foreign literature was more moderate in tone than it had been in the recent past: "Since passions in Europe have cooled, everything has settled into its normal order, and literature too has taken the path of legal activity." The censorship now could concentrate its efforts on "truly harmful works instead of seizing upon petty details or single words." Novels, stories, and children's books were reviewed with particular strictness (a practice maintained right up until 1917); most decisions to ban for the public only, or to excise passages, were made with regard to works of these types.[17] The absolute ban, used rarely even under Krasovskii, nearly disappeared under Tiutchev; censors (mostly in the provinces, far from Tiutchev's influence) recommended it from time to time, but were overruled. Indeed, Tiutchev proposed that the absolute ban be dropped altogether. As for the practice of excising passages, in 1850 the Chief Censorship Administration, overwhelmed by vast quantities of "doubtful" foreign publications sent over by the committee, reminded the latter of its rights: "'If a work is written with good intentions but contains some intolerable passages, then with the consent of the owner those words or expressions may be destroyed by means of excising pages or by some other means.'"[18] Whether the item in question was confiscated from an individual or was part of a bookseller's stock, the owner presumably would have preferred to have the book with excisions than to forfeit it altogether. This suggestion, made in order to keep the flow of publications moving, was accepted enthusiastically by the committee and used frequently—too frequently for Tiutchev, who viewed it as petty.

In his 1858 report Tiutchev remarked on a recent development calling for vigilance on the part of the committee: the rise of émigré Russian

presses in Western Europe that were issuing "reprehensible works." He
assured his superiors that these works were being handled "in the strictest
possible manner and were not being distributed to anyone on any account."
The émigré publications were causing his staff a good deal of trouble, he
complained; they had to examine each packet from abroad with special
care since "books which seem perfectly innocent to judge by their titles
might have lists, or even a large number of brochures pasted inside the
covers."[19] Note the contrast between this assertion of successful censorship
in the official report and Tiutchev's assessment of the problem in his
earlier letter to Gorchakov:

> It would be useless to try to conceal the progress already made by this
> literary propaganda. We know that right now Russia is flooded with
> these publications, that they are avidly sought after, that they pass
> from hand to hand with a great ease of circulation, and that they have
> already penetrated, if not the masses, who do not read, at least the
> lower strata of society. On the other hand, it must be owned that
> without having recourse to positively vexatious and tyrannical mea-
> sures, it would be most difficult effectively to thwart either the impor-
> tation and sale of this printed matter or the exportation abroad of
> manuscripts intended to feed it.

As to the significance of Herzen's journal, in his letter to Gorchakov,
Tiutchev wrote:

> Now how can we overlook the fact that what gives it its strength and
> that to which it owes its success is that for us it represents free discus-
> sion, in bad conditions, it is true, of hatred and bias, but nevertheless
> free enough—why deny it—to permit the competition of other more
> reflective, more moderate, and even some positively reasonable
> opinions.[20]

But in this and subsequent annual reports publications such as Herzen's
were simply denounced as "reprehensible works."

The 1858 report concluded with a plea for change. There had been a
significant increase in the number of foreign publications received that
year, as well as in the number of items examined and permitted. Although
the staff had worked diligently, all the new titles simply could not be
examined; a still greater increase was to be expected in the future. Tiutchev
referred to "significant reforms" already presented to his superior and
asserted that "the future course of foreign censorship depends on these

reforms." Nothing came of the proposal and subsequent reports (at least those available for examination) contain no further mention of reforms.

Not recorded in the report for 1858 was an incident concerning Dumas's *Le Comte de Monte-Cristo*, which Tiutchev described rather ruefully in a letter to his wife on 26 July of that year:

> At this point in my letter I was brutally interrupted by the arrival of a courier sent to me by Minister Kovalevskii bearing a very hurried letter in which I was requested to confirm whether it was our censorship committee which had permitted passage of a certain issue of a journal published [*sic*] by Dumas called Monte-Cristo.
>
> By chance I learned yesterday at Peterhof from Princess Saltikov about the existence of this issue, which apparently contains some rather indiscreet details about the Russian court, so much so that the excellent princess, while savoring them very much, could not conceal from me her astonishment that such things should be circulated in print.
>
> Happily, our poor committee need not reproach itself for such criminal leniency, at least not as a whole committee, and one must suppose that one of the censors, on his own responsibility, allowed the unfortunate issue to pass. Meanwhile, on orders from above we must proceed with an investigation, an investigation made much more difficult by the circumstance that today is a holiday, you can imagine what sort of fix we are in, and in what poor condition I find myself to write the kind of extensive letter which I would have liked.
>
> You will not begrudge me if I do as George Sand does, who always cuts short her novels toward the end.[21]

The inquiry is not mentioned again, so we must remain in ignorance of the identity of the guilty censor.

In his report on the year 1860 Tiutchev commented on the characteristics of contemporary foreign literature. The struggle between hostile religious, philosophical, and political ideas reflected in the writing of a few years ago had died down, he remarked, and had in any case presented no real danger to Russia, for although those burning issues had been known to Russian readers, they were viewed as objects of curiosity far removed from Russian life rather than as battles to be fought by Russians. In fact, observed Tiutchev, Russians might even profit from the lessons of history to be learned from Western Europe's struggles. It was impossible, he maintained, to keep the Russian public in a state of total blindness and ignorance; "it was the task of the foreign censorship painstakingly to select from the masses of books entering the country those with a positively harmful influence on all readers and to restrict them for the public."[22] But one had to be cautious even when dealing with scholarly publications. In 1857, shortly before Tiutchev became chairman, Minister of Education Norov, his future superior, had issued a circular to censorship authorities that the competition sponsored by the Academy of Sciences for the best historical works on the changing status of landlords' property rights in various European countries could be advertised only in the academy's French-language *Bulletin* and in foreign magazines and newspapers.[23]

Tiutchev went on to enumerate five categories of harmful works that had surfaced in the past year. First were "books of philosophical content with an extremely rationalistic or materialistic tendency, rejecting every possibility of the existence of God and every hope for the immortality of the soul beyond the grave." These were primarily German publications, since "the spirit of rationalism rules practically all classes of society in Germany."

The second group comprised "religious books of a polemical nature or directed against the dogmas of the Russian church, which is, in the words of the fanatical advocates of Catholicism, dead, heretical, and accursed." Also reprehensible were works directed against Western Catholicism, the pope, the priesthood, the Vatican. These works, written by Catholics as well as Protestants, were mainly in French.

Third were historical works dealing with Russia. Tiutchev noted that, in general, writers of history were now much more moderate than they had been ten or fifteen years earlier and assured his superiors that those incendiary works of the past era were still under ban, even though they had by now lost most of their influence. The committee had concentrated on references to Russian history, excising them if they were found to be contrary to the censorship statutes. The majority of these excised passages were descriptions of the deaths of Emperors Peter III and Paul I. Both men were murdered, but the facts were never officially acknowledged nor permitted to appear in print; the censors' concern with this matter is discussed in chapter 6 of this volume.

A fourth category of publications consisted of pro-Polish, anti-Russian pamphlets or collections of patriotic poetry, written for the most part in Polish by Polish émigrés and having the aim of "drawing down curses upon Russia—the land of the knout, as her bitter enemies call her—and proving the absence of all human qualities in the people as well as in its rulers." These works were banned for the public by the committee. Finally, immoral novels and stories (mostly in French) were stopped by the censors, while publications in Russian received by Tiutchev's staff were sent on to the ecclesiastical and internal censorship authorities for examination if they were "unknown to the censorship." The implication is that émigré publications were handled directly by the Foreign Censorship Committee only when the decision to permit or ban already had been made by others.

Tiutchev devoted a paragraph of the report to English publications imported during 1860. A very small number of these works had to be banned: "books on travels in Russia, prejudiced descriptions of the Crimean campaign, or anecdotes and stories dealing with the reign of Emperor Nicholas I." In general, however, he found that most English writers had achieved the true aim of literature: "to promote the moral development of society; the censorship cannot point to a single immoral novel or story, to a single philosophical work refuting Christianity; to a single political pamphlet preaching hatred for Russia, or war, or revolution."

In 1860, as in the preceding year, Tiutchev reported, the majority of foreign publications reviewed by the committee were serious, scholarly works. Unlike lighter literature, "written to make the time pass pleasantly," these volumes were of relatively little concern to the censorship; their "difficult, dry, metaphysical language cannot be easily understood by the superficially educated mass of readers, and thus cannot have the same influence on them as works on the very same subjects written in light, popular language."

The report concluded with some figures: 2,255,359 volumes had been imported in 1860, as compared to 1,422,157 volumes in 1859. The number of new titles was increasing steadily, resulting in a heavier workload for the committee staff, which Tiutchev praised for its conscientious work.

The 1863 report opened with a parade of figures to document the steady increase in the volume of imported foreign publications.[24] Twenty years earlier, in 1843, 534,372 volumes had passed through the committee; ten years later the number had grown to 958,533; by 1858 it had reached 1,614,874; and in 1863, 2,727,302 volumes and issues had been received. Tiutchev stressed the significance for Russian advancement of this quadrupling of the number of imported foreign publications, pointing with pride to the large number of titles in "useful" fields such as mechanics, technology, and natural sciences, "many of which are accessible to the masses of the Russian public in Russian translation."

While the number of imported foreign publications was increasing each year, the number of banned works was decreasing. In 1862 the committee had banned 285 works, as compared to 464 banned in 1852. Of the 3,670 titles examined in 1863, only 142 were banned and 87 permitted with excisions. Probably in answer to expected criticism, Tiutchev stated that "this gradual decrease in the number of banned books . . . cannot be attributed to weakness on the part of the Foreign Censorship Committee, from whose attention not one single harmful book can be hidden; rather, this condition and its cause can be explained by historical events in the West, as well as by the more liberal attitude of our government toward domestic and foreign literature." In the 1840s and 1850s, he explained, literature had had an undeniable effect on politics in Western Europe: "The teaching of Feuerbach, Strauss, Louis Blanc, Proudhon, the ideas of Lamartine, Heine, and the school of rationalists and materialists formed in Germany could not but rock the foundations of foreign society." Given this relationship between literature and revolution, Tiutchev acknowledged the Russian government's obligation to protect its people from such influences by means of strict censorship of foreign and domestic publications.

However, time had passed. Napoleon III had calmed France and in Germany it was no longer true that "the ideas of Heine, Karl Vogt, Büchner, and others were avidly read and devoured and considered infallible, and the literature of these peoples became more hopeful and more useful for Russia than it had been previously." Thus the foreign censorship had been able to be more tolerant, Tiutchev explained, while still remaining strictly within the limits of the law. As in the 1858 report, the chairman stressed his concern over the Russian émigré presses, especially Herzen's establishment in London, "where well-known people of Russian extraction have made a plan to disseminate revolutionary propaganda in Russia by means of the printed word." Tiutchev assured his superiors that the committee was sparing no effort to prevent such vicious publications from reaching Russian readers. Note the contrast here, as in 1858, between Tiutchev's official assurance that no harmful publications might escape the committee's attention and his private admission to Prince Gorchakov in the letter on censorship that there was simply no way to curb the influx of harmful literature.

Commenting on the five groups of banned publications, Tiutchev observed that although the Germans had published many unacceptable works on philosophy in recent years, few had entered Russia during the past year "because the leading figures of this school have for the most part exhausted their inspiration, and if they are still writing, it is with far less sharpness than formerly." The committee had banned forty-four works viewed as antireligious in general or anti-Orthodox. Tiutchev viewed this large number as significant: "It proves that a new danger for society has arisen in the West which threatens to take away from man his dearest and most cherished beliefs." He singled out Renan's *La vie de Jésus* and Strauss's *Das Leben Jesu* as particularly virulent examples of this category.[25] Tiutchev considered Renan's book to be the more dangerous of the two: "It is written in a popular style and thus can do more harm than Strauss' strictly scholarly book." Accordingly, *La vie de Jésus* was permitted only for "a few people who, by virtue of their positions, enjoy the trust of the government." A few of these forty-four books were in Polish and praised Catholicism while abusing the Greek-Russian rite.

Since 1863 was the year of the Polish uprising, it is not surprising that most of the political works banned dealt with the Polish question: five in German, twenty in French, and fifty-seven in Polish. The committee confiscated a large number of copies of the Polish works and, in addition to these new titles, the staff searched incoming packages for copies of "previously banned and positively harmful works" by Mickiewicz, Chojecki, Krasiński, and other Polish writers. The committee worked closely with the internal censorship in regard to French books on the Polish question; since these works already had been criticized in the Russian press, it was possible for the Foreign Censorship Committee to be more lenient and permit at least some, such as Comte Charles Forbes René de Tryon Montalembert's *L'insurrection polonaise*. Even English literature, so benign in 1860, had grown malignant as a result of the events of 1863. "Articles appeared there in many periodical publications and even in magazines for young people preaching hatred for Russia, with reprehensible anecdotes and improper references about Grand Duke Konstantin Nikolaevich, the late emperor Nicholas, and members of our present government." Numerous copies of twenty-two offending publications were confiscated by the committee.

Only ten historical works were banned absolutely in 1863, mostly Polish books without "general literary interest." Permitted with excisions were sixty-two titles "painting in gloomy colors the lives of Empresses Anna, Elizabeth, and Catherine II and describing in detail the death of Peter III and the demise of Emperor Paul." Improper anecdotes or disrespectful references to Emperor Nicholas occurred in historical novels, of which a large number of copies entered the country. The offending passages, Tiutchev reassured his superiors, were always blotted or cut out by staff.

As for erotica, the committee's reputation for strictness was well known to the booksellers and few titles made their way into the office. Tiutchev included two titles by Eugène de Mirecourt warranting the committee's special attention: *Les femmes galantes de Napoléons: Secrets de cour et de palais* (1862) and *Napoleon III: Nach dem Leben gezeichnet* (1860). When the latter book was banned in 1860, the censor had written that "the author portrays [Napoleon] as some sort of degenerate of the human race."[26]

Tiutchev ended the 1863 report with comments on the ever-increasing flow into the country of Russian-language works published in France, Germany, and Switzerland. In the course of the year twenty-eight titles (1,652 volumes and issues) had been received. Many more titles, amounting to thousands of volumes, had entered the country between 1859 and 1862, causing Tiutchev to conclude that the Russian press abroad was growing in strength each year. He described its publications as "negative and harmful, directed primarily against Russian internal policies, the clergy, and government leaders," and concluded that under the circumstances it was not surprising that of eighty-two works known to the censorship, only twelve were permitted. Most dangerous of all, in Tiutchev's opinion, were émigré writers such as Herzen, Ogarev, Bliummer, and Dolgorukov, who "chose as the motto of their literary activity revolution and destruction." The committee was especially vigilant where such reprehensible works were concerned. Perhaps by ending the reports of 1860 and 1863 with strong statements against Russian émigré literature and assurances of the committee's strict measures to control it, Tiutchev hoped to divert his superiors' attention from the true situation and from the fact that the censorship was becoming more lenient toward foreign works in general.

The concluding section of the 1865 report opened with a philosophical discussion. In considering works banned that year because of rationalistic and materialistic ideas, Tiutchev observed that the attempts of philosophers through the ages to deal with big questions often have led them away from religious truths and that, although the answers they found were of necessity erroneous, "there is still a measure of truth in philosophical systems." He stressed the importance of the legacy of these great thinkers, whose "systems and views . . . passed from century to century, from generation to generation and, as the fruit of centuries of labor, now belong to the history of civilization. For this reason it is not appropriate that the censorship, on the basis of the statutes, should continue to uphold a ban on this type of book, which is in any case not accessible to the masses due to its contents and exposition." Such books, he urged, should be permitted in a small number of copies and only for specialized scholars. Indeed, he continued, there were very few such books imported in 1865—six rationalistic and two materialistic—and all had been banned for the public.[27]

Tiutchev repeated his assurances of 1863: rationalist writers such as Büchner, Vogt, and Comte, "known for their bold teachings against the authority of the Bible," were no longer influential. The materialists were still active, but had moved away from philosophy: "Their age-old argument with the theologians has now been transplanted to new soil, namely religious ground, as is evident from the seventy works in the area of religion banned in the past year." In his remarks on several English and German scholarly attempts in recent years to reconcile science and biblical teaching, Tiutchev made the case for permitting such works. Writers, he maintained, were expressing the opinion that "progress in the natural sciences does not have to lead to atheism, since in addition to matter and energy there is still . . . the atomic principle, which does not disappear without a trace either in matter or in the soul. Such a view, although in disagreement with teachings contained in the Holy Scripture, does not in fact contain anything hostile to the Bible and is not offensive to the feelings of the faithful."[28]

Moving on to works on the subject of religion, Tiutchev expressed his disapproval of those followers of Strauss, Renan, and others who attempted to "lower the Savior to the level of man." Indeed, some went even further: "The skepticism of the rationalists and materialists has now been replaced by total denial. Science and knowledge are to be higher than any religion, and an educated man can manage without the teachings of the Church, now necessary only for the masses, and in general only for those at the lowest stage of development." As an example of religion for the masses, he cited a play intended for popular audiences, A. B. Dulk's *Jesus der Christ*:

In this drama the author's imagination pictures the conception of Jesus not by the Holy Ghost but by a young Essene [a member of an ascetic brotherhood] who had stolen into the Virgin Mary's bed while she lay half asleep in an ecstatic state. According to this fiction Jesus, born of an Essene, was taken into their sect, which taught its pupil various sciences, among them therapeutics, with the help of which he later healed the sick. With the same kinds of fantasies the author portrays the death and resurrection of the Savior. The half-dead Jesus, removed from the cross, is brought back to life by the Essene elders; to convince the apostles of the actuality of resurrection and ascension they resort to an optical illusion, to mirages and other tricks. Such are the main features of a drama intended by the author for the popular stage![29]

The play was, of course, banned in entirety by the committee. Tiutchev added that while this piece could not be considered literature, it did "demonstrate clearly the results of contemporary unbelief." In the course of the year seventy such items had been banned (only three specifically anti-Orthodox), while twenty-seven articles in periodical publications had been permitted with excision of antireligious passages.

There had been relatively few offensive foreign political works in 1865, but a few pieces critical of Russian rulers had made their way into the country. Tiutchev remarked that lately such literature had been increasing as foreigners paid closer attention to Russian affairs, motivated perhaps by envy of Russia's strength and power. These attacks on Russia's eastern policies and treatment of peasants were now particularly hostile in regard to the Polish question. "One cannot deny that almost every event important for Russia has resulted without fail in false counsel, rumors and censure of us by foreigners," Tiutchev asserted. One might have expected, he observed, that Polish propaganda would have subsided by 1865, after the uprising had been put down, but this was not the case; he reported that the committee had banned sixty-nine political works and excised passages from thirty-nine periodicals. French and Polish works were particularly anti-Russian, including in their hostility the imperial family, government officials, and common people. Furthermore, the Poles were incited to rebel and their revolutionary leaders were praised. English literature was again offensive and contained "improper stories, allusions and anecdotes in journals and even in children's books."

Works dealing with history, including novels, stories, and biographies, were also suffused with sympathy for Poland and anti-Russian sentiments. "The censorship could not be anything but strict with these works, since the authors not only falsely portrayed common Russians in a hateful manner, but also subjected our rulers, members of the imperial family, and official personages to abuse and slander, reprehensible anecdotes and allusions." As in previous years, textbooks, magazines, and newspapers had to be examined for references to the deaths of Emperors Peter III and Paul I. In all, fifty-three works categorized as "history" were banned or permitted with excisions in 1865.

Again in 1865 erotica and pamphlets presented only minor problems—seven titles in French or German, and only a few copies of each, had come to the attention of the committee—and again Tiutchev explained this fact by noting that booksellers were well aware of the strictness of the foreign censorship.

Products of the Russian émigré press were not even reviewed by the censorship this year, Tiutchev explained, because their reprehensible contents were already well known. Herzen's publications no longer posed much of a threat, he remarked; this literature had "worn itself out and lost all significance." Other producers of Russian literature abroad were now more positively inclined toward Russia, and of twenty-three works reviewed the Saint Petersburg Censorship Committee had been able to permit sixteen (five had been banned by that committee, the remaining two by the ecclesiastical censorship).

The 1865 report ended with Tiutchev's assurances to his superiors that "the Committee entrusted to me acted moderately in its decisions about books if this seemed possible and harmless, and severely when the work under consideration warranted it. Thus the censorship statute served as the basis for the Committee's actions." He added that "in applying the statutes to specific questions, especially political ones, the Committee sometimes took into account statements in the domestic press, since special instructions are sometimes given by the Higher Authorities in the process of internal censorship."

Tiutchev's relations with Minister of the Interior P. A. Valuev, his superior after 1863 when censorship was transferred out of the Ministry of Education, and with other high officials were not always smooth. He had been appointed to the Council on Press Affairs (the executive committee of the Chief Administration for Press Affairs) in March 1864; almost two years later, in December 1865, he reported to his friend Nikitenko a conversation with Valuev in which he had "explained frankly to the minister that the repressive system which he had adopted could not lead to anything good." Nikitenko continued:

> Tiutchev also told me indignantly about the Council, in the affairs of which he had absolutely declined to take part. Goncharov confirms the same thing. None of this is the least bit surprising. The minister himself views the matter as a bureaucrat and not as a statesman and, it seems, does not have any understanding of the importance of thought,

which he intends to stifle by means of bureaucratic routines and measures.

(The "Goncharov" referred to by Nikitenko is Ivan Goncharov, another famous writer who worked as a censor, in this case of Russian publications.) As an example, Nikitenko cited a recently published circular to censors in the Baltic regions which was "remarkable for its uncommon illiteracy and for such a muddle of ideas that one tried in vain to discover what the Chief Censorship Administration wanted." Nikitenko also noted that at a meeting of the council in October 1866, concern was voiced over the effect of some literature on young readers; "Tiutchev rightly observed that literature does not exist for schoolchildren, and that it must not be given a juvenile orientation."[30]

Six months later, in June 1866, Tiutchev wrote to his friend A. I. Georgievskii about censorship and its effect on the press: "It is rather like curing a toothache by smashing the teeth with one's fist."[31] Matters apparently came to a head at the end of 1866: Valuev wrote Tiutchev a coldly official letter (in French) in December offering to accept his resignation.

Some time ago your Excellency expressed to me your lack of sympathy with the orientation of press affairs, and your confessed difficulty in continuing to take part in this branch of official service. For my part, I also have formed an absolutely firm opinion on this count. The personal esteem in which I hold you, the feelings of sincere respect which I have presented to you and my natural aversion toward making a decision which might be less than pleasing to you have not until now permitted me to act upon the intention of which I informed the emperor long ago. Changes in the personal composition of the Chief Censorship Administration force me nonetheless to take this action.[32]

He invited Tiutchev to call on him that evening to arrange satisfactory terms. However, the letter apparently was never sent and, in any case, Tiutchev continued to serve both as a member of the council and as chairman of the Foreign Censorship Committee.

His complaints continued as well. In April 1867, he wrote to his son-in-law Ivan Aksakov that "absolute honesty, absolute candor of the press require absolute honesty, absolute candor in legislation of press affairs, and not that hypocritical, arbitrary rule by force which now prevails in our country." On the bright side, in October 1867, Tiutchev wrote to his wife that he had given a soiree: "It was a political-literary soiree. Long ago I had promised to arrange one for the gentlemen of the Administration of Press Affairs and the committees. Tea, ice cream and punch were the refreshments for this festive occasion, which was moved from my bedroom to the large living room. The party broke up at one o'clock in the morning."[33]

A year later, he was unhappy again. In a letter to his brother Nikolai, Tiutchev wrote bitterly about Pokhvisnev (then chairman of the council), Timashev (Valuev's successor as minister of the interior), and others: "All of them are more or less scoundrels, and looking at them is simply nauseating, but it is our misfortune that this nausea never reaches the point of vomiting." This "vulgar department" should, he wrote, be defamed because of its "calculating stupidity." Tiutchev used the same metaphor in a poem:

> The well-wishers of the Russian press
> And, in fact, all of you gentlemen
> Nauseate her. The trouble is,
> Not quite enough to cause vomiting.[34]

He also occasionally permitted himself some sarcasm at the expense of his colleagues, as in the case of the Slavophile Iurii Samarin, who had published a pamphlet that displeased the internal censorship. In a letter to his wife dated 30 September 1868 Tiutchev observed that "Samarin's pamphlet is still engaging universal attention. This is a true event. They decided to ban its sale after practically the whole thing had already appeared in the journals. But its success would not have been complete if such measures had not been taken."[35] Not so light-hearted was this little poem that Tiutchev wrote in 1870 in the album of P. A. Vakar, a member of the Chief Administration for Press Affairs and of his own committee:

> Obedient to a higher command,
> Standing guard over *ideas*,
> We were not very mirthful,
> Although we held carbines in our hands.
> We wielded them unwillingly,
> We threatened rarely,
> It was rather a *guard of honor*
> Than *guarding prisoners*.[36]

Early in 1871 an incident occurred that resulted in the curtailment of the Foreign Censorship Committee's power. Until that time the committee had had the authority to decide which foreign works could be translated into Russian. One such title was a biography of Robert Owen, the British reformer and socialist. In his report Polonskii had recommended permitting the book both in the original and for translation into Russian. The following year the Russian translation was detained by the internal censorship in Saint Petersburg, which brought charges against the publishers on the grounds that the book contained "extremely blasphemous censures of religion and attacks on marriage and property." When it was learned that the Foreign Censorship Committee actually had approved this book for translation, the case was discussed at the Council of the Chief Administration for Press Affairs. It was agreed that Polonskii would be reprimanded, but the matter did not end there; the council also gave this highly negative assessment of the work of the Foreign Censorship Committee:

> The present case is *by no means unique* in the activities of the Committee, and the actions of the foreign censorship *in general* are *extremely unsatisfactory*, because by its censorship decisions the Committee has repeatedly paralyzed the actions of the internal censorship in regard to its prosecution of translators, and because, permitting themselves serious dereliction of duty, the censors of the foreign censorship almost always occupy themselves with the excision of short, insignificant phrases and expressions, stopping at details which signify nothing, while at the same time allowing for circulation *truly harmful* books, thus displaying a *completely erroneous view of their work*, which they do not regard with the proper attention.[37]

As a result of this judgment the committee lost its right to make decisions regarding translations into Russian.

In general the question of translation was a delicate one. In 1865 both Tiutchev's ministries—education and foreign affairs—had been involved in the case of an illegal translation of a work by Emperor Napoleon III, *Histoire de Jules César*. The French ambassador protested the circulation in Russia of illegal translations, reminding the Russian authorities of an 1861 convention under which the Russians had agreed to forbid the sale of any translation of a French work published in a foreign country deemed by the French to be unacceptable. The Russians agreed that this particular translation should be banned but pointed out that the responsibility for identifying other illegal translations would have to lie with the French ambassador.[38]

The chairman of the Chief Administration for Press Affairs at this time was M. R. Shidlovskii, with whom Tiutchev did not see eye to eye. On one occasion, in the course of an argument between the two men, Tiutchev is reported to have exclaimed:

> "What is the purpose of literature and the press if we deny the significance of its statement?" "For amusement, for amusement!" shouted Shidlovskii in a voice not his own. "To provide people who have nothing to do with something to read. Literature and the press in general have no other significance!" Everyone was silent. Many squirmed in their chairs.

Shidlovskii, who had formerly been the governor of Tula province, served the writer Saltykov-Shchedrin as the model for a town governor with a "little musical box" in his head in his piece entitled *The History of One Town.*[39]

Tiutchev spent a fair amount of time away from Saint Petersburg and his official censorship duties, although he continued on the official payroll. In March 1860, for example, Tiutchev had been paid part of his salary—653 rubles, 20 kopeks—for the period of his absence abroad in 1859. Three months later, instead of the per diem to which he was entitled as chairman, it was authorized that he be paid by the state treasury a lump sum of 1,333 rubles, 33 kopeks for his four-month leave abroad.[40] Tiutchev's superiors had to approve his proposed absences, which they did in June 1863 and again in June 1864. The first of these two leaves, extending from 5 June to 14 August 1863, was spent in Moscow, where Tiutchev underwent a course of homeopathic treatment. The second leave, less than a month in duration, was also spent in Moscow.

On his return to Saint Petersburg in July 1864, Tiutchev met immediately with Prince Gorchakov, his superior at the Ministry of Foreign Affairs (as mentioned above, Tiutchev continued to work for both ministries at once) to arrange an extended diplomatic tour abroad, where his family was then residing. Valuev, his other chief, approved this leave too, and Tiutchev left for Germany at once on his diplomatic mission. His signature was missing from committee documents from 25 August 1864 through 17 March 1865.

Shortly after his return from Moscow Tiutchev had suffered a great blow: the death of E. A. Denis'eva, his mistress of many years. It has been speculated that his urgent desire to leave the country was due at least as much to his grief as to his eagerness to begin his mission for Prince Gorchakov. In any case, in Tiutchev's absence his per diem was paid to Z. M. Dobrovolskii, the committee's executor and treasurer. Count E. E.

Komarovskii, a senior censor since 1859, who had been appointed to his post at Tiutchev's urging, filled in for him as chairman. Komarovskii caused Tiutchev some anxiety by falling ill that first winter. In a letter to Polonskii from Nice in December 1864, Tiutchev remarked, "I almost wish that I might be summoned to Saint Petersburg in the name of our committee, for which, it seems, there is also cause—on account of Count Komarovskii's illness—what is the matter with him, poor man?"[41]

In general, extremely warm relations appear to have existed between Tiutchev and his committee staff. In 1860, for example, Tiutchev wrote to his second wife, "Yesterday I took leave of my committee, and not without some difficulty at parting from these gentlemen, who are so kind to me." Returning from another trip abroad in August 1862, he wrote, again to his wife, "Yesterday I resumed control of my committee. All these gentlemen showed great pleasure at my return."[42]

Tiutchev's benign influence became evident very soon after he took office in April 1858 but it took some time for the new attitude to penetrate the lower levels of the committee. One of the censors, Baron von Bistram, recommended for banning for the public the fifth edition of Dupont's *Muse populaire*, a collection of popular songs and poems, because many of the verses included were "against the Christian faith, our government, a summons to revolution, to socialism, with a democratic tendency and in general inclined toward the destruction of social tranquility. . . . For these reasons I would suggest banning the book for the public, all the more so because these folksongs can be only of local interest, for the French nation." However, the committee declined von Bistram's recommendation and permitted the book without even any excisions. This show of tolerance may be attributed to the general liberal attitude of the time. A. V. Golovnin, future minister of education, complained that "well-known ideas are disseminated in the air, despite all the police and all the censorship." However, by 1878 the mood had changed and an 1875 edition of Dupont's work was banned. This time the situation was reversed: although the censor, L. O. Ivanovskii, found certain poems to be imbued with hatred for Russia, he concluded that they were not important and were no longer even a novelty. But despite his recommendation to permit it, the committee decided to ban the entire collection.[43]

Moderate decisions were made in 1860 and 1862, in regard to works by Béranger and Louis Blanc, respectively. In the first case, censor N. Lebedev found a new edition of Béranger's poems to be mainly acceptable and recommended treating this author with greater leniency than in the past:

The complete collection of Béranger's poetry has been banned by the foreign censorship, partially for the public and partially absolutely. Earlier editions were subjected to this ban because they contained a great many anti-religious or erotic poems which had to be excised; but, as is well known, a small volume of his poems has been published in Russian, translated by Kurochkin, and for that reason it seems to me that the foreign censorship too is not obligated to hold absolutely to its former decision not to permit any of Béranger's poems for the public.

Lebedev recommended the excision of five poems or parts of poems, but the committee permitted the whole collection with the excision of only two poems.[44] In the case of Louis Blanc's *Histoire de dix ans*, which had been banned previously, censor Lebedev was charged by the chairman with the task of reviewing the book. He found that because of its "social democratic tendency" it would be necessary at least to exclude certain passages, but the committee determined that it should be permitted, having "outlived its epoch."[45]

Heinrich Heine continued to attract the attention of the Russian censorship authorities during Tiutchev's years as chairman. In 1862–63 eighteen of the twenty-two volumes of the new edition of Heine's *Sämmtliche Werke* (Collected Works), published in Hamburg between 1861 and 1863, were examined by the committee. This case is especially interesting not only because Maikov wrote most of the reports but also because it illustrates many of the concerns of this period and the committee's response to them. Maikov was, of course, superbly qualified to deal with a poet of Heine's stature; not only was he at home in German but he was himself a poet. This is not to suggest that there was a general policy of matching censors with publications examined—this was obviously not true and, indeed, would have been impossible—but surely a great advantage of employing men such as Maikov and Polonskii in the foreign censorship was precisely their ability to deal with foreign literature (both major and minor works) in appropriate terms. Tiutchev, himself a great poet and well-versed in foreign literature, must have appreciated the presence of such men on the committee. As for Maikov's knowledge of German, it was well known to his contemporaries.[46]

Reporting on the first and third volumes of the Heine collection, Maikov opened with a statement that very few of Heine's works had been reviewed by the foreign censorship and that only *Reisebilder* and *Englische Fragmente* were banned for the public. However, in his study of Heine and the Russian censorship Fedorov points out that, in fact, almost all of Heine's works had been not only reviewed but banned, and reminds us that Maikov himself had recommended the banning of a French translation of *Götter im Exil* in 1853 (discussed in chapter 2 of this book). Fedorov suggests two possible explanations: either Maikov was unaware of the entire corpus of reports on Heine or he was attempting to make Heine seem less dangerous, in which case he must have been counting on the ignorance of his fellow members of the committee.[47]

Maikov went on to assert that Heine had assumed his place among classic German writers, in the light of which fact he suggested that the censorship might change its opinion. "Heine is a phenomenon characteristic of his epoch; he shares its suffering, its aspirations, participating in what it destroyed and what it created." Times have changed, Maikov said, and "his political and philosophical ideas recede into the background, and what appears before the reader is the artist, for whom the whole world is undifferentiated and all its history is no more than colors, images; more the poet than the thinker, he constantly falls into contradictions." Maikov noted that Heine himself changed his views and that the introduction to this edition of the *Sämmtliche Werke* reflects that change. He concluded that "on the basis of everything which I have said, and taking into account also the fact that an eighteen-volume set will be quite expensive, but will nonetheless be a necessary acquisition for every decent library, I recommend permitting the set as a whole."[48]

Before leaving these volumes Maikov cited several passages that might be seen as questionable but which he recommended leaving intact in the German edition. He did concede, however, that these passages should not be included in the Russian translation, which would reach a different audience. For example, in volume 1, *Reisebilder*, he proposed to keep page 37, which contains a description of the sky as "so transparent that one could gaze into it deeply all the way to the Holy of Holies, where the angels sit at God's feet and in the features of his countenance study the continuo." Maikov did not specify it but it is probably safe to assume that this passage is the objectionable one on the page, since the same image was excised years later from a German-language anthology (see chapter 7 of this book). Indeed, this phrase about the angels was excised even from the last prerevolutionary Russian-language edition of Heine. At one point Heine refers to the beheading of royalty during the French Revolution and the *trommeln* (drumming) of the guillotine march; Maikov maintained that "the sharpness of this *trommeln* is softened by the impression of the whole passage, in which, among other things, Napoleon's curbing of anarchy is discussed." This passage too was excised from Russian editions of Heine's works through 1904. Certainly the most amusing example is page 269, which Maikov suggests should be permitted only with a general consensus of the censors (since a picture is better than a thousand words, see figure 3-1). The committee agreed with Maikov's opinion and excised only two pages containing a discussion of the legitimacy of certain German princes, as well as a reference to "mein Unglaubensgenosse [my unbeliever-comrade] Spinoza." Thus page 269 was ultimately permitted; apparently, the Russian censors saw no harm in poking fun at their German counterparts. The page is chapter 12 (in its entirety), *Ideen: Das Buch Le Grand* (Ideas: Book Le Grand).[49]

In volume 3, *Englische Fragmente und Shakspeare's Mädchen und Frauen*, Maikov found almost nothing to ban. He singled out a number of possibly questionable passages that he recommended permitting, such as two pages in praise of English freedom and the beginning of *Das neue Ministerium*, recounting an irreverent discussion with an inmate of London's New Bedlam on God, the devil, and the state of the world. Typical is a passage in which the mad philosopher informs Heine that "dear God was very short of cash when he created the world. He had to borrow the money from the devil, and mortgage all of creation to him." Maikov also recommended permitting the beginning of *Shakspeare's Mädchen und Frauen*. This essay begins with an analogy between the feelings of a good Christian, who must reconcile himself to the fact of Jesus' Jewish origins, and Heine's own feelings about Shakespeare, who he must acknowledge as an Englishman even though he hates the English. Heine was a Jew who converted to Christianity but many doubted the sincerity of his conversion. Maikov and the committee obviously saw no harm in allowing Russians to read a defamation of Jews written by an author who was Jewish in fact, if not in name. The only passage recommended for excision is the six pages where Heine glorifies the French Revolution, claims freedom as a new religion, sanctions regicide, and expresses anticlerical attitudes.

In his report on volumes 2, 4, 5, and 6 Maikov reaffirmed his opinion of Heine's works as harmless. He found some troublesome spots in volume 2 (the continuation of *Reisebilder*), such as ribald and disrespectful remarks about biblical characters, Heine's dislike of state religions, and his threat of revolution. But Maikov also pointed out some positive passages, such as the pages where Heine is "most respectful toward religion, and his inspired

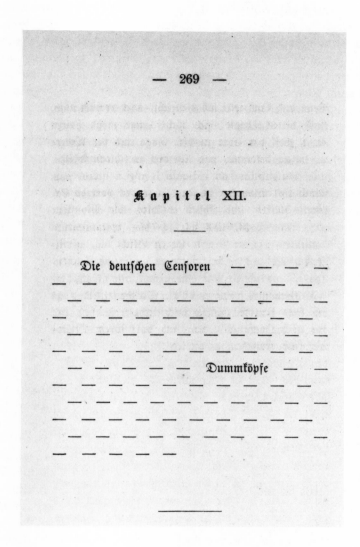

Fig. 3-1. Heinrich Heine on the subject of censors. From Heine's *Sämmtliche Werke* (Hamburg, 1861), vol. 1, p. 269.

words on page 361 about Christ himself," while not traditional, of course, are not offensive either. Finally, Maikov pointed to Heine's own statement to the effect that *Reisebilder* had been written in response to conditions in Germany at an earlier time and that many of his critical remarks were no longer applicable. Despite Maikov's efforts, volume 2 was banned for the public, probably because it was simply too hostile toward the church and Christianity. Chapters 12 and 14, dealing with state religions, were considered so objectionable that they were dropped from prerevolutionary Russian translations and replaced with ellipsis points.[50]

Maikov found nothing objectionable in volume 4, *Novellistische Fragmente*, although he did note the possible impropriety of "one comical character, a pietist, who reads only the Bible and who, being of a voluptuous temperament, dreams of various Biblical women, Esther, Magdalen, and others, for which his wife beats him out of jealousy." The piece in question is *Aus den Memoiren des Herrn von Schnabelewopski*. The committee apparently was willing to overlook the impropriety since they agreed to permit the volume.

Nor did Maikov see any problem with volume 5, *Zur Geschichte der Religion und Philosophie in Deutschland* (the first part of *Über Deutschland*), since in his own introduction Heine "admits that he was carried away when he wrote this history, but that now he has been directed toward other views by the world's premier book, the Bible." The power of the preface must not have convinced the committee, however, because the volume was banned for the public. As Fedorov rightly observes, much of the material deals with philosophy and religion, and Heine's free thinking and irony must have made a stronger impression on the censors than his alleged switch to the Bible.

Only two pages of *Die romantische Schule* (the second part of *Über Deutschland*) were recommended for discussion. In this passage Heine expresses his distaste for the dogma of damning all that is fleshly; in his view this breeds sin and hypocrisy, and people will no longer tolerate such an idea. "People have now recognized the nature of this religion, they no longer allow themselves to be put off with directions to heaven, they know that matter has its value too, and does not belong wholly to the devil, and now they vindicate the pleasures of the earth, of this beautiful garden of God, our inalienable inheritance." The committee accepted Maikov's recommendation and permitted this volume with the excision of these pages.[51]

One report on this edition of Heine *not* written by Maikov was submitted by censor Kestner to the Riga committee in 1863. It deals with volume

17, containing the long poems *Atta Troll* and *Deutschland* and a group of shorter poems under the general heading of *Zeitgedichte*. The two censors approached Heine very differently. The problems presented by volume 17 are the familiar ones: hostile political and religious views, biting satire, and irreverence often verging on blasphemy. But whereas Maikov took a broad view, emphasizing Heine's distance from the current battlefield and raising him above it, Kestner grappled with the poet on a petty level, challenging him line by line.

Kestner began by observing that although this volume, which had previously been banned, was not entirely reprehensible and much of what was previously objectionable was no longer so pernicious in view of altered circumstances, there were nonetheless quite a few passages that the censorship could not approve. He singled out, for example, a portion of *Atta Troll* showing heaven filled with dancing bears and another part of the same poem where Herodias caresses the severed head of John the Baptist. (Kestner's comment here is that she "plays ball with the head.") This scene, as discussed earlier, also had been criticized by the censorship in Krasovskii's time. In *Deutschland* Heine "blasphemes against the Savior" with this verse:

> The sight of you, my poor cousin,
> Always fills me with melancholy.
> You, who wanted to redeem the world,
> You fool, you savior of mankind.

He pokes fun at the German King Ludwig of Bavaria in *Lobgesänge auf König Ludwig*:

> As soon as the apes and kangaroos
> Convert to Christianity,
> They will certainly honor Saint Ludwig
> As their patron saint.

By citing these and other examples Kestner hoped to persuade the committee to excise a series of passages in volume 17.[52]

However, Maikov's view prevailed. His last report on Heine, covering volumes 15, 16, and 18 (16 October 1863), was an eloquent plea for tolerance:

> We have before us the works of the poet who, in the assessment of critics in the entire cultured world, now occupies the third place in

the triad of the greatest poets of Germany: Schiller, Goethe, and now Heine. To the highest degree a poetic nature, he reflected in himself, as in a mirror, all the intellectual ferment of his time in regard to politics, religion, and philosophy and in the sphere of art.

Maikov maintained that Heine was no propagandist but, rather, an artist, "a man who wanders among the ruins, through the battlefields of humanity and is moved by every victim, by every fallen one." This was not a writer, said Maikov, who stood firmly by one position and might carry readers with him. Furthermore, times have changed: "The political element in his writing has lost its meaning, and only the great artist and a series of pictures remain. He has passed already into the pantheon of classics, which is, alas, a sort of honorary graveyard." Here we should note the parallel with Mark Twain's definition of a classic as a book which everyone wants to *have* read but no one *does* read. How dangerous, after all, can such a book be? The same argument was applied in Russia to Shelley's *Queen Mab*. Banned in 1866 as demagogical and atheistic, the poem was permitted three years later because of Shelley's status as an established literary giant.[53]

Maikov's final argument, also mentioned in an earlier report, quoted above, was a particularly persuasive one: "I am convinced that there would be no danger whatever in presenting Heine to our public in a complete collected works, all the more so because the cost of the edition, sold not as individual volumes, but complete, will render it inaccessible to the masses." Furthermore, he reminded the committee that a Russian edition of Heine's complete works was in preparation—with excisions, of course, made by the internal censorship—and that this would shrink the market for the German original. The committee—chaired, we must remember, by Heine's old friend and admirer, Tiutchev—accepted Maikov's proposal (which, he assured his colleagues, was his sincere opinion, "based not on a literal interpretation of censorship principles, but, rather, on an organic view of society"), and the set was made available for sale to that segment of the public that could afford it. Fedorov notes that "this decision was a compromise and, in fact, contradicted earlier decisions in which individual volumes of Heine (e.g., 4, 8) had been permitted, in their entirety, that is, without the excision of pages." Fedorov is convinced that the decision to permit the set could be made safely only because of the restrictive effect of the high price.[54]

Another well-known writer of belles lettres discussed by the committee in the 1860s was Victor Hugo, who was persistently criticized for his anti-Russian sentiments. For example, the words "Nicholas assassinating Poland" were excised from his novel *Les travailleurs de la mer* in 1866 (and again in 1892). Hugo's *Napoléon le petit* which, we recall, had struck an angry chord in censor Dukshta-Dukshinskii in 1852, was still irritating twenty years later. In 1872, toward the end of Tiutchev's term, the book was permitted only with the excision of the passage comparing Nicholas I with Louis Napoleon; this decision was reaffirmed in 1879 under Viazemskii and again in 1883 under Maikov.[55] Volumes 7 and 8 of *Les misérables* came before the committee in 1862. Censor Komarovskii found Hugo's political views difficult to accept but he had the insight to recognize that the work already was well known and read all over Europe. The report contains one sentence that is quite remarkable, a sentence acknowledging the futility of banning books at all: "Banned books do ultimately reach the public (since there are no books which you could not get in Saint Petersburg if you wanted them), and in this case they would have added attraction in the eyes of the readers due to their secret fame and the splendor of forbidden fruit." He concludes that "in such circumstances—rather rare, by the way—it might be more harmful to ban than to permit." Komarovskii proposed that the volumes be permitted with several necessary excisions, since the rest of the novel already had been released and to hold back the last volumes would mean disfiguring the entire work. His advice was taken.[56]

Darwin and his followers began to be noticed in Russia in the 1860s. Darwin himself was amazed by the lively interest in his work in Russia, which he learned about during a visit from the Russian scientist Vladimir Kovalevskii. Indeed, the first volume of *The Variation of Animals and Plants under Domestication* was published in Russia, in Kovalevskii's Russian translation, seven months before the publication in England of the original, and *The Origin of Species* had been republished four times by 1867.[57] However, works about Darwin's theories, especially popularizations, were not so welcome. A volume of essays on Darwinian theory by Ludwig Büchner was banned in 1868 because the essays were "written in a popular style, easily understood by anyone" and were directed against the dogmatic teachings of the Christian church. Three years later Theodor Herzka's *Die Urgeschichte der Erde und des Menschen* was banned. This explanation was given: "The author is a follower of Darwin. . . . The tone of this book is polemical and has neither Darwin's calm tone nor a strictly scientific tendency. . . . the materialistic tendencies are sharply pronounced."[58]

In March 1872, a little over a year before he died, Tiutchev signed a resolution on behalf of the committee directing that the London edition of the *Manifest der Kommunistischen Partei* (1848) be banned for the public. This action was taken in response to the recommendation of censor A. P. Esipov, who found that although this manifesto might not

> preach those horrors of destruction for which the international association of workers in Paris is celebrated, it has nonetheless sown its seeds in the productive soil of the proletariat, so hospitable to every form of disorder, and these seeds have grown, matured, and borne their fruits in recent developments.[59]

It would be interesting to know whether any Soviet biography of Tiutchev mentions the beloved poet's role in the banning of the *Manifesto*.

4

The Committee
and the Poet-Censors:
From Tiutchev to Maikov

In 1873 Tiutchev died and Prince P. P. Viazemskii took his
place as chairman, where he remained until his appointment in 1881
as head of the Chief Administration for Press Affairs. According to
Zlatkovskii, secretary of the committee at the time, the change caused
"Tiutchev's admirers to rally even more closely and impelled us to maintain Tiutchev's traditions in a more united way." While not damning him
altogether, Zlatkovskii was quite critical of Viazemskii and clearly did not
admit him to his company of poet-heroes, consisting of Tiutchev, Maikov,
and Polonskii.

> Our new chairman, son of the well-known poet Petr Andreevich—a
> contemporary of Pushkin's—although not stupid and a good man,
> had an uneven character, nervous and hot-tempered. He recognized
> no traditions, especially Tiutchev's. In work-related matters he was
> distrustful and over-anxious, not to say timorous, despite his high
> position in society. This instability and constant apprehension—not
> to make any kind of little mistake or error in form—sometimes made
> the job of secretary extremely onerous, and so quite frequently I had
> to unburden myself in conversation with our two poets and to recall
> with them the old days when Tiutchev was still with us.[1]

Another staff member critical of Viazemskii was A. E. Egorov, who had
joined the committee in the last year of Tiutchev's administration and
remained until 1881, when he left to become chairman of the Odessa

Foreign Censorship Committee. Thus his service on the committee coincided almost exactly with Viazemskii's term as chairman. Egorov came to the committee via the Saint Petersburg Censorship Committee (dealing with Russian publications), where he served for a couple of years as assistant to the secretary and to the censor for foreign publications. Before coming to the capital he had worked as a censor in Simbirsk (a city famous later as Lenin's birthplace), where his job had been to read the correspondence of Polish political prisoners exiled to Simbirsk province after the uprising of 1863. The position as assistant to the secretary was to be an interim appointment, until a high position in the Foreign Censorship Committee could be arranged. The man pulling the strings was M. N. Pokhvisnev, that same head of the Chief Censorship Administration who Tiutchev had found so nauseating. Pokhvisnev, a friend of Egorov's father in Vilno, also had planned to have Egorov named censor in the Riga Foreign Censorship Committee but was transferred from his Chief Censorship Administration job before he could make those arrangements.[2]

Egorov devotes several pages of his memoirs to his committee colleagues.[3] He had first met Tiutchev before joining the committee, while he was still working for the Moscow Censorship Committee. Tiutchev had visited the Moscow office and had made a strong impression on Egorov:

> He came to our department in winter, wearing his great raccoon coat thrown open, the way he always did, and a fur hat, his long grey hair sticking out from underneath, with a woolen scarf wound carelessly around his neck. His face was expressive, with its fine features and large forehead, and he wore spectacles through which he gazed with his clever but somehow weary eyes, which drew attention to him and compelled one to suspect that the man's senile appearance really concealed an uncommon personality.

The Foreign Censorship Committee offices in Saint Petersburg were located in the Shol'ts house on Obukhovskii Prospekt, near Sennaia. Egorov describes how "packages of books were hoisted up to us by a pulley strung to the window from the courtyard below." He writes that Zlatkovskii, the committee secretary, lived in an official apartment in the same building; a retired army officer, he had returned from the Crimean campaign with a head wound that made it impossible for him to bend his neck. Egorov was assigned to the German-Italian department, headed by Esipov, who he describes as a man "of advanced years," so senile that he would drop off to sleep in his armchair; after his death he was replaced by

Miller-Krasovskii, known, says Egorov, for his brochure on the importance of the rod in educating schoolchildren. The French and English department was run by Liubovnikov, while Maikov supervised the department handling newspapers and periodicals as well as works in Polish and other Slavic languages. Esipov, Liubovnikov, and Maikov were all senior censors.

Books were distributed among the junior censors according to the languages they knew: Polonskii read French, English, and Italian works; Miller-Krasovskii read only German; Dukshta-Dukshinskii handled Polish; and Shul'ts—a "censor-polyglot"—took on works in every conceivable language. Egorov, who knew five foreign languages himself, calls Shul'ts a "titan in his field," and tells how everyone watched with awe each Saturday as he brought back the enormous heap of books he had taken to read that week, producing a report on each one. No one ever learned his secret. Egorov mentions as possible competition Pevnitskii, formerly with the committee, later the censor for foreign publications in Dorpat, and finally a colleague in Odessa, a man with a degree in philology and remarkable linguistic ability, but concludes that even he was no match for Shul'ts.

Prince Pavel Petrovich Viazemskii resembled a boyar of Ivan the Terrible's time, reminisces Egorov; the painter Makovskii may have used him as a model for one of the boyars in his well-known piece, *Wedding in a Boyar's Home* (Svad'ba v boiarskom dome). As Egorov describes him:

> He always wore a monocle in his eye, his shabby frock-coat was stained with traces of food, and he was constantly rolling a ball of wax nervously in his fingers with their huge nails. . . . Sympathetic in appearance, he gave the impression of being a good-natured simpleton, but in fact he lacked that softheartedness which is a distinguishing feature of the Russian character.

To illustrate Viazemskii's attitudes Egorov relates an incident that occurred after the prince's term on the Foreign Censorship Committee, when he was head of the Chief Censorship Administration. It involved Egorov's cousin, N. V. Egorov, who had at one time been the censor for foreign publications in Moscow but at this time dealt with Russian publications at the Moscow Censorship Committee. He had permitted for publication in a magazine a caricature that seemed perfectly harmless. A few days later, however, instructions came from Viazemskii in Saint Petersburg to dismiss the censor responsible for permitting the caricature. No one in the Moscow office could understand why this drawing should be the cause of such drastic punishment. N. V. Egorov decided to go to Saint Petersburg and talk to

Viazemskii. The prince informed him that the caricature was really about socialists and chided the thunderstruck censor, remonstrating that ignorance was no excuse: "A censor is obliged to know and understand everything!"

Egorov's cousin happened to drop by the Foreign Censorship Committee office, where he told his friends about his misfortune. One of the censors remembered seeing the same caricature in one of the German humor magazines and recalled that it had been permitted for circulation in Russia. They found the issue and gave it to Egorov's cousin, who took it to Viazemskii; convinced that the drawing really was nothing more than an ordinary German joke, the prince reported this new fact to the minister and the innocent censor got his job back. According to Egorov, this incident attracted a good deal of attention in high places.

When Egorov was offered a position in Odessa as senior censor and chairman of the Foreign Censorship Committee there, Viazemskii was upset because the head of the Chief Administration for Press Affairs proposed to promote one of his own subordinates so prematurely, and without even asking his advice. When Egorov told Viazemskii about his move, "he frowned at me and observed morosely: 'I shall not congratulate you on this appointment; impossible things are going on there and you will have to get yourself out of a terrible mess.'" Egorov observes that Viazemskii was not known for benevolence toward his subordinates.[4]

Viazemskii was succeeded as chairman by Apollon Nikolaevich Maikov, whose committee service under Krasovskii and Tiutchev was discussed in chapters 2 and 3 of this book. Like Tiutchev, Maikov is far better known as one of Russia's outstanding poets than as a censor. But through his job in the Foreign Censorship Committee he had a great deal to do with the official response to Western ideas in Russia; seen in this light, his career as a censor, like Tiutchev's, is certainly worthy of attention. Since this chapter deals with the period of Maikov's chairmanship, the last years of his life, let us look back briefly at Maikov's youth and see how this great poet came to be connected with the Foreign Censorship Committee in the first place.

As a boy Maikov had dreamed of following in his father's footsteps and becoming a painter, but his early success as a poet, combined with near-sightedness, had caused him to devote himself to literature. (Maikov's brothers Vladimir and Leonid were also well-known literary figures, the former a journalist and translator, the latter a historian of literature and a folklorist.) In his biography of Maikov, Zlatkovskii tells of the young poet's last flirtation with painting and his decisive turn to literature. In 1842 Emperor Nicholas I saw a painting of Maikov's in his father's studio and wanted it (since the artist refused remuneration for his picture, the emperor presented him with a diamond ring). At the same time Maikov's first collection of verse was published. When Count S. S. Uvarov, then minister of education, presented the volume to the emperor, the latter asked what the young man wanted to do. Learning that Maikov wished to go to Italy, Nicholas ordered that he be given one thousand rubles for the trip, so Maikov went off to Europe on a royal subsidy, traveling for nearly two years in Italy, France, Germany, and Bohemia.

Not only the emperor and the minister were impressed with Maikov; his professors at Saint Petersburg University recognized him as an extraordinarily versatile and excellent student. He had graduated from the law faculty in 1841 and, apparently, could have been a mathematician as well, having written an exceptionally fine entrance examination in that field. His Russian literature professors all thought very highly of him. Among them was A. V. Nikitenko, already discussed as a censor; Zlatkovskii credits Nikitenko with being one of the first to take Maikov seriously as a poet. Recognition came also from the highest level of the university: the rector publicly praised Maikov when his book of verse appeared.

Shortly after his graduation from the university in January 1842, Maikov began his career in government service with a posting to the Department of the Exchequer in the Ministry of Finance. Zlatkovskii points out that this appointment was unusual since ordinarily a young person just out of the university had to spend several years in the provinces before being given a position in the capital. Maikov had been such a brilliant student that an exception was made in his case.[5]

Upon his return from Europe in September 1844, Maikov was transferred from his position in the Department of the Exchequer to the Rumiantsev Museum, where he worked as an assistant to the librarian. (Known today as the Lenin Library, the Rumiantsev Museum library collection was destined to become the largest in the country.) He remained at that post until October 1852, when he began his new job as junior censor at the Foreign Censorship Committee where he was to remain, rising in rank and position, until his death nearly forty-five years later.[6] Incidentally, one cannot help but wonder whether Maikov's unusual first name and his career in the civil service might have influenced a later Russian writer, Andrei Belyi; in his novel *Peterburg* Belyi called the senior bureaucrat Apollon Apollonovich, and his son, Nikolai Apollonovich.

It was Krasovskii who hired Maikov. Zlatkovskii searched the committee archives and found a letter written by "the unforgettable Krasovskii" to Prince Shirinskii-Shikhmatov, then minister of education and his superior, justifying his choice of Maikov to fill the vacancy. Krasovskii had preferred Maikov to the other two candidates—Klepfer, formerly director of a Moscow high school, and Karpov, a professor at a Saint Petersburg seminary—although all three were clearly capable of doing the job.

> In my apartment each of them examined approximately twenty works of varied contents in French and German, and Maikov examined two additional books in Italian. From the opinions written by them about the various books and the comparison of these opinions with each other and then with the reports on these books written by the censors it was possible to reach the general conclusion that each of the above-named applicants for the position of censor would appear to be capable of doing the job. However, of the three applicants for the one opening on the Committee for junior censor I must give preference to the first, that is, to Mr. Maikov, not only because he appeared for his examination before the other two, or because he examined two more books than the others and, indeed, in three languages, but, rather, because by appointing him to the Committee censor Nagel', who has been discharged but who has served on the Committee for more than fourteen years, will not lose his entire salary, because the authorities at the Rumiantsev Museum have promised to give him the position of librarian which Mr. Maikov now holds there. For this reason I have the honor to recommend to your Excellency the appointment of Mr. Maikov to the post of acting junior censor in the Committee as my first choice.

As far as foreign languages are concerned, we know that in addition to French, German, and Italian, Maikov read the classics and Roman law in the original Latin while at the university. He did not know Greek and had to read the Greek poets in French translation. However, he studied modern Greek in 1858 thus enabling him to use modern Greek material in connection with his own poetry. His study of Greek came about as the result of an imperial order: Grand Duke Constantine Nikolaevich had him transferred to the Naval Office for one year so that he might join a naval expedition to Greece and the Archipelago; in preparation for this assignment Maikov studied the language.

Zlatkovskii gives no explanation as to why Maikov in particular should have been chosen for this mission but he does report that as a result Maikov was unable to take part in a project that Minister of Education A. S. Norov had organized in November 1857. The project was the review of the 1828 censorship statutes mentioned in chapter 3 of this book. Norov had appointed a temporary committee and wanted Maikov not only to be a member but to be in charge of the business of the committee. However, the grand duke's wishes obviously took precedence over those of the minister and Maikov went over to the navy. Maikov had another chance in 1869 to participate in a review of the foreign censorship statute but nothing appears to have come of that review either.[7]

Zlatkovskii's opinion of Krasovskii was more temperate than Ryzhov's, perhaps because he only joined the committee after Krasovskii's death and was able to take a more objective view. He saw the chairman's letter to the minister about Maikov as a perfect illustration of Krasovskii's personality, in which two diverse qualities—his strict sense of duty, justice, and humanity, and his pettiness as a "pedant-bureaucrat and a fool"—somehow managed to coexist harmoniously.

On the one hand, as a man known for scrupulous fairness for whom personal preferences played no role in the choice of a man, in his capacity as a chief concerned about the office entrusted to him, he practically locked himself up in his apartment with three aspirants for a vacancy to determine beyond all doubt which was the most worthy one, and when all three turned out to be equally suitable, his sense of justice made him prefer the man who appeared first and who, moreover, had examined two more books than the others. But a humane feeling also surfaced in him: by appointing Mr. Maikov he could also give the censor who was leaving the Committee (his eyesight had been destroyed by too much reading) the opportunity to occupy the place left vacant in the Rumiantsev Museum.

Having given Krasovskii his due, Zlatkovskii then went on to describe the comical aspects of the case:

The chief of an administrative office seats in different corners of his apartment — like schoolboys at an examination — a poet who has already made a great name for himself, the former director of a *gimnaziia*, and a former professor at a seminary, a translator of Plato—and performs on them curious experiments in the course of four whole months and appoints himself as the sole expert judge—even though he was undoubtedly less educated than his so-called aspirants who were being examined! And also one must ask whether it was ultimately worth the expenditure of so much time, energy, and, at the very least, one-hundred sheets of "official" paper!

(In Russian government offices special notarized paper was used for all written communications.)

Even after Maikov had been appointed as junior censor, he remained on probation, as it were, because, in Zlatkovskii's words, "Krasovskii, in his nervousness, was not yet quite convinced that our poet was capable enough to carry out the duties of a censor." Maikov finally was confirmed in 1854, when Krasovskii felt confident enough to inform the minister in his annual report for 1853 that

> Mr. Maikov is sufficiently skilled as a censor, and because of his capabilities and his knowledge of many languages and his constant diligence he has always been a useful official in the Committee. . . . in the last two months of 1852 and in the course of 1853 Mr. Maikov examined 223 books in four languages: French, German, Italian, and English; these books contained 101,329 pages in octavo. To do justice to the proven capabilities and labors of Mr. Collegial Assessor Maikov in fulfilling the duties of junior censor in the Foreign Censorship Committee, and at the same time wishing to encourage him to continue his active and useful service here, I now have the honor humbly to request your Excellency to confirm this official as a junior censor in the Committee entrusted to me.[8]

In the second edition of his biography of Maikov, published the year following the poet's death, Zlatkovskii reminisces about his years on the committee, thus providing us with a few new details, some further definition and color for our woefully incomplete picture. Zlatkovskii obviously revered Maikov who emerges from the narrative not only as a great artist, but as a warm and endearing human being. Zlatkovskii joined the committee in 1862, when Tiutchev was chairman, Polonskii was secretary, and Maikov was a member of the staff. This august company totally overwhelmed the young man: "I completely lost my head, I imagined that I had boldly penetrated Parnassus, that the Olympian gods were beings of a higher order who think and speak not as we ordinary mortals do, and finally, that they would judge my every awkward step, my every ill-timed remark."

At first he had no contact with the poets and was satisfied merely to stand near the "holy of holies, as we then called the meeting room" on meeting days to catch a glimpse of "our coryphae." Once, he relates, Maikov came in, grief-stricken by the death of his only daughter. Noticing Zlatkovskii and recognizing him as a junior member of the committee, Maikov approached and greeted him. Without thinking, the younger man blurted out his sympathy: "I am sorry for you . . . your only daughter!" . . . Apollon Nikolaevich gazed at me through his spectacles for the second time, both astonished and touched; without a word he shook my hand firmly and walked away. . . . I heard as in a dream A. N. asking someone: 'Who is this young man?' then 'Has he been at the Committee long?' " Deeply embarrassed, Zlatkovskii resolved not to appear on Wednesdays anymore,

> so as not to meet A. N. and commit new stupidities. Two or three weeks passed, I relaxed a bit and thought to myself: "Perhaps he's forgotten!" But I was seriously mistaken: A. N. *never* forgot the kind of action which may seem stupid but comes from a sincere heart. On one of those Wednesdays I was sitting at my desk, absorbed in some sort of tedious work, when suddenly I felt someone's hand on my shoulder. I glanced up and saw Maikov in front of me. Before I could become embarrassed A. N. managed to overcome my timidity by his tender, compassionate tone. He plied me with questions: "What kind of wisdom are you so absorbed in? . . . Why have you disappeared? Did you think it would be impossible to find you? You see, I have sought you out! So? What do you think of that? Well, give me a cigarette . . . there's still a quarter of an hour before the meeting . . . We have time to smoke and have a chat . . ." Word by word Ap. Nik. inquired about my work, my employment, gave me some friendly advice, interspersing all this with jokes and anecdotes, and not only charmed me completely, but gave me back my peace of mind. Thus he was able to guess what was going on in someone else's soul and to reconcile a person with himself.[9]

Egorov too relates some impressions of Maikov gathered during the 1870s, when they worked together at the committee. Although Maikov was in charge of the department dealing with publications in Slavic languages and with newspapers and periodicals received by the committee, Egorov maintains that he had no interest at all in these materials and left them entirely in the hands of his colleague Dukshta-Dukshinskii, who had worked in the department for almost fifty years and who later succeeded Maikov as head.

> Our poet used to run to his department with his quick step, stick a few newly received books requiring review into his briefcase, and, passing back through the room where the Committee's longtime watchman, Dolotov, "worked" with mechanical composure, cutting out and blotting over passages in books and magazines as indicated by the censors to be excised and banned, Maikov would call out to him as he passed: "Well done, old man! Are you printing? Print, old chap, print!"—and he would dash to the exit.

This watchman with whom Maikov loved to joke was, according to Egorov, a characteristic figure in such offices, which depended in large part on these honest, hard-working men to keep the machine functioning. Dolotov had been senior watchman at the committee for as long as anyone could remember.

> Of course, he did not know a single word of any foreign language, but he had excellent mastery of all our methods and manipulations, he knew what was going on in all the departments, what was located where, what was supposed to be distributed, where excisions were to be made, and what was to be retained. In his sphere of activity he was in truth invaluable—an excellent type of Russian self-taught common man with the addition of the self control and discipline of a soldier of Nicholas I. We all treated him with respect, and if in their bureaucratic arrogance our young people occasionally permitted themselves to speak scornfully to him, he unceremoniously checked them, calling them young whippersnappers. Protecting the stock of books in their cupboards, he watched over them like a true and constant sentry, and no book ever left his storehouse without being accounted for.

Maikov took the old man's promising son under his wing, saw that he received a proper education, and sent him to the Academy of Arts, where he was trained to be an architect. The young man was a success and wanted to support his father but Dolotov was so devoted to his committee that he insisted on spending the rest of his life as watchman.

Egorov compares Dolotov with his watchman at the Odessa committee, a man who did his job as well as Dolotov, "sorting them [foreign publications] without errors after taking them out of the heavy containers and laying them on tables for the censors to examine, arranging them by categories." But this man, a Catholic from Lithuania, was not as trustworthy as Dolotov. Egorov began to hear rumors that he had some sort of dealings with local booksellers, and after he had been caught twice Egorov had to dismiss him. Apparently the watchman had had an arrangement with one bookseller to put aside certain publications, marked before shipping so he could identify them as he unpacked the boxes. Naturally, says Egorov, "the designated books were all ones forbidden for circulation in Russia, and by letting them through, the Odessa censorship took the full blame, and I was the person held responsible."[10] We do not know how common this sort of incident was but one can assume that not all watchmen were as dedicated as Dolotov, and that Odessa was only one of numerous similar holes in the fence around the empire.

Zlatkovskii drew closer still to the poet-censors after 1870, when he was named secretary of the committee. In addition to his own narrative, we are fortunate to have an outsider's views of the committee (and of the functioning of the foreign censorship in general) at this time. This was the period, we will recall, when Tiutchev was rather discouraged about the pettiness of his colleagues who had, he felt, lost sight of the higher purposes of censorship. Furthermore, his committee had been placed under much stricter supervision as a result of its alleged laxity and it was necessary to adhere strictly to the rules. An old university friend of Maikov's, A. Chumikov, had an encounter with the committee in 1873 that illustrates not only the absurdity of the system, but the sort of method that an enterprising citizen might devise to circumvent that system.

Chumikov's problem revolved around a German edition of essays by the Polish poet Mickiewicz. Chumikov was living in Helsingfors (now Helsinki); Finland was at this time part of the Russian Empire. A friend in Revel (now Talinn) in the Baltic province of Estonia (also part of the empire) owned the edition in question and mailed it to Chumikov in Helsingfors. He read it and returned it to its owner in Revel, also by mail, but after some time his friend informed him that the volumes had not arrived. Chumikov made inquiries at the Helsingfors post office and learned, to his great annoyance, that the books probably had been held back at the Saint Petersburg Customs office and forwarded to the Foreign Censorship Committee. Chumikov notes that although Mickiewicz's works were on the index in the Saint Petersburg Foreign Censorship Committee, in Vilno and Warsaw they were available with approval of the censorship, and that Heine's banned works "were sold freely by every Saint Petersburg German bookseller." Thus, he concludes that to the proverb "Every city

has its mores" should be added the words: "and its laws!" He decided that
he would have to

> rescue the books in Petersburg, where I counted heavily on the help of
> my university comrade, Apollon Nikolaevich Maikov, then working at
> that committee. . . . Having sought out A. N. Maikov in Petersburg
> and told him about my adversity, I encountered on his part complete
> readiness to help me rescue the confiscated work of Mickiewicz. We
> went immediately to the censorship committee located not far from
> his apartment (on the Bol'shaia Sadovaia Street). But to our common
> astonishment a *non possumus* awaited us there, announced by the
> secretary of the committee. This limb of the censorship laws indicated
> the volumes of the *Lectures* sitting peacefully in the bookcase and
> explained that it was impossible to give them to me, since they had
> already been entered into the register of confiscated books. You can
> imagine the embarrassment of the good Maikov, who had come to the
> committee with complete assurance that he, as senior censor, would
> not have any difficulty in helping me.

In desperation Chumikov came up with a plan to "outwit" the censorship. "The plan I thought of could not, in fact, deceive either A. N.
Maikov or the secretary of the committee, but they grasped at it with
pleasure as a means of helping me without breaking the law."

> I ascertained that in the book trade there was the practice of returning
> foreign books not cleared by the censorship to those booksellers abroad
> from whom they had been received. Let us do the same with my
> books: suppose that I bought them in Helsingfors, and since Finland
> has separate censorship regulations and its own Customs office, let us
> send the books to the latter, which has its office at the Finland rail-
> road station; the Customs office there will send them back to the
> bookseller.
> My proposal was accepted, and the very next day I prepared to go to
> Helsingfors. Before my train departed I stopped at the Finnish Cus-
> toms office out of curiosity, to see whether a package of books had
> been received from the censorship committee to be returned to
> Helsingfors. "Yes, it has been received," they told me, "and if you
> want to deliver it to the address, take it with you." And they handed
> me my Mickiewicz, without asking my name or demanding any kind
> of paper. And so the *Lectures* found themselves in my hands once

again and on the shelves of my library, and were later returned to their owner, but not, of course, through the mail.[11]

Maikov became chairman in 1882 after Viazemskii had been named head of the Chief Administration for Press Affairs. Zlatkovskii was, of course, delighted by his appointment: "Ideal relations between the chairman and his secretary such as we had are difficult to imagine: he gave me his full confidence, being convinced that I would never in any way "let him down," hide anything from him, that I would always remind him in time what needed to be done." Zlatkovskii recalls that, unlike Viazemskii before him, Maikov relied on him to run things properly at the committee: "He often said that he could sleep peacefully, for 'the guard was at his post.'" (We recall that some years earlier Minister of Education Uvarov also had claimed to sleep peacefully, knowing that his watchdog, Krasovskii, was on duty.) In Zlatkovskii's estimation Maikov was the perfect chief: "A cleverer, more erudite, encyclopedically educated and humane chairman would be difficult to imagine. On Wednesdays, the meeting days, A. N. proceeded with great solemnity. He loved these days, loved to preside and was extremely distressed if he had to be absent on those days due to ill health or some other reason."[12]

Reminiscences by men who knew Maikov as a censor add to our picture of the poet in his official capacity. N. N. Beliavskii had met Maikov through his uncle, A. S. Liubovnikov, head of the committee's French-English department, whom he describes as "the well-known linguist, the first translator of Dickens into Russian [Little Dorrit], who wrote reviews of foreign literature in Golos [Voice], Petersburgskie vedomosti [Petersburg bulletin] and other publications, and who chaired the Committee in place of Apollon Nikolaevich in view of his frequent indispositions." After 1882, when Maikov was chairman, Beliavskii recalls delivering books to him at his apartment on Bol'shaia Sadovaia Street at the corner of Ekateringofskii Prospekt: "I invariably found A. N. in the depths of his study, sitting in an armchair with a book in his hands, his legs covered with a rug. On the table lay piles of new books, neatly stacked, awaiting examination, which A. N. devoured in incredible quantities." Also on the table, continues Beliavskii, were "several Badmaev powders of a brick-red color: having lost confidence in our allopathy A. N. had at this period of his life become a regular patient of Badmaev, a physician practicing Tibetan medicine."

Looking back twenty-five years, Beliavskii remembers Maikov as

an old man of good color; his radiant eyes had a stern gaze which penetrated into one's soul. He wore spectacles with round lenses and was very thin. Even indoors he generally wore a long summer-weight coat over his clothes, since he was very sensitive to cold—he gave the impression of an ascetic. . . . strict with himself and others, his whole life was incessant labor and enrichment through knowledge.

Maikov's work-ethic is illustrated by a conversation he had with V. A. Alekseev on the subject of work in 1889, when Alekseev was a young man. Maikov asked him why he so stubbornly refused to take a job. Alekseev replied that he wanted above all to be a literary man and was afraid that if he worked he would not have time for literature. "That is all very well, but in Russia it is difficult for a writer to live without a job or a fortune. If you worked, you would also become accustomed to neatness and promptness. It is having a job which teaches one to be neat, prompt."[13]

Another man who knew Maikov at the committee was N. Mardar'ev who, like Egorov, also served as a censor of both foreign and Russian publications in other cities (Kiev, Odessa, Rostov-on-the-Don). He began work as a censor at the Saint Petersburg committee in 1886 and recalls Maikov as

> a little old man, graying, not very tall, always calm and quiet, who usually appeared at the Committee once a week for the meeting. Quietly, noiselessly he slipped into the office of A. S. Liubovnikov, the senior censor who ran the Anglo-French section, and only his quiet voice: "Good morning, gentlemen," caused us, his co-workers, to raise our heads and answer the chairman's greeting.[14]

The third member of the committee's poetic triumvirate, Iakov Petrovich Polonskii, was born and raised in the province of Riazan'. Like Maikov, he began writing poetry as a schoolboy and attracted the attention of the great poet Zhukovskii when he passed through Riazan' with his royal pupil, the future Emperor Alexander II. In 1840 Polonskii entered the law faculty of Moscow University but, unlike Maikov, he was not a brilliant student. After finishing his studies he spent some years in Odessa and Tiflis, supporting himself by giving private lessons, doing editorial work, and continuing to publish his work. (He had his difficulties with the internal censorship, as did most writers.) He traveled in Germany, Switzerland, Italy, and France; married a young Russian woman but was soon widowed (he was married again to a sculptress in 1866); and served as editor of the journal *Russkoe slovo* (Russian Word) in 1859 and 1860. He left this job when a new publisher took over the journal and, being in need of a regular position, he applied for the job of secretary of the Foreign Censorship Committee, which happened to be vacant at the time, and was hired by Tiutchev.

Of Polonskii's term as secretary we know of one incident. His friend Elena Stackenschneider wrote in her diary on 5 February 1863 that Polonskii had received a letter from the writer Fedor Glinka in regard to his book, published in Berlin, which had been sent to the Foreign Censorship Committee. Glinka, a metaphysical poet, had written a book-length poem entitled *Kaplia tainstvennaia* (The Secret Drop) based on a legend about the Virgin Mary. The book had been banned by the Russian internal censorship and Glinka apparently thought that his poet-colleagues at the foreign censorship might use their influence to help him. He wrote asking Polonskii to "give protection to the Berlin orphan," and referred to squeezing his "warm poetic hand." Stackenschneider obviously found the letter amusing: "you could laugh yourself to death over it."[15]

In the spring of 1863 Polonskii was promoted to the position of junior censor. It seems that he had made arrangements to reduce the burden of his new job to the minimum. On 4 April Stackenschneider wrote in her diary, "When Polonskii becomes a censor I shall censor the German books." I. N. Rozanov, who wrote the commentary on Stackenschneider's diary, notes that "when Polonskii got the job of censor she transferred the burden of censorship work almost completely from his shoulders to hers and in the course of many years she was the actual and secret censor of foreign books." Rozanov adds that, according to A. Ia. Polonskii, the poet's son, the job "troubled the poet very little: Elena Andreevna looked through practically all the foreign works, not only the German ones, and in most cases Iakov Petrovich merely sanctioned her opinion." In October 1868, Stackenschneider mentioned giving Polonskii English lessons, but either he was a poor pupil or simply unwilling to dispense with the services of his unpaid assistant, for twelve years later she wrote that Polonskii was sending her English books and newspapers to be censored.

It seems likely that other censors made similar arrangements with friends, especially well-educated ladies such as Elena Stackenschneider who were fluent in foreign languages. In at least one case censoring was done openly by a husband and wife team; Egorov mentions Baron Gan in Odessa, an elderly and mild-mannered gentleman who headed the internal and foreign censorship in Odessa for twelve years and worked in tandem with his much stricter baroness. One Odessa resident suggests that the couple's two pet parrots also had a voice in their decisions. (The baron was asked once by a superior what award he would choose, to which he responded, "I would like to be a German, Your Excellency!")[16]

Polonskii continued to work as a censor until the mid-1890s, when he was recommended by Maikov to serve on the Council of the Chief Administration for Press Affairs, in which position he remained until his death in October 1898. He apparently was required to appear at the office only for the weekly meeting, since he was not head of a section and thus had no administrative responsibilities. Mardar'ev notes that Polonskii's arrival rarely went unnoticed.

> Despite the distance between our section and the hall porter we heard Iakov Petrovich's powerful voice while he was still taking off his overcoat or fur coat as he conversed with Pavel, the courier. Then the door opened noisily and Iakov Petrovich, banging his crutches (needed because of a caries in his leg) boomed: "Good morning, gentlemen," and as he walked he was already talking about something or other, disturbing the peace and quiet which usually reigned at the Committee. And we co-workers did not confine ourselves to a simple response to Iakov Petrovich's greeting; rather, we rose from our places as if involuntarily and hurried to shake his hand and listen to his story. . . . A few minutes later we heard Iakov Petrovich's voice from another section of the Committee, and then it thundered in the meeting room while the censors' reports on the books they had read were being examined.

As for Polonskii's orientation as a censor, Mardar'ev portrays him as

> a great advocate of the free circulation of foreign literature in Russian society. And his reports on the books which he had reviewed very rarely concluded with the stereotypic conclusion: "In view of all this I find that the work in question should be banned for circulation in Russia." He held the same free view in regard to the issuing of banned books requested by individuals. Iakov Petrovich's voice was usually heard to boom: "Give it to him!"

While the written opinions were probably the work of Polonskii's "assistant," Elena Stackenschneider, we can assume that he agreed wholeheartedly with her conclusions.[17]

Mardar'ev recalls Polonskii's "stout figure . . , his powerful, somewhat coarse voice, his good-natured smile." Describing the committee meetings, Mardar'ev pictures Maikov as completely overwhelmed by Polonskii, who was "always boisterous, constantly inveighing against someone or something." Mardar'ev and Zlatkovskii do not quite agree on Maikov's role at the weekly meetings. Zlatkovskii portrays him as quiet, to be sure, but definitely in control of the meetings, which he chaired in an animated fashion. Mardar'ev, on the other hand, sees Polonskii as dominant, drowning out his less boisterous friend. Since both Zlatkovskii and Mardar'ev attended the weekly meetings regularly, we can only conclude that we are dealing here with quite natural differences in perception. There is no doubt, however, that Maikov and Polonskii were very different types.

Beliavskii too emphasizes the contrast between the quiet, scholarly asceticism of Maikov and Polonskii's exuberance: "Polonskii . . . had the appearance of a man who wore his heart upon his sleeve, whose heart ruled his head. . . . [He] was happy-go-lucky and indulgent towards others." Beliavskii describes Polonskii as "emanating sympathy from his large figure and frank face." But although he saw Polonskii as "very affable, a good comrade," Beliavskii characterizes him as a

> not very diligent official. At the Committee meetings, where they discussed questions of retaining or excising passages from books, or blacking out certain places (the so-called application of "caviar"), Iakov Petrovich would grow bored and his colleagues, taking advantage of his habit of constantly drawing, frequently supplied him with sheets of paper with ink blots, which Ia. P. would sketch, connecting all the blots into one picture. My uncle saved several of these sheets with landscapes by Polonskii, skillfully done with a pen during the meetings. These impromptu drawings reveal Ia. P. as a remarkably clever graphic artist.[18]

Zlatkovskii often mentions his close friendship with Maikov and Polonskii. Beliavskii confirms that relationship, adding that Maikov and Zlatkovskii often had to join ranks to prevent their naive and absent-minded comrade Polonskii from squandering all his money. He passes on this anecdote about Polonskii, which he learned from Zlatkovskii. While a house guest at the country home of his friend Fet, another famous poet, Polonskii was continually borrowing small sums of money from Zlatkovskii. Curious to learn where he was spending all this money, Zlatkovskii watched him closely and discovered that he stuffed it all into his pockets and then left his clothes to be cleaned at night by the servants, who not only cleaned the clothes, but cleaned out their owner! Thereafter, Zlatkovskii himself quietly emptied his friend's pockets, and upon their departure to the city returned all the money to Polonskii.[19]

Another man who knew Polonskii as a censor was Ieronim Iasinskii, who came to Saint Petersburg at the end of the 1870s and "discovered that the poet Polonskii worked in the censorship — the foreign censorship, to be sure, which was not considered to be so disgraceful." The question of how writer-censors viewed their work and themselves and were viewed by the intellectual community is, of course, of great interest. Iasinskii relates a revealing conversation with Ivan Goncharov, the novelist, who worked in the internal censorship. Goncharov complained that Turgenev, with whom he was quarreling at the time, had attacked him because of his censorship activities. But what about Maikov and Polonskii, who were also censors, Goncharov asked, why were they not also under attack? Someone responded that they worked in the foreign censorship.

> "Well yes, foreign, but censorship all the same. What's the difference?" shouted Goncharov. "It's true that they don't do anything, while I worked night and day. It's true that I worked in the general censorship. And do you know how I earned my reputation as a strict censor? By battling against stupidity. I let through the clever authors without argument, but I saw to it that the road to literature was closed to fools. I lowered the barrier and told them to make themselves scarce. Yes, I myself am against censorship, I am not an advocate of arbitrary rule, I am a literary man *pur sang*. But one must protect literature against the invasion of stupidity. Not one single editor would permit a stupid story or article in his journal. So why should literature have to be free in this respect?"[20]

The artist Aleksandr Serov, who censored foreign newspapers, was more cynical. When the fact that he was a censor was greeted with horrified astonishment he hastened to say that he was in the *foreign* censorship and, when asked why he continued such disagreeable work, he responded that it was not more disagreeable than any other stupid job. Egorov, who hated working in the internal censorship, positively welcomed the opportunity provided by the foreign censorship to spend his time reading books and magazines in all languages. He saw in his Moscow job a chance to broaden his perspectives and acquaint himself with world literature: "In this respect working in the foreign censorship undoubtedly has its agreeable aspects, compared to any other kind [of censorship]."[21]

Egorov recalls Polonskii spending most of his time up in the clouds with his music (in the company of another censor, G. A. Lishin, known for his recitations to music), and Iasinskii too tells several amusing anecdotes about the poet's absentmindedness. For instance, he once fell asleep still holding the hand of a guest who had come to greet him. The guest sat for half an hour, not wishing to awaken his respected host, and was only released when Polonskii's wife came in and shrieked, "My God, he forgot he had you in his hand!" He was known to extinguish his cigar in the jam pot and, once, dining at Maikov's house, he forgot where he was, imagined that the guests were at his house, and rose to apologize for the poor meal. Fortunately, Maikov was his dear friend and did not take offense.

Most amusing perhaps was Polonskii's conversation with Emperor Alexander III, to whom he was presented in 1887, on the occasion of his jubilee. In the Russian civil service a civilian might hold military rank, and Polonskii was a general. Iasinskii remarks that he "did not seem like a general; one might say that he was a bureaucrat due to a misunderstanding." But a general he was, and so Polonskii donned his moth-eaten general's cap (worn only on this occasion and at his own funeral) and set off for the palace. When the emperor asked his name, Polonskii grew confused and forgot it:

> He shrugged his shoulders helplessly and said, "Pardon me, your Highness, I simply can't remember it." Pointing to his forehead, he said, "It's spinning, spinning, and I couldn't tell you to save my life!" Then, turning to the master of ceremonies: "Please announce my name to his Highness!" "This is the famous poet, your Highness: Iakov Petrovich Polonskii!" announced the master of ceremonies.

The emperor is reported to have smiled graciously and done Polonskii the great honor of inviting him to join the royal family for breakfast, but Polonskii refused, explaining that he had already eaten breakfast. "'What a fool you are!' Maikov told him when he heard about this answer to the emperor. 'What can I do? In general I'm stupid,' admitted Polonskii. He considered stupidity to be in general a virtue for a poet." Polonskii may have borrowed this idea from Pushkin, who held the same view; he wrote that "poetry must be a little stupid."[22]

The same familiar themes run through censors' reports from the Viazemskii and Maikov periods. Predictably, perhaps, Maikov's influence softened the Viazemskii hard line in some cases. Voltaire is a good example; he was one of those foreign writers not protected by their status as authors of classics, and individual volumes of his collected works were still being banned or permitted with excisions. In 1877 and again in 1883

Voltaire was accused of "sharply expressing his atheistic views. He questions the traditions of the Holy Writ with his caustic satire and profanes them with characteristic relentlessness." In 1878 censor L. Ivanovskii wrote a similar report on a new edition of *Oeuvres choisies*, recommending that the section entitled "Religion" be excised, but the committee chose to ban the entire book. Editions of Voltaire's works continued to demand the censors' attention in the 1880s, but now the attitude had shifted; it would seem that Voltaire finally had lost his sting. As Polonskii wrote in his 1884 report on *Extraits des oeuvres*, "Voltaire struck me as the most naive fool and a poor wit after Byron, Heine, and the scientific school of German materialists." And of *Extraits en prose* he wrote in 1888 that "for us Russians the works of Herzen represent more deadly poison than does Voltaire, but even Herzen has lost his fascination."

Earlier in the 1888 report Polonskii observed that

> after everything which has been written and published about Voltaire not only abroad, but even here in our journals, when you actually read him he does not seem at all frightening. On the contrary, everything he wrote seems insipid after the narcotic effect of contemporary literature. To our half-baked philosophers and atheists Voltaire will undoubtedly seem like a believer, and our anarchists and nihilists will find him unpleasant, since Voltaire preaches that the happiest country is the one which voluntarily bows to laws. . . . One does perhaps encounter dubious passages in this book, but nowhere in this collection does he reject religion or touch upon the essence of Christianity.

As Aizenshtok points out, Polonskii's technique here is of interest; he compares Voltaire to contemporary writers and shows him to be by far the lesser evil. Nevertheless, Aizenshtok reminds us, Polonskii wrote at least one later report in which Voltaire is portrayed again as a dangerous writer. He apparently had not convinced all his colleagues either, for in 1896 a censor reviewing a Russian translation of *La Princesse de Babylone* wrote that Voltaire's works would have the same effect on Russians as they had had in France in the eighteenth century; that is, "to prepare for the revolution and give it an anti-religious character."[23]

Victor Hugo was still seen as an anti-Russian troublemaker in the 1870s and 1880s; his collection of essays, *Actes et paroles pendant exil*, was permitted in 1876 only after the excision of an article that assailed the Russian government and expressed sympathy for the Poles. (The decision was reaffirmed in 1886.) Another French writer immensely popular in Russia was Emile Zola; as in Darwin's case, some of his works were published in Russia before they appeared in France.[24] In 1885 *Germinal* was permitted by the committee in the original. The book was brought to the attention of Konstantin Pobedonostsev, the reactionary head of the Holy Synod of the Russian Orthodox church and one of the most powerful men in Russia at the time. He wrote to Evgenii Feoktistov, then head of the Chief Administration for Press Affairs, quoting from a friend's letter to him about the book:

> "Have you seen Zola's new novel *Germinal?* This book deserves attention. *Translation into Russian must be absolutely forbidden.* Do you know that our thick journals vie with one another to translate Zola's novels, and that they are read eagerly by the *rural clergy* and *factory workers? Germinal* may be the best thing Zola has written. It is the story of a strike exactly like the ones taking place in our own factories. It is written with filth and blood and is saturated with the conviction of the imminence and lawfulness of a worldwide socialist revolution. The hero is a *Russian nihilist. . . .* The translation must not be permitted, not even with excisions. The original is harmless—the French language is dying out here."

Pobedonostsev concluded his letter to Feoktistov by instructing him to see that no translation of *Germinal* appeared. He was too late, however; as he was writing his letter a translation was being published in a Russian journal.[25] It is interesting that in this case the French original was viewed as harmless because "French . . . is dying out here"; certainly the reports from the Foreign Censorship Committee during this period do not support that statement. On the other hand, it would not be to the committee's advantage to voice such a view, since by doing so the censors might talk themselves out of their jobs.

Numerous works were banned for their socialist bias, free thought, or antimonarchical stance. The censor reporting on August Bebel's *Der deutsche Bauernkrieg* (The German Peasants' War) found that "the peasant uprising is portrayed here with sympathy for the peasants, and with contempt for the rulers, the nobility, and religion." Bebel's ideas on history and politics were judged unacceptable in the 1880s and 1890s. *Die Frau in der Vergangenheit, Gegenwart und Zukunft* (Woman in the Past, Present, and Future) was banned in 1884 and not permitted until 1907 (despite the banning this book was extremely influential among Russian radicals and feminists). Also banned that same year, on the basis of anti-Christian views, was *Die*

Mohammedanisch-Arabische Kulturperiode (The Mohammedan-Arabic Cultural Period). In 1893 Bebel's speech *Zukunftsstadt und Sozialdemokratie* (The City of the Future and Social Democracy) was seen by the censor as dangerous because of its popular exposition, making revolutionary ideas so easily accessible to the masses.

The same criticism was leveled in 1891 against Koch's *Natur und Menschengeist im Lichte der Entwicklungslehre* (Nature and Human Spirit in Light of the Theory of Evolution), which the censor saw as an anti-Christian treatise written for the people and all the more dangerous because it was well written. In 1893 the censor saw Aulard's *Etudes et leçons sur la revolution française* (Studies and Readings on the French Revolution) as unscholarly: "In view of the fact that we have so many classical, serious, and scientifically objective tractates and courses of history on the French Revolution, the desirability of disseminating these popular lectures about revolution written in a spirit so hostile to religion and the principle of monarchical power seems doubtful."[26]

Friedrich Nietzsche's individual works were not permitted in Russia until after 1906. Polianskaia cites an 1880 report on *Der Wanderer und sein Schatten* (The Wanderer and His Shadow) in which the censor describes the work as "a collection of aphorisms expressive of bold free thinking." *Die fröliche Wissenschaft* (The Joyful Wisdom) was banned in 1882 for antireligious ideas and mockery of religion, and *Götzen-Dämmerung, oder Wie man mit dem Hammer philosophirt* (The Twilight of the Gods, or How to Philosophize with the Hammer), in 1888. ("The author is revealed as an extreme materialist, repudiating freedom of will.") A German book about Nietzsche's ideas was objectionable because the author was not critical of Nietzsche. The censor maintained that while this sort of objective treatment might be suitable for people already familiar with the philosopher's work, naive readers could take this book to be a guide to morality—with disastrous results.[27]

The censors' concerns are understandable in light of the substantial Nietzsche cult that had developed in Russia during this period, reaching its peak after 1905. Vulgarized ideas of "superman"—sexual liberation, individualism, and justification for crime and violence—were floating in the air. Nietzsche's ideas had been popularized in Russian in the early 1890s by the critics N. K. Mikhailovskii and V. P. Preobrazhenskii, and by the novelist P. D. Boborykin (e.g., *Pereval* [Pass], published in 1894). After 1898 Russian translations of Nietzsche's writings were available and widely read by students. Novels reflecting Nietzschean ideas, such as

Artsybashev's *Sanin*, Verbitskaia's *Kliuchi shchast'ia* (Keys of Happiness),
and Andreev's *Rasskaz o Sergee Petroviche* (Tale of Sergei Petrovich) and
Mysl' (Thought) were enormously popular among Russian readers.[28]

Büchner's *Sämtliche Werke und Handschriftlicher Nachlass* (Collected
Works and Unpublished Materials) was banned in 1880 and again in
1910, Polianskaia reports, because of its aim of "undermining the foundations of monarchy and at the same time turning the poor class against the
rich." Several of his books were forbidden on the grounds of materialism;
his *Die Darwinische Theorie von der Entstehung und Umwandlung der Lebe-
Welt* (The Darwinian Theory of the Origin and Transformation of the
Natural World) was judged in 1890 to be especially pernicious because of
the association of these two famous names—Büchner's own and Darwin's
—with materialist ideas. Espousal of Darwinism was the reason given for
banning a number of books in these years. Bartholomäus Carneri's *Sittlich-
keit und Darwinismus* (Morality and Darwinism) was banned in 1879 not
because it was incendiary, but because the author maintained that "the
struggle for existence brought about the development of man's moral and
spiritual forces. He denies the existence of God, life beyond the grave,
miracles."[29]

Darwinism was a problem throughout the period. In 1890 a popular
collection entitled *Darwin und seine Lehre, Aforismen, gesammelt aus Darwin's eigenen Werken und seiner Vorgänger und Zeitgenossen* (Darwin and His
Teaching, Aphorisms Collected from Darwin's Own Works and Those of
His Predecessors and Contemporaries) was found to be unacceptable because it was seen not as a "learned tractate from the field of natural
science, but rather as a catechism of materialist negation of religious
truths." Along the same lines, a German translation of a study of Darwin
by the prominent Swiss botanist Alphonse de Candolle was banned in
1893 because of its aim of "making the famous Darwin's research results
available even to the uneducated reader." Jean de Lanessan's *La transformisme:
Evolution de la matière et des êtres vivants* (Transformism: The Evolution of
Matter and Living Beings) had been attacked ten years earlier because the
author applied Darwinism and the views of other modern scholars "to the
social question and, denying the existence of God and the soul, . . .
expresses the conviction that the chief evil for man is his belief in God."
Similarly, Thomas Huxley's *Science and Christian Tradition* was banned in
1896 for its "criticism and denial of religion in general and Christianity in
particular. As a naturalist the author acknowledges and believes only in
experimentation. Everything supernatural or incomprehensible seems to

him to be merely temporarily inaccessible to scientific research."[30]

The French socialist Louise Michel—perhaps more a firebrand than a writer—was the subject of a number of reports in the 1880s. Her *Mémoires écrits par elle-même*, published in Paris in 1886, arrived at the committee in February of that year. Polonskii wrote a violently negative review in which he concluded that

> Louise Michel is a psychopath or a madwoman for whom gunfire, the smell of powder and blood are the most delightful things on earth; who accepts no government, neither monarchist nor republican, and no authority, who craves some kind of unprecedented freedom and equality, the freedom of wild beasts, and who is deeply convinced that behind her stand thousands, millions such as she, and that the old world of governments, families and all kinds of religions will soon perish forever, never to return. But this kind of outrageous behavior is infectious for young people. The heroism of fanaticism wins over a weak will and captivates a romantic imagination—that is why I propose that this book must not be permitted.

In his capacity as chairman Maikov sent a copy of the book directly to Feoktistov at the same time as he gave it to Polonskii to review. Feoktistov responded promptly; he had not even considered it necessary to examine the book: "For me it is completely sufficient that the book bears the name of a bitch such as Louise Michel: why should we allow her foul works into our country?" The same concern for weak-willed readers was expressed in 1891 by the censor reporting on Schopenhauer's *Metaphysik der Geschlechtsliebe*: "Even without this our reading public is undermined enough by rationalism and skepticism."[31]

In October 1886, Polonskii was given Michel's novel *Les microbes* to review. Here his contempt for her literary ability is the overriding feature of the report: "Louise Michel, well known in Paris as a socialist and communist, has written the stupidest, most mediocre work to appear in a long time." Not only does he consider her ideas objectionable but he finds fault with her style and language, and suggests that the book actually should be recommended to Michel's admirers: "She could not find a better way to show what confusion, what a mess she has in her head." In his 1888 report on Michel's novel *Le monde nouveau* Polonskii continues in the same vein. He is particularly offended by her misspelling of the name of the Russian folk hero, Stenka Razin, who appears in the novel as "Stenkorate," and again regrets that the book cannot be given to her admirers: "Unfortunately, it must be banned in accordance with the censorship statutes."[32]

Two writers controversial in their own countries were presented to the committee in the 1890s. Anatole France's novel *Les opinions de M. Jerome Coignard*, published in 1893, was reviewed by the committee that same year. Censor Dukshta-Dukshinskii found the book unacceptable for its antimonarchical views and for the peculiar opinions expressed on the subject of marriage. The ban was upheld in 1907 after a review by censor A. Gents. Oscar Wilde's only novel, *The Picture of Dorian Gray*, reached the committee in 1895, just after Wilde's second trial for homosexual offenses, at which he was found guilty and sent to prison with hard labor. The censor recommended banning the book, noting that even though the author had "assiduously avoided descriptions of the hero's orgies and debauchery" and "cleverly sidestepped ambiguous passages, . . . now, after the author has been sentenced to hard labor, the reader will be able to understand them unambiguously."[33]

Turning, finally, to Karl Marx, let us review briefly the fate of *Das Kapital* during this period. We recall that the committee had been lenient toward Marx in earlier periods, on the grounds that his writings were too abstract and serious to be dangerous, and that in any case they were not applicable to Russia. According to Polianskaia, the first two volumes of *Das Kapital* had been permitted in 1871 (two years later in French translation), and it was not until 1890 that the fourth edition of volume 1 was banned. (The censor had argued in favor of permitting it with some excisions but was overruled.) The third volume was reviewed in 1895, just at the end of the period under consideration. In a seventy-one-page report Count Golenishchev-Kutuzov reviewed the censorship history of *Das Kapital* and concluded by recommending that the committee permit all three volumes of the original, as well as any complete translations into other foreign languages, with the excision only of one of Marx's forewords. He expressed his conviction that if the foreign and internal censorship continued to keep *popularizations* of Marx's teachings out of Russia, the original would not be harmful and that it would, in fact, "divest this book of the lure of forbidden fruit." The committee agreed with the censor and permitted *Das Kapital* on the conditions proposed in the report.[34]

In the second half of the nineteenth century the censorship of foreign publications changed not only with the times, but under the influence of the men who directed the committee. Zlatkovskii notes the contrast between Krasovskii and Tiutchev—"What a chasm between these two rulers of the destiny of the foreign press in our country!"—and describes the appointment of Tiutchev as a

> revolution in the internal life of the Committee. Of course Fedor Ivanovich's personal influence on its entire structure goes without saying: everyone was imbued with a new spirit, and for Apollon Nikolaevich this was the occasion for a still closer rapprochement with the man who was always able to stand above his era; knowing the past and correctly foreseeing the future, he exerted no small influence on the direction of Russian foreign policy in the great events of his time.[35]

Tiutchev may have been unable to bring about the "significant reforms" to which he had referred in his first annual report but he did manage to introduce some changes: he decreased the number of absolute bans and attempted to curtail the use of excision as a method of censorship. What is perhaps most important is that he raised the intellectual level of censorship from the depths into which it had sunk under Krasovskii, when learned men such as Odoevskii and Maikov were the exception rather than the rule. Under Tiutchev's direction books and articles were still censored, to be sure, but with a greater degree of intelligence, understanding, and circumspection, and we must view this as progress.

Unfortunately, all the foreign censorship offices were not like Tiutchev's. Egorov's chief in Moscow in the late 1860s, Vladimir Maksimovich Vëdrov, had been a professor of history at Kazan University; he gave up his academic career after having some problems with colleagues (Egorov calls him a very petty character) and became the censor for foreign publications attached to the Moscow Censorship Committee. Although generally well educated, Vëdrov was not comfortable with any foreign languages and wrote his reports with great difficulty. Still, says Egorov, he was far better than many colleagues with whom he worked in the foreign censorship who did not know the languages at all.[36]

Viazemskii's nine-year term was certainly more conservative than Tiutchev's, at least in part a return perhaps to the Krasovskii style. We must not forget, however, that this was a very troubled decade in Russia. The age of the great reforms was definitely over. Acts of terrorism were occurring with increasing frequency, and it is not surprising that censorship should become a matter of greater concern. We saw Tiutchev's disappointment shortly before he died over the new press regulations, which he considered a step backward. It was against this background that Viazemskii became chairman, and although he was undoubtedly not Tiutchev's intellectual equal, even Tiutchev, had he lived, might have been defeated in those years leading up to the assassination of the emperor in 1881.

As for Maikov, Zlatkovskii portrays him as deeply involved in his work. He did not merely sign papers prepared by his secretary; on the contrary, he took a genuine interest in the affairs of the committee and worked hard at his job. Zlatkovskii observes that at the beginning Maikov, like Tiutchev before him, had been inexperienced at office routines. But Tiutchev had been

> an enemy of any kind of formalism, it was irksome for him to read through what he signed; two words were sufficient to communicate to him the contents of a paper and if it did not contradict his views he was satisfied; he did not concern himself at all with the manner of formulation or expression—he left the tone and phrases completely up to the secretary and signed the paper without reading it. Apollon Nikolaevich, on the other hand, was always interested in how some conclusion or other was expressed in a paper, and to what degree the tone of the paper corresponded to the prevailing circumstances. He was an enemy of bureaucratic "evasion," "passing the buck," "giving somebody the business," and blaming other institutions or holding them responsible for this or that action. Nor did he like verbosity, details, or numbers. He demanded brevity and clarity of exposition and a proper tone. When it was necessary to advocate the inclusion of some idea or some numbers in a paper, Ap. Nik. disputed them with such tact, good nature and humor that one sometimes had to yield against one's will. But when, as sometimes happened, one could not agree with him and announced with conviction that this was impossible, then Ap. Nik. yielded, repeating, "well, if you are going to insist on having your own way so stubbornly—have it your way: it means you are right. . . . After all, you have the books in your hand—do it your way!"

Zlatkovskii comments that Maikov never made him aware of the difference between them, although he himself never forgot it. "I never permitted myself to decide a question beforehand, even in those matters about which Ap. Nik. knew little. He appreciated this and dealt with me on all occasions as a colleague and a friend." On two occasions Zlatkovskii turned down promotions offered him so that he might remain Maikov's secretary. He quotes Maikov as saying, " 'No, don't leave me! For goodness' sake, what will I do without you!' " The third time it was impossible for Zlatkovskii to decline his promotion, so Maikov arranged matters so that Zlatkovskii would still manage the office: "He announced to me with joy: 'See here, I won't allow it; you are my right hand, you must agree, and what would I do without my hand!'"[37]

Maikov himself spoke very warmly of Tiutchev as chairman. S. Umanets recalls Maikov reminiscing about his friend in the late 1880s or early 1890s:

> "This was a man of splendid wit"—he said of him—"and his talent was strong, brilliant, he raised us up off the ground and bore us upwards, into the heavens. . . . This was a charming, amiable, good-natured, noble man. When he was our chief we all loved him very much. His conversation was always so lively, interesting, simple. On Wednesdays, our meeting days, we all used to be especially animated and in good spirits. Tiutchev always told us something interesting, in connection with some new foreign book he would remember an historical case, an anecdote, an event from diplomatic life, something from the reservoir of his impressions. . . . And all of this cleverly, wittily . . . "And now"—added Apollon Nikolaevich—"we all live together amicably, remembering our dear Fedor Ivanovich. Together we form such a harmonious scale, it is simply lovely!"[38]

Zlatkovskii's description of Maikov's own Wednesday meetings sounds very similar:

> At the beginning of every session A. N. inquired about the news of the day and he himself always told us a mass of interesting rumors, facts, anecdotes on the subject of politics, literature and social life. Then we began with the reports. There was no scientific, literary, or artistic question which A. N. Maikov did not elucidate with a whole series of interesting commentaries of the most varied kinds. Possessed of an excellent memory and following the development of religious, philosophical, historical, political, literary and artistic questions in the West, A. N. always discovered in himself a whole arsenal of facts with which he explained or enriched the material in the reports. If it should happen that he was not knowledgeable about the subject touched upon, then he administered a real examination to the author of the report with the aim of clarifying for himself comprehensively the subject treated and then, with a full feeling of responsibility, offering his conclusion. I may say with confidence that our Wednes-

days were our academy, where we enhanced our knowledge and broadened our intellectual horizons.[39]

The notion of "our academy" surfaces repeatedly in accounts of the censorship careers of the three poets; they supported and protected one another and formed a sort of literary seminar centered at the committee.

It is probably true, as Egorov claims, that the chairman's position was a sinecure, always occupied by someone "with connections and protection in high spheres." Tiutchev had his daughter at court, one of the empress's ladies. Viazemskii's wife was close to Emperor Alexander II. Maikov was a favorite of the next emperor, Alexander III, and the last chairman, Count Murav'ev, was the brother of the Minister of Foreign Affairs. Egorov was clearly critical of Maikov for accepting a position that he saw as being in conflict with his poetic nature, although he did notice a "tendency toward careerism" in Maikov.[40]

Yet the chairmanship was not *just* a sinecure for Tiutchev and Maikov, and the committee was not just another government office. These men cared for one another and for their art. On at least one occasion Tiutchev came to Maikov's aid in regard to censorship attacks on the latter's own poetry. In February of 1864 Tiutchev received a letter from Minister Valuev complaining about one of Maikov's poems, "Il'e Il'ichu," in which some people had seen an allusion to Alexander II. The next day Tiutchev approached his friend about the matter; on the following day Maikov brought Tiutchev a letter for Valuev; and the day after that Maikov dined with Tiutchev, the incident having ended happily.

Zlatkovskii praises Maikov for his aid—both financial and intellectual —to beginning writers. As secretary, however, he thought Maikov was far too generous with casual petitioners, who accosted him in the hallway when he appeared at the committee offices for the Wednesday meetings. Tiutchev wrote of his friendship with the two poets in his letter to Polonskii from Nice: "It will be very, very gratifying to me to see you again, my dear Iakov Petrovich. Please give Maikov the same message from me. I thank you both from the bottom of my heart for your friendship, and I prize it very, very dearly."[41]

Zlatkovskii writes of Maikov that "he had not sought this career, and desired neither a promotion nor any other positions with higher status or salary; he was completely satisfied with his chairman's armchair and felt at the Committee as if he were in the bosom of his own family. 'I do not need anything else; I want to die, as Tiutchev did, in the Committee which is so dear to my heart,' said A. N." According to Zlatkovskii Maikov considered his other appointments—corresponding member of the Academy of Sciences, member of the Academic Council of the Ministry of Education, and others—as more honorary, official, and marginal to his true interest, which lay in his Foreign Censorship Committee. Maikov died just after his last committee meeting, which had been postponed from Wednesday until Thursday so that he might attend a special session in memory of the late Emperor Alexander III. Zlatkovskii reports that the chairman was in a very good mood that Thursday and that "when he took his leave of us it did not occur to anyone that we were seeing him in our midst for the last time." The following evening he caught cold and died of pneumonia a few days later.[42]

Why was Maikov so happy at the committee? Certainly his colleagues and the atmosphere they created together must have been a factor. His friend and fellow poet, Count Arsenii Golenishchev-Kutuzov, points out the benefits to Maikov of having Tiutchev and Odoevskii as professional colleagues.

> While they were his immediate supervisors at work, they were also his personal friends, intellectual advisors, and fully competent judges and critics. The intellectual and moral influence of F. I. Tiutchev strongly promoted the ultimate elaboration of those views on Russian history and the foundations of the Russian state to which Maikov remained committed all his life. In general Apollon Nikolaevich considered himself very fortunate in his personal ties and friendships, and often, during friendly conversations in recent years, he expressed a touching gratefulness to fate for constantly bringing him into contact and intimacy with people whom, with his infinitely good smile and with irresistible persuasiveness in his voice, he called "the most excellent people."

This "literary seminar" also provided opportunities for good, stimulating gossip. Mardar'ev remarks that despite Polonskii's habit of always "inveighing against someone or something," he was "a very good-natured and sympathetic man" who "always found something interesting to tell us . . . about Russian or foreign life which he had read in the newspapers or gotten from some other source and which was the news of the day—anyone could get it hot from Iakov Petrovich."[43]

The presence of men such as these guaranteed some measure of bright light and good cheer in the committee offices, even as the sky darkened outside.

Part
Two

Dangerous Friends:
Foreign Publications in Russia

5

Patterns of Banning:
German Publications in Russia
under Two Tsars

In 1870 and 1898 the Chief Administration for Press Affairs issued for official use two alphabetical catalogs of banned foreign publications, both of which are available in published form.[1] The first lists titles in French, German, and English; the second also includes Polish and a small number of Lithuanian titles. As we have seen, periods of stringent censorship were followed by periods of relative relaxation, when earlier decisions were reviewed and sometimes modified. The 1870 catalog, including items examined between 1856 and 1 July 1869, reflects the changes that had taken place in the censorship during the first fifteen years of the reign of Alexander II—Tiutchev's term as chairman of the committee, when many works previously banned were reviewed and permitted. However, the next thirty years were increasingly tense in Russia, and there was growing concern over harmful foreign publications entering the empire. The 1898 catalog, which covers decisions made between 1 July 1871 and 1 January 1897, is less liberal than its predecessor and a good deal larger. Although Polianskaia maintains that this later catalog excludes serious scientific or scholarly works and items such as encyclopedias, historical studies, memoirs, works of well-established authors, and items containing references to the violent deaths of Emperors Peter III and Paul I, it does in fact contain numerous titles in these categories.[2]

This chapter deals with the German-language works—more than six thousand entries—included in the two catalogs, which are arranged alphabetically by language and list the author, title, place and date of publication, and type of ban imposed on each item examined. In addition, in order to compare banned German publications with permitted ones, two more lists covering this period were utilized. The official monthly record of banned and permitted imported publications prepared by the Chief Censorship Administration was available in published form only for the years 1866–69, 1882–92, 1894, and 1896,[3] but was supplemented for the years 1864–65 and 1870–81 with the list of foreign accessions to the Imperial Public Library in Saint Petersburg, the most important library in the country at that time.[4] Taken together, these two lists provide the data necessary for a comparison of banned and permitted German publications during all but the first few years of the period.

In order to determine patterns of banning, a formal analysis was conducted. Since the period in question coincides closely with the reigns of Emperors Alexander II (1855–81) and Alexander III (1881–94), the study would suggest the differences in censorship, if any, between the two reigns. Since the German publications imported between 1856 and 1896 exceeded seventy thousand titles, it was necessary to draw samples from the group of imported works banned and the group of those permitted for dissemination in Russia. A 40 percent systematic sample (2,456 items) was drawn from the two catalogs of banned publications, and a 2 percent systematic sample (1,286 items) from the two lists of permitted publications.

It should be noted that the term "imported" as used here includes those items that arrived at the Foreign Censorship Committee offices for review, or were accessioned by the Imperial Public Library in those years for which the monthly list was unavailable.[5] Some of those items that ended up at the committee had been confiscated from individuals but it seems reasonable to assume that the vast majority came via the book trade. (In any case, those confiscated items can also be considered "imported"; they were subject to the same censorship as were publications entering the country through regular channels.) Additional copies of works previously reviewed by the committee are not included in the official catalogs, so all entries are for new material (except for the occasional reexamination of an earlier decision).

Using a computer and standard programs the items in the samples were cross-classified and other statistical procedures were applied, resulting in an overall profile of subjects and bans and indicating detailed differences in the treatment of various subjects, given the limitations of statistical samples. A classification scheme was devised and applied to the two samples in

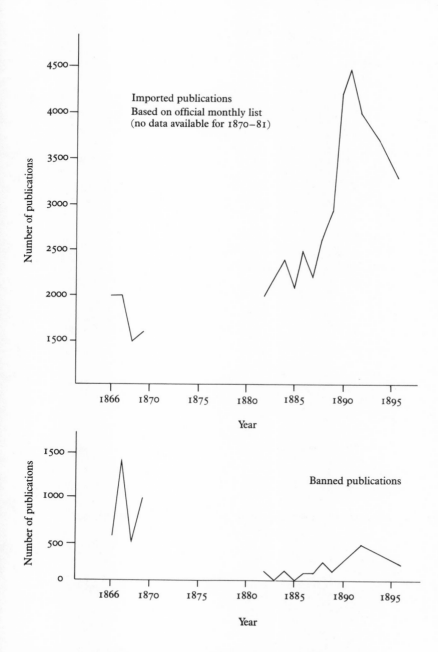

Fig. 5-1. Imported and banned German publications (1866–96).

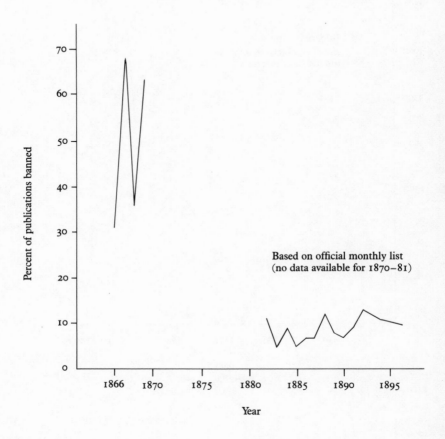

Fig. 5-2. Percentage of imported German publications banned (1866–96).

order to discover the distribution of subjects and certain other features among the two groups. A discussion of this scheme and coding procedures can be found in appendix 1.

IMPORTATION AND BANNING

Figures 5-1 and 5-2, based on a tally of all banned and permitted German publications in the years for which the monthly list was available, show a rather surprising pattern. In the late 1860s quite a high percentage —from one-third to two-thirds—of the German works imported were banned. This is in sharp contrast to the figures for the 1880s and 1890s, when the percentage of banned publications remained very low although the number of publications imported had increased tremendously. (The decline in the number of works imported in the early 1890s, shown in figure 5-1, might be explained by the general economic situation at that time; still, even with that decline the numbers are considerably higher than in the earlier period.) What might explain these differences? Clearly valid explanations cannot be derived from these incomplete data alone. There might, of course, be some problem with the figures themselves that is not immediately evident. However, even if they are accurate, the issues involved are far too complex to permit simple answers, although some conjectures are possible.

First of all, the large number of publications requiring review in the later period simply may have overwhelmed the committee, resulting in more books being permitted out of sheer necessity. Or perhaps German publications were perceived to be less threatening than they had been earlier. Another related possibility is that fewer German works imported in the 1880s and 1890s were on subjects seen to require banning; indeed, as will shortly be shown, some subjects were permitted far more often than they were banned.

As for the late 1860s, perhaps the increase in the percentage of publications banned in 1867 was a result of the general crackdown on the press following the attempt on the life of Alexander II by Karakozov in April 1866. It is impossible to say whether the increased percentage of banned publications in 1869 was maintained for any part of the 1870s, nor is it clear what the pattern for that decade might have been as the data are unavailable. Perhaps the rise can be attributed to increased government repressiveness. But if so, then why the low level of banning in the 1880s and 1890s, generally considered to be a highly repressive period? This question will be addressed later.

Table 5-1. Distribution of Major Subject Categories (in sample[a] of imported publications permitted and banned)

Subject	Percentage
Belles lettres	23.7
Government	12.7
Religion	12.3
History	9.1
Health	6.1
Pure science	5.6
Biography	5.2
Philosophy	3.9
Generalities	3.5
Literary history and criticism	2.7
Arts	2.5
Geography	2.4
Social conditions	2.3
Technology	2.1
Language	2.0
Education	1.9
Sex	0.8
Unable to assign	0.7
TOTAL	99.5[b]
Number	3,742
Estimated total	70,791

[a] This table represents a pooled sample combining the samples of permitted and banned publications.
[b] Column does not total 100% because of rounding error.

MAJOR SUBJECT CATEGORIES

As can be seen from the last section of this chapter, Russians were importing German-language publications on a wide variety of subjects during the second half of the nineteenth century. Table 5-1 shows the percentage of the total number of imported German publications by major subject category.[6] A note of caution must be sounded here: the sample of permitted publications drawn for this study was intended chiefly to serve as a backdrop for the banned works, the subject of primary interest, and is too small to provide a very accurate estimation of the number of publications on each subject, especially those categories represented by very few items. The sample is sufficient, however, to give a general idea of the types

of publications permitted and their relative strengths, as long as one resists
the temptation to interpret the results too finely.

For example, it does seem clear that belletristic literature was the largest
subject imported. That sex and erotica take last place among subjects is
hardly surprising; we recall that Tiutchev commented several times in his
annual reports that the booksellers knew better than to import such publications. The relatively small percentage of items in the field of technology
may be explained if, as seems likely, most publications in this category
were sent directly to the educational institutions and government agencies
that had requested them, thus avoiding the general censorship altogether.
(There also may have been some arrangement for cookbooks, classed here
with technology, to bypass the committee, or perhaps Russian cooks simply
were not interested in German recipes.) The pure sciences are better represented; apparently there was more demand by the general public for works
in these fields than for publications on technology and agriculture. Health
and medicine, also fairly high on the list, still represent only a very small
percentage of imported publications. Presumably the bulk of publications
on these subjects also entered the country through different channels.

ASPECTS OF FORM AND CONTENT

From the title information given in the catalogs it was also sometimes
possible to assign works to one or more categories on the basis of form
(e.g., encyclopedias, almanacs), mode (humorous or serious), or groups
treated (e.g., Jews, Russians). Table 5-2 shows the percentages of the total
represented by these groups.

The censors' reports examined in chapters 2, 3, and 4 revealed considerable concern with publications "for the people," especially young and
unsophisticated readers. The first five form categories contain some of the
kinds of material intended for these audiences: non-technical, written in
popular style, and aimed for the most part at the general public. Together
these educational and reference works account for the largest percentage of
the total (for purposes of discussion they will be treated henceforth as one
group). There were too few advertisements to permit generalization (most
were promoting food products, patent medicines, or contraceptives), so
the category was dropped from the study.

One might ask how advertisements and prospectuses found their way to
the Foreign Censorship Committee in the first place. It seems that no
category of printed paper was exempt; earlier in the century, during the

Table 5-2. Aspects of Form and Content of Imported Publications[a]

Type	Percentage[b]
Form	
Yearbook	6.3
Encyclopedias	3.5
Books for youth	2.7
Readers	2.3
Textbooks	1.9
Advertisements	0.1
Mode	
Humor	5.0
Groups treated	
a. Religions	
Protestants	2.5
Jews	2.2
Catholics	1.9
Freemasons	0.4
b. Nationalities	
Russians	6.2
Poles	0.9
c. Other	
Revolutionaries, etc.	1.8
Women	1.5

[a] This table represents a pooled sample combining the samples of permitted and banned publications.
[b] Column does not total 100% because some titles had none of these characteristics and some had more than one.

most intense period of censorship under Nicholas I, even candy wrappers were considered potentially dangerous because of the undesirable mottoes often printed on them. These imported candies probably were sold at the same shops that dealt in imported publications. Posters also were seen as a problem; in 1849 the committee received complaints that posters of foreign revolutionary leaders were displayed in bookstore windows. Musical scores of patriotic songs, even without accompanying words, were a matter of concern in those years too. Among such songs of fifteen countries carried by an Austrian bookseller in Odessa the only clearly acceptable items were "Hymne National Russe" and "Rule Britannia," on the grounds that both were well known; just as clearly forbidden were "Chant

National Polonais," "La Marseillaise," and "Choeur des Girondins."[7]

Another complaint frequently registered by the censors of foreign publications was lack of proper respect and reverence for serious and sacred subjects. Since these qualities are often characteristic of humorous and satirical works, an attempt was made to identify works in the samples that appeared to be written in the humorous mode. The percentage, although small, is still worth considering; clearly some Russian citizens enjoyed reading German literature of this type.

The representation of literature on "foreign" (i.e., non-Orthodox) religious groups is of interest because there were substantial numbers of Jews and Roman Catholics in the western part of the empire (Poland, Lithuania, White Russia), large settlements of German Protestants on the Volga, and a significant German population in the Baltic Provinces, especially in Latvia and Estonia. The amount of imported literature dealing with these groups appears to be rather small, and items such as Roman Catholic catechisms or Protestant calendars undoubtedly were intended mainly for the use of these groups themselves, rather than for the general public. Ban types such as "banned, permitted for Protestants" and "permitted for Jews" occasionally were imposed on this kind of specialized religious literature (see the last section of this chapter for a discussion of ban types). Freemasonry has had a long and stormy history in Russia; the category was included in order to learn whether many works on the subject were imported. Perhaps dealers knew that such publications were unlikely to be permitted; in any case, so few appeared in the samples that the category was dropped.

As one might expect, works dealing with Russians are fairly well represented, perhaps because people always like to read about themselves. Books on Poles are of interest because Poland was a rebellious part of the empire during this period, and a fairly large number of publications dealing in one way or another with Polish independence might be expected. In fact, however, very few were identified. But the perennial "Polish question" was a major theme characterizing the excised passages examined.

As far as works dealing with revolution and antimonarchist movements are concerned, it is not too surprising that rather few with these ideas clearly reflected in the title were imported. Again, this theme was much more widely represented in the excised passages. There was also a rather small number of items dealing with women, mostly reference works and biographies about famous women or educational works written specifically for female readers. There were also a few serious works on prostitution and several items of erotica.

Table 5-3. Major Subject Categories: Percentage of Publications Banned

Category	Percentage banned	Standard deviation
Sex	39.7	0.8
Philosophy	15.8	0.6
History	14.0	0.8
Religion	13.5	1.0
Social conditions	12.3	0.5
Biography	10.3	0.6
Generalities	9.4	0.5
Geography	8.2	0.5
Belles lettres	7.8	3.6
Government	6.5	1.9
Literary history and criticism	5.7	0.4
Health	5.4	0.8
Education	3.9	0.4
Language	1.3	0.6
Technology	0.7	1.2
Pure science	0.6	6.3
Arts	0.3	4.1

BANNING BY MAJOR SUBJECTS AND
BY ASPECTS OF FORM AND CONTENT

What was the likelihood that a work in any one of these categories would be banned in Russia? It should be emphasized that out of a total of nearly 71,000 publications, only a little over 6,000 were banned, resulting in an overall probability of banning of less than 10 percent. Nonetheless, as indicated by tables 5-3 and 5-4, some subjects and types of publications were more likely than others to be banned. For example, the estimates show that 40 out of 100 publications on sex were forbidden, whereas only 6 out of 100 science publications met with disapproval. While 26 out of 100 works dealing with revolutionaries were found to be objectionable, only 8 out of 100 humorous works were banned.[8] It is possible to make statements about gross differences between groups of categories on the basis of these data and the pattern that emerges makes intuitive sense. For instance, it stands to reason that works on sex would be seen as more likely to corrupt readers than would chemistry books. It is also not difficult to imagine why publications dealing with the dangerous topic of revolution should have a greater chance of being banned than humorous works. It seems that the censors could be more tolerant if a publication were not intended to be taken seriously. However, as the analysis of excised passages will show, there were limits to this tolerance; on some subjects the censors proved to be totally humorless.

BANNING BY REIGN

So far the probability that a work on a particular subject would be banned has been considered. But tables 5-5 and 5-6 show that the situation did not remain constant throughout the period.[9] For example, table 5-5 shows that under Alexander II 16 out of 100 belletristic works were banned, as contrasted to only 4 out of 100 in the reign of Alexander III. In this case, the explanation may be that so many more literary works were imported in the second reign (867 per year as opposed to 116), the censors simply may have been so inundated by novels that they were inclined to permit most of them, or perhaps German novels were simply seen as less harmful than they had been earlier. The same might be true, although on a smaller scale, for biographies: the number of publications imported increased from 34 to 182 per year with a corresponding decrease in the likelihood of banning, from nearly 20 percent down to almost 5 percent. The most striking example of this type in table 5-6 is the case of humorous works: despite a very large increase in the number imported per year— from 19 to 175—the percentage banned dropped dramatically, from 27 percent to 3 percent. Perhaps the official standard of "acceptable" humor became more relaxed in the course of the century, or Germans may have been addressing fewer sensitive subjects in a humorous vein.

Table 5-4. Aspects of Content and Form: Percentage of Publications Banned

Category	Percentage banned	Standard deviation
Revolutionaries, etc.	25.7	0.7
Catholics	16.9	0.6
Poles	16.7	0.6
Jews	13.7	0.6
Women	13.3	0.6
Russians	10.4	0.6
Educational and reference books	10.2	0.9
Protestants	8.7	0.5
Humor	7.5	0.6

Table 5-5. Publications Banned by Major Subject Categories
in Two Reigns (1864–94)

Category	Alexander II (works published 1864–81)		Alexander III (works published 1882–94)	
	Average number imported per year (18 years)	Percentage banned	Average number imported per year (13 years)	Percentage banned
Generalities	27	15.6	132	3.7
Philosophy	64	12.5	93	17.0
Religion	143	12.6	362	10.6
Government	272	2.9	205	9.8
Social conditions	41	5.8	61	11.9
Education	40	2.5	13	13.3
Language	64	0.3	16	0.0
Pure science	181	0.5	20	2.0
Health	163	1.2	62	13.6
Sex	4	100.0	13	39.4
Technology	28	0.0	19	0.0
Arts	50	0.3	31	0.0
Literary history and criticism	59	0.5	33	7.0
Belles lettres	116	16.1	867	3.8
History	161	11.8	191	9.6
Geography	41	4.1	53	5.1
Biography	34	19.1	182	4.7
Total books imported	27,195		30,570	
Percentage of total	47.1%		52.9%	

Total number of works imported with publication dates 1864–94 = 57,765

Some subjects, however, were treated the same way in both reigns, regardless of increases or decreases in the number of publications imported. As shown in table 5-5, sex was the subject most likely to be banned under both emperors, while arts, language, and technology remained the least likely. But, as table 5-6 shows, works dealing with Jews, imported in about equal numbers per year during both reigns, were banned five times more frequently under Alexander III than in the preceding reign, perhaps in keeping with the increasingly virulent anti-Semitism of the 1880s and 1890s.

DISTRIBUTION OF BAN TYPES

The sample of banned works drawn for this study consists of 40 percent of all publications banned between 1856 and 1896, and with this large a proportion of the total it is possible to speak with considerable confidence. (Since only banned publications are being considered, those published in the first eight years of the reign of Alexander II also may be included.) Until now banned publications have been treated as a single entity, but in fact there were several ways to ban a book or magazine. Table 5-7 shows the distribution of ban types over the whole period (1856–96). The most prevalent type was the ban in entirety, imposed on more than half of the banned publications. The second most popular method, permission with excisions, was used in one-third of the cases. The option of permitting a publication for a few favored readers while banning it for the public was chosen relatively rarely, in only a little over 10 percent of the cases. Other options, such as permitting publications for Jews only or banning for the public while permitting for doctors, were imposed so rarely as to be almost negligible.

Table 5-8 reveals distinct differences in the patterns of banning between the two reigns. Under Alexander II the censors frequently made qualified decisions, permitting with excisions more often than banning in entirety.

Table 5-6. Publications Banned by Aspects of Content and Form in Two Reigns (1864–94)

Category	Alexander II (works published 1864–81)		Alexander III (works published 1882–94)	
	Average number imported per year (18 years)	Percentage banned	Average number imported per year (13 years)	Percentage banned
Educational and reference books	204	10.1	432	7.4
Humor	19	26.5	175	3.4
Jews	32	5.2	36	24.4
Protestants	19	9.9	86	5.7
Catholics	14	23.1	53	13.4
Russians	150	5.3	71	19.2
Poles	19	13.8	9	16.6
Revolutionaries, etc.	24	17.7	51	24.0
Women	18	7.7	34	9.7

Table 5-7. Distribution of Ban Types (1856–96)

Type of Ban	Percentage
Banned in entirety	56.1
Banned for public	11.5
Permitted with excisions	32.2
Other	0.2
Number	2,456

However, during his son's reign the ban in entirety was the rule, applied in three-quarters of the cases, and banning for the public was no longer an option. The process was reduced to a simple choice: an objectionable work either was banned altogether or permitted with excisions, and when in doubt the tendency was obviously to opt for the former.[10] This pattern would seem to reflect general trends in Russian society in the second half of the century. By the 1870s the mood had definitely swung toward the reactionary end of the spectrum and the assassination of Alexander II in 1881 often is viewed as the beginning of a repressive period that continued unrelieved until the Revolution of 1905.

BAN TYPES BY MAJOR SUBJECT CATEGORIES
AND ASPECTS OF FORM AND CONTENT

How were these ban types imposed on various categories? Table 5-9 shows the distribution over the whole period of types of ban by subject; table 5-10, by aspects of form and content. The ban in entirety appears to have been imposed most heavily on technology, philosophy, religion, government, society, education, health, and, of course, sex. Of the aspect categories only educational and reference works, humorous works, and

Table 5-8. Distribution of Ban Types in Two Reigns (1856–94)

	Alexander II (1856–81)	Alexander III (1882–94)
Banned in entirety	38.3	76.3
Banned for public	20.4	—
Permitted with excisions	46.4	23.7
Other	0.3	—
Number	1,076	882

Table 5-9. Ban Types by Major Subject Categories (1856–96)

Category	% banned in entirety	% banned for public	% permitted with excisions	% other	Number in sample
Generalities	17.2	5.4	77.4	0.0	93
Philosophy	79.5	10.8	9.7	0.0	176
Religion	70.9	15.3	13.6	0.2	470
Government	70.5	9.8	19.7	0.0	234
Social conditions	71.6	7.4	21.0	0.0	81
Education	71.4	14.3	14.3	0.0	21
Language	42.9	0.0	57.1	0.0	7
Pure science	44.4	33.3	22.2	0.0	9
Health	98.9	0.0	1.1	0.0	94
Sex	85.9	9.8	4.3	0.0	92
Technology	100.0	0.0	0.0	0.0	4
Arts	50.0	0.0	5.0	0.0	2
Literary history and criticism	23.3	4.7	72.1	0.0	43
Belles lettres	45.6	14.4	39.7	0.2	526
History	31.9	8.6	58.3	1.1	360
Geography	34.5	5.5	60.0	0.0	55
Biography	33.1	17.9	49.0	0.0	151

publications dealing with women were permitted with excisions more often than they were banned in entirety. In no subject was a majority of publications banned for the public, and only in a few categories did this method exceed one of the other ban types. For instance, slightly more publications on philosophy, religion, and pure science were banned for the public than were permitted with excisions, but in the first two subjects most items were banned outright. (Although most sex publications were banned in entirety, a small number were banned for the public; one wonders who qualified for the honor of obtaining this material legally.)

Other categories, including history, geography, biography, belles lettres, generalities, language, literary history and criticism, educational and reference works, humor, and women, all had a large proportion of items permitted with excisions. In chapters 6 and 7, where a number of the excised passages themselves are examined, the rationale for using the excision method on these categories will become apparent. In many instances, only a small section of the publication was objectionable—perhaps a single chapter or article, certain encyclopedia entries, one humorous poem, or

Table 5-10. Ban Types by Aspects of Form and Content (1856–96)

Category	% banned in entirety	% banned for public	% permitted with excisions	% other	Number in sample
Educational and reference books	35.4	5.5	59.1	0.0	575
Humor	44.8	6.7	48.6	0.0	105
Jews	65.1	11.6	22.1	1.2	86
Protestants	65.6	23.0	11.5	0.0	61
Catholics	66.3	12.4	21.3	0.0	89
Russians	68.5	17.9	12.5	1.1	184
Poles	61.4	27.3	11.4	0.0	44
Revolutionaries, etc.	79.4	7.6	13.0	0.0	131
Women	30.0	10.0	60.0	0.0	55

Table 5-11. Ban Types by Major Subject Categories in Two Reigns (1856–94)

Category*	Alexander II (works published 1856–81)				Alexander III (works published 1882–94)		
	% banned entirety	% banned public	% permitted with excisions	Number in sample	% banned entirety	% permitted with excisions	Number in sample
Generalities	8.3	10.4	81.3	48	24.0	76.0	25
Philosophy	64.4	23.3	12.3	73	92.7	7.3	82
Religion	57.6	33.2	9.2	184	84.5	15.5	200
Government	48.8	23.3	27.9	86	85.6	14.4	104
Social conditions	60.9	17.4	21.7	23	78.9	21.1	38
Education	70.0	30.0	0.0	10	77.8	22.2	9
Language	33.3	0.0	66.7	3	66.7	33.3	3
Pure science	42.9	42.9	14.3	7	50.0	50.0	2
Health	100.0	0.0	0.0	14	100.0	0.0	44
Sex	73.5	23.5	2.9	34	96.2	3.8	26
Arts	0.0	0.0	100.0	1	0.0	0.0	0
Literary history and criticism	7.7	15.4	76.9	13	41.7	58.3	12
Belles lettres	31.4	23.0	45.6	226	65.1	34.9	169
History	21.1	10.1	67.5	225	60.0	40.0	95
Geography	16.1	6.5	77.4	31	78.6	21.4	14
Biography	21.2	22.4	56.5	85	59.1	40.9	44
Number	406	219	438	1063	658	209	867

*No data were available for the technology category.

Table 5-12. Ban Types by Aspects of Form and Content in Two Reigns (1856–94)

	Alexander II (works published 1856–81)				Alexander III (works published 1882–94)		
Category	% banned entirety	% banned public	% permitted with excisions	Number in sample	% banned entirety	% permitted with excisions	Number in sample
Educational and reference books	16.2	8.5	75.3	25.9	58.1	41.9	167
Humor	32.7	12.2	55.1	49	58.1	41.9	31
Jews	39.3	32.1	28.6	28	84.4	15.6	45
Protestants	39.1	56.5	4.3	23	84.0	16.0	25
Catholics	54.1	29.7	16.2	37	81.1	18.9	37
Russians	53.0	30.1	15.7	83	88.7	11.3	71
Poles	53.6	28.6	17.9	28	100.0	0.0	8
Revolutionaries, etc.	66.7	15.4	17.9	39	87.3	12.7	63
Women	16.7	16.7	66.7	24	70.6	29.4	17

isolated statements in a history book. But a work on religion or philosophy was more likely to be built around a unifying principle and permeated with a certain type of idea; if the basic concept were objectionable the whole work was tainted and the censors were likely to ban it outright. There were numerous examples of this phenomenon in the reports discussed in chapters 2 through 4.

BAN TYPES BY REIGN

Table 5-11 shows the distribution of ban types over major subject categories in the two reigns; table 5-12 shows the distribution over aspects of form and content. In both periods the proportion of generalities, belles lettres and other literary works, history, and biography permitted with excisions was high, but in the second reign, without the option of banning for the public, the percentage banned in entirety increased in every category. Educational and reference works, humorous works, and works dealing with women were the only categories to be permitted with excisions on a large scale under Alexander II and, although they were treated more harshly in the second reign, these types of publications were still permitted, albeit with cuts, to a much greater extent than were works on non–Eastern Orthodox religious groups, Russians, or revolution.

There is no doubt that the reign of Alexander III was characterized by a more negative attitude toward foreign works than was his father's. However, it also appears to be true that many more publications entered the country during this period and that fewer were found to be objectionable, for whatever reason. But those publications that did not pass muster were handled more harshly: the number of options available to censors was reduced and most objectionable works in most categories were simply forbidden.

6

Applying the "Caviar":
Respect for Royalty and the Social Order

Ideas traveled from the West and, transmuted by Russian logic and Russian passion, acquired an influence which would have astonished some of their authors. The Russian intelligentsia was bred on Western doctrines, movements, and events: French eighteenth-century skepticism, scientific materialism, and positivism; German historicism, romanticism, and idealism; the principles and dogmas of the French Revolution and of its aftermath; the new rational organization created by Napoleon; European revolutions in the early years of the nineteenth century, for which centralized France acted as a model; the Utopias of Saint-Simon, Fourier, Owen, Cabet, Leroux; the counterattacks of Maistre, Bonald, Schelling; the destruction of metaphysics by Comte, Feuerbach, Strauss; the social doctrines of Sismondi, Mill, Spencer, and the Darwinians. All had their fervent disciples in Russia. —Isaiah Berlin[1]

Between 1856 and 1896 nearly two thousand German-language publications were permitted by the Russian censorship only with the excision of certain passages, ranging in length from a single line to many pages. Examination of nearly 20 percent of these cases reveals the kinds of material the censors found it necessary to excise from German publications to make them suitable for Russian readers and makes it clear why certain kinds of publications were banned in particular ways.[2] The passages are not usually entire works but surely many of the characteristics leading to their excision were the same as those causing entire books and articles to be banned. Certain objectionable themes recur in passage after passage, on widely diverse subjects. German prejudices and ignorance concerning

Russia, especially in regard to Russian history, also become evident. As noted in the Introduction, four major themes emerge from the study of excised passages: disrespect toward Russian royalty, opposition to the existing social order, Russians as non-European barbarians, and ideas contrary to religion and morals.

While these same themes are already familiar from the censors' reports discussed in earlier chapters, here we examine the raw material directly, as the censor himself (or herself) did. Tracking down the indicated editions and leafing through the volumes in search of pages or lines to be excised — rather like following clues laid in the distant past for a peculiar sort of literary treasure hunt — the researcher feels an eerie connection with the censors who traveled the same path one hundred years ago. Indeed, sometimes their ghosts are uncomfortably close; unlikely as it seems, several of the German volumes examined evidently had been in Russia before arriving in this country, for the precise passages sought had been obliterated. Five examples are reproduced in figures 6-1 through 6-5. These volumes belonged to the late Professor Simon Litman of the University of Illinois, who brought his library with him when he emigrated from Russia. Since Professor Litman came from Odessa, it is quite likely that members of Egorov's staff were responsible for the excisions.

Identifying the specific lines and pages to be excised is a valuable and rather sobering experience because it forces the researcher to assume, quite literally, the censor's role. After a relatively short time one is able to spot the offending lines instantly, without first consulting the catalog for guidance, and a bit later one even begins to feel a certain pleasure in the process. Now the researcher has really become the censor: "Aha!" he or she says, "This line must go, that paragraph will never do — cut them out!"

These excised passages, interesting enough in their own right as samples of the censor's work, become still more interesting when viewed in the broad context of the importance of foreign publications in Russia. The printed word played an enormously important role in shaping Russian national consciousness and the contribution of foreign publications to that process is incalculable. From the beginning, however, Western influence was a two-edged sword. Translations of some European popular scientific and belletristic works were undertaken in mid-seventeenth-century Muscovy but most remained in manuscript. Russians were also not publishing their own work at this period; Mirsky notes that the first original Russian novel was not published until 1763 and that whatever demand there was for fiction was being met by translations from French, German, and

594   Sechstes Buch. Das Zeitalter Friedrichs des Großen.

1717 und 1733 gehalten worden waren, nicht weniger als elf, welche mit Gewalt gesprengt wurden: es war kein Schade, daß nunmehr einige Jahrzehnte vergingen, in denen gar keine dieser wilden Adelsvolksversammlungen zu stande kam. Charakteristisch war, daß was durchgesetzt werden sollte, nicht auf diesen Versammlungen, sondern nur durch regellose Verbindungen oder Konföderationen, die sich nach denselben bildeten, durchgesetzt wurde: auch der König, dem die Konstitution dieses unvergleichlichen Freistaats nur eine Leibwache von 1200 Mann gestattete, konnte nur durch den Anschluß an eine solche Konföderation, in der eine oder ein paar der großen Familien den entscheidenden Einfluß übten, einige gelegentliche Bedeutung erlangen. Die wirtschaftlichen Zustände kann man sich denken, wo das ganze Leben der herrschenden Klasse auf das Gegenteil angestrengter und ehrlicher Arbeit gestellt ist — schmutzige Pracht, Bettlerhochmut, Schulden: daher denn auch das Land das Eldorado der Juden war, die allen Handel und Geschäftsverkehr vermittelten und sich nach ihrer Weise unentbehrlich machten. Und nur eines ist noch zu ergänzen, um dieses Zerrbild der Freiheit vollständig zu machen — die religiöse Unduldsamkeit. Auch diese hatte sich zeitig eingestellt. Die Gegenreformation seit Sigismund (1581—1632) hatte die vielversprechenden Keime des Protestantismus verkümmern lassen: die Jesuiten bemächtigten sich, indem sie nach ihrer Weise sich dem aristokratischen Charakter dieser Staatsgesellschaft anschlossen und nur Edelleute als Ordensmitglieder zuließen, der Erziehung des herrschenden Standes: und um 1733 hatten die Dissidenten — Protestanten und Griechen — keine politischen Rechte mehr. Vieles hat man den Jesuiten zu Unrecht nachgesagt, manches Gute und vieles Schlimme: in einem aber, der Kunst Staaten zu ruinieren, sind sie ohne Zweifel unerreicht und ihr Meisterstück hatten sie an diesem unglücklichen Lande gemacht.

Seit lange überwog nun der russische Einfluß und wir sahen, wie während des siebenjährigen Krieges die russischen Heere über den Boden dieses Landes verfügten, als wenn es ihr eigener wäre. Die Gefahr war vorhanden, daß dasselbe in absehbarer Zeit die Beute dieses übermächtigen Nachbars würde. Es war der Klugheit Friedrichs gelungen, mit der neuen Herrscherin dieses Reiches, Katharina II. in ein gutes Verhältnis zu kommen, und diese ihrerseits wußte wohl, daß es auch für sie, eine Fremde auf einem an verborgenen Gefahren fruchtbaren Boden, von Wert sei, mit dem bedeutendsten Manne der Zeit im Einvernehmen zu sein: in einem geheimen Vertrag vom 11. April hatten sich die beiden Mächte zu einer gemeinsamen Behandlung der schwedischen und der polnischen Dinge verbunden. Insbesondere betraf dieses Abkommen die Lage der polnischen Dissidenten, und als nun am 7. September 1764 mit einem Aufwande von drei Millionen russischer Bestechungsgelder — denn daß dieses Unkraut vor allem auf diesem verwahrlosten Acker üppig sproßte, versteht sich von selbst — der Kandidat der Zarin, ▆▆▆▆▆r, Stanislaus Poniatowski zum König gewählt worden war, mußte dieser gemäß den Versprechungen, welche er Rußland und Preußen gegeben, dem Reichstag von 1766 eine Vorlage in Betreff der Dissidenten machen. Sie ward durch wilden Tumult unterdrückt, noch ehe sie zur Beratung kommen konnte. Dies gab das Signal zum Bürgerkrieg: eine Konföderation bildete sich zu Radom, im Sinne der russisch-preußischen Forderung, und von den Russen unterstützt: auf einem

Fig. 6-1. Pasting over with "caviar." The obliterated words identify Poniatowski as one of Catherine the Great's lovers. From Oskar Jäger, *Geschichte der neueren Zeit, 1517–1789* (Bielefeld: Verlag von Velhagen & Klasing, 1888), p. 594. Reprinted by permission of Velhagen & Klasing.

608   Sechstes Buch. Das Zeitalter Friedrichs des Großen.

sich leicht bestimmen, um dann in anderen Fällen um so eigensinniger auf seinem Sinne zu bestehen: den ins Unmögliche schweifenden Ehrgeiz, die großen Projekte teilte er mit Katharina, die überdies bei ihrem Reformieren in einer sehr besonderen Lage war.

Rußland und Katharina II.   Sie war eine Fremde und das altrussische Volk betrachtete, wie sie auf einer Reise nach Moskau im Jahre 1774 deutlich zu merken bekam, ihren Sohn, den Großfürsten Paul Petrowitsch als den eigentlichen Zaren; wiederholt kam man Verschwörungen auf die Spur, welchen man doch aus guten Gründen nicht allzugenau nachzuspüren wagte; im Jahre 1773 erhob sich ein ungemein gefährlicher Aufstand durch einen donischen Kosaken, Pugatschew, der sich für Peter III. ausgab, und der nun, da er mannigfaltigen Haß seiner Volksgenossen gegen kaiserliche Beamte, vieler Leibeigenen gegen ihre Herren, der Altgläubigen gegen die herrschende Geistlichkeit für sich in die Waffen rufen konnte, einen Augenblick ernstliche Gefahren erregte, indes doch überwältigt und Juni 1775 in Moskau hingerichtet wurde. Katharina war von den liberalen Grundsätzen der französischen Philosophen und Encyklopädisten wo nicht durchdrungen, so doch angeregt; fleißige Korrespondentin Diderots und Voltaires, der Schmeichelei mit Schmeichelei zu bezahlen wußte, schriftstellerte sie wohl selbst, errichtete und förderte Schulen; eine Übersetzungskommission wurde geschaffen, an deren Arbeiten sich die Kaiserin persönlich beteiligte. ▬▬▬▬▬▬▬▬▬▬▬▬▬▬▬ ...heuchelte, übte sie doch ▬▬▬▬dung, gewährte wie Friedrich der Große selbst den Jesuiten, die damals in den katholischen Ländern so üble Tage hatten, ihren Schutz; und die Bibel, wie der Koran und Schriften Voltaires wurden zugleich in den toleranten Staatsdruckereien gedruckt. Von mehr als zweifelhaftem Werte war eine gesetzgebende Versammlung, welche im Jahre 1767 in Moskau eröffnet wurde: eine freisinnige Komödie, bei der schon durch die Zusammensetzung der Versammlung dafür gesorgt war, daß nichts herauskam. Im zweiten Jahre wurde sie auf Nimmerwiedersehen vertagt, nachdem sie ihrer Kaiserin noch einige volltönende Titel — der Großen, der Weisen, der Mutter des Vaterlands — dekretiert hatte. Vieles was diese that, war wohlthätig. Sie gab dem Reich eine neue und zweckmäßige Organisation, in Gubernien mit 3—400000 Einwohnern, welche allemal in Kreise von 30—40000 Menschen zerfallen sollten; Kreisgerichte, ein Zivil- und ein Kriminalgerichtshof für jedes Gubernium; Rechtspflege, Finanzen, Verwaltung getrennt. Es mag sein, daß manches bloß Schein war, aber in einem solchen Reiche war schon dieser Schein nicht ohne Wert: es war schon etwas, daß man der Kaiserin mit einer Thätigkeit in diesem fortschrittlich-humanitären Sinn zu gefallen hoffen konnte: aber freilich war die Schranke dieses Fortschritts bald erreicht. Von einer Aufhebung der Leibeigenschaft durfte nicht ernstlich die Rede sein, und weder unter dem Adel, geschweige unter dem Volke konnte sich eine Partei bilden, welche ein folgerichtiges Fortschreiten auf dem Wege der Reform möglich gemacht▬▬▬ Und so wenig gefähr▬▬▬

Fig. 6-2. Excision by "caviar" and paper. The first passage accuses Catherine of feigning devotion to the Greek Church; the second refers to her lovers Potemkin and Orlov. From Oskar Jäger, *Geschichte der neueren Zeit, 1517–1789* (Bielefeld: Verlag von Velhagen & Klasing, 1888), p. 565. Reprinted by permission of Velhagen & Klasing.

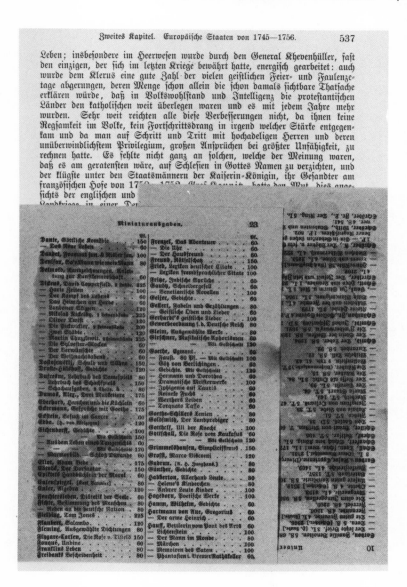

Fig. 6-3. More "caviar" and paper. Obliterated is an unfavorable account of Empress Elizabeth's reign. Underneath the loose edges of the paper one can see that the print is completely covered with ink. From Oskar Jäger, *Geschichte der neueren Zeit, 1517–1789* (Bielefeld: Verlag von Velhagen & Klasing, 1888), p. 537. Reprinted by permission of Velhagen & Klasing.

538   Sechstes Buch. Das Zeitalter Friedrichs des Großen.

Elisabeth, Kaiserin von Rußland.
Gestochen von C. F. Schmidt.

Er war ein Mann von überlegenem Genie und
einen solchen pflegt die Mittelmäßigkeit zu allen Zeiten und in allen Lagern
zu fürchten: er hatte soeben ein großes und einfaches Ziel mit den Mitteln
des Genies erschritten und die Mittelmäßigkeit glaubt bei genialen Naturen
nicht an weise Selbstbeschränkung, worin doch eben das Geheimnis ihrer Erfolge
mitberuht, sondern sie dichtet ihnen ihre eigene vage Begehrlichkeit an: so kam
es Juni 1746 zwischen Österreich und Rußland zu einem Schutzvertrag gegen

Fig. 6-4. "Caviar" with paper removed. The passage continues from the preceding page. Someone—perhaps an angry reader—tore off the covering paper to reveal the ink underneath. From Oskar Jäger, *Geschichte der neueren Zeit, 1517–1789* (Bielefeld: Verlag von Velhagen & Klasing, 1888), p. 538. Reprinted by permission of Velhagen & Klasing.

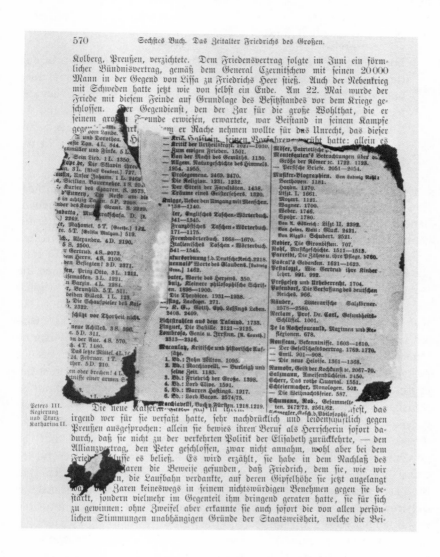

Fig. 6-5. Excision of references to the murder of Emperor Peter III. From Oskar Jäger, *Geschichte der neueren Zeit, 1517–1789* (Bielefeld: Verlag von Velhagen & Klasing, 1888), p. 570. Reprinted by permission of Velhagen & Klasing.

English.[3] While some products of Western technology and culture were accepted and admired, their foreign producers were often viewed with suspicion. Chyzhevs'kyi notes:

> For a long time the attitude of the Russians toward elements of culture and technology which they borrowed from the West remained unchanged: in everything which came from the "infidels" they detected some sort of threat to the fundamentals of Russian life and the Christian faith. Unless we keep this constant suspiciousness and caution in mind, we cannot understand many of the episodes in the history of Russia's later relationship with the West.[4]

Certainly it is true that, due to suspicion, national pride, or a combination of both, Russians always have felt uneasy about this cultural dependence on the West. In his panegyrical odes written in the mid-eighteenth century Mikhail Lomonosov, the great writer and scientist, exhorted his country to produce "her own Platos and quick-witted Newtons." In 1802 the historian Nikolai Karamzin, himself a writer of fiction, bemoaned the fact that "there are in our country many more translations than original works, and consequently the foreign authors' fame outshines that of the Russians." These feelings did not prevent Karamzin from being a translator, however, and he had his own run-ins with the censorship, to which he referred in exasperation as "a black bear standing in the road." He was not permitted to publish translations of Demosthenes, Cicero, or Sallust because, he was told, they were republicans and such authors should not be translated. Some Russians, on the other hand, were quite willing—indeed, eager—to borrow from the West. Ivan Pnin, a prominent intellectual during the early years of the reign of Alexander I, proposed that the government should "compile a list of the books it deems most useful for translation into Russian and announce to all practicing men of letters that the best translation will be accepted [for publication] and the translator duly rewarded by the government. In this way we shall soon have available in our language the most needed and the best works of foreign writers."[5]

Uneasy or not, a degree of dependence on the West was a fact after Peter the Great broke with the Muscovite past and made the connection between Europe and Russia. As Riasanovsky observes:

> From the beginning of Peter the Great's reforms to the death of Catherine the Great, the Russians applied themselves to the huge and fundamental task of learning from the West. . . . The eighteenth cen-

tury in Russia then was an age of apprenticeship and imitation par excellence. It has been said that Peter the Great, during the first decades of the century, borrowed Western technology, that Empress Elizabeth, in the middle of the period, shifted the main interest to Western fashions and manners, and that Catherine the Great, in the course of the last third of the century, brought Western ideas into Russia. Although much too simple, this scheme has some truth.[6]

The French Revolution was the great watershed. Before 1790 Catherine, herself an author, was proud of her enlightened European attitudes. She corresponded actively with Voltaire, Diderot, and Grimm, and her famous *Nakaz* (Instruction) of 1767 was liberal enough to be banned by the *French* censorship. In the years following the Revolution, however, official receptivity to Western ideas changed to official caution and the printed word, seen as the carrier of these now dangerous ideas, was subjected to rigorous review. As we have seen, Catherine's son Paul—sometimes suspected of madness—took the extreme position of banning all imports from the West. Fifty years later Nicholas I, maintaining that the writings of Goethe and Schiller had contributed directly to the 1848 Revolution, demanded the strictest possible surveillance of foreign publications entering the empire.[7]

From 1790 on the authorities worried about the presence in Russia of "radical" Western literature dealing with religion, philosophy, morals, and the social order, and their concern deepened when they saw these ideas being translated into Russian and published before their very eyes. Their concern would seem to be justified: reminiscing about the importance of foreign publications for young people in the first years of the reign of Alexander II, Nestor Kotliarevskii recalls that while those who knew foreign languages had the easiest time, others learned about current Western thought from bibliographic notices for new books and discussion of these books in journals, and by talking with people who had read the originals. Translation was not always possible due to the censorship and was in any case highly disorganized in these years: "The risk was great, the market precarious, the choice of books often accidental, occasionally depending on the number of printer's sheets." Kotliarevskii stresses the importance of those Russian journal articles about foreign works: "There is no doubt that in many cases the journal articles expedited and accelerated the circulation of the foreign original or its Russian translation among the readers."[8]

The novelist Ivan Goncharov, who, we recall, served as a censor for domestic publications in the 1860s, was not inclined to place so much importance on these journal articles. In an 1865 report he observed:

> Articles devoted to these theories are printed in the pages of our reviews with virtually no result. Almost nobody reads them except perhaps a few specialists who in any case prefer to learn of the works of Schulze-Delitzsch and Lassalle in the original. The difference between the situation of the working classes abroad and in Russia, and their different ways of life, make these articles almost incomprehensible to the public.

Franco Venturi suggests that Goncharov's use of "perhaps" and "almost" indicates a lack of conviction and this may indeed be an example of that variance between official reporting and personal opinion that we saw to be characteristic of Tiutchev. In any case, enough of those articles were permitted by the internal censorship to yield the results observed by Kotliarevskii.[9]

Clearly it was too late to retreat. Russians had become Europeans and they shared in European intellectual movements. Indeed, Isaiah Berlin calls Russia an intellectual dependency of Germany in the second quarter of the nineteenth century.[10] Educated Russians traveled and studied in the West, mixed with their European colleagues, and read voraciously. Home again in Russia they continued to read; some became professors and shared Western ideas with their students. They might identify themselves as "Slavophiles," convinced that Russia and Orthodoxy were superior to anything the West had to offer, or as "Westernizers" who saw Russia's future as tied to Western civilization; but all had read the same works of German idealistic philosophy and were thoroughly steeped in Western culture.

European literature was readily available in nineteenth-century Russia and what could not be found at home was obtained abroad. By the end of the eighteenth century, Riga censor Tumanskii was permitting numerous foreign publications without even subjecting them to thorough scrutiny, including some church-related literature; works on mathematics, physics, and geography; medical books (but not medical journals, which often contained inappropriate material); works of ancient and classical authors; Italian writers such as Petrarch, Tasso, Dante, Ariosto, Metastasio, Beccari (but not Boccaccio); works of French writers such as Étienne, Malherbe, Marot Racine, Corneille, La Fontaine, Fénelon, Fontenelle; works of English authors, including Bacon, Shakespeare, Newton, Swift, Addison, Milton, Pope, Richardson, Steele, Fielding, Locke, Sterne,

Thomson (probably James Thomson, the Scottish poet), and Goldsmith; and works of many German authors.[11] It is important to remember that while we are concentrating in this book on banned works, most imported publications were in fact permitted (see chapter 5).

During the reign of Alexander I educated Russians in the provinces as well as in Moscow and Saint Petersburg knew French as well as, if not better than, Russian, and many had mastered German and English as well. Pushkin read and was strongly influenced by Byron, Sterne, and Hoffmann, and he and other writers of the period were much taken with Sir Walter Scott and his "Waverley" novels. In the 1830s and 1840s the dramas of Schiller and especially of Shakespeare were popular. The importance of George Sand and Balzac for the development of the great Russian realistic novels cannot be overestimated, and Turgenev's exposure to Merimée, Flaubert, and other French writers in Paris certainly affected his own writing. The poet and critic Apollon Grigor'ev was very partial to Byron, Victor Hugo, Schiller, Carlyle, Emerson, and Michelet. In the 1860s and 1870s, translations of Byron, Béranger, and Heine enjoyed great popularity; according to Mirsky, the latter two were "more popular with the wide mass of the intelligentsia than any Russian poet."[12]

Russians, then, were definitely in the mainstream of European culture and the censor's task was an impossible one. From the time of Peter the Great until 1917 European literature of all kinds was to be found in the empire in increasing abundance and most of it had entered legally. The censors were supposed to check all incoming works for dangerous ideas and this they tried to do. But what exactly *is* a dangerous idea? It is apparent, with hindsight, that ideas that later proved dangerous often lurked in dry and uninteresting tomes and were overlooked altogether, while considerable attention was paid to what seem to be rather petty concerns. The excisions described below give a wholly negative view of the Russian response to Western literature because the censor's function here *was* negative: he was to excise from foreign publications unacceptable passages. However, in discussing these negative actions we must constantly remind ourselves that they represent only one aspect of Russia's complex and ambivalent response to the West. (Unless otherwise identified, all quotations in this and the following chapter are taken from excised passages.)

148 Dangerous Friends

DISRESPECT TOWARD RUSSIAN ROYALTY

Russian royalty as murderers and victims. In 1882, the year following the assassination of the Russian Emperor Alexander II, a German writer named Ernst Hellmuth published an article in a popular journal entitled "The Russian Imperial House." He wrote:

> The tragic fate prepared by nihilist murderers for Emperor Alexander II on 13 March 1881 has resulted in a general interest in the Russian ruling house of Romanov. It seems, in fact, as if dark powers had sworn that joy in existence and in the pleasures of life should be but a vain desire for the proudest throne on earth. A glance at the history of this family—raised so high, ruling over the largest empire in the world—will show that in the past two hundred years these powers of fate have touched the destinies of its members with violence all too frequently.[13]

Hellmuth then proceeds to review the history of the Romanovs, beginning with Michael in 1613 and ending with the then-reigning emperor, Alexander III. This article, which the Russian censors would not permit to circulate within the empire, serves as a good starting point for the discussion of one of the most sensitive and frequently encountered topics dealt with by the Russian censorship. It should be emphasized that the article is filled with extreme statements based on gossip and misinformation; the same can be said of numerous pieces examined in this and the following chapter. Thus an additional motivation for censorship may well have been to protect Russian readers from the gross inaccuracies of foreigners regarding Russia. (No attempt is made here to correct these errors.)

Indeed, all four prevalent themes can be found in the banned passages of this article. Hellmuth devotes three pages to Peter I ("the Great"), who came to the throne in 1682 as the result of a palace revolution of a type already familiar to him: "Acts of violence and the murder of relatives for the sake of succession had already filled his childhood." Peter combined barbarism with a desire to be civilized and these unreconciled opposites were to characterize the imperial house from then on. Hellmuth passes quickly over the brief reigns of Peter's widow, Catherine I, and his grandson, Peter II (whose father, Alexis, had died in prison under torture), but devotes two pages to Peter the Great's niece, Anna, who reigned from 1730–40, after Peter II had been dispatched to Siberia. Empress Anna was guided by her favorites and especially by her lover, one Bühren from

Courland, who ruled "in the manner of a tyrannical sultan." Anna died childless and Bühren named as her successor an infant, Ivan, great-grandson of Peter the Great's stepbrother. (This feeble-minded stepbrother, says Hellmuth, actually should have been emperor instead of Peter the Great, but had been pushed aside by his cleverer relative.) However, a stronger claimant to the throne was Peter the Great's own daughter, Elizabeth, who became empress in 1741 by means of a coup, imprisoned the baby Ivan, and reigned until her death in 1762. Hellmuth characterizes Elizabeth as "a cruel, vengeful woman, extremely licentious [äusserst zügellose] in her private life."

Elizabeth named as her successor her nephew, son of the Duke of Schleswig-Holstein Gottorp, who reigned for a few months as Emperor Peter III before being dethroned and murdered on the orders of his wife. She was a princess of the house of Anhalt-Zerbst who took the name of Catherine at her marriage and who became the most famous Russian empress, Catherine II ("the Great"). Hellmuth calls her "a vain, sensual, but highly gifted and energetic woman"; she reigned until her death in 1796.[14] (Note that Hellmuth calls the notoriously promiscuous Catherine merely "sensual," while Elizabeth is "extremely licentious.") Catherine the Great was succeeded by her son, Paul I. Hellmuth calls him a "tyrannical nature who, in the wielding of limitless power, committed abuses which had to be traced back to a mental illness. In his imperial madness, which had gruesome features, he appeared to be so dangerous to his own family that they agreed upon his downfall." Paul was murdered in March 1801. His son, Alexander I, succeeded to the throne "under the bloody shadow" of the murder, and reigned until 1825.

> The most varied and contradictory ideas of the time were reflected in him; he embodied the striving for enlightenment and freedom, and at the same time held views aimed at despotism and spiritual repression. Softhearted and of noble inclinations, he fell into religious fanaticism, depression, and distrust of everyone after his brilliant successes against Napoleon I. . . . he died on 1 December 1825, just as an extensive plot to topple him and Russian despotism was being prepared.

The plot, of course, was the so-called Decembrist uprising, which was brutally suppressed by Alexander's successor, his younger brother, Nicholas I. Actually another brother, Constantine, should have been Alexander's successor, but "this boisterous, wild prince with an Asiatic mentality had voluntarily renounced his rights in 1822 to marry a Polish woman and persisted, declaring that he lacked the attributes necessary to rule." Hellmuth writes that the reign of Nicholas I "was to oppress Russia with rigid despotism for thirty years." Under this emperor Russia was recognized in Europe as a world power but the defeats of the Crimean War, in Hellmuth's view, destroyed Nicholas; he died in 1855.

Nicholas was succeeded by his son, Alexander II, a "mild and peace-loving character. . . . He sought to be worthy of the expectations he aroused." Hellmuth maintains that the admirable reforms carried out by Alexander created unbearable tensions in Russian society resulting in general dissatisfaction which gave rise to

> a revolutionary agitation which, under the name of nihilism, was to become fearsome through a series of murderous attempts against high officials and even against the life of the emperor. Alexander II fell victim to such a nihilistic attempt, a dynamite bomb. Thus the dark powers of fate were to reach into his life too. . . . And just as Alexander II's reign was to be ended with another murder, so was it necessary for the reign of his son, Alexander III, to begin with a criminal trial of the perpetrators of this murder. . . . Surely it can be said that no other ruling house in recent history has had such a fearful destiny.[15]

The Russian censorship had to deal with countless books and articles similar to Hellmuth's, ranging from brief references comprising only a few damaging words to entire, often lengthy, sections of books or magazine issues. Genealogical tables of the Romanovs appended to, or included in, history textbooks crop up rather frequently in the sample, the presence of the word *ermordet* (murdered) after some names clearly having led to the excision of those lines.[16]

As we have seen, the two royal deaths attracting most attention in Europe, and thus in the Foreign Censorship Committee, were those of Emperors Peter III and Paul I. Peter, described by Hellmuth in an excised passage from another work as "an ugly, crude, childish crank who played with dolls and dogs," was murdered on 17 July 1762, a few days after being deposed by his wife, Catherine. This account of the murder by German historian Wolfgang Menzel was excised from his twelve-volume world history:

> A few days later Alexis Orlov [brother of Gregory Orlov, Catherine's lover] came to him to inform him of his imminent release and to drink

with him to that event, but gave him poison. Peter's strong constitution withstood the poison, but then Orlov and his companions, Teplov and Baratynskii, all strong men, threw themselves upon him and strangled him with a serviette, on 17 July.[17]

Peter's murder is described in gruesome detail in a number of poems, plays, and novels. An example is *Die Hofdame der Kaiserin* (The Lady-in-Waiting of the Empress), a novel by A. Oskar Klaussmann, which appeared in serialized form in numbers 4 and 7 (1894) of *Bibliothek der Unterhaltung und des Wissens*. This embellished account of the murder was excised from the conclusion:

> Alexis Orlov was the first to lay his hands on the unfortunate Peter. He knelt on the chest of the man who had been thrown on the ground, and he and Teplov were trying to strangle him when the young Prince Baratynskii, commander of the guard, came up. He knew immediately what had to be done, and made a noose out of a serviette, and he and Teplov threw it around the neck of the lamentable victim. In so doing, Baratynskii was wounded in the face by Peter so extensively that he bore the traces, like a brand, for a long time afterward.

Indeed, the subject was so sensitive that the censors would not even permit accounts in which the murder was *not* mentioned; a statement in a history textbook to the effect that Peter III was dethroned by his consort was excised.[18]

Even a direct denial of the murder was banned: in a biographical sketch of Catherine the Great the author maintains that she has been falsely accused. It is well known, he writes, that the empress spent this time in great anxiety and tears and that it took great effort to cheer her up. "People who are guilty of a deliberate crime are rarely capable of tears." Furthermore, he continues, the emperor would surely have lost his life in the revolution anyway and "it is certain that the death of the emperor saved the empire from internal unrest and disorder." The author concludes by remarking that while no just man can praise the way in which Catherine assumed power, still she is surely to be forgiven "and her subsequent life and deeds as empress, the fame and success she achieved for the good of Russia . . . permitted this shadow to disappear from her history." After all, he asks, is it any wonder that a beautiful and talented young princess should have preferred the crown of the greatest empire on earth to the undeserved imprisonment in a convent with which Peter had threatened her? Considering that the book from which this passage was excised bears the ultrapatriotic title of *Princely Portraits, Historical Sketches and Characteristics of Nobility of Soul, High-mindedness, Bravery and Kindheartedness of European, Especially German, Princes and Princesses. For the Strengthening in Youthful Hearts of Love for, and Loyalty to, Princely House and Fatherland*, one should expect nothing less than a complete exoneration of Catherine, who was, after all, a German princess.[19] A denial, of course, no matter how convincing (and this one could not have been considered convincing), must come in response to an allegation and, since any mention of the allegation itself was forbidden, the denial had to be forbidden as well.

However, accounts of foreign ambassadors that do mention the death, but not the murder, were published in the 1870s by the Russian Historical Society and Russian historians did discuss the "revolution" of 1762 in some detail in scholarly works in the second half of the nineteenth century. Russian reference works for educated general readers also handled this topic with kid gloves. In the entry for Peter III in the venerable *Entsiklopedicheskii slovar'* (Encyclopedic Dictionary), the murder is not mentioned —the officials responsible for the censorship of domestic publications were obviously no less cautious than their colleagues in the foreign branch—but the reader is directed to other works for details of Peter's death, among them Bil'basov's *Istoriia Ekateriny II* (History of Catherine II). Anyone attempting to find this book in a Russian library or bookstore, however, was likely to be disappointed. One of the excised passages examined contains an advertisement for the German translation of volumes 1 and 2 of Bil'basov's book, with the following notation:

> Since the Russian original of this book, we are told, was destroyed at the orders of the censorship with the exception of only a very few copies, the German edition of this volume is of all the more interest. Bil'basov's statements earn the special attention of experts and the public because of the unusual detail with which he related the process of the great empress' accession to the throne and the first period of her reign, and because of some completely new documentary material which the author had at his disposal.[20]

Emperor Paul, too, was portrayed as a murder victim in all sorts of historical and literary works. In his *Die Geschichte der Welt* Carl Wernicke wrote this account of Paul's murder, excised for Russian readers:

> During the night of March 23, 1801, the conspirators rushed into the bedroom of the emperor, who sprang out of his bed, enraged. Prince

Zubov showed him a document according to which he should abdicate in favor of Alexander, and when Paul shouted: "I am emperor and intend to remain emperor!" and tried to make his way to the window with drawn sword, Nicholas Zubov threw him to the ground, abused [*misshandelte*] him, and without consideration for his plea that he be allowed a few moments to pray, the emperor was strangled with a scarf.[21]

References to Alexander I's guilt in regard to his father's murder were carefully purged by the censors. In the same passage Wernicke maintains that while Alexander certainly knew of the plot, he probably did not guess that the conspirators intended to kill the emperor. The dramatist Gustav Felix, on the other hand, in his play *Moskau 1812* portrays Alexander as guilt-ridden, although he protests his innocence. Russians had to read the play without this soliloquy:

Why do you climb threateningly out of the dark grave
And look at me with such a reproachful glance?
My clean hand is not stained by murder;
Not by my wish in dastardly fashion
In the dark of night was the sword drawn against you
And your bright life light extinguished.
My conscience is blameless and free!

The censors also found references to Paul's murder in some unexpected places; for instance, a paragraph on Paul turned up in a collection of crime stories, in the middle of a piece about an attempt on the life of King William I of Prussia.[22]

As in the case of Peter III, the fact of Paul's murder was not acknowledged in Russian sources, at least prior to the easing of internal censorship after 1905. The article on Paul in the *Russkii biograficheskii slovar'* (Russian biographical dictionary) deals with Paul's death as follows: "During the night of 11–12 March Emperor Pavel [Paul] Petrovich was no more . . ." (ellipsis points in the original). "A higher destiny," proclaimed the manifesto of the new emperor, Alexander Pavlovich, "saw fit to end the life of our dear parent, the Sovereign Emperor Pavel Petrovich, who died suddenly of an apoplectic fit." However, among sources cited in the lengthy bibliography following the article are several in which the murder is mentioned specifically in the title, including one German article excised in its entirety by the Foreign Censorship Committee. The author of that article,

Heinrich von Sybel, a prominent German historian and editor of the journal in which the article appeared, noted in his introduction that "our story is based completely on direct communications from people who were at that time close to the Russian court and to the events in question."[23]

In his biography of Marshal von Blücher the historian Johannes Scherr quotes a "knowledgeable Russian" to the effect that in those days

> a man in Russia who wanted to make his fortune would hatch a plot to change a monarch or a dynasty the way one now undertakes an industrial venture: one "became a conspirator, an assassin of emperors, the way one becomes today the founder of a joint-stock company." . . . On the day after the murder of Peter III Count Simon Vorontsov met one of the murderers, Prince Fedor Baratynskii: "How could you do such a thing?" asked the count. To which the prince responded, shrugging his shoulders: "What do you want, my friend? I had too many debts!"

That passage was excised by the Russians, as was this observation on Peter III's fall by Heinrich von Sybel: "In this empire all important events end the same way. They have no concept of legitimacy. Force alone is the means of attaining justice: the possessor is then considered to be God's representative until a new conqueror thrusts him back into oblivion."[24]

Slurs on the Russian royal house were no more palatable to the censors when blame was shifted to the Germans responsible for the line. Eduard Reich wrote:

> Sometimes great misfortune can be visited upon a less advanced nation by the implanting of foreign stock in its ruling house. For example, all the evil in Russia dates from the transplantation of German stock from Holstein and Anhalt to the throne of the tsars. The old dynasties of the Muscovite tsars never inhibited the natural development of the Russian people; the servants of the Holstein-Anhalts, however, fettered the people in the chains of an unheard-of physical and spiritual absolutism.[25]

The combination of unattractive assumptions in this passage—that the introduction of the German line was a misfortune, that the Russians were a less advanced people than the Germans, and that there is evil in Russia— would seem to account for its excision.

Russian Royalty as dissolute, corrupt, despotic, insane. In a study entitled *Die Frau in der Kulturgeschichte* (Woman in the History of Culture) published in 1892 Otto Henne am Rhyn writes of Russia:

> The peculiar phenomenon which characterized Russia during the greater part of the eighteenth century, the union of mistress and female monarch in one person, is not to be found in other lands. In different ways this anomaly was personified in Catherine I, Anna, Elizabeth and Catherine II. If we were to write the history of Russia in that period we would describe how the Livonian of obscure origins, Catherine I, arrived through dubious intermediate stages at the side of the mightiest despot of the century and usurped the throne; how Peter's niece, Anna, herself without energy, relinquished the empire to her lover Bühren; how Peter's daughter, Elizabeth . . . , of a similar character, sank far deeper, and how Catherine II, who curbed her temperament still less, but who still, like the English Elizabeth, enlarged her empire, despite her good intentions attempted more for her people's welfare than she was able to accomplish.

In this banned passage Henne am Rhyn was far more generous toward Catherine the Great than were numerous other writers, as we shall see shortly, but neither he nor anyone else in the works examined had anything good to say about the other "mistress-monarchs." Elizabeth, for example, is portrayed in other excised passages as a "common alcoholic," a woman "who apportioned her empire amongst her prevailing gaming and drinking comrades: musicians, non-commissioned officers, medics, and even married one of them—the peasant's son, Razumovskii, in church."[26]

Catherine the Great fares a little better. Some writers acknowledge her accomplishments but with reservations; for example, the historian Karl von Rotteck calls her "powerful, prudent, bold and successful, a great woman insofar as greatness can exist without morality." Sybel, in the same excised passage cited above, says of Catherine that "her self-assurance matched her sovereign power, the force of her ideas filled the atmosphere completely, the ardor of her passions required the moral corruption of her empire. Her whole being was made up of contradictions: she was benevolent and merciless, extravagant and hard-working, cautious and impetuous; but all the contradictions cancelled each other out in the development of colossal ambition, of an all-embracing sense of power."[27] Not wholly flattering views, perhaps, but not wholly negative either, although too much so for the censorship.

Other writers concentrate on Catherine's dissoluteness and are censored accordingly: a statement that she had as lovers "more than fifty grenadiers of the Preobrazhenskii regiment" is cut, as is her description in a novel (by an upright female character) as a "merciless, immoral woman . . . a blemish upon our sex." (This last phrase was excised from a novel intended as a companion piece to a novel by Leopold von Sacher-Masoch—the same Masoch whose name, paired with that of the Marquis de Sade, became a well-known "ism.")[28] In another excised passage Catherine is compared unfavorably to Maria Theresa, the virtuous empress of Austria-Hungary:

> While Catherine had her husband murdered in order to ascend his throne, the great empress-queen mourned the husband whom she loved until her death, and never took off her widow's veil. While Maria Theresa provided for the well-being of her children with maternal care, naming her eldest son as co-regent, the heir to Catherine's throne languished in his mother's shadow. As a woman Maria Theresa was a model of purity and modesty, while Catherine changed lovers, in the choice of whom she was not very fastidious—indeed, she often had more than one.

The paternity of Catherine's son Paul was questioned by several German writers. Both Scherr's observation that "the current ruling dynasty entertains the fiction" that it descends from the Romanovs, and Constantin Frantz's assertion in 1882 that "everyone has known for a long time that the present Russian emperor is descended just as little from the house of Holstein as from the house of Romanov" were cut by the censors.[29]

The males of the dynasty are no more gently treated than the females. Grand Duke Constantine, Emperor Nicholas I's elder brother who had renounced the throne in Nicholas's favor, is mentioned in one excised line of a letter to Varnhagen von Ense and his wife Rahel as "such a scoundrel: he is a completely dissolute fellow." In another passage, excised from an article by Sybel, one of Alexander I's ministers expresses concern in the event of the emperor's death: "If we lose him we would have another one (Grand Duke Constantine) who would have to be killed." Portrayals of Peter the Great as a sexually voracious giant occurred frequently and were excised. Menzel tells how Peter is supposed to have received a straight-laced and respectable Prussian statesman while "sitting between two half-naked mistresses, without allowing their caresses to be interrupted"; Neigebaur describes the empress's four hundred ladies in waiting "mostly German chambermaids, laundresses, etc., who carried children in their arms, and who answered the question of whose children they were: the Tsar has honored me in giving me this child" (*le Czar m'a fait l'honneur de me faire cet enfant*).[30]

The immoral behavior of Emperor Alexander II seems tame indeed when contrasted with that of his illustrious ancestor; he appears to have maintained a decorous and homely relationship with his mistress, Princess Dolgorukii, which lasted many years and culminated in marriage after the death of the empress. The wedding announcement, which appeared in the *Schulthess' europäischer Geschichtskalender* for 1880, was excised for the Russian reading public. It might pass for an item in a contemporary newspaper or magazine:

> July 31. The emperor and Princess Dolgorukii were married in a private ceremony in the chapel of the Winter Palace. He has had a relationship with her for years and she has borne him several children. Neither the Grand Duke heir apparent nor Grand Dukes Constantine and Vladimir were present. . . . Witnesses at the wedding were Generals Loris Melikov, Miliutin and Adlerberg. The existing children of this union received the princely name of Iur'ev. The deceased empress had known about the relationship for a long time.

Russians were not the only dissolute monarchs, however, and the Russian censors were unwilling to subject readers to accounts of royal misdemeanors wherever they might occur; a page of poetry by King Louis of Bavaria was excised from an anthology because mention was made in the annotation of his affair with the adventuress and dancer Lola Montez, which became such a scandal that he had to abdicate the throne in 1848.[31]

Alexander II is reported to have been deeply shocked to learn that his younger brother, Grand Duke Nicholas, had been involved in fraudulent wartime dealings with army contractors in order to pay his debts. Because of this prodigality Nicholas had to be placed under the care of a guardian and limited to an allowance of seven thousand rubles per month. Part of the entry on the grand duke in the thirteenth edition of the *Brockhaus' Conversations-Lexikon* had to be excised because these details were included. It was no such stink of corruption that concerned the censorship in regard to Emperor Nicholas I. Only one excised passage contained a rather low-key hint of immoral behavior; according to this article, within his own family Nicholas was viewed as a "tender, solicitous father and a gallant, loving husband, even though, in later years, especially, his record of marital fidelity was no longer spotless." What did worry the censorship were the numerous references to Nicholas as a cruel and inhuman despot, such as this one:

> During his whole life his motto for his people was "to your knees!" An unlimited despot, he ruled by fear alone, and this fear of him was so great that once, shortly after his death, when the conversation at a social gathering turned to his cruelty and tyranny, a very well-known general who just happened to be present fearfully removed the emperor's portrait from its place on the wall, turned it over and hung it up again backwards—people still feared even his picture. He did not know the meaning of the words forgiveness and clemency; he intensified every sentence to Siberia with some pitiless marginal observation. By nature crude and brutal, he became even more sinister when he was in a bad mood. . . . His slavish people, governed only by means of the knout, suffered in dull silence. . . . When the news [of his death] spread through Europe everyone breathed a sigh of relief, as if freed from a terrible nightmare.[32]

The poet Lermontov accused Nicholas I, in verse, of a particular act of cruelty: of being personally responsible for the death of Alexander Pushkin, Russia's most famous poet, who was killed in a duel in 1837. Nicholas had appointed Pushkin to the humiliating position of *Kammerjunker* (gentleman of the bedchamber) in order to make Pushkin's wife available to Dantes, with whom he then had to fight a duel. Lermontov's bitter poem, which made him famous, was banned by the Russian censors both in German translation and in romanized Russian. Only the last sixteen lines of the original Russian were banned in the Austrian bilingual edition. Nicholas I also was accused by a German critic of insensitivity to his country's needs, of pursuing a disastrous foreign policy to feed his own insatiable ego:

> This man, preoccupied with arrogance and lust for power, had as little judgment as he had great strength of character. In his own country he would have had a rich field for the execution of the most beautiful and the highest sovereign duties, but he neglected them in the most irresponsible way in order to stick his finger into all the affairs of other countries, which were absolutely none of his business. The fate of this despot should serve all sovereigns as a warning example, which they should study closely instead of constantly admiring his arrogance, his pride, and his lust for power.

It is interesting that the censor stopped cutting where he did, since the text continues with more unflattering comments about Nicholas.[33]

The German poet August, Count of Platen-Hallermünde, dedicated an epigram, entitled *To a Despot*, to Nicholas I:

> Devilish hypocrite! With your right hand
> you make the sign of the cross,
> But with your left hand
> you nail the people to the cross.

These lines were excised from an 1895 edition of Platen's work, as was a group of poems entitled "Polenlieder" in which Nicholas I was vilified. The German historian Rotteck describes the results of the emperor's despotism in these words, excised for Russian readers: Nicholas "saw Russia bleeding more staunchly from the internal wounds which he, the emperor, had inflicted upon his empire by his completely misspent life and reign than from the wounds with which the English, French, Sardinians, and Turks together defeated his troops." In a note (banned by the Russian censors) to his *Geschichte der Deutschen* Menzel reports that some people believed Nicholas "ordered his physician to give him poison because the failure of his great undertaking wounded him so deeply."[34]

Another forbidden subject was Nicholas's alleged belief in spiritualism. He was said to "consult wood, and indeed, on trips he supposedly made use of his boot-tree for this purpose, but he was also in communication with other spiritualists." According to the author of this excised passage, Nicholas regularly consulted oracles. (In general, references to spiritualism were banned by the censorship; for example, a passage explaining the miracles of Jesus in spiritualist terms was excised, although in that case the rest of the book was permitted.)[35]

As far as insanity is concerned, there is certainly good reason to believe that Emperor Paul was at the very least mentally unbalanced. One German writer maintains in a banned article on Nicholas I that Paul's sons had inherited his illness. He writes of Nicholas:

> Concerning his internal illness, it was without doubt an inherited one which then took on the character of megalomania. As early as the 1840s the emperor's personal physician of many years, Dr. Arndt, who had known him since his youth, complained of signs of an inherited mental disorder with the words: "I must be on guard day and night, for the emperor and his brothers all have the affliction of

Emperor Paul." The latter, Nicholas' father, was mad, as everyone
knows, and in his frenzy was murdered by officers of the Guards. His
eldest son, Alexander I, died, afflicted with the inherited disease, at
the age of forty-eight in brooding melancholy, sick of life, alone in
faraway Taganrog; Paul's second son, Constantine, considered himself
incapable of governing on account of his melancholia and relinquished
the throne, where he probably would only have met the tragic fate of
his father. He did not live beyond the age of fifty-two. Death from
apoplexy overtook Paul's youngest son, Michael, even earlier, as a
result of his irritability which had already intensified to the point of
insanity. And Nicholas, Paul's third son, had shown such unequivocal
signs of mental eccentricity [Geistesüberspanntheit] that an English
doctor, Granville, had predicted with certainty in July 1853 in a letter
to Lord Palmerston that the emperor had at most two years left to
live, which was then confirmed.

Whether or not he was clinically insane, Paul remains the classic model of
a mad ruler. The censorship had to contend constantly with references to
his insanity. Nothing could illustrate this point more beautifully than the
following exercise in English, excised from a German reader for schoolchildren studying English:

36. The Emperor Paul.

Fits of rage frequently rendered Paul insane. One day, being incensed
against England, he ordered a favourite general to march immediately
to Calcutta. The commander begged to know which line of march
would in his majesty's judgement be best? Calling for a map of the
world, the Emperor soon answered this by drawing a straight line
from St. Petersburg to Calcutta. The marked map is still in existence.
What frequently rendered Paul insane?
What orders did he give his general?
What did the commander enquire?
In what manner did the Emperor answer?[36]

The prevailing European view of the Romanovs as licentious and mad is
nicely summed up in an advertisement excised from the back of the book
containing the Bil'basov advertisement mentioned above. This one is for a
book by Bernhard Stern entitled *Die Romanovs: Intime Episoden aus ihrem
Hofleben* (The Romanovs: Intimate Episodes from Their Court Life). The
table of contents shows the following chapters:

Morals, lack of morals, and sex life [Frauenleben] among the first Romanovs. Love affairs of Catherine the First. Marriage and love affair of Crown Prince Alexis. The children of Peter the Great and Catherine the First. Love affairs of Empress Anna Ivanovna. Love affairs of Empress Elisabeth Petrovna. Marriage and love affairs of Peter the Foolish. Love affairs of Catherine the Second. From the life of Paul the Insane. The descendants of Paul the Insane.

After Paul's murder in 1801 a highly placed Russian is said to have made the following observation to the ambassador from Hannover: "Despotism, tempered by assassination, is our Magna Charta."[37] This *bon mot*, excised over and over again from German works sent to Russia, must have been a constant source of irritation to the censors, especially when combined with numerous insulting remarks about royal morals, manners, and mental states. The Russian royal house was indeed vulnerable to attack and German writers obviously relished the opportunity to prod their neighbor to the east.

These excisions by the Russian censors strike the modern reader as trivial and ineffective. After all, there can be no doubt that educated Russians already knew how Emperors Peter and Paul died, that they were aware of the sexual reputations of their rulers, and so on. Why, then, go to such pains to erase every petty reference to well-known facts? The answer seems to be that once a government embarks on a course of censorship, there can be no stopping. There are two ways to deal with the authority of the printed word: The first diminishes authority by allowing a free press so that opposing views may be published, and the second enhances authority by acknowledging the printed word as a formidable power and attempting to control it. Once committed to the second position, as the Russians were, the government must maintain that control at all costs. In the case of foreign publications, this meant cutting out passages seen as demeaning to the royal family, ridiculous as it may seem.

OPPOSITION TO THE EXISTING SOCIAL ORDER

Nineteenth-century Russians approached ideas with a ferocity, an eighteenth-century intensity. As Isaiah Berlin observes:

No matter where an idea may have been born, writers, artists, critics, the educated minority in the capitals, and, at their hands, a growing number of sincere and idealistic semi-educated Russians elsewhere sought to discover the truth in its light and to shape their lives accordingly. A capacity for rigorous reasoning from premises believed to be true even if they led to unpalatable conclusions, intellectual enthusiasm, integrity, courage, and the rational conviction that only if a man understands the truth and lives by it can he rise to his full stature and be happy, creative, wise, and virtuous—these convictions, inherited from the Age of Reason, were never abandoned by the vanguard of Russian society. It is this faith that, for good or ill, has enabled it to move mountains.

Berlin distinguishes between Western thinkers who, though deeply concerned with great intellectual issues, were for the most part content to leave these ideas in the realm of theory, and Russian thinkers, for whom

> they were questions of desperate urgency, causes for which men were prepared to risk their prospects and their lives. . . . Nothing like it existed in the West; the total and unquestioning, at times fanatical dedication of the intelligentsia, its purity of character and unswerving pursuit of the truth, and the horror with which any lapse from integrity—collaboration with the enemy, whether state or Church or other obscurantist powers—was regarded by it, are probably unique in human history. Unless this is grasped, the later history of Russia, not merely intellectual but social, economic, and political, cannot be adequately understood.

Ideas had to be translated into action in Russia, and Kotliarevskii saw the Western book as the agent of change: "The book gave them [young people] that concentration of thought, that courage, and that lifting of spirits which have the property of being transformed into events."[38]

There is no doubt that those educated Russians who criticized their system of government and agitated for change did rely heavily on Western ideas. Aleksandr Radishchev, one of the first Russians to take on the government in print, wrote his *Puteshestvie iz Peterburga v Moskvu* (Journey from Petersburg to Moscow), a scathing indictment of social and political conditions published in 1790, under the influence of men such as the French philosophers Helvétius, Raynal, Rousseau, the English economist Adam Smith, and the German historian Herder (whose works Radishchev read as they appeared). He also admired the new American constitution, especially those articles dealing with freedom of the press. In the 1830s Nikolai Chernyshevskii, whom Franco Venturi calls the politician

of populism, as Herzen was its father, learned to read Latin, Greek, [?]
Hebrew, French, English, German, Polish, Italian, Persian, and Tatar,
devouring every book he could find in his native Saratov, a provincial town
on the Volga. Writing of the 1860s, Venturi notes that "the future popu-
lists were all reading much the same books at this time, even in the most
remote corners of Russia, for there were only very few Russian works to
assist their development."[39] Among the authors they read were Schelling
and Hegel, Schlosser, Herder, Niebuhr, Ranke, and Feuerbach.

The "Petrashevtsy," followers of Fourier who met in Saint Petersburg
from 1845 until their arrest in 1849, maintained a library at the home of
Petrashevskii, their leader. A description of the collection reveals the
group's involvement in the contemporary intellectual life of Europe:

> It contains most of the French Socialists before 1848 and, to a far
> smaller extent, those of the revolution itself. The collection, too,
> shows their concern with propaganda, and contains many works of
> popularization. All the different trends are represented, most fre-
> quently those of the Fourierists, but also many of the works which
> had by then been published by Proudhon, the Christian Socialists,
> Flora Tristan, Leroux, Pecqueur, Raspail, Vidal, Villegardelle, Louis
> Blanc. The Communists, too, were represented with Cabet, Dézamy,
> Engels (*Die Lage der arbeitenden Klasse in England*) and Marx (*La
> misère de la philosophie*). Besides these and a large number of books by
> economists and planners, there was a very full collection of works on
> the most varying political, legal and social problems, chiefly French,
> but including a number of books published in the West on Russia and
> Poland; as well as studies of other European countries, including
> Italy. The library reveals a deep interest in social theories and a
> passion—which might be called journalistic—for life in Europe
> around 1848.

As Kotliarevskii observed, "At the end of the '40s the Petrashevskii affair
showed that despite the strictest system of defence, forbidden ideas penetrated young heads and that the spectre of 'socialism' stepped across the
Russian border."[40]

Not all such books crossed the border illegally. Venturi recounts a curious story about Ivan Krasnosperov, a young revolutionary who served a
prison sentence in the fortress of Kazan in the 1860s:

> In that two-storeyed tower he continued the life of reading and discus-
> sion that he had led as a free man. The university library provided

him with books, and so he was able to read Holbach's *System of Nature*, Cabet's *Voyage to Icaria* and also Fourier, Proudhon, Louis Blanc and Boerne. He read Engels's *Condition of the Working Classes in England* and translated it for his friends. But he was unable to obtain two books which he specially wanted—Louis Blanc's *History of Ten Years*, and the works of Lassalle. One day, after he had saved up his pay for three or four months, he got permission to come out of prison accompanied by a guard. He went to the only foreign bookshop in the town and found the books that he was looking for. He paid for them and took them back to his cell, incidentally giving the German bookseller a bad fright at the sight of the policeman.[41]

On the other hand, there are numerous documented cases of illegal entry: Prince Peter Kropotkin, the anarchist, used a smuggler to get forbidden pamphlets across the border and another anarchist, Nikolai Sokolov, returned from a trip to Brussels, where he met Proudhon, and to London, where he saw Herzen, with a load of forbidden books that he got into the country "thanks to the sailors of Kronstadt." The importance of Russian émigré publications already has been stressed. Disaffected Russians living abroad always have followed the example of Prince Kurbskii, who fled Muscovy in 1564 and sent his famous epistles to Ivan the Terrible from Lithuania. Herzen is probably the best-known émigré of this type but there were many others; Solzhenitsyn is a contemporary addition to the list.[42]

Venturi maintains that during the last years of the reign of Nicholas I, socially conscious young people in Russia had to educate themselves: "As the revolution in the West struck deeper roots, persecution in St. Petersburg grew more severe. The university more and more took on the appearance of a barricade raised by Nicholas I against the spread of Western ideas." Kotliarevskii confirms this: "Young people, as is evident from the memoirs of contemporaries, viewed their professors and their teaching methods with great distrust." When the new reign began and Western publications could enter the country more easily, Russians were overwhelmed by the influx of reading matter—older titles missed during the bad years as well as a great flood of current titles. Kotliarevskii reels off the names of western giants in philosophy, science, history: Feuerbach, Comte, Mill, Claude Bernard, Vogt, Moleschott, Büchner, Darwin, de Tocqueville, Schlosser, Thierry, William Prescott, Guizot, and many others. It is impossible, he says, to pinpoint precisely the effect of any one work but taken together, "The foreign book helped the young reader above all in his struggle with the old traditions—that is, with the prevailing religious views, the reigning political order and the current social system."[43]

From the 1860s on Russian revolutionaries maintained close ties with European social thinkers and activists. The Social Democrats were in touch with Swiss and German socialist movements, the labor movement, and the Marxists. As we have seen, a number of Marxist works appeared in Russia legally; as Chyzehevs'kyi notes, "The censors paid no heed to the political threat of books devoted to questions of national economics and the philosophy of history." Some Russians, such as G. Lopatin, who translated part of *Das Kapital* into Russian, were personally acquainted with Marx and Engels. Another active revolutionary, A. Serno-Solovevich, was sent a presentation copy of *Das Kapital* by its author, although they had never met.[44] (There is some speculation as to just why Marx sent him a copy of the book; in any case, Serno-Solovevich committed suicide in 1869 without ever having met Marx.)

The excised passages discussed below contain general criticisms of autocracy and specific complaints about the Russian system of government. The authorities, as we know, had long been nervous about such attacks; in Catherine the Great's time Princess Dashkova, then president of the Academy of Sciences, instructed the editor of the newspaper *Sanktpeterburgskie vedomosti* (Saint Petersburg news) to avoid selecting from foreign newspapers and translating into Russian any articles containing political material hostile to Russia or her allies. In some of these passages violence is advocated as a means of bringing about change. Venturi comments that in the 1860s "the idea of an attempt on the life of the Tsar was probably more widespread than is generally thought. The words of Lincoln's assassin, 'Sic semper tyrannis,' were fairly well known in Moscow."[45] It is not surprising, then, that such passages should have been viewed as objectionable in Russia during the second half of the nineteenth century, especially in view of growing discontent and the increasing incidence of terrorism. However, seen in the context of the country's intellectual climate at this time, when Western ideas were crossing the borders quite freely and foreign publications were readily available (legally or otherwise), these excisions do seem ineffectual indeed.

Criticism of the Russian system of government. In a book on the Roman satirist Lucian, the German author praises the Roman imperial government—"Every region had its former freedoms and rights insofar as they

were compatible with the whole"—and then contrasts the Roman system
with "Russian despotism, which smothers life in suffocating fear for thousands of miles." The page containing these lines was banned, as were
passages from two books comparing Russia with China. In the first, the
author pairs the emperor of Russia with the "son of heaven" in Peking,
since they "indulge themselves in the same feelings of sovereignty and
divinity." In the second, the Russian system is shown to be worse than
Chinese despotism "not merely because it is sustained by a greater physical
power but even worse, because the entire spiritual power is in the hands of
the rulers. The Chinese government is not a despotism supported by
physical power, but rather an autocracy which exists by the free consent of
the people."[46]

These unfavorable comparisons of their country with ancient Rome, and
especially with modern China, were understandably distasteful to the Russians. The Roman Empire may have been infamous but at least it was far
removed in time, while contemporary China was uncomfortably close,
especially from the point of view of a country that wished above all to be
considered part of "civilized" Europe rather than of "barbarian" Asia. We
shall return to this point in the next chapter. However, the Russian censors
would not tolerate *any* negative view of absolutism, whether or not Russia
was mentioned. A sentence in a history of Schleswig-Holstein that dispar-
aged the theory of the divine right of kings was excised, as was a passage
from an article on the English in India in the seventeenth century; con-
trasting the successful East India company with its unsuccessful French
counterpart, the author concludes that French despotism was to blame:
"How could . . . grand trade ventures flourish in a country the energy of
which was dissipated by the capricious actions of absolute power? The ill
will, ignorance and indolence of a single minister in such despotic states
could easily ruin the entire community and impede the most profitable
undertakings." One of the worst aspects of Russia's despotic system was
seen by some observers to be the corruption that plagued the country.
Discussing Central Asia, Karl Friedrich Neumann wrote these unflattering
lines about Russia:

> The demoralization is frightful. Karamzin, the historian of his
> people, Alexander's [Alexander I] friend, could not find fifty
> virtuous and scrupulous men among all Russians who could curb
> their insatiable greed and live for the happiness of the people, for
> the well-being of their subjects. . . . The final cause for such

general corruption lies in a bad principle of government. If the master rules by despotism, the servant too will rule by despotism; if the master takes whatever he likes, the servant too will take whatever he likes.[47]

The entire page was excised.

In addition to describing the unsatisfactory state of Russian government, German observers discussed prospects for change. *Schulthess' europäischer Geschichtskalender* for 1878 described a student demonstration at which the crowd shouted, "Long live the constitution! Long live freedom!" and the historian Ludwig Stacke noted that by 1881 even members of high officialdom were inclined towards a constitutional form of government. (Both passages were banned.) Statements stressing the attainment of constitutional government by force also met with disfavor. This comment about England is one example: "Its constitution is no gift of kings; it was won, sword in hand, despite princely rulers and noblemen."[48]

The view that Russia was not ready for constitutional government was objectionable when linked with revolt, as in this banned passage: "So one must say that the 'Decembrists' did not understand their time or their people correctly, and that they were wrong in believing in the necessity of a constitutional reform for Russia." (Understandably, the Decembrist uprising was a forbidden topic; Scherr's essay, *Die Dekabristen* was cut in its entirety from the second edition of his *Neues Historienbuch*.) And even the statement that "were they to vote, the Russian people would choose absolute monarchy by a vast majority" was banned, perhaps because the rest of the sentence reads "this fact, however, would still not protect the emperor from nihilist bombs."[49]

Violent change: the tsar trembles in his palace. Nihilism and the inevitability of revolution in Russia were themes discussed frequently by German writers in the 1880s and 1890s, and the Russian censorship was kept busy cutting references to these highly sensitive topics. "The tsar trembles in his palace" were the only words cut from an installment of a serialized story called *Zwischen drei Reichen: Erzählung von unserer Ostgrenze* (Between Three Empires: A Tale from Our Eastern Border).[50] This is an interesting example of inconsistent cutting; the lines preceding the excised words refer to a proclamation in Polish, calling on the Polish people to "throw off the yoke which Russian tyranny has laid upon you." Perhaps the dreadful image of the emperor trembling in his palace blinded the censor to other dangers. Of course, a positive view of revolution anywhere, at any time, was considered dangerous: "Old freedom died because of the tyranny of emperors," wrote one author in 1856, referring to the Roman Empire, "and emperors will die because of the new freedom of the future."[51] (The entire page was cut.) But in the last two decades of the nineteenth century German observers were concentrating on the scene unfolding before their eyes, viewed by many of them as the decline and fall of the Russian Empire. A few examples of banned passages from this period, taken in chronological order, illustrate the problems confronting Russian censors reviewing German publications.

In a review of an Italian book on nihilism published in the December 1880 issue of *Der Kulturkämpfer*, the author discussed the ideas of Herzen, Chernyshevskii, and Bakunin—all personae non grata in their native Russia—and assessed the impact of nihilism on Russian society. He suggested that the government's method of dealing with the problem was likely to worsen the situation rather than improve it: "Peace cannot be re-established by exiling hundreds or thousands of people who, justly or unjustly, were accused of major or minor crimes." Reflecting on the condition of Russia in 1880, the author of *Schulthess' europäischer Geschichtskalender* observed that "tsarist absolutism has become simply impossible." It is also impossible, he added, that "a band of desperate men who call themselves nihilists could play such a role for such a long time and hold an entire great empire in fear and terror if all of the upper classes of Russian society, all those who can think for themselves, were not consciously or unconsciously sympathetic to them. . . . the conspiracy . . . draws its circle ever closer around the emperor."[52]

Alexander II was assassinated in 1881. The following year a book review in *Der Kulturkämpfer* ended with these words: "The entire great empire of the tsars is trembling upon a volcano." The work under review was *La Russia sotterranea*, published in Milan in 1882 and written by "Stepniak" (S. M. Kravchinskii), former editor of the revolutionary journal *Zemlia i volia* (Land and Freedom), with a preface by Peter Lavrov, a prominent revolutionary. That same year *Schulthess' europäischer Geschichtskalender* for 1882 reported on trials of terrorists and demonstrations by university students. In a study on the psychology of crime published in 1884 a scholar concluded that nihilism arose and thrived in Russia because of the

general dissatisfaction of the people with existing political conditions, the necessity (which had penetrated deep into the popular consciousness) of replacing the personal caprice of the ruler with the security of an existence ordered by law. Had the Russian people not lacked this solid foundation for national life, the legal basis, then all the destructive forces coming from outside would have been ineffective.[53]

Two years later, in 1886, Ludwig Stacke discussed the development of the "revolutionary-terrorist party" and described in detail a series of attacks on Russian officials between 1878 and 1882. Terrorism took its toll on Russian society, noted a German journalist in 1890:

> The events of recent times have forced a constant expansion of the secret political police, for which shockingly large amounts of money must be spent. As is the case everywhere, in Russia too this secret police has caused great harm to innocent and peace-loving people, since a denunciation is sufficient to make an honorable man suspect and thus miserable. Thousands of extortions are committed by agents of the secret political police, and unfortunately, well-known conditions prevail in Russia which enable the really guilty to lead undisturbed lives or to flee, provided they understand that they must silence the secret political police with money.

In a more dramatic vein is this prediction of doom aimed at the Russian royal house in 1890:

> I can already hear the thunder, deep in the bowels of the earth. Soon the earth will open and swallow up those who trample with their feet upon Justice and Truth. And where the "almighty" throne of the tsars now stands will be nothing but a cloud of smoke.

But according to another commentator, writing in 1892, the emperor was no longer almighty:

> Emperor Alexander III is absolute now only to the extent that the all-powerful court clique, together with the bureaucracy and the upwardly striving elements of the nationalist movement, humor him. . . . the elements which have actually been ruling Russia for a good decade now are the dignitaries, generals, and bureaucrats, and the Autocrat of All the Russias can only play the dignified and graceful puppet by means of which the St. Petersburg court camarilla keeps the great masses, corroded by nihilism, in their customary state of dependence.[54]

The Russia portrayed in *Schulthess' europäischer Geschichtskalender* for 1892 is imbued with a strong sense of impending doom:

> Famine, cholera, preparations for war despite everything, and secret, undermining policies in the Balkans are the characteristics of Russian politics this year. Many people maintain that the economic emergency in Russia is no temporary condition, but rather the beginning of an incurable malady. Russian agriculture is said to have been maintained in recent decades only by exhaustion of the soil and is facing complete ruin. The gradual clearing of the forests, sacrificed to the beginnings of industry and railroads, is said to have resulted in a climatic change. The rivers are supposed to have run dry, the previously fertile land turned barren and no longer capable of supporting its inhabitants. A very energetic and intelligent government might, by expenditure of the greatest means, be able to check the disaster through many years of work. But since all surplus resources are being used exclusively for the continued escalation of military preparedness, the downfall would appear to be inevitable.

Finally, the censor assigned to review the tenth issue for 1894 of *Bibliothek der Unterhaltung und des Wissens* banned an article entitled "Aus der Werkstatt der Anarchisten," an amply illustrated guide to explosive devices used by terrorists around the world.[55] (Numerous contemporary parallels come to mind, such as the recipe for a "Molotov cocktail" in a 1968 issue of the *New York Review of Books*, or the recent controversy over plans for constructing a hydrogen bomb published in the *Progressive*.)

One of the most sensitive spots in this generally tender area was, not surprisingly, the assassination of a ruler, with special emphasis on the reigning emperor of Russia. It was not necessary, however, that the place be Russia, or the time the present: a description of the murder of Julius Caesar was cut from an 1856 German account of an Italian journey, and there is no mention of Russia in this banned 1876 justification for political murder:

> When the people are convinced that the murderer for political motives is to be compared with a warrior who frees his people from a fierce and wicked enemy; when the infringement of the law is clearly a lesser evil than the continuation of unbearable national suffering, and thus is an appropriate means for healing the most terrible ills, they will condone even murder, if it is committed with these patriotic aims.[56]

Assassination of a reigning Russian emperor was clearly different from murder within the royal family, as described in the preceding section. The latter sort of murder was not acknowledged officially, being a family affair, and so could not be allowed to appear in print. But the former was far more serious, committed by riffraff and posing a threat to the established order; references to this type of killing were cause for genuine alarm rather than mere displeasure.

Several allusions to assassinations of Russian royalty by terrorists, some quite oblique, were expunged from works examined. A character in a play by Hermann Bahr expressed himself thus: "If we could begin again from the beginning we could drop the explaining and the agitation, *buy ourselves a rifle, shoot the Emperor of Russia*, and then let ourselves be merrily hanged." Only the italicized words were excised. And this toast, proposed by a drunken Russian in a historical novel by J. Rettcliffe, was cut: "Down with the emperor!"[57]

More subtle was the excision of part of an essay on Dostoevskii's novel *Crime and Punishment* by the Danish critic Georg Brandes that included the author's observation that Dostoevskii was making an obvious, though veiled, reference to the murder of the emperor when he had Porfirii say to Raskol'nikov: "It is certainly good that it was only a miserable old woman you murdered; if your theory had taken another direction your crime might have been a hundred million times more terrible." In the eyes of the Russian censorship Brandes himself may well have appeared to be a dangerous radical. He wrote on Nietzsche and corresponded with him, and had even given the German philosopher contacts in Saint Petersburg. Brandes had visited the Russian capital in April 1887 to participate in the celebration of Polonskii's fiftieth birthday, at which he spoke (in French) on the significance of Russian literature; one wonders whether Polonskii had any part in the censorship of Brandes's books in German translation, several of which appear in the 1898 catalog of banned publications.[58]

The censorship of censorship. In their examination of German publications Russian censors occasionally encountered references to the theory and practice of censorship itself. Among the passages examined for this study there were several of these, dealing with censorship in general, in European countries, or in Russia. The work of Karl Gutzkow, a writer of the "Young Germany" group, was a rich source for this material, since he had strong opinions on the subject of censorship and expressed them passionately. In one passage banned in Russia he complained that it was painful enough to have one's work judged by anyone but to be forced to turn it over to the state was particularly unfortunate:

> Censorship might still be bearable if from the outset it did not, as a branch of the administrative bureaucracy, bear the stamp of literary incompetence. An official who has perhaps studied all the commentaries on the laws of the land but who has never studied a work of a different scholarly discipline, not to mention art, an official whose ideas are all directed towards small spaces in the administrative buildings, who has only one God, namely his superior, and only one heaven, namely promotion—such a man should pass judgment on your writing.

He wrote about the absurd demands made of authors by the state:

> They must feel and comprehend things only in the direct interests of the state. What an unreasonable demand at a time when governments have to admit that forcible suppression of the opposition is impossible and that the solution to disagreements will be possible only when the government settles them, when it consents to so-called concessions and knows how to make good use of the gradual waning of passions! Why should literature, which could be the best mediator between the conflicting interests, think and write only as the government demands!

Gutzkow conceded that there had to be some kind of censorship "in the higher sense of the word. . . . Censorship should be the law, and freedom of the press should be in the form of execution of this law."[59]

In his *Wiener Eindrücke* (Viennese Impressions), published in 1845, Gutzkow made an ardent plea for freedom from the theatrical censorship practiced in the Austro-Hungarian empire. "The lightly frivolous, the drolly suggestive is most willingly tolerated, but any serious attempt to solve some social problem is viewed with suspicion. History, politics, religion are completely closed subjects." The expression of moral values is controlled too: "No illegitimate children are permitted on the stage, fathers may not quarrel with their sons, nor sons with their fathers, kings must always be admirable. . . . I would be ashamed to be ruler of a country, minister of a government which glosses over such absurdities." A few pages later Gutzkow described in great detail the censoring of foreign publications by the Austro-Hungarian authorities, which, we will recall, corresponded very closely to the Russian system.[60] Indeed, everything he wrote about censorship was applicable to Russia and, although he never mentioned that country specifically, it comes as no surprise that the Russian authorities tried to keep these pieces of Gutzkow's writing out of the country. (Indeed, it is surprising that the Austro-Hungarian censors permitted Gutzkow to publish these critical passages.)

Another hostile and detailed description of the Austrian censorship was excised from a historical novel by L. Mühlbach. In this passage the zealous Jesuit censors give Emperor Joseph II himself a hard time when he comes to the office, disguised as a simple traveler returning home from abroad, to claim his confiscated foreign publications.[61] Again, there are too many unwelcome parallels with Russia. Both authors challenge the Austrian system: Gutzkow maintains that the rulers should be ashamed of themselves for countenancing such stupidity and Mühlbach portrays the emperor as outraged by the actions of his own censorship. From an official point of view, clearly, neither passage could be considered appropriate for Russian readers.

Judging by the direct references to Russian censorship in passages examined, German writers were well aware of the Russian situation. As one writer observed, "Even the Slavic earth has produced its Pushkin, but this earth is not hospitable to the development of literature. The gardener who is supposed to tend this precious blossom of the human spirit has never been kindly disposed toward it. The chief impediment to Russian literature was, and remained, censorship." In banned passages from *Dichterkönige* (Kings of Verse), Johannes Scherr discusses the difficulties that Mickiewicz, Pushkin, and Lermontov had with the censorship. Alexander von Reinholdt's history of Russian literature was permitted only with the excision of the section on Herzen, Bakunin, Dobroliubov, and colleagues, which included a list of Western authors banned in Russia such as Mill, Vogt, Moleschott, Buckle, Darwin, Stirner, Ruge, Feuerbach, and Louis Blanc.[62]

Readers of foreign works were given some details of the functioning—or malfunctioning— of Russian censorship which probably amused them, but must certainly have irritated and embarrassed the censors themselves. In the entry on Herzen in the third edition of *Meyers Konversations-Lexikon*, for instance, one reads that "it is taken for granted that the emperor at that time always read *Kolokol* (Herzen's London journal, banned in Russia) to inform himself of matters which were kept secret from him." Not only the emperor was known to have had access to forbidden publications, however. As one German observed:

The life of fine society in Saint Petersburg under the strict despotism of Nicholas I did not have to suffer in regard to freedom of expression. In these regions people paid no attention to the Russian censorship or to the fear of the Third Section of the Foreign Office, and the same people who collaborated with the machine of government to keep the minds of Holy Russia in slavish discipline talked carelessly about forbidden books and candidly about political conditions and people.[63]

It was taken for granted that the more strictly a work was forbidden, the more attractive—and available—it would be. One author reports that "the work by Marquis [de] Custine on Russia is so strictly forbidden in the lands of the lord of all the Russias that a bookdealer is fined five thousand rubles for the first copy he sells, ten thousand rubles for the second, and for the third he is exiled to Siberia. Because of this strict ban the book has been disseminated everywhere; in fact, good breeding demands that one have read it." The page containing this passage is from a book by Karl Friedrich Neumann on the history of the English-Chinese War, proving that a Russian censor could not be too diligent in his search for dangerous material. It was to be found in the most unlikely places.[64]

How do we imagine the Russian censors felt when they encountered passages such as these, stating boldly that their work was in vain? Were they angry or discouraged, resigned or indifferent? Or was it perhaps just part of the day's routine?

7

Applying the "Caviar":
Defending Country,
Religion and Morals

How and why was it possible," Chyzhevs'kyi asks, "that as late as the nineteenth century people in the West felt the 'Europeanized' Russians to be 'Tatars in European clothing' whose patina of European culture, as Napoleon asserted, could easily be scratched off to reveal the Tatar underneath it?" In responding to this question Chyzhevs'kyi looks back at the Russia of the fifteenth, sixteenth, and seventeenth centuries, when "in a certain sense the Muscovite tsar considered himself the successor to the disposed Tatar khans." He notes that Russians at that time did accept the absolute power of the tsar: "Even in the time immediately before the Revolution of 1917 the notion of the blind allegiance of the Russian people to the tsar was still quite widespread."[1]

Russian rulers were viewed by the West as "Oriental" or "Asiatic" potentates—a view shared by Belinskii, who referred to "our Tatar censorship," and by other alienated Russians—but it was not only the system of government which was seen as "Tatar." Europeans responded to what Chyzhevs'kyi calls the "'lack of polish' in the Russian character, which manifested itself in crudity, in violent impetuosity, and in extreme immoderation."[2] In European eyes, Russians were simply barbarians who behaved barbarously toward one another and toward the peoples they subjugated.

Beginning with Peter the Great, Russians were extremely sensitive about the low opinion of their country and citizens held by Europeans. Hans Rogger observes that the eighteenth-century historian Tatishchev was eager to have his history of Russia published in English translation by the Royal

Society of London as "part of a larger ambition which he shared with Peter—of presenting to Europe a favorable picture of the state of learning and civilization in Russia." Rogger relates a charming story to the same effect about Princess Dashkova:

> A touchingly naive instance of the desire not to seem inferior in the eyes of Europe is related by the Princess Dashkova. Putting up at a Danzig inn for a couple of nights, she was horrified to see that its large dining room was almost completely dominated by two paintings depicting battles lost by Russian troops "who were represented in groups of dead and dying, or on their knees, supplicating mercy of the victorious Prussians." The Princess was scandalized that this evidence of Russian pusillanimity and defeat should be so openly displayed for all to see, and she upbraided the Russian *chargé d'affaires* for allowing such an "abominable monument of our disgrace to exist." That gentleman assured her that it was quite outside his province to influence the art work in Prussian inns, so that the Princess took it upon herself to redress this grievous slight to the national honor. She and a few companions barricaded themselves in the dining room, and with the help of paints and brushes regained these lost battles for Russia by "changing the blue and white of the conquering Prussians into the red and green uniforms of our Russian heroes." . . . This redemption of the national honor was not much more than the prank of a spirited young woman; but it reveals the deep sensitivity of many Russians in the face of a Europe which seemed still to deny them recognition.[3]

"BEYOND THE BORDERS OF CIVILIZATION"

With these words Heinrich Berghaus placed the Russian people unequivocally outside the cultural boundaries of Europe and left his readers little doubt as to his attitude toward what he calls the "Slavic nationality." In a similar handbook of geography another writer described the gulf between educated Russians and the common people and the low state of the latter, portraying them as a physically and spiritually impoverished, largely undifferentiated mass of serfs, corrupt and excelling mainly at petty theft. A third textbook emphasizes the backwardness of Russian culture and the gap between Russia and her European neighbors: "Absolutism still reigns today in Russia, in contrast to all other European countries. . . . The concept of honor among civil servants is generally lacking still; public office is viewed as an opportunity for feathering one's nest. In this respect too Russia presents a picture of bygone centuries. . . . This people is not yet ready for a modern constitutional system of government." These three examples all come from simply written books intended for broad popular audiences, for use in schools and home libraries. Russians with a fairly low level of German reading skill could handle books such as these; it is no wonder, then, that the censors decided to excise such clearly unflattering descriptions of the local scene.[4]

In German discussions of every period of Russian history we find Russian culture assessed as crude, backward, barbarous, cruel. (Most of the excised passages dealing with this theme come from works on history and geography and from travel accounts.) The common people are portrayed as archconservatives who resist all attempts from above to impose Western culture upon them. As one textbook writer describes the medieval period:

> The despotism of the emperor kept the nobles in servitude too; the lower orders were kept in the filth of serfdom. Characteristic of the Russians were a servile disposition and a fawning adoration of the emperor, lack of a sense of honor, indifference to pain and privation as well as to hardship and abuse, cheerfulness in the face of the most profound external distress, superstition, fearful observance of the fasts and church rites, hatred for other religious groups, cunning and delight in trickery, indifference to keeping one's word, a lack of moral feeling and stupidity in regard to every high and noble idea.[5]

Peter the Great traveled in Europe and soon had a reputation as a barbarian on a grand scale. The same banned passages cited in the previous chapter describing Peter's dissoluteness tell also of his barbaric destructiveness: "When in the course of his travels through Germany Peter visited the Prussian court, his servants totally ruined all the furniture and tapestries, as he himself had warned they would. He was constantly drunk. In order to become familiar with the punishment of the wheel, as yet unknown to him, he wanted to have it demonstrated immediately, on the first of his servants at hand." The empress, who accompanied Peter on some trips, is described in similar terms in these excised lines: "The [Prussian] queen had made her palace Monbijou in Berlin available to the consort of the emperor, but had had all breakable items removed because she knew how the Russian visitors dealt with such things; despite her precautions, after their departure she had to have the palace almost completely redecorated."[6]

Russian absolutism at the time of Catherine the Great was described as having more characteristics of "Asiatic brutality than European culture." The attack of the Russian general, Suvorov, on Warsaw's suburb Praga, which resulted in the defeat of Poland, became infamous in Europe. Writing for schoolchildren, one textbook author described the attack this way: "The hardhearted Russian General Suvorov now stormed Warsaw's suburb Praga and allowed murder and bloody frenzy as only a barbarian could." Catherine's son, Emperor Paul, is often described in terms such as these: "a peculiar prince who combined an Oriental-Tatar character . . . with European manners and culture in the strangest mixture."[7]

The masses at the time of Nicholas I were called "half savage," and Nicholas himself, as we have seen, was frequently described as a cruel despot. In his article on the Russian royal house—excised in its entirety, as we recall—Ernst Hellmuth enumerates the sentences Nicholas imposed on the participants in the Decembrist uprising:

> Five of them were to be drawn and quartered, thirty-one beheaded, seventeen were condemned to lifelong forced labor in the Siberian mines, thirty-five were to atone for their crime with exile and military reduction in rank. The emperor showed mercy only to the extent of permitting the first five to be hanged and sending the thirty-one to the mines at Nerchinsk.[8]

A sentence to be drawn and quartered must have seemed as medieval and barbarous to nineteenth-century German audiences as it does to us today.

Alexandre Dumas (*père*) toured the Caucasus in 1858–59 and in the book resulting from his trip made some interesting comments about Russians. The censors excised several passages from the authorized German translation, including one containing the following observations: "Russia is an element: it expands, but only to destroy. In modern conquerors there remains a residue of the barbarism of the Scythians, Huns, and Tatars; from the point of view of today's civilization and intelligence one cannot comprehend this need for conquest combined with disregard for improvement." Dumas continues with the prediction that Russia will conquer Constantinople: "Blond people have always been conquerors; conquests of dark-haired tribes are always of short duration." The Russian Empire, he continues, will be divided into four parts: the northern empire with its capital in Saint Petersburg, the western empire of Poland, the southern empire of the Caucasus, and the eastern empire of Siberia. The present emperor will maintain the throne of the northern empire, a popular commander-in-chief supported by France will rule in Poland, a disloyal general will reign in the Caucasus, and a "brilliant, bold exile will proclaim a federated republic between Irkutsk and Tobolsk." Not surprisingly, this passage was also banned.[9]

In an 1878 handbook chronicling events in European history, the German author reported that at the July 1867 trial in Paris of Berezowski, a Pole who had attempted the preceding month to assassinate Alexander II, the accused named the emperor as the criminal rather than himself, calling Alexander "not the tsar, but rather the Tatar." (Here is another case of inconsistent cutting; only the line containing these words was excised, while the preceding lines cataloging the emperor's crimes were permitted.)[10] This insult, coming from a dissident element within the empire, was perhaps at least as bitter as goading from an outsider. But outsiders—in this case Germans—made themselves quite unpleasant in regard to Russia's Baltic provinces, which retained their German character. Twenty-two years later, in the reign of Alexander III, *Schulthess' europäischer Geschichtskalender* for 1889 referred to the "barbaric, anti-European character" of Pan-Slavism at the point where it "encounters real culture and civilization," the "real" culture being, of course, German and thus European.[11] Five years after that, at the end of the reign of Alexander III, a Prussian schoolteacher equated Russia with Asia by putting this motto on the title page of his book: "In Prussia, of course, there are still philosophers and patriots, but that is also where they are most needed. Only philosophers and patriots shall go there, and Asia shall not advance over the borders of Courland."[12] Both passages were, of course, excised before the publications were permitted for circulation in Russia.

In German writing about Russia the knout stands out as a symbol of barbarism and cruelty. One writer claims that Russian aims to "reach its greedy claws into Europe's heart and degrade Germany, the motherland of civilization, the source of knowledge, to the status of a zealous client of the Russian knout." In the same poem Poland is described as suffering under Russia's blows: whipped, shot, and exiled. (It might be added that there is no mention in the poem of *German*-occupied Poland.) A cartoon excised from a collection published by *Kladderadatsch*, the German humor magazine, is entitled "an armchair for the president of the Bundestag (Masterpiece by a native of Saint Petersburg)."[13] The high back of the chair is straddled by a fierce, bearded Russian clutching a cross in one hand, a knout in the other; civilized European heads are perched on the chair's arms and legs.

The terrible reputation of the knout reached even into the wilds of

Central America, where a German traveler observed that "the aversion to the Russian knout had even taken hold in the minds of natives of the new continent, accustomed as they were to Spanish slavery, and the brutality and violence of the Russian system had attained an even more dismal fame than they deserved." Such excised passages present a clear view of Russia as a loathsome, fear-inspiring, nightmare of a country "at the name of which little children stick their heads under the covers and dream of long beards and strokes of the knout, and which big children imagine as a monstrous spider-web in the middle of which the eternally watchful rob-ber-lady sits, waiting to catch and kill every fly that comes into her territo-ry." Aversion for the Russians was not limited to Westerners. A German poet portrays the proud response of a young Circassian prince to imperial messengers hoping to buy his allegiance with promises of riches, weapons, and women. The prince disdainfully declines to be bought; he is the noble savage while the Russians are corrupt aggressors. The entire poem was banned.[14]

Fearsome as the empire might appear to some, other observers had a low opinion of the Russian army, which they saw as bumbling and incompetent rather than threatening. (Princess Dashkova's Prussian innkeeper undoubt-edly shared this view.) Sometimes the emperor himself is blamed; in one banned passage Alexander I is held responsible for the poor showing of the Russian army at Austerlitz by a writer who says his "vanity and youthful carelessness" were at fault. In another passage a military analyst writes that General Suvorov's campaign in Italy and Switzerland in 1799 was the only campaign in which *"the Russians defeated the troops of a Western Great Power on the open field under approximately equal conditions of manpower and ter-rain"* (emphasis in original). Another military analyst writing on the Cri-mean War considers the Russian cavalry to be "the worst in all of Europe"; the officers were acknowledged to be brave enough, but the common soldiers "remained at the rear like a herd of sheep." Even the wounds they inflicted on the enemy were considered inferior: "The bayonet thrusts, sword cuts, and blows from rifle butts which the Russian soldiers dealt to the French and English in frequent skirmishes were said to have rarely caused very dangerous wounds, since the Russian soldiers proved to be very weak and inept at hand-to-hand combat, and also because their weap-ons were extremely poorly made."[15]

However, bumbling as the army might be, Russia was still viewed as a military threat to Europe: "As long as the spirit of the Russian government remains Asiatic, that is, absolutely autocratic, every increase in the intellectual as well as the physical, military, and monetary strength of the northern giant is a misfortune for the remaining civilized world." Those banned lines were written in 1861; in 1895 a skeptical observer noted that

> the emperor's personal love of peace sometimes paraded in the press is cobwebs and moonlight. A man who stands at the head of an internal political system such as Russia's and who has the intention of maintaining the system and perfecting it where possible must be ready at every hour for the most brazen war of aggression, because war can be indispensable to his internal politics at any moment.[16]

The Russian censors were sensitive not only to slurs on their country's military prowess; they were also on the lookout for antimilitary, pacifist sentiments such as those expressed in these excised words: "Now, too, hundreds and thousands of men capable of work are torn from their homes and families so that instead of the nurturing plow or tool, infertile weapons can be thrust into their hands so that they might protect the people, which could protect itself so easily and so much better." Mention of a Russian pacifist was particularly unwelcome. Parts of an 1895 article about Tolstoi were excised, including a picture of the count plowing and a discussion of his pacifism: "He has decided that he would rather be locked up or transported to Siberia than to pay taxes which would be used to mobilize soldiers and make war."[17]

RUSSIFICATION AND RELIGIOUS PERSECUTION

German writers, Catholic and Protestant alike, described with horror Russian treatment of non-Orthodox Christians within the empire. As one Catholic phrased it, the Russians "made use of religion to sharpen their sword, and made use of the sword to spread their so-called Orthodox faith." References to the sad state of the Catholic church in Poland— "written indeed with blood and tears"—abound in the sample of excised passages examined.

> One cannot imagine the persecution which the Catholic population of Lithuania and White Russia must endure. The poor rural population is threatened with banishment and complete destruction of all their property; prosperous Catholic peasants are burdened with extraordinary taxes; the father wishing to have his child baptized according to the Catholic rite must pay thirty rubles, while he who brings his child

to the Orthodox priest for baptism according to the Greek Orthodox rite receives, on the contrary, a fifteen ruble reimbursement; officials and employees who do not wish to convert are hounded mercilessly from their jobs without concern for their support and that of their families. The confiscation of Catholic churches and the incessant deportation of priests also contribute to the driving of Catholics into the schism.

This passage, by the historian Menzel, continues with a description of a forced conversion in Lithuania:

While a large group of rural people was gathered in a Catholic church the troops surrounded the church and the Orthodox priest, chalice in hand, was let in. The people waited quietly for what would follow. The priest went from one person to the next and administered Communion. If a person gritted his teeth and refused to accept the Holy Sacrament, the soldier accompanying the priest opened the mouth of the recalcitrant one with his bayonet. This is how the Muscovite missionaries proceed!

According to Menzel, this story came from a Krakow publication and was related by an officer who had been present.[18]

Catholic priests apparently were persecuted with special vigor; according to the author of one excised passage, they were often denied passports and, since they were not permitted to leave their dioceses without passports, they were unable to travel to help one another, "not even when a priest who had no vicar was dying; thus it happened frequently that a priest had to die without the Holy Sacrament." Poland is called "the Christ of nations," while the Russian autocrat is portrayed with "one hand in the bowels of the earth, taking out his gold" and his other hand grasping the knout with which he drives his "thousands of armed slaves." Nevertheless, prophesies one writer in a banned passage, "Poland still has a future."[19]

The policy of Russification was not limited to religion; in Poland and the Baltic provinces attempts were made to replace local languages with Russian. German observers reported the effects of this policy in numerous books and articles that subsequently were banned or permitted only with excisions by the Russian censorship. Menzel, for example, reported:

On July 9, 1868, Potapov, the new governor of Lithuania, issued an order . . . forbidding the Polish language not only in official business, in the church, the theater, and on the streets, but also in all inns, restaurants, beer halls, coffee houses, in all shops and even in all private houses where more than two people were present, in respect to which only children were excepted. Instead of the Polish language everyone except foreign travelers was to use Russian. This tyranny was unprecedented, since in all of Lithuania there are only six thousand Russians along with a majority of Poles, Jews, and Germans. It was also learned that anyone heard speaking Polish on the street would be arrested. Also all the German governesses who did not speak Russian were expelled.

(Note that Menzel does not acknowledge the existence of Lithuanians in Lithuania.) Similar actions in the Baltic provinces were reported in—and subsequently excised for Russian readers from—the *Deutscher Geschichtskalender* for 1892:

Beginning of July. Several German educational institutions are being closed down, since schools with German as the language of instruction are not permitted to continue. . . . 18 July: At the railroad station of Walk all the machinists and machinists' apprentices who are Lutherans or Catholics are being relieved of their duties and their positions occupied by Russians. . . . Six pastors in Dorpat have been sentenced to loss of their posts and further employment opportunities, and then they are being "reprieved" with lifelong banishment from the Baltic provinces. . . . Professor Richland in Dorpat is suddenly dismissed because a Russian is to take his place.[20]

"Where did Christ teach that the Jews should be persecuted?" Heinrich Zschokke posed this question in 1844 in a passage banned for Russian readers. The ban is no surprise since persecution of Jews was official policy in the Russian Empire during parts of the nineteenth century. Anti-Semitism was less virulent at some times than others and in 1837 Isaac Baer Levinsohn could write that "only Russia was a laudable example: here the Jews were spared persecution." This statement was permitted by the censors but the accompanying footnote added by the translator in 1892 was excised: "These beautiful times are unfortunately long past."[21]

Those times were certainly past by 1855, judging by these (excised) observations of a Dutch Jew:

In general the system of the present emperor seems to have a strange, yet easily explicable similarity to the most extreme tendency in Germany, which aims not only to absorb Jews into the nationality of the peoples among whom they live, but to merge them with those peoples. . . . It is well known that the Russian government is striving to unite its subjects not merely under one secular absolute power, but also under the ecclesiastical sovereignty of the emperor.

Although events such as the visit of Sir Moses Montefiore in 1846 to plead with the emperor for a more favorable disposition toward the Jews alleviated the situation temporarily, he continues, the condition of the Jews in Russia remains pitiable. By 1888 the situation had deteriorated further and a page containing a portrayal of a desperate Jewish population, crying out in pain: "Is there no Montefiore?" was excised. (The answer, the author declared sadly, must be "No!") Also cut was a page from the *Schulthess' europäischer Geschichtskalender* for 1882 reporting "the most abominable persecutions of Jews, which were transplanted from one city to another and naturally affected the guilty and the innocent alike."[22]

Russian sensitivity to "the Jewish question" must have been acute indeed in the 1880s; a volume on ancient Jewish history was permitted only with the excision of passages describing atrocities suffered by the Jews and their militant response. Evidently it was deemed unwise to expose Russian readers—among whom there were Jews, of course—to such accounts. Something similar has been occurring recently in the Soviet Union; Michael Heller reports that "all mention of the Jews has been removed from textbooks on ancient history and on the Middle Ages, as if such a people had never, in the entire course of history, existed."[23]

"SIBERIA: A PRISON OF MONSTROUS DIMENSIONS"

The author of an 1888 article about famous prisons published in a popular German magazine used these words to describe Siberia. (The page containing this remark was excised.) This view was a common one in the West, especially after the publication of George Kennan's report on Siberia, issued first as a series of articles in *Century* between 1888 and 1891, and then as a book. In his memoirs Prince Kropotkin writes with admiration about Kennan:

> When Kennan came back to London from his journey to Siberia, he managed, on the very next day after his arrival in London, to hunt up Stepniak, Chaikovsky [an émigré revolutionary], myself, and another Russian refugee. In the evening we all met at Kennan's room in a small hotel near Charing Cross. We saw him for the first time, and

having no excess of confidence in enterprising Englishmen who had previously undertaken to learn all about the Siberian prisons without even learning a word of Russian, we began to cross-examine Kennan. To our astonishment, he not only spoke excellent Russian, but he knew everything worth knowing about Siberia. One or another of us had been acquainted with the greater proportion of all political exiles in Siberia, and we besieged Kennan with questions: "Where is So-and-So? Is he married? Is he happy in his marriage? Does he still keep fresh in spirit?" We were soon satisfied that Kennan knew all about every one of them.[24]

Numerous German-language editions of Kennan's book were published—and banned in their entirety by the Russians—in the early 1890s. Kennan's observations on the horrors of the Russian penal system aroused tremendous interest in Germany as well as in other countries and the Russian censorship had to deal with numerous objectionable works and passages on the subject published during these years.

Sometimes material on Siberia was included in works on a completely different subject and the censors had to be alert. Advertisements at the back or front of a book were often offenders. In the same publisher's list containing the references to that sensational history of the Romanovs mentioned in the preceding chapter are notices of Kennan's books as well as a volume of letters by a Russian professor sentenced to forced labor in the Siberian lead mines. This latter book, writes the publisher, goes beyond even the horrors described by Kennan: "Everyone knows that the people sentenced to lifelong forced labor perish; what we did not know is that people are treated there in a manner in which in civilized countries one cannot treat cattle."[25] In his 1897 study of penal reform Julius Vargha devotes several pages (all excised) to a discussion of the facts and figures made available by Kennan and in an article—completely excised—published in a popular journal in 1891, while the revelations were still fresh and emotion ran high, M. Piehlmann concluded: "Siberia and exile there will remain what it is today: a blemish on the face of humanity and an affront to European culture, to which Russia boasts unjustly that she belongs."[26]

German publications of this period abounded in Siberia horror stories. Most of the censored accounts examined could just as well be set in a Nazi concentration camp or, without leaving Siberia, in the Gulag Archipelago. A few examples will suffice. In a chapter (excised in entirety) entitled "Die

Gezwungenen" (The coerced ones) Karl Emil Franzos told of mass marriage at gunpoint among prisoners, in this case the particular victims being
a Polish man and a Jewish woman. A passage excised from the second
edition of Franzos's book deals with the persecution of the great Ukrainian
poet Taras Shevchenko: "At the age of thirty-three he was flogged and sent
as a common criminal to Orenburg." His spirit was not yet broken, but
then he was sent on to a worse place:

> It was a dreadful existence; the garrison consisted of the dregs of
> humanity, the duties were terribly rigorous; aside from the depraved
> rabble of soldiers there was no communication, no book, no newspa-
> per. This devilish medicine had its effect; the pitiable poet became
> sickly and apathetic. When, in 1857, his Petersburg friends, espe-
> cially Countess Tolstoi, after many vain attempts, finally brought about
> his release, it could be granted without any difficulty. "The man is
> harmless," the commander of the fort had reported.[27]

One of the most moving excised passages—effectively written in mat-
ter-of-fact language, the drama provided by the events themselves—tells
the story of a Polish Catholic priest who had been deported to Siberia in
1796. After refusing repeatedly, under the knout, to convert to Orthodoxy,
he was banished for life and sent into the wilderness, where he was shown a
cave to live in, given minimal supplies, and required to deliver pelts
monthly to the Russian inspectors who came to his cave to collect them.
On each visit an Orthodox priest made further attempts to convert him.
After three years of solitude—the only other humans he saw were the
inspector and the priest—he stumbled upon another cave, where he discovered the frozen corpse of his own bishop. After fourteen years he
became ill and in his delirium vowed to visit the Holy Land if he should
ever regain his freedom. In 1813 Alexander I granted him amnesty and he
returned to Europe. Thirty-seven years later, at the age of seventy-eight, he
finally fulfilled his vow and made the pilgrimage to Jerusalem.[28]

An effective contrast between Siberia and Saint Petersburg is shown in a
banned chapter from *Die Höllenmaschine* (The infernal machine), a historical novel by Franz Isidor Proschko. The scene is set in Kamchatka, in a
native hut. The characters are an exile—perhaps a Pole—and a native.
The exile bemoans his fate:

> "Paul! Paul!" he cried, beginning a monologue with himself.
> "Emperor Paul! How long still must I prolong my life by eating

birchbark and fish-oil in this miserable smoky prison! What did I do that was so monstrous that I was banished to the farthest boundaries of vegetation in the company of foxes and dogs and must nourish myself on birchbark, while you fill your bellies with champagne and oysters in the salons of Saint Petersburg!"

The Kamchadal crouched next to the hunter on the bearskin.

"Eat bear grease if you can't stand birchbark," he said, comforting kindheartedly in broken Russian, "hunt with our dogs across the snow and fish for seals in the bay below—there's probably nothing better than that in your fatherland, what else could you possibly want?"[29]

The authors of the *Kladderadatsch* volume mentioned earlier obviously thought there were enough Polish exiles in Siberia to refer their readers from the entry "Poland" to the entry "Siberia." This volume, published in 1851, is a satirical account of an international industrial exhibition held in London. The index of objects supposedly sent to the exhibition includes jibes at several countries. The Russian censorship instructions for excision specify two places on the page but unfortunately we are not told precisely which two. Some likely candidates are "Siberia, costly vases, bowls, etc. made of petrified blood"; "Moscow, a deceased person who is not yet dead"; "Petersburg, a fox pelt. Not like other pelts, to be beaten only in summer, but, rather, every day"; and "Warsaw, a conservation machine, most solidly constructed, including a tax-collecting machine and an easily mobilized steam machine fired by burning questions."[30]

AGAINST RELIGION AND MORALS

It would be difficult to find a country whose government had not at some time in its history attempted to curtail freedom of expression in regard to religion or morality or both. However, by the second half of the nineteenth century most Western governments had loosened up considerably, and a wide range of publications was available, from scholarly works disputing the basic tenets of Christianity to anthologies of naughty poems. According to Kotliarevskii, Russian young people in the 1850s and 1860s were prepared to break with the traditional form of religion, Russian Orthodoxy, and wanted to learn more about the historical and scientific study of religion, including historical criticism of the Bible, being pursued in the West: "The major works of Strauss and Feuerbach were known in

Russia, as were the works of some scholars of the Tübingen school working on criticism of the Holy Writ."[31] Publications on these topics, of great interest to them, were a matter of considerable concern to the censorship.

As for morality, this was the Victorian age and Russia was certainly not the only country where the authorities frowned on printed matter containing immoral ideas or blasphemous expressions. However, given the combination of Victorian attitudes and the pre-1848 mode of censorship, foreign publications of these types in Russia were surely destined for scissors or "caviar" pot.

"No reasonable man believes anymore that Jesus is a God." Assertions such as this one by Moritz Müller were hardly favored by the Russian censorship. While not always banned outright, the writings of Friedrich Schleiermacher, Ludwig Feuerbach, and other philosophers were subjected to careful scrutiny. Selections from Schleiermacher's writings on religion included in an anthology were cut, as was an obituary of Feuerbach by Otto Henne am Rhyn, in which the philosopher was held to be worth "more than all the gods together." Feuerbach always was viewed with deep suspicion by the Russian censorship. In 1863, when N. G. Chernyshevskii published his revolutionary novel *What Is to Be Done?* he was forced to refer to the philosopher by his first name only. In a Soviet edition of the novel the editor informs the readers that "the mention of Feuerbach's name in print was forbidden at that time by the imperial censorship."[32]

Gotthold Lessing had to be censored when he maintained that "a revelation that all people can believe in one established way is impossible." The assertion that "we are not created to believe blindly, we are human beings, and have the human right to think—to what end the train of thought may lead an individual is something he must settle with himself" was also unacceptable. The traditional view of the world, with man on earth and God in heaven, was the only acceptable one. A statement such as this one by Henne am Rhyn was forbidden:

> Why seek at all for a final cause? It is, after all, a scientifically proven fact that all things and creatures of nature have their motivating force within themselves; consequently the world in general has its cause within itself. . . . The assumption of a principle establishing the world is therefore superfluous; the world was never established, never created, but rather it establishes and creates itself from eternity to eternity.[33]

What is wrong with all these statements from the censors' point of view, of course, is that they are incompatible not only with established religious views in general, but also with Christian doctrine in particular. These writers take Christianity off its pedestal, as it were, subject it to critical review, and find it wanting. Karl Grün writes:

> The basic view of Christianity is: all humans are worthless, with their own best efforts they cannot become anything else; they are lost simply because they are human. The first human couple is responsible for this because once they went against God's direct prohibition. Finally God took pity on this indescribable disaster and, coming down himself from heaven, permitted himself to be born of a virgin as God the son, endured every kind of humiliation, even the death of a criminal on the cross, satisfied himself thus regarding the sins of humanity, and all that he now asks from man is that he believe obstinately in this remarkable story, which no mortal can grasp. His holiest intermediaries explain to us positively: you must believe in this story all the more indefatigably the more absurd it appears to you, *credo quia absurdum*.

Another writer noted that the concept of the Trinity always had been perplexing to philosophers, whereas the common people "comforted themselves with the thought that the Heavenly Schoolmaster was accustomed to teaching arithmetic according to a different primer"; regarding Adam's sin, he concluded that "the death on the cross caused by Adam's sin was explained with such monstrous logic that anyone concerned about the health of his mind would be advised to leave it alone."[34]

The censors encountered a good deal of German skepticism in regard to Mary. Johannes Scherr points out the absurdity of the Virgin birth:

> The same church which passed off the Jewish wife of a carpenter as the consort of God and the son of this Jewess as the co-god of his god-father preached rabid contempt and hatred, fire and sword against the entire Jewish people because the Jews were unfortunate enough not to be able to comprehend the mystery whereby Mary was gotten with child not by her fiancé Joseph, but with the intervention of the Holy Ghost by God himself, gave birth to a god, but still remained a virgin and finally was formally raised to be "Queen of Heaven."

One theologian discusses her as a cult figure and compares her to her heathen counterparts; Michelet, after studying a picture of the Madonna in Bologna, refers to the "childish myth" of the Virgin Mary. Another writer simply dismisses her as "the alleged Virgin Mary," and still another considers the Virgin Birth to be "a nut for the doctors to crack, but a theme beloved of celibate church fathers, and completely comprehensible to them."[35]

Praise of other religions was not appreciated by the Russian censorship: writing of Egypt, one traveler remarked that "its priests raised and educated the lawgiver of the Jews, Moses; on the precepts of worship of Isis he based the structure of the religion of the Israelites, still respected and admired by us today." This remark is doubly distasteful; not only does the author praise the Jews but he traces their religion, on which Christianity itself is founded, back to the worship of a heathen Egyptian goddess. And if mere praise of Judaism was unwelcome, an unfavorable comparison with Christianity was bound to be even less welcome; for example, the following statement, excised from a novel by Karl Gutzkow: "While the Christian became in the course of time ever more of a philistine, the Jew became the connoisseur of the world."

Another traveler praised Islam, and his juxtaposition of the precepts of that religion with those of Christianity resulted in what must have appeared to the censors to be too positive a view of the former:

> These are the precepts of the Koran. For a full appreciation of its teachings, however, one must picture what it does not teach. It teaches no Trinity, it recognizes no church impregnated with the Holy Ghost; it teaches no forgiveness of sins through the blood of Christ; it does not place faith above deeds, it teaches no persecution of heretics, it teaches no eternal damnation of unbelievers. "Jews, Christians and Sabaeans will get their reward from the Lord if they only believe in God and in Judgment Day and do what is right."

Religious tolerance was never characteristic of the imperial Russian government and the attitude of the English toward Mormonism must have seemed threatening indeed, as illustrated by this portion of an excised passage from a book entitled *Englische Freiheit* (English freedom): "Very rarely is a voice raised in England calling for limitation of Mormon religious practices, and the voice is immediately drowned out by the universal objection that beliefs may only be combatted by means of beliefs. . . . Mormonism tests the strength of English tolerance."[36]

Another comparison unpopular with the censorship was between Christian and Greek beliefs and world views. Saint Peter's cathedral in Rome caused Michelet to reflect "that the beautiful humanity of the Greek artistic world will serve to break through the constraining limits of medieval Christianity and to pave the way for a new form of Christianity, the triumphant, truly universal church, a new world religion." The philosopher Friedrich Paulsen's study of ethics has a cool, intellectual tone; in a banned passage in which he compares Greek and Christian virtues and vices, for example, Paulsen never asserts the superiority of the Christian over the Greek system. In his history of literature Scherr exhibits the same unfortunate objectivism; he views the Hebrew Scriptures as a literary continuation of heathen writings and maintains that some early Christian poetry is "very thin and monotonous, even stupid."[37]

Religion as the object of "scientific" study. Christianity may have been functional in more primitive times but it has lost its meaning in the contemporary world, since the techniques of modern science have revealed the absurdity of Judeo-Christian tenets. This proposition, expressed in a variety of ways by numerous German authors, was unacceptable to the Russian censorship and was banned when encountered. Christianity has been doomed, according to one writer, "since the universal acceptance of the Copernican system in the civilized world." Specific biblical events have now been shown to be impossible: "The truth and actuality of the Mosaic story of the Creation became untenable in the face of scientific results; geognosy and geology moved the "creation of the earth" back millions of years into the past; historical research has discovered traces of peoples who must have already died out long before Adam was set down in Paradise." The story of Noah's ark is shown to be ridiculous in the light of modern knowledge:

> One need only reflect for a moment on creation today if it were limited in that way to the existence of two individuals. Continued existence would clearly be impossible. Would the carnivorous animals suffer hunger until the parent-animals which serve them as food produced their young? What about the anteater, which must eat thousands of ants each day in order to live, or the whale, which can maintain its bulk only at the cost of swarms of herring: are they perhaps supposed to have originated only at a much later time?

One writer looks ahead with certainty to the time when men will be able to "cook up and assemble a complete human being according to scientific recipes."[38]

Archaeologists cast doubt on the authenticity of various biblical sites, including that of the Holy Sepulcher: "Thus we are finally brought to the conclusion that the authenticity of the present Holy Sepulcher is not supported by well-documented historical fact, nor by an earlier tradition, nor by archaeological foundations." David Friedrich Strauss in Germany and Ernest Renan in France became controversial figures when they published books treating the life of Jesus as historical fact, stripped of what they considered mythical elements. As mentioned in chapter 3, the works of both men were banned in Russia and discussion of their ideas was excised from the works of other authors. A lengthy review of both books was excised from Sybel's *Historische Zeitschrift* of 1864, as was a long article on the Tübingen historical school in the 1860 volume of the same journal, probably because historians of this school specialized in criticism of biblical texts "according to the same rules as any other historical source." The entry for Jesus in the 1892 edition of *Meyers Kleines Konversations-Lexikon* was cut, perhaps because the writing was too prosaic and because Strauss, Renan, Schleiermacher, and other suspicious characters were cited in the bibliography.[39] It is this kind of material that Kotliarevskii found to be so much in demand in the 1860s.

Criticism of Orthodoxy. The official state religion of the Russian Empire was Eastern Orthodox Christianity, generally viewed with raised eyebrow and curled lip by Russia's Catholic and Protestant European neighbors. The practice of requiring conversion to Orthodoxy of all foreign princesses marrying into the imperial Russian family aroused the indignation of some German writers; the censors did their best, however, to prevent these indignant remarks from reaching Russian audiences. One writer accuses the German princely houses of submitting "unblushingly" to this disgraceful practice. Another claims heatedly that it is "an abuse of the free, high position of the Protestant church, not to mention the religious wrong done to these poor children, who must resolve to forget the Reformation and pray to graven images." A third writer ventures the opinion that Friedrich Wilhelm III of Prussia would never have allowed his daughter to marry a Russian (Nicholas, son of Emperor Paul) had he not suspected that Nicholas would become emperor instead of Constantine, the implication being that it was worth compromising one's principles if the reward were great enough, and to be consort of the emperor of Russia was no small prize.[40]

Other writers met with the censors' disapproval because they were critical of the close ties between church and state in Russia. Franz von Baader viewed the Orthodox church as no more than a tool of Russian propaganda in the Baltic provinces, and a writer for the *Historisch-politische Blätter für das katholische Deutschland* accused the Russian government continually "of proclaiming to the people in a truly blasphemous manner the solidarity of God and Russian politics." Criticisms of the church-state union in general were not permissible. A section of a theological work with the heading "The true Christian community cannot be dependent on civil society" was excised, as were excerpts from essays by Heinrich Heine including *Über Staatsreligion*, beginning with these typically biting words: "Precisely because I am a friend of the state and of religion I hate that monster which is called state religion, that ridiculous creature born of the love affair between secular and ecclesiastical power, that mule begotten by the stallion of the Antichrist on the she-ass of Christ."[41]

The Orthodox rite itself is viewed with distaste by some authors and its practices portrayed as primitive, uncivilized, disgusting:

> The divine service is extremely disagreeable to someone unaccustomed to it. It consists of nasal chanting and mechanical recitation of the passages concerned, accompanied by swinging of the censer. And from what I have seen, it loses that dignity and impressiveness which often takes hold even of Protestants in a Roman Catholic service. I have seen how on the most important Greek holy day, Easter, . . . a priest, in other respects a handsome, stately man, used his finger instead of his handkerchief in front of the altar during the service.

Another observer calls the service on Saturday afternoon before Easter at the Church of the Holy Sepulcher in the Holy Land "shocking beyond description" and then proceeds to describe it. Passing Turks were highly amused by the goings-on, he observes, especially when the patriarch's beard caught fire. Another traveler among the Muslims, Sandreczki, warns that "we may not assume that Christianity could be preached with success among the Mohammedans as long as they see around them nothing but a complete caricature of Christianity and Christians who—and it is hard for me to say this—are in general not only not a whit better than they are, but are morally even lower."[42]

The Russians come off no better than their coreligionists to the east. They are accused by Sandreczki of an unseemly worship of Saint Nicholas, and in another banned passage a critic blasts the priesthood for its ignorance and corruption: "The degradation of the lower clergy due to excessive dependence, domestic need, avarice and drunkenness is completely incomprehensible to us. In 1839 the Holy Synod punished 5,000 priests, out of a total of 102,000, for dishonorable offences." This observer continues with derogatory remarks about the low standards of Russian Orthodox convents and monasteries, quoting a comment that "with the exception of the non-monastic Russian clergy, in all of Christianity there is no more miserable race of men than the monks of this country." Finally, he notes the regrettable lack of martyrs in the Russian church: "Their apostles must support their families, sacrifice for the emperor, but must not shorten their lives for the love of God. For this reason one seeks in vain for martyrs in the annals of the Russian church and finds only sacrifices to imperial tyranny."[43] (This is, of course, untrue; the Russian church has its martyrs.)

Some Germans considered the Russians to be incompetent even as missionaries for their own religion. In a banned passage from an article on the official Russian mission society in a Protestant theological work the Russians are shown to be much more successful in Japan than in their own country: "Apparently the mission thrives far better in the free air of Japan and because of the independent character of the Japanese than in Russia itself, under the soul-destroying power of the state." Indeed, these same Protestants maintained that the Russians (along with Catholics and others) were not really engaged in true missionary work at all but were merely interested in making converts, "a kind of egoism." The page containing these words was excised.[44]

Whether or not they were effective as missionaries, it is clear from the actions of the censorship that Russia was concerned about the reverse; that is, the success (and hence the threat) of rival religions within the empire. The introduction to a book on the Turks was cut; it contained, among other disturbing elements, the prediction that "the slumbering lion" of Islam would rise soon in a spirit of vengeance. Included in the lion's territory were the Caucasus and the Volga. Also considered unsuitable for Russian readers was the observation that "in Russia too there is hope again that freemasonry will gain ground"; the censors obviously did not want this idea to circulate in Russia. Sometimes missionary activity could have political implications as well; the Odessa censorship kept an anxious eye on John Melville, an agent of the English Bible Society who imported thousands of bibles in various languages each year and took them to the Caucasus and surrounding areas.[45]

The actions of the censorship in regard to Catholicism and Protestantism, the major religions of the West, reflect an ambivalent attitude. On the one hand, praise and reports of successful proselytizing—especially within Russia—were inadmissible. Sybel's comment that by 1811 the Roman church was beginning to win important converts from "the highest circles of Petersburg society" was part of a passage excised from his article on Joseph de Maistre; in the same article Sybel maintains that Alexander I had "as little enthusiasm for the Russian Church as his subjects had." On the other hand, these religions were still Christian and thus deserving of respect, so offensive remarks about Catholicism or Protestantism ought to be banned too. For example, a page was excised from Johannes Scherr's *Blätter im Winde* (Leaves in the Wind) in which one character complains that "after all, one ought to be able to expect that after so many thousands of years of cultural work mankind would have produced and become accustomed to a rather decent religion, one less anxious about the multiplication table, less philistine and more civilized." When another character suggests that the "Catholic and Lutheran bigwig religions, as they are now, answer the religious needs of the overwhelming majority of our more or less civilized fellow men," the first responds that "then all our great thinkers and poets have lived in vain."[46]

It was not advisable to praise one form of Western Christianity while damning another; a poem by Ludwig Bechstein, *Johannes Hilten*, which praises Martin Luther and his teachings and bitterly criticizes the pope, was excised from an anthology. Also unacceptable were passages in an autobiography describing some unattractive aspects of Catholicism that Scherr's character certainly would consider uncivilized. From his travels in Poland, Galicia, Austria-Hungary, Belgium, and France the author concludes that "the less ideal the beauty embodied in a painting or sculpture and the more horribly dehumanized the figures in such holy pictures appeared, the more miracles they had already performed and the more faithful worshippers they attracted. . . . The gloomy, dark, horrible and ghastly is for such people an expression of holiness." He goes on to enumerate and ridicule Catholic sacred superstitions and to condemn practices such as celibacy and self-flagellation and concludes by confessing that to his great shame he had once believed in all this nonsense but had fortunately freed himself before it was too late.[47] The censorship could have permitted this unflattering account of Catholicism in the hope of turning Russians against that religion but apparently the need to protect *all* forms of Christianity from slander was stronger than the temptation to gain points for Orthodoxy at the expense of Catholicism.

Immorality and blasphemy. Just as the censorship would not permit slurs to be cast on the morals of Russian royalty, so too did it attempt to protect Russian readers from exposure to immoral behavior in general. In a story entitled *Madonna* excised from a collection by Alexander Engel, the character Paul, who has just made love with his sweetheart, lectures her on their situation: "Banish all these banal, moralistic scruples, for us there is only one divine morality, the morality of the heart. . . . Yes, I have possessed your body, but not without first having mastered your heart. And one heart which conquers another has an indisputable right to the body which belongs to this heart." Here traditional morality is rejected and love alone legitimizes a sexual relationship.[48]

Also banned was a discussion of the sexual activity of military officers. The author of a manual for officers argues for a tolerant, relaxed attitude:

> One must not be too strict a judge of young, vigorous officers. . . . According to our observation it is about the same in all European armies and young, high-spirited officers are never found to be strict adherents to the doctrine of renunciation of all pleasures of the flesh. After all, an officer's uniform is not a monk's cowl, and along with one's oath of allegiance one is not also required to take a vow of absolute chastity.

Dueling too is acceptable for a young officer, although it was forbidden at that time in Russia as well as in most European countries. The author contends that dueling is not really wicked; that it is, in fact, a knightly virtue, a "relic of the chivalrous age." As far as sex is concerned, he does argue for sexual moderation, however, warning that "imprudence in youth is all too often punished with chronic ill health in old age."[49] Since there cannot be anything in this passage that Russian readers did not already know about the military—their own or that of any other country—we must assume that in cases such as this the censors were simply declining to put the official stamp of approval on such behavior by permitting it to be discussed in print. As in the case of the murders of Emperors Peter and Paul, it was possible to deny facts merely by withholding acknowledgment.

In general sex was a forbidden subject but it became even more untouchable when combined with blasphemy. For example, a naughty poem *cum* drinking song about the attempts of Potiphar's wife to seduce Joseph was excised from an anthology of poetry by the Swede Carl Bellman; the woman is portrayed as a heroine who failed only because Joseph was sober, and her husband as a fool who deserved to have been cuckolded. The verse ends: "Long live Mrs. Potiphar! To her Health! She still lives today!" This anthology contains several more banned poems in the same vein, including one on Abraham's remarkable sexual prowess at an advanced age and another on Lot's sexual relationship with his own daughters, ever-popular subjects for pornographers.[50]

Sometimes a poet exceeded the boundaries of good taste in his own country to such a degree that even his publisher refused to print parts of his work. An example is Richard Dehmel, whose poem *Venus Domestica* appeared in Germany with a number of blank lines. (In a note accompanying the poem Dehmel protested the publisher's action.) Following the example set in Germany, the Russian censors also refused to permit the poem. They also excised another Dehmel poem in the same volume, *Venus Adultera*, although the German publisher had allowed the whole work. A third poem, *Venus Perversa*, was permitted for Russians. Some banned passages are irreverent rather than blasphemous, reminding one more than anything else of puerile college humor; for instance, this epigram attributed to "Moses the Lawgiver": "In order to attain your goal you shouldn't be afraid of a path through the Red Sea, but you should never wet your pants."[51]

The much-maligned Virgin Mary also received a good deal of attention from humorous poets exploring the possibilities in her relationships with Joseph and the Holy Ghost. God and Jesus were not spared either; Otto Bierbaum had God singing a love song (which he had written himself) to a girl named Josephine, and Jesus and Lilith are portrayed in a very erotic scene excised from a verse-play. In another banned poem an angry poet proclaims that he would happily exchange Christ the Messiah, whom he hates, for any woman, and that his faith—and God himself—are dead. Heinrich Heine, always an object of suspicion for the Russian censorship, had the audacity to dream that he himself was God, sitting in heaven surrounded by angels who praised his verse. In another banned passage from this same volume Heine pictures the angels sitting at God's feet studying the continuo and criticizes a crucifix for being too lifelike: "Only material suffering is carved into this face, not the poetry of pain. Such an image belongs in an anatomy classroom, not a place of worship." (We recall that the phrase about the angels is the same one discussed in chapter 4, judged by Maikov to be harmless for Russians.)[52]

In a banned humorous short story called *Der Traum* (The Dream) author Ludovic Halévy also found himself in heaven, observing God and his assistants as they dealt with a new arrival, a young woman who now had to decide with which of her two husbands she would spend eternity. (She settled in the end on a third possibility, her lover.) Halévy's portrayal of heaven as just another earth and God as just another judge also was bound to offend the Russian censors. In a more serious vein, the ominous legend of the Antichrist was excised from a German translation of Alphonse Daudet's novel *Port Tarascon*.[53]

Sometimes the offending passage was not only blasphemous but had unwelcome social connotations as well. The reader was reminded that Rothschild and Jesus were both Jews, or reference was made to a revolution in heaven, the rebels' demand being that God's son finally take power and appoint the Holy Ghost as his minister. It was even suggested that the archtraitor Judas Iscariot might not be all bad: "From a religious point of view, of course, one must damn him, but from a political point of view he was actually not completely wrong to inform the authorities of what seemed to him to be dangerous intrigues against the laws and security of the state. The authorities also recognized this by rewarding him." However attractive it might seem to encourage informing for the good of the state, the Russian censorship was obviously not prepared to go quite this far.[54]

Russia, as we know, was not alone in attempting to control blasphemy. In 1875 Scherr wrote:

> Don't you know how the so-called freedom of the press actually operates in the new German empire? Don't you know that what counts as "blasphemy" today was presented to the people without further ado in the medieval mystery plays, and was told laughingly to contemporaries by the humanists of the fifteenth and sixteenth centuries.[55]

The German regulations may have seemed harsh to Scherr but from a Russian perspective the situation looked quite different. Scherr's criticism of government policy on blasphemy could be published in Germany, the country against which it was aimed, but could not be circulated in Russia.

Conclusion
The Futility of Fences

Beginning with the reign of Catherine the Great in the mid-
eighteenth century and ending only in the twilight years of the empire,
the Russian government maintained continuous efforts to protect Russian
readers against dangerous foreign ideas. This was a time of great flux in
Russian society—a time of industrialization, of secularization, and, perhaps most significant, of rapidly growing literacy. As the nineteenth century progressed the number of people able to read increased enormously
and educated society expanded to include new groups. *Raznochintsy*—
from country doctors to petty bureaucrats, very often sons of merchants
and village priests—fed the revolutionary movements. Jews and other
minorities were rapidly learning Russian. The government feared that
these voracious consumers of the printed word, many of them harboring
grievances against an autocracy that did not always treat them well, would
not merely *read* forbidden works. Poisoned by the ideas contained in them,
they might, it was feared, turn against the established order of Russian
society, against the institution of autocracy itself.

The antagonistic relationship between autocracy and educated society—
between Russia's rulers and the producers and consumers of the printed
word—has always been at the heart of the dilemma of the institution of
censorship. Russian autocrats, like many reigning European monarchs,
distrusted writers—not only those living and working within their own
empire, but *all* writers, everywhere, whose works might enter their realm.
The royal thinking presumably went something like this: writing dealing

with private, personal concerns or aimed at sheer entertainment of the reader should be encouraged by all means. Unfortunately, some writers, whether ill-intentioned or merely misguided, also produce books, poems, plays, and articles containing ideas which, sometimes unbeknownst to them, may be dangerous. Readers may be influenced by these dangerous ideas and therefore, like it or not, the state must assume the onerous duty of maintaining control over the printing and dissemination of these works in order to protect readers from corrupting influences. We can truly call the resulting phenomenon "sovereign censorship," control exercised directly by the autocrat over the reading and writing of his or her subjects.

As we have seen, Western literature always has been of the greatest importance to educated Russians. The Soviets have an insatiable appetite for it, as did their forebears in tsarist times, who devoured whatever Western works were permitted to circulate, both in the original languages and in Russian translation. A Russian shopping for books in the 1860s at Bazunov's in Saint Petersburg—one of the largest bookstores in the empire—would find, for instance, that forty percent of the titles on history of philosophy and thirty percent of those on political economy and general history were translations from German, English, and French; almost one third of the belletristic offerings were also translations from various languages.[1] Western books and magazines were imported in ever larger quantities for bookstores, libraries, educational institutions, government agencies, and private citizens.

Foreign publications had not been imported into Russia for very many years, however, before the government began to exert control over them —to erect that elaborate fence around the empire intended to keep out dangerous ideas. With the 1828 censorship statute and the establishment of the Foreign Censorship Committee procedures were created that would remain in effect until the fall of the empire in 1917. This censorship was a reflection of the ambivalence toward things foreign that had been characteristic of Russia at least since the time of Peter the Great, and which is still evident today. The government wanted the country to be part of the "civilized" West but at the same time felt threatened by outsiders and their dangerous ideas.

As a government agency the committee naturally reflected to some extent the political climate in the country. Krasovskii's rigidity was ideal during the reign of Nicholas I, as Tiutchev's more liberal attitudes with regard to foreign literature were suited to the period of the great reforms. But even after the decline of the reforming spirit, intelligent, well-educated, and artistic censors such as Tiutchev, Maikov, and Polonskii continued to exert a beneficient influence on the committee. There is a common view of censors as hacks, small minds caught up in small questions. Krasovskii may fit this image but the poets certainly do not.

In his letter on censorship and other writings Tiutchev demonstrated that he was concerned with big questions; he argued eloquently that censorship could play a positive role and tried to extricate the committee from the small questions, as Maikov did when he defended Heine from petty attacks. Zlatkovskii recalls Maikov as a "European-educated man" who observed the West with an enthusiastic, yet critical eye—a censor eager to accept from the West what he saw as good for Russia and prepared to reject what he saw as harmful or inappropriate. He worried because his countrymen lacked the "conscientiousness and perseverance of Germans, the enterprising spirit of Englishmen and Americans, the energy and taste of Frenchmen"—qualities vital for the development of native Russian talent.[2] Polonskii urged his committee colleagues to permit foreign works to circulate in Russia. These were not small minds.

The results of my study of German publications (chapter 5) generally support the assertion that the reign of Alexander III was more repressive than his father's. Although it appears that a smaller percentage of imported works was banned in the second reign, those works that were banned were treated more harshly than was the case under Alexander II. It is also true, however, that the tendency in this direction was already quite strong in the late 1860s and 1870s before the assassination of Alexander II. The change under the new emperor was really a matter of degree rather than a totally new policy.

The analysis of excised passages serves to clarify and illuminate the statistical findings and to enhance what has already been learned from the censors' reports about the themes that concerned them. What emerges from these passages is a picture of Russia as a thoroughly nasty place: an uncivilized backwater inhabited by barbarians and ruled by morally degenerate tyrants. A steady diet of this sort of bombardment from outside might be expected to raise the hackles of reasonably conscientious and patriotic officials anywhere. And when the country under attack has a tradition of censorship, it is hardly surprising that the government should counter the attack by attempting to keep such offensive literature out of the country.

The fear of popularizations, translations, and cheap editions for the masses that runs through the censors' reports, amply illustrated in my sample of excised passages, is equally understandable. Well-to-do Russian intellectuals traveled abroad and read freely and widely; despite the best efforts of the censorship they would devour George Sand, Darwin, and Marx, carrying the pernicious ideas of these writers and thinkers back home with them to Russia. However, the common people were another story; there were so many of them and they might be difficult to control if aroused. (In fact, there were probably relatively few "common" readers capable of handling even simply written works in foreign languages.) Such people simply could not be allowed to read attacks by foreigners on the institutions of marriage and the family, on the church's view of the divine origin of man, on the legitimacy of autocratic rule, on Russia. This sort of literature was not permitted for publication within the empire; why, then, should it be allowed to penetrate from without? As Marc Raeff observes, "it was not the contents of second-rate scientific popularizations that influenced the history of Russian thought but rather the use the Russian intelligentsia made of them to provide the sanction of scientific evidence for their own moral and social ideals and their critique of contemporary Russian society."[3]

How effective was the censorship of foreign publications in Russia? Did this elaborate mechanism actually work? Was the government really able to stem the flow of "undesirable" foreign works into the empire? The question is difficult to answer authoritatively since statistics of this sort are scarce. It is clear that the number of publications imported legally increased steadily in the course of the century and that the Foreign Censorship Committee was kept busy over the years. However, we also know that seditious literature made its way into the country despite obstacles, through secondhand book dealers and other channels, and that Odoevskii, Tiutchev, and other less well-known censors of foreign publications were painfully aware of the futility of their censorship activities.

Furthermore, the foreign censorship failed to keep up with the times. Writing about events of 1906, when it seemed as if Russia finally had a free press, Egorov sees the operation continuing to function as though nothing had changed, banning works in their original languages which were "abundantly and legally available in Russian throughout the empire." He complains of the extremely awkward position in which the censors found themselves with regard to firms selling foreign publications and individuals ordering foreign works from abroad or bringing them into the country. "These people would show me copies of works permitted in Russian translation but banned in the original language by us in the foreign censorship, and would demand the release of the latter, refusing to understand our bureaucratic arguments, which were incomprehensible to them and were indeed absurd."[4] After one such incident involving a translation of Renan, Egorov handed over the original to the requester and complained to the Chief Administration for Press Affairs; his complaint may or may not have had anything to do with the subsequent withdrawal of the 1898 catalog of banned foreign publications.

The real problem was neither the failure of the mechanism nor the foreign censorship's ability to adapt to change; these were accepted, albeit irritating, facts of life. Baron Korf, who played a central role in the development of the censorship apparatus from the time of Nicholas I through the reform period, states flatly that "everyone knows that despite the continued existence of censorship of foreign books there is not, and never has been, a banned book which was impossible to get. . . . when we are increasingly concerned with protecting our young people from the doctrines of materialism and socialism, it is difficult to find a student, or even a pupil in the higher *gimnaziia* classes who has not read such works." Coming to the crux of the matter, he continues:

> These facts are not strictly a phenomenon of our own life; similar things happen wherever foreign publications are censored. This gives rise to the well-known . . . comparison that to try to protect a society from the influx of harmful ideas from outside by means of censorship is like trying to protect one's garden from birds by closing the gates.[5]

Why, then, did the Russians continue such seemingly vain efforts? The internal censorship underwent some reform in the 1860s and again after 1905; why not the foreign branch? Let me suggest four possible reasons. First, the censors probably *were* successful in keeping a certain percentage of "harmful" material out of circulation in Russia—low-flying birds, as it were. Second, the government may not have been officially aware of the extent of its failure in this area, the opinions of individuals such as Baron Korf notwithstanding. Third, it is very difficult to dismantle a bureaucracy once it has been established and this one had been functioning quite smoothly since 1828. Finally, even in their most liberal moments the rulers of Russia were not given to throwing open the gates, let alone tearing down the fence with which they had so painstakingly encircled the empire.

Control, or at least the illusion of control, was not to be laid aside lightly. Censorship of foreign publications had been woven tightly into the fabric itself in 1828. In Isaiah Berlin's assessment:

The censor was the official enemy, but unlike his modern successor, he was almost wholly negative. The tsarist censorship imposed silence but it did not directly tell professors what to teach; it did not dictate to authors what to say and how to say it; and it did not command composers to induce this or that mood in their audiences. It was merely designed to prevent the expression of a certain number of selected "dangerous ideas." It was an obstacle, at times a maddening one. But because it was, like so much in old Russia, inefficient, corrupt, indolent, often stupid, or deliberately lenient—and because so many loopholes could always be found by the ingenious and the desperate, not much that was subversive was stopped effectively.[6]

The Soviets, of course, wove the censorship of foreign publications into *their* new fabric—but that is another chapter.

Appendix 1
On Classification and Coding
of Banned and Permitted
German Publications

I examined a 10 percent systematic sample of the banned publications to learn what subjects were represented and which other aspects of the works might be of interest. I then tested the resulting scheme (based on the Dewey Decimal Classification) against the lists of permitted publications and added a few categories, such as beekeeping and cookbooks. I assigned a serial number to each publication in the two samples (40 percent of the banned publications and 2 percent of the permitted publications) and coded for subject, form, mode, groups or movements treated, year of publication, and ban type. The categories of subject, form, mode, groups treated, and ban type are as follows:

SUBJECT

Generalities. Includes various subjects; too general to be assigned to any single category.
Philosophy. Includes freemasonry, atheism, materialism, occult, mysticism, parapsychology, astrology, prophecy, ghosts and spirits, superstition, hypnotism.
Religion. Includes church history and affairs, life of Jesus.
Government. Includes economics, politics, political philosophy and theory, law, statutes, appeals, regulations, instructions for government workers, life insurance, military affairs, nihilism, anarchy, patriotism.
Social conditions. Includes customs, sociology, ethnology, crime, marriage and family, population statistics, welfare, psychology.
Education.
Language. Includes philology, linguistics.
Pure science. Includes botany, zoology, biology, oceanography, etc.
Health. Includes medicine, folk medicine, homeopathic medicine, insanity, veterinary medicine, phrenology.
Sex. Includes sex manuals, contraception, homosexuality, venereal diseases, erotica.
Technology. Includes food processing and products, agriculture, beekeeping, cookbooks.

Arts. Includes architecture, art history, graphology, music (if scores included).
Literary history and criticism.
Belles lettres. Includes stories, plays, poetry, novels, historical novels, folklore, myths, proverbs.
History. Includes *Kulturgeschichte*, genealogy, courts and courtiers, archaeology.
Geography. Includes travel, *Land und sein Volk* types.
Biography. Includes autobiography, memoirs, letters, *Schriften.*

FORM

Advertisements, prospectuses
Yearbooks, almanacs, calendars, periodical publications
Encyclopedias, dictionaries, handbooks, self-instruction
Textbooks
Readers, anthologies, prayer books
Books for young readers

MODE

Humor, satire

Groups or movements treated
Jews
Protestants (including Evangelicals, *Freireligion*)
Catholics (including Jesuits and other orders)
Freemasons (including Carbonari)
Women (not including belles-lettres with women's names as titles)
Poles
Revolutionaries (including socialists, communists, revolution, terrorism, assassinations, working-class movements, nihilism)

YEAR OF PUBLICATION

Ban type
Banned in entirety
    Banned
    Banned unconditionally
    Whole publication banned unconditionally
    Entire work banned
    Entire edition banned
    This and subsequent editions banned
    Banned, permitted for Protestants
    Banned in separate edition
    Earlier decision reviewed, book banned
Banned for the public
    Banned for the public

    Entire edition banned for the public
    Banned for the public, permitted for Protestants
    Banned for the public, permitted for doctors
Permitted with excisions
    Permitted with excisions
    Excisions in original and translation
    Excisions in original, banned for translation
    Excisions in translation, permitted in original
    Excisions, permitted for Protestants
    Excisions for public, permitted for Protestants
Other
    Permitted for Jews
    Permitted for Lutherans
    Mixed decision (different decisions for different volumes of same title)
Permitted

Classification is difficult enough with the book in hand; clearly any attempt to classify on the basis of title alone is bound to be risky. Still, for many works in the sample the subjects were indeed obvious from the titles. For example, a book entitled *Grundriss der Weltgeschichte* (Outlines of World History) clearly belongs to the history class; *Des Zweiflers Umkehr: Roman* (The Skeptic's Conversion: A Novel) is identified in the title as a novel; and *Der Ursprung der Evangelien* (The Origin of the Gospels) deals with religion. In hundreds of other cases, however, I had to search intensively to learn more about the works in order to be able to assign them to subject categories. I was fortunate to find some in the *National Union Catalog*, which often indicates how the work was classified by one or more libraries. A Dewey Decimal or Library of Congress number or a library's subject heading was often helpful in determining subject. Since such classification is based on examination of the piece itself, I considered it generally acceptable for my purposes. However, libraries fail to distinguish between belles lettres and other types of literature by a single author; in these cases I consulted reference works to determine, for instance, whether a specific book should be classed as belles lettres or history. If I could not find the work in the *National Union Catalog* I consulted other library catalogs and bibliographies, chiefly the British Museum *Catalogue of Printed Books* and the two main German national bibliographies for the period (Kayser and Heinsius). These sources were often helpful for determining place and date of publication. Those suspected of being erotica I checked in *Biblioteca Germanorum Erotica & Curiosa*, edited by Hugo Hayn and Alfred Gotendorf (Munich: Georg Müller, 1912–68, 9 vols.). I also consulted these and other sources to establish publication date if none was given. In cases where date of first volume only was given, or where publication extended over several years, I used the first year given. If only the decade was indicated, I selected the middle of the decade as the year of publication (e.g., I coded "187?" as "1875"). I gave calendars the date of the year of publication rather than the year in the title since they are published for the following year. In the case of serial publications running over several years, I selected the middle year of the run. If no other date was given for periodicals in the Public Library list, I chose the date of the year in which they appeared in the list.

Appendix 2
Who Were the Censors?

In the course of gathering data for this study I noted the names of a number of people associated at one time or another with the censorship of foreign publications. Most of these names were then checked in various reference works and other sources to obtain more information about the censors. Three groups emerge: (1) people for whom there is no information beyond the fact that their names appear in connection with reports on foreign works or who are mentioned in some sources as censors of foreign material, (2) people about whom there is fragmentary information, and (3) people identified as censors and described more or less fully in one or more biographical works or in other sources. This list is admittedly incomplete and should be viewed as the first draft of a "directory" of Russian censors of foreign works.

The names are presented in alphabetical order (Russian spelling of foreign names is used), followed by information—if any—about the censors and numbers referring to sources, listed at the end of this appendix, in which the individuals are mentioned. For those people discussed in the text reference is made to the appropriate chapter.

Albrand, V. N. He wrote a report in 1908 (2, p. 829).

Al'fonskii, Arkadii Alekseevich. He was assistant to A. P. Fedotov, censor for foreign publications in the Moscow Censorship Committee, and had the rank of collegiate secretary in 1896 (1).

Annikov, Aleksandr Aleksandrovich. He was secretary of the Foreign Censorship Committee in 1895 and 1896 with the rank of collegiate secretary. He is listed in the 1895 *Spisok chinov* (List of Ranks) as Orthodox, unmarried, and serving in this post since 1891. He was certified as having received the equivalent of the education required of an official of "first class rank" (1; 35).

Barg, Genrikh Karlovich. Mez'er gives his first name as Leonid. A junior censor in the Warsaw committee in the 1870s, a German who had previously been a Protestant pastor in a district (*uezdnyi*) city of Poland (7, no. 1, p. 133; 24).

Berte (Bertier?), Nikolai Aleksandrovich. He was a junior censor in the Saint Petersburg Foreign Censorship Committee in the 1840s and 1850s. By 1859–60 he was a senior censor with the rank of state councillor (1; 11, p. 658).

Boas, Viktor Karlovich. He was a censor for foreign publications in Vil'no in 1896 and senior censor at the Saint Petersburg Foreign Censorship Committee in 1905 with the rank of collegiate councillor (1; 2, p. 843).

Boborykin, Nikolai Nikolaevich (1812–88). Educated at home in Moscow, he began his government service in the provincial government there in 1831. He retired and spent the years 1843–72 abroad, studying foreign literature. Upon his return he worked as assistant to the librarian of the Rumiantsev Museum in Moscow for two years; in 1874 he became a censor of English publications and Russian drama for the Chief Administration for Press Affairs. He was also known as a poet (4, 24, 31).

Butovskii, Dmitrii Petrovich. He was a censor of foreign publications in Kiev in 1896 with the rank of collegiate assessor (1).

Delakroa (Delacroix), Aleksandr Ivanovich. He was a censor in Dorpat in the 1850s. Mez'er refers to Andrei Ivanovich, which is probably an error. Aleksandr is listed first in the 1853 *Adres-kalendar'* (Address-Calendar), the year after Johann Anton Friedrich Delakroa's death (see below). Perhaps he was Johann's son? By 1858–59 he held the rank of collegiate councillor (1, 24).

Delakroa (Delacroix), Johann Anton Friedrich (1781–1852). The son of a Belgian nobleman in the service of Austria, he was born in Saratov, where he was educated at home. In 1793 he served with the Voronezh hussars. Four years later he began work in a government office dealing with Livonian, Estonian, and Finnish affairs. Two years later he was teaching French in a local *gimnaziia* in Kazan. He then moved to Mitava (now known as Elgava, in Latvia), where he worked in the office of Governor General Prince Golitsyn; he also taught Russian in a *gimnaziia* there. Soon he transferred to Saint Petersburg, where he worked for the commission charged with compiling Russian laws and, later, for another government agency. In 1808 he went to Paris with Duke Aleksandr Virtembergskii; he remained for two years at the Russian embassy there. Back in Saint Petersburg, he joined the Ministry of Police. Two years later he returned to Mitava, where he remained until his death. He spent thirty-six years as director of the office of the governor of Courland (part of present-day Latvia). One year before his death he was appointed to be a censor in Dorpat. His literary activity was extensive: he published German translations of Russian works as well as a political journal, and while in Paris he published music. He also published works in Russian, French, and German. The *Adres-kalendar'* for 1851 lists Ivan Ivanovich; this is probably just the Russianized form of Johann's name. The rank given is aulic councillor (1; 2, p. 821; 8; 12; 31).

Demchinskii, M. M. He chaired the committee from 1828 until 1830 (29, p. 68).

D'iakonov, Nikolai Vasil'evich. He was a junior censor at the Saint Petersburg Foreign Censorship Committee in 1905 with the rank of collegiate assessor (1).

Dobrovol'skii, Zakharii Mikhailovich (died 25 November 1875). He was executor and treasurer of the Saint Petersburg Foreign Censorship Committee during Tiutchev's chairmanship (16, p. 223; 17, p. 596; chap. 3).

Drozdov, N. M. He wrote a report in 1889 (2, p. 850).

Dukshinskii, G. D. He wrote reports in the 1830s (30, pp. 929–32).

Dukshinskii, G. R. He is mentioned in Krasovskii's diary and wrote a report in 1829

(2, p. 781; 32, p. 137).

Dukshta-Dukshinskii, Gavril Rafailovich. He was a senior censor from the 1840s through the 1870s. He is listed in 1858–59 with the rank of high state councillor. This and either or both of the two preceding names could possibly refer to the same individual (1; 6, vol. 1, p. 145; 24; 27, p. 72; chap. 4).

Dukshta-Dukshinskii, Nikolai Gavrilovich. He was a senior censor in the Saint Petersburg Foreign Censorship Committee 1895–1905. His rank in 1905 was high state councillor. The 1895 *Spisok chinov* lists him as Roman Catholic, married, educated at the Fourth Saint Petersburg *gimnaziia,* and serving in this post since 1882. Perhaps he was the son of Gavril Rafailovich (see above) (1, 35).

Egorov, Anatolii Evgen'evich (born 1842). He was a censor for foreign publications in Moscow, Saint Petersburg, and Odessa from the 1860s through the early 1900s. His memoirs are the source of a great deal of information about other censors (6, 24, chap. 4).

Egorov, A. N. He was chairman of the Kiev Foreign Censorship Committee around 1900 (23, p. 388).

Egorov, Nikolai Vladimirovich (or Georgievich?) (died 1902). Cousin of Anatolii Evgen'evich Egorov, he worked in the Moscow Censorship Committee from 1865 through 1902, first as a clerk, then as secretary, finally as a censor. He was a bibliophile who amassed an important collection, sold after his death to the bookseller P. P. Shibanov. In his memoirs A. E. Egorov notes that his cousin became interested in rare books while serving as a censor of foreign publications (6, vol. 1, pp. 213–14; 24; chap. 4).

Ellenbogen, Aleksandr Solomonovich. He was a censor for Hebrew publications in Vil'no in 1846, listed as "honorary citizen" (1).

Emmausskii, Khristofer Vladimirovich. He was a junior censor in the Warsaw Censorship Committee, later a senior censor and director of its foreign section. In 1896 he was listed with the rank of state councillor (1, 7, 24, chap. 2).

Esipov, Aleksandr Pavlovich. He was assistant senior censor in the late 1840s and 1850s and librarian 1858–60 in the Saint Petersburg Foreign Censorship Committee. His rank in 1859–60 was aulic councillor (1; 21, p. 106).

Esipov, Grigorii Vasil'evich (died 1899?). He was a censor for foreign publications from the 1840s through the 1870s. There is some confusion about the two Esipovs (see above). In his memoirs A. E. Egorov names Esipov (without any initials) as head of the German and Italian department of the Foreign Censorship Committee in Saint Petersburg (see chap. 4). According to Mez'er, Egorov is referring to G. V. Esipov. In the absence of further information, I assume that these are two different men (24, chap. 4).

Fedorov, F. He wrote a report in 1905 (2, p. 781).

Fedotov, Aleksei Prokhorovich. He was a censor for foreign publications in the Moscow Censorship Committee in 1896. His rank is given as aulic councillor (1).

Fekht (Vecht?), Vil'gel'm Aleksandrovich. He was a senior censor in the foreign section of the Warsaw Censorship Committee. A German, he had worked forty years for the Russian government but allegedly spoke no Russian; he spoke French to other censors and German to book dealers. The *Adres-kalendar'* for 1859–60 gives his patronymic as Fridrikhovich; in 1858–59 and in Mez'er he is listed as Fridrikh Aleksandrovich. He is designated in 1859–60 as "honorary citizen" (1; 7, no. 1, pp. 130–31; 24; chap. 2).

Feodorov, Vladimir Vasil'evich. Born in the province of Kiev, he began life as a Jew named Gersh Birnbaum. He was a rabbi but converted and took his Russian name. After his baptism he worked in Kiev as a civil servant in the office of the governor general, where he dealt with Jewish affairs. He then moved to Warsaw as a senior censor. He reviewed Polish and German newspapers and other works for the committee and censored all Jewish publications. Because he had been a rabbi, he knew both ancient Hebrew and contemporary "jargon" (Emmausskii's term for Yiddish) and was an expert in Jewish literature. When pestered by authors he was known to throw their manuscripts at them (7, no. 1, pp. 132–33; 24).

Fomin, Aleksandr Dmitrievich. He was a senior censor for foreign newspapers and magazines in Saint Petersburg, a privy councillor, and for some years head of the "secret department of censorship" (15, p. 93; 24).

fon (von) Bistram, Baron. He wrote a report in 1859 (2, p. 844).

fon (von) Budberg, Baron Otton Ottonovich. He was a junior censor in the Riga Foreign Censorship Committee in 1896 with the rank of state councillor (1).

fon Fok (von Vock), Maksim Iakovlevich. He was responsible for foreign censorship in the 1820s and was director of what later became the Third Section (13, p. 711; 24).

Gan (Hahn?), Iulii Fedorovich, Baron. He was chairman of the Odessa Censorship Committee from the end of the 1860s until Egorov's arrival in 1881. There is a suggestion that his pet parrots participated, along with his wife, in his censorship decisions (6, vol. 2, pp. 63–64; 24; chap. 4).

Gedekhen (Hedechen, Heidechen?), Gotlib (Gottlieb) Viktorovich. He was a senior assistant censor in the Saint Petersburg Foreign Censorship Committee in the 1890s and early 1900s. His rank in 1905 was collegiate assessor; that year he also was listed as secretary of the committee. The 1895 *Spisok chinov* lists him as unmarried, an Evangelical Lutheran who had attended the Saint Petersburg Commercial School and had been serving at his post since 1889 (1; 21, p. 196; 35).

Geispits (Heispitz?), Stepan Frantsovich. He was a senior assistant censor in 1895 and 1896. The 1895 *Spisok chinov* lists him as an Evangelical Lutheran, unmarried, who had attended the Saint Petersburg Reformed School and had been serving at his post since 1891. His rank in 1896 was collegiate secretary (1; 2, p. 851; 35).

Genikes. A Jewish teacher who worked in the Odessa School District Administration, he was the first censor in Odessa of publications in Hebrew and of Hebrew works imported from abroad (6, vol. 2, p. 56).

Gents (Henz, Heinz?), A. He wrote a report in 1907 (2, p. 830).

Gin'e (Heine?), Emil Ivanovich. Perhaps he and Iulii (see below) were brothers; he too was a junior censor in Warsaw in the early 1850s and became a senior censor in 1855. In 1859–60 his rank was collegiate assessor, two ranks lower than Iulii's (1).

Gin'e (Heine?), Iulii Ivanovich. He was a junior censor in Warsaw in the early 1850s and became a senior censor in 1855. In 1859–60 he had the rank of collegiate councillor (1; 2, p. 814).

Gintsburg (Ginzburg?), Boris Solomonovich. He was a junior assistant censor in the Saint Petersburg Foreign Censorship Committee in 1901 with the rank of titular councillor (1).

Gol'mbladt (also Gol'mbliad, Gol'mblad; Holmbladt?), Burg (?) Reingol'dovich. He was a censor for foreign publications in Vil'no in the 1850s. His rank in 1859–60 was state councillor (1; 2, p. 780).

Gol'mblatt (Holmbladt?), F. B. He was head of the Odessa "black office" (22).

Gol'mstrem (Holmstrem?), V. A. The illegitimate son of V. K. Plehve, minister of internal affairs under Nicholas II, he worked in the Department of Police and was transferred to the Chief Administration for Press Affairs to work on surveillance of the foreign press (24).

Golenishchev-Kutuzov, Petr Arkad'evich, Count. He was a junior censor in 1895 and 1896. His rank in 1896 was collegiate councillor. The 1895 *Spisok chinov* lists him as married, Orthodox, and a graduate of Moscow University, serving in this post since 1890 (1, 35).

Goriainov, A. A. He wrote a report in 1912 (2, p. 831).

Grave. He was a censor in Riga who wrote reports in the 1830s (11, p. 636; 30, p. 929).

Iablochkov, V. M. He was head of the Moscow "black office" (22).

Iakovlev, Lev Vasil'evich. He was a junior assistant censor in 1895, Orthodox, married, who attended the School of the Ministry of Communications, and who had been serving in his post for only three months, according to the 1895 *Spisok chinov* (35).

Ivanovskii, L. O. He wrote a report in 1878 (2, p. 845).

Karpinskii, Vladimir (Milovidov). He was a junior censor, head of the "black office" in Tiflis. The authorities did not want him to be suspected of involvement with this secret operation by the Tiflis Committee for Press Affairs, so he was attached to the Ministry of Education and sent to Tiflis allegedly to study Eastern languages (15).

Kaul'bars, Baron. He was a junior censor in the Saint Petersburg Foreign Censorship Committee in 1907, and wrote a report on a German edition of Herzen's memoirs. He almost certainly belonged to the Russian baronial family of this name, among whose illustrious members were Barons Aleksandr Vasil'evich and Nikolai Vasil'evich (see 8). It is possible that either of these two gentlemen was serving as a censor in 1907 in addition to other activities, or perhaps the baron in question was another relative (18, p. 260).

Kestner (Koestner?), K. He was a censor for foreign publications in Riga in the 1850s. His rank in 1859–60 was state councillor (1; 11, p. 656).

Kokh (Koch?), Eduard Fedorovich. He was an assistant senior censor in the Saint Petersburg Foreign Censorship Committee in 1859–60 with the rank of titular councillor (1).

Komarovskii, Egor Evgrafovich, Count (1803–75). He was a senior censor under Tiutchev's chairmanship in the Saint Petersburg Foreign Censorship Committee. In 1859–60 he held the rank of state councillor. It was to Komarovskii that the Slavophile Ivan Vasil'evich Kireevskii wrote his 1852 letter, "O kharaktere prosveshcheniia Evropy i o ego otnoshenii k prosveshcheniiu Rossii" (On the character of European enlightenment and its relationship to Russian enlightenment) (1; 2, p. 788; chap. 3).

Konopatskii, Kasimir Viktorovich. He was a senior assistant censor in 1895 and secretary in 1901 and 1902 in the Saint Petersburg Foreign Censorship Committee. His rank in 1902 was collegiate councillor. The 1895 *Spisok chinov* lists him as a graduate of the Rovno *Realgymnasium,* a Roman Catholic, unmarried, serving in this post since 1889 (1, 35).

Kopylov, Adrian Fedorovich. He was a senior censor in the Saint Petersburg Foreign Censorship Committee in 1895. He is listed in the 1895 *Spisok chinov* as a graduate of Saint Vladimir University, Orthodox, married, and serving in this post since 1890. His rank in 1895 was high state councillor (1; 2, p. 850; 35).

Kosogovskii, Aleksandr Nikandrovich. He was a senior assistant censor in the Saint Petersburg Foreign Censorship Committee in 1902 with the rank of collegiate councillor (1).

Krasovskii, Aleksandr Ivanovich (1776–1857). He chaired the Foreign Censorship Committee in Saint Petersburg 1832–57. His rank in 1857 was privy councillor (1, 24, 31, 32, chap. 2).

Kurganov, Vladimir Filipovich. He was secretary and assistant censor in the accounting department of the Odessa Foreign Censorship Committee in 1896, with the rank of collegiate registrar (1).

Kurts (Kurz?), Eduard Genrikhovich. He was a junior censor in the Riga Foreign Censorship Committee in 1896 with the rank of state councillor (1).

Lamkert, Ferdinand Iosifovich. He was a senior censor in the Saint Petersburg Foreign Censorship Committee in 1901–2 with the rank of collegiate assessor (1).

Langer, V[alerian Platonovich] (born 1800). He wrote a report in 1860. Mez'er describes Valerian Platonovich Langer as an artist and teacher of the theory of fine arts at the Lycée in Tsarskoe Selo. She does not identify him with the foreign censorship but he may have written this 1860 report (2, p. 845; 24).

Lappo, Mikhail Romual'dovich. He was a junior assistant censor in the Saint Petersburg Foreign Censorship Committee in 1905 with the rank of collegiate assessor (1).

Lebedev, Nikolai Egor'evich. He was an assistant senior censor in the Saint Petersburg Foreign Censorship Committee in 1856 and 1857 with the rank of titular councillor. He wrote a report in 1860 (1; 2, p. 798; 24).

Lishin, Grigorii Andreevich (1854–88). A poet, composer, and music critic, he was an assistant censor at the Foreign Censorship Committee in Saint Petersburg (6, vol. 1, pp. 148–50; 24; chap. 4).

Liubovnikov, Aleksei Stepanovich (1829–90). He was a senior censor at the Saint Petersburg Foreign Censorship Committee and secretary at least for the years 1858–60. Son of a civil servant, he was educated at Saint Petersburg University in philosophy and Oriental studies. In 1853 he began service at the committee. He was very energetic and hard working, an expert in history and philosophy who knew almost all the romance languages and some Oriental languages as well. He advanced rapidly in his career; in 1855 he became an assistant senior censor and two years later was named secretary of the committee. In 1863 he was made head of the English section with the rights of a senior censor; in 1870 he became a senior censor officially and head of an important section of the committee dealing with French, English, Italian, Spanish, and Portuguese works. He was awarded the rank of state councillor in 1877. He held the position of senior censor for twenty-nine years; in the view of his biographer in the *Russkii biograficheskii slovar'* this was a job requiring care, tact, and great knowledge. He followed Russian literature closely and constantly read foreign literature, especially works in English. He also worked for the foreign sections of two periodical publications—*Sanktpeterburgskie vedomosti* (Saint Petersburg Bulletin) and *Golos* (Voice)—writing on contemporary foreign literature. He also translated many works, especially of English writers, including Dickens, George Eliot, the Brontës, and Collins (1; 2, p. 792; 3; 6, vol. 1, p. 144; 23; 31; chap. 4).

Maikov, Apollon Nikolaevich (1822–97). One of Russia's greatest poets, he chaired the Foreign Censorship Committee from 1882 until 1897. His rank in 1896 was privy councillor (1, 35, chap. 4; also see the Notes and Bibliography).

Maiskii, S. (pseud.). He served more than ten years as a censor of foreign newspapers and journals in Saint Petersburg and was involved with the "black office" (22).

Mardar'ev, Mikhail Georgievich. He was a senior censor and head of the Saint Petersburg "black office" (15, p. 95; 22, 24).

Mardar'ev, Nikolai Georgievich. He began work at the Foreign Censorship Committee in Saint Petersburg in 1886 and rose to be a senior censor. Beginning in 1907 he was a member of the Council of the Chief Administration for Press Affairs. He also served as a censor in Kiev and Odessa. Perhaps he and Mikhail (see above) were related (23, 24).

Martini. He wrote a report in 1827 (11, p. 637).

Mikhailov, Vladimir Vasil'evich. He was executor and treasurer of the Foreign Censorship Committee in Saint Petersburg in the 1890s and early 1900s. His rank in 1902 was aulic councillor. The 1895 *Spisok chinov* lists him as a graduate of the Imperial Institute at Gatchina, Orthodox, unmarried, and at his post since 1892 (1; 35).

Miller-Krasovskii. He was a censor of German publications at the Foreign Censorship Committee in Saint Petersburg, succeeding Esipov as head of the German-Italian department (6, vol. 1, pp. 144–45; chap. 4).

Murav'ev, Aleksandr Nikolaevich, Count. He was a senior censor in 1895 and chairman of the Foreign Censorship Committee in Saint Petersburg 1897–1917. His rank in 1905 was high state councillor. The 1895 *Spisok chinov* lists him as a junior censor with the rank of state councillor, a graduate of the imperial Lycée at Aleksandrovsk, Orthodox, unmarried, and at this post since 1890. Egorov says Murav'ev's brother was minister of foreign affairs (1; 6, vol. 1, p. 146; 29, p. 68; 35).

Nagel', Egor Egor'evich. He was a censor in the Saint Petersburg Foreign Censorship Committee in the 1840s and 1850s. Fedorov calls him G. Nagel' but the *Adres-kalendar'* for 1846–52 lists Egor Egor'evich Nagel', first as librarian and in 1851 as junior censor and office manager. His rank in 1852 was aulic councillor (1; 11, p. 649; chap. 4).

Nepomilov, Ivan Mikhailovich. He was a junior assistant censor in the Foreign Censorship Committee in Saint Petersburg in 1895 with the rank of titular councillor. According to the *Spisok chinov* for that year he was Orthodox, married, educated at home, and had served in his post since 1894 (35).

Nikiforov, Nikolai Dmitrievich. He was a junior censor in the Saint Petersburg Foreign Censorship Committee in 1901 with the rank of state councillor (1).

Odoevskii, Vladimir Fedorovich, Prince (1803–69). He was a prominent Russian intellectual who served as librarian and occasionally as censor in the Saint Petersburg Foreign Censorship Committee in the 1820s (8; 11, pp. 642–44; 12; chap. 2).

Paleolog, Mikhail Grigor'evich (1800–61). An educator and translator, he was born in Constantinople and died in Odessa. At the age of eleven he moved to Bucharest with his family (his father was at the Wallachian court). He was educated at a lycée in Bucharest but had to leave the country after taking part in an unsuccessful uprising against the Turks. He moved to Odessa, where he became a teacher of ancient Greek at a Greek commercial school; in 1827 he became head of the school. In 1838 he was teaching modern Greek at the Richelieu Lycée in Odessa. He became a censor of foreign publications in the Odessa Censorship Committee in 1846, while remaining head of the Greek commercial school. He published a Greek grammar in Russian, Russian-French-Greek conversation books (*razgovory*), several works in Greek, including collections of Greek prose and poetry, and translations from Greek, French, and Italian. The *Adres-kalendar'* for 1851 and 1852 gives his patronymic as Dmitrievich. His rank in 1859–60 was state councillor (1; 2, p. 813; 31).

Pevnitskii, Aleksandr Ivanovich (died 1905). Egorov's predecessor as senior assistant censor at the Foreign Censorship Committee in Saint Petersburg in the 1860s, he moved from there to Dorpat as censor in 1875 and then to Odessa, where he joined Egorov's staff and served in the 1880s as censor there (1; 2, p. 784; 6, vol. 1, p. 145, vol. 2, p. 65; 24; chap. 4).

Pletnev, A. He wrote a report in 1909 (2, p. 858).

Polonskii, Iakov Petrovich (1820–98). He was a great Russian poet and a censor of foreign publications in Saint Petersburg (serving first as secretary and later as censor) from 1860 until the mid-1890s. In 1896 he was a junior censor with the rank of high state councillor (1, chap. 4; also see the Notes and Bibliography).

Ponomarev, Andrei Andreevich. He was a junior assistant censor in the Saint Petersburg Foreign Censorship Committee in 1902 with the rank of titular councillor (1).

Reinvot (also Reinbot), Evgraf Antonovich. He was an assistant senior censor and office manager in the Saint Petersburg Foreign Censorship Committee in the early 1850s. He held the rank of titular councillor in 1854 (1).

Rochfort (Rochefort?), Aleksandr Osipovich. He was a senior censor in the Saint Petersburg Foreign Censorship Committee in the 1840s and 1850s. His rank in 1857 was state councillor (1, 24).

Rode, Lev L'vovich. A censor at the Foreign Censorship Committee in Saint Petersburg in the 1840s and 1850s, he apparently wrote all his reports in French. In his diary Krasovskii tells of a dream in which Rode banned a play in English. In 1859–60 he was a senior censor with the rank of state councillor (1; 11, p. 635; 30, p. 932; 32, p. 131).

Roskovshenko, Vladimir Ivanovich. He was a senior censor in the Saint Petersburg Foreign Censorship Committee in 1905 with the rank of state councillor (1).

Rozen (Rosen?), Platon Vladimirovich. He was a censor of Hebrew publications in Vil'no in the 1850s. His rank in 1859–60 was collegiate assessor. Through 1857 he is listed as "honorary citizen"; in 1858 he became a titular councillor and, in 1859–60, a collegiate assessor (1).

Ryzhov, Aleksei Ivanovich (1829–72). He was educated at home, then entered the law faculty of Moscow University, where he was influenced by the liberal and idealistic trends of the time. He began his government service at the criminal court in Saint Petersburg but soon transferred to the Foreign Censorship Committee, where he served from 1854 through 1858 as secretary. His biographer in the *Russkii biograficheskii slovar'* writes that in that difficult period Ryzhov was a relatively liberal censor who always tried to smooth the way for foreign works; he often broke the rules when he felt that a particular work was important. In 1859 he moved to a different ministry. He also published works on literature and law in *Otechestvennye zapiski* (Notes of the Fatherland), *Golos* (Voice), and other periodicals, usually under the pseudonym of O. Koliadin; he translated Shakespeare's *Titus Andronicus* into Russian. He was killed by a relative in a family quarrel. His rank in 1857 was titular councillor (1, 31, 32, chap. 2).

Rzhepetskii, Vikentii Lavrent'evich. He was an assistant censor in the Saint Petersburg Foreign Censorship Committee in the 1840s and served as librarian in the 1850s. His rank in 1859–60 was aulic councillor (1; 2, p. 844).

Salias de Turnemir, Evgenii Andreevich, Count (1841–1908). His mother was the writer E. V. Salias de Turnemir (pseud. Evgenii Tur) and his uncle was the writer A. V. Sukhovo-Kobylin. He received an excellent education at home from his mother, and also spent a great deal of time around artists in her salon. He traveled extensively in Europe, living abroad (primarily in Spain) from 1862 until 1869 after having been expelled from Moscow University for taking part in student demonstrations. After his naturalization in 1876 (his father was French) he worked at the Ministry of Internal Affairs, with Moscow theaters, and as an archivist. He was associated with the journal *Poliarnaia zvezda* (North Star) in 1881–82. He was a censor at the Committee under Maikov's chairmanship (3; 9; 19; 23, p. 372; 25; 26).

Savel'ev, Pavel Stepanovich (1814–59). He was born in Saint Petersburg to what his biographer in the *Russkii biograficheskii slovar'* refers to as a cultured (*intelligentnaia*) merchant family. His father was apparently well educated and saw to it that the children learned French and German. Savel'ev attended Saint Petersburg University, where he studied philology and Oriental languages, toyed with a diplomatic career, and worked on the journal *Biblioteka dlia chteniia* (Library for Readers), writing on English literature for this and other journals and encyclopedias. Because he needed a regular job he became a civil servant in the Ministry of Education, where he worked on that ministry's journal. In February 1841 he became secretary of the Foreign Censorship Committee, which he remained until 1852. (His rank in 1851 was collegiate assessor.) He was active in the Russian Geographical Society and was an enthusiastic student of numismatics (1; 4; 31; 32, p. 119).

Serov, Aleksandr Nikolaevich (1820–71). Serov was a composer and music critic, born in Saint Petersburg, where his father had a rather important job in the Ministry of Finance. His father was intelligent and energetic but not of a particularly good family. Serov's mother was the daughter of a baptized Jew (Karl Ivanovich Gablits) who had been a very capable senator under Catherine the Great and had worked with Potemkin. From childhood Serov spoke and read French and German fluently and loved to read and draw. He attended a pension for three years, then a Saint Petersburg *gimnaziia*, and in 1835 he entered law school. His father thought that everyone ought to have a job, so Serov went into the civil service. He moved from job to job, usually connected with the courts. He worked for various ministries between 1840 and 1868; he must have been a censor in the 1860s. In 1863 he told V. S. Serova that he worked as a censor of foreign works for thirty rubles per month and let through unacceptable articles, to the horror of his chief. This job, he said, was no more disagreeable than many other stupid jobs! He appears to have dealt with foreign newspapers at the postal censorship office. Finally he left government service to become a music critic and compose music (5, 3d ed.; 24; 31; 33, p. 25; chap. 4).

Shirinskii-Shikhmatov, Platon Aleksandrovich, Prince (1790–1853). He was associated with the Ministry of Education from 1842 on, becoming minister in 1850. He may have chaired the committee 1830–33 (29, p. 68).

Shirinskii-Shikhmatov, P. P., Prince. He is named by Mez'er as chairman of the committee from 1830 until 1833, but the reference is probably intended to indicate P. A. Shirinskii-Shikhmatov (see above) (29).

Shlitter (Schlitter?), A. F. He was head of the Warsaw "black office" (22).

Shmidt (Schmidt?), Ivan. He was an assistant censor in the accounting department of the Riga Foreign Censorship Committee in 1896 with the rank of titular councillor (1).

Shtein (Stein?), Vladimir Ivanovich. He was a junior censor in the Saint Petersburg Foreign Censorship Committee in 1901, with the rank of state councillor. According to his son, Sergei, he was author of a biography of Schopenhauer; he was a friend and correspondent of the Russian poet Fet (1, 24).

Shul'ts, (Schultz?), Evgenii Khr. He was a "censor-polyglot" who worked for the foreign censorship in Saint Petersburg in the 1870s (6, vol. 1, p. 145; 24; chap. 4).

Sots (Sotz?), Vasilii Ivanovich (1788–1841). He was a censor, writer, and translator, born in Moscow and educated at Moscow University. He became a teacher at the Iaroslavskii Demidovskii School. In 1809 he worked as a translator for the government. Beginning in 1810 he worked for the Ministry of Police, where he advanced over the next few years; in 1816 he was named secretary of the Russian section of the censorship committee. He remained there until 1828, when he left to become senior censor at the newly established Foreign Censorship Committee. During his years as a censor he was given various medals and awards. He remained senior censor at the committee for the rest of his life. His name appears on numerous reports of German and French works (11, p. 639; 31).

Teodoridi. He was a Greek, employed by the Warsaw Censorship Committee to deal with the foreign periodical press. He read several foreign languages fluently (7, no. 1, p. 131).

Terent'ev, Sem'en Sem'enovich. He was secretary of the Riga Foreign Censorship Committee in 1896 with the rank of collegiate assessor (1).

Timkovskii, Fedor Osipovich. He was a very strict censor in Riga in the last years of the eighteenth century. Between 1797 and 1799 he was responsible for banning 552 of the 639 books detained by the Riga censorship. Included were works by Swift, Boccaccio, Wieland, Schiller, Kant, Herder, Klopstock, Rousseau, Voltaire, and Goethe (30, p. 915).

Tiutchev, Fedor Ivanovich (1803–73). One of Russia's foremost poets, he chaired the Foreign Censorship Committee in Saint Petersburg from 1858 until 1873. His rank in 1859–60 was high state councillor (1, 24, chap. 3; see also the Notes and Bibliography).

Treier, Rudol'f Fedorovich. He was a senior censor in the Riga Foreign Censorship Committee in 1896 with the rank of state councillor (1).

Treiman, I. G. He wrote a report in 1908 (2, p. 820).

Trusman, Georgii Georgievich (born 1857). He was a censor for foreign publications in Revel in 1896 with the rank of collegiate assessor. A specialist on the history, philology, and ethnography of the southern Baltic Finns (the people of present-day Estonia), he was born into an Estonian peasant family and was educated in Saint Petersburg at an ecclesiastical academy, where he took a master's degree in divinity in 1884. He published numerous works in his specialty (1, 4, 8).

Tugendgol'd, Vol'f Isaevich (1796–1864). A writer and censor, son of Isaiah Tugendgol'd, one of the first enlighteners (*prosvetiteli*) in Galicia, he was born near Krakow and died in Vil'no. He was educated at Breslau University. In 1827 he was appointed censor of Hebrew publications in Vil'no—in 1859 he was listed as "honorary citizen"—and also served as a teacher of history in a Vil'no rabbinical seminary. He played an important role in the circle of local *Maskilim* (proponents of Moses Mendelsohn's enlightenment) and was close to such important Jewish figures as S. Fine, Isaac Baer Levinsohn, M. A. Ginsberg, and others. He published stories and linguistic works in German; some also were translated into Hebrew (1, 10, 25).

Tumanskii, Fedor Vasil'evich (died 1805). He was a writer and translator at the end of the eighteenth century, a corresponding member of the Adacemy of Sciences, and a member of the Russian Academy who served as a censor of foreign works at the Riga customs office. Like Krasovskii and Timkovskii, his colleague in Riga, he is portrayed as a censor whose vigilance bordered on fanaticism (2, p. 775; 8; 34).

U———n. He was a censor in Odessa. According to Egorov he was not suited for his job as a censor of foreign publications because he lacked the proper education and knew no foreign languages at all. He handled only clerical tasks and occasionally censored minor Russian publications for the internal censorship. Egorov's predecessor, Baron Gan, depended heavily on U———n for his correspondence, since Gan's native language was German and he did not know Russian well. U———n's position changed radically when Egorov came, since neither he nor the censor for Russian publications needed a clerk. U———n was finally dismissed because of an incident involving a pamphlet in Russian (6, vol. 2, p. 66).

Utechkin, Vasilii Nikolaevich. He was secretary and junior censor of Russian and foreign works in Odessa in the 1870s and 1880s (24).

Vakar, Platon Alekseevich. He was a member of the Chief Administration for Press Affairs in the 1870s and 1880s and a censor in the Foreign Censorship Committee under Tiutchev's chairmanship. Tiutchev wrote a verse about censorship in his album (24, chap. 3).

Vasentsovich-Makarevich, Nikolai Aleksandrovich. He was a junior assistant censor in 1895 and 1896. His rank in 1896 was aulic councillor. The 1895 *Spisok chinov* lists him as a Roman Catholic, unmarried, a graduate of Saint Petersburg University who had held this post since 1894 (1; 2, p. 822, 35).

Vashkevich, Ivan. He was a censor in Vil'no in the 1840s and 1850s. His rank in 1850 was collegiate assessor (1; 11, p. 655).

Vasil'ev, Ivan Vasil'evich. He was a senior assistant censor in the Saint Petersburg Foreign Censorship Committee in 1901 with the rank of aulic councillor (1).

Vĕdrov, Vladimir Maksimovich. He was censor for foreign publications at the Moscow Censorship Committee during Egorov's employment there, 1866–68 (6, vol. 1, pp. 116–17; chap. 4).

Veisman (Weisman?), Karl Karlovich. Former head of the "black office," he is said to have taught the Viennese censors excellent methods developed by the Russians for opening and sealing letters (22).

Vereshchagin, Sergei Andreevich. He was a junior censor in the Saint Petersburg Foreign Censorship Committee in 1902 with the rank of state councillor. He also may have been a censor of dramatic works in the internal censorship (1, 25).

Viazemskii, Pavel Petrovich, Prince (1820–88). He chaired the Foreign Censorship Committee from 1873 to 1881 (6, vol. 1, pp. 145–46, 210–13; 8; 24; 36, p. 84; chap. 4).

Vinch, Iosif Frantsovich. He was assistant for foreign censorship to Boas in Vil'no in 1896 with the rank of aulic councillor (1).

Viskovatov, P. A. He was a member of the Saint Petersburg Foreign Censorship Committee during Maikov's chairmanship (36, p. 100).

Vladimirov, Ivan Vasil'evich. He was a senior assistant censor in the Foreign Censorship Committee in the early 1850s and under Tiutchev's chairmanship. In 1854 he had the rank of titular councillor (1; 16, p. 84).

Vladimirov, Petr Petrovich. He was a censor under Krasovskii's chairmanship. An invalid, he worked in his quarters in the same building as the committee offices (32, p. 120).

Volochaninov, Nikolai Glebovich. He was a censor in Warsaw in the 1870s who had served in the administration in the western region before joining the Foreign Censorship Committee. He was known as a very cautious censor (7, no. 1, p. 133; 24).

Volovskii, Fedor Frantsovich. He was a junior censor and office manager in the Saint Petersburg Foreign Censorship Committee in the early 1850s. In 1854 he had the rank of state councillor (1).

Zakharov, Iakov Dmitrievich (1765–1836). Zakharov was *not* a censor but he had to fight not to be one. He was a professor of chemistry, an academician, and state councillor. Born in Saint Petersburg, he attended the Academy of Sciences *gimnaziia*, of which he was one of the first graduates. He was sent to Germany to study at Göttingen University, where he spent four years. Upon his return to Russia he was selected to lecture at the Academy of Sciences and was named an academician by Emperor Paul himself. The director of the academy, Bakunin, recommended him for the post of censor at the Radziwill Customs office. He refused, protesting that he was a chemist who did not know anything about literature and that he had to wish to be a censor. His colleagues supported him against the director; in their statement they said Zakharov was known as a chemist only, and that they could not judge his knowledge of literature, politics, etc. (8, 31, 34).

Zaks (Saks?), Naum Grigor'evich. He was a censor for Hebrew publications in the Warsaw Foreign Censorship Committee in 1896 (1).

Zeiberling (Seiberling?), Iosif Isak'evich (died 1882). Born in Vil'no, he died at an advanced age in Vienna. His father, Isaak Markovich, was one of the few Jewish doctors to graduate from Vil'no University. Iosif Isak'evich was educated at one of the German universities, returned to Kiev as doctor of philosophy, and was appointed censor of Hebrew publications, at which job he served for about fifteen years. (He is listed in the *Adres-kalendar'* in 1846, 1850, and 1851, but without rank or title.) Later he worked for the Ministry of Education on questions concerning Jewish schools, succeeding L. Mandel'stamm. He lived in Saint Petersburg, where he played an important role in Jewish life. He was connected with such prominent scholars as Isaac Baer Levinsohn, Abraham Baer Gottlober, and Perez Smolenskin. He made a large fortune but earned the disfavor of the Jewish community for his official activity. After retiring he moved to Vienna, where he published a number of works (1, 10).

Zibert (Silbert, Siebert?), K. F. He was head of the Kiev "black office" (22).

Zlatkovskii, Mikhail Leont'evich (1836–1904). He was secretary of the Foreign Censorship Committee in Saint Petersburg and later senior censor. His rank in 1902 was high state councillor. The 1895 *Spisok chinov* lists him as a member of the First Cadet Corps, Orthodox, unmarried, and serving as senior censor since 1890 (1; 3; 6, vol. 1, p. 145; 24; 36; chaps. 3, 4).

SOURCE LIST FOR APPENDIX 2

The number of each source in appendix 2 refers to the list below.

1 *Adres-kalendar'. Obshchaia rospis' nachal'stvuiushchikh i prochikh dolzhnostnykh lits po vsem upravleniem v Rossiiskoi imperii.* Saint Petersburg: n.p., 1765–1916. (Examined 1846, 1850, 1851, 1852, 1853, 1854, 1855, 1856, 1857, 1858–59, 1859–60, 1896, 1901, 1902, and 1905 volumes.) For those censors listed in more than one year of the *Adres-kalendar'* the rank included in appendix 2 is from the latest available year. Ranks given in the *Adres-kalendar'* and *Spisok chinov* (source no. 35) are translated as follows: rank 3, *Tainyi sovetnik,* privy councillor; rank 4, *Dieistvitel'nyi statskii sovetnik,* high state

councillor; rank 5, *Statskii sovetnik*, state councillor; rank 6, *Kollezhskii sovetnik*, collegiate councillor; rank 7, *Nadvornyi sovetnik*, aulic councillor; rank 8, *Kollezhskii Assessor*, collegiate assessor; rank 9, *Tituliarnyi sovetnik*, titular councillor; rank 10, *Kollezhskii sekretar'*, collegiate secretary.

2 Aizenshtok, I., and Polianskaia, L. "Frantsuzskie pisateli v otsenkakh tsarskoi tsenzury." *Literaturnoe nasledstvo* 33–34 (1939): 769–858.

3 Beliavskii, N. N. "Stranichka iz vospominanii o A. N. Maikove i Ia. P. Polonskom." In *Sertum Bibliologicum v chest' Prezidenta Russkogo bibliologicheskogo obshchestva Prof. A. I. Maleina*. Saint Petersburg: Gos. izd., 1922.

4 *Bol'shaia entsiklopediia*. 22 vols. Saint Petersburg: Prosveshchenie, 1903–9.

5 *Bol'shaia sovetskaia entsiklopediia*. 3d ed. 30 vols. Moscow: Sovetskaia entsiklopediia, 1970–78.

6 Egorov, Anatolii Evgen'evich. *Stranitsy iz prozhitogo*. 2 vols. Odessa: Tip. E. Krisogelosa, 1913.

7 Emmausskii, Kh. "Iz vospominanii varshavskogo tsenzora." *Novaia zhizn'* (January 1914): 124–40; (February 1914): 136–51.

8 *Entsiklopedicheskii slovar'*. 41 vols. Saint Petersburg: F. A. Brokgauz, I. A. Efron, 1890–1904.

9 *Entsiklopedicheskii slovar' Russkogo bibliograficheskogo instituta Granat*. 7th ed. 58 vols. Moscow: Granat, 1933–40.

10 *Evreiskaia entsiklopediia*. 16 vols. Saint Petersburg: Obshchestvo dlia nauchnykh evreiskikh izdanii i Izdatel'stvo Brokgauza-Efron, 1906–13.

11 Fedorov, A. "Genrikh Geine v tsarskoi tsenzure." *Literaturnoe nasledstvo* 22–24 (1935): 635–78.

12 Gennadi, G. N. *Spravochnyi slovar' o russkikh pisateliakh . . . s 1725 po 1825 g.* 3 vols. Vols. 1–2, Berlin: Rozental', 1876–80; Vol. 3, Moscow: Tip. Shtaba Moskovskago voennago okruga, 1908.

13 Grech, N. I. *Zapiski o moei zhizni*. Moscow: Academia, 1930.

14 Grigor'ev, Vasilii Vasil'evich. *Zhizn' i trudy P. S. Savel'eva preimushchestvenno po vospominaniiam i perepiske s nim*. Saint Petersburg: Tip. Imp. Akademii Nauk, 1861.

15 Kantor, R. "K istorii 'chernykh kabinetov.'" *Katorga i ssylka* 37 (1927): 90–99.

16 Kazanovich, E. P., ed. *Uraniia. Tiutchevskii al'manakh 1803–1928*. Leningrad: Priboi, 1928.

17 Kirillov, P., Pavlova, E., and Shakhovskoi, D. "Neizdannye pis'ma Tiutcheva i k Tiutchevu." *Literaturnoe nasledstvo* 19–21 (1935): 579–602.

18 [Kovalev, I.] "Gertsen i tsarskaia tsenzura (k 70-letiiu so dnia smerti)." *Krasnyi arkhiv* 98 (1940): 240–62.

19 *Kratkaia literaturnaia entsiklopediia*. 9 vols. Moscow: Sovetskaia entsiklopediia, 1962–78.

20 *Literaturnaia entsiklopediia*. 11 vols. [Moscow]: Izd. Kommunisticheskoi akademii, 1929–39; reprint ed., Ann Arbor, Mich.: J. W. Edwards, 1948–49.

21 Lur'e, M. L., and Polianskaia, L. I., comps. "'Kommunisticheskii manifest' i tsarskaia tsenzura." *Istorik-Marksist* 66 (1938): 106–19.

22 Maiskii, S. "'Chernyi kabinet.' Iz vospominanii byvshego tsenzora." *Byloe* (July 1918): 185–97.

23 Mardar'ev, N. "Nechto iz proshlogo (Iz vospominanii byvshego tsenzora)." *Golos minuvshego* (May–June 1916): 372–91.

24 Mez'er, A. V. "Tsenzory." In *Slovarnyi ukazatel' po knigovedeniiu*. 3 vols. Moscow: Sotsekgiz, 1934.

25 Muratova, K. D., ed. *Istoriia russkoi literatury XIX veka. Bibliograficheskii ukazatel'*. Moscow: Izd. Akademii Nauk SSSR, 1962.

26 Nikitenko, Aleksandr Vasil'evich. *Dnevnik*. 3 vols. Leningrad: Gos. izd. khudozhestvennoi literatury, 1955–56.

27 Oksman, Iulian. "Mery nikolaevskoi tzenzury protiv fur'erizma i kommunizma." *Golos minuvshego* (May–June 1917): 69–72.

28 Opochinin, Evgenii Nikolaevich. *Pamiati kniazia Pavla Petrovicha Viazemskogo*. Saint Petersburg: n.p., 1888.

29 Polianskaia, L. I. "Obzor fonda Tsentral'nogo komiteta tsenzury inostrannoi." *Arkhivnoe delo*, no. 1 (1938): 62–116.

30 Reiser, S., and Fedorov, A. "Gete v russkoi tsenzure." *Literaturnoe nasledstvo* 4–6 (1932): 915–34.

31 *Russkii biograficheskii slovar'*. 25 vols. Saint Petersburg: Tip. I. N. Skorokhodova, 1896–1918.

32 Ryzhov, Aleksei Ivanovich. "Aleksandr Ivanovich Krasovskii." *Russkaia starina* (January–April 1874): 107–40.

33 Serova, V. S. *Serovy, Aleksandr Nikolaevich i Valentin Aleksandrovich*. Saint Petersburg: Shipovnik, 1914.

34 Sipovskii, V. V. "Iz proshlogo russkoi tsenzury." *Russkaia starina*, April 1899: 161–75; May 1899: 435–53.

35 *Spisok chinov Ministerstva vnutrennykh del* (1895): 365–69.

36 Zlatkovskii, Mikhail Leont'evich. *Apollon Nikolaevich Maikov. Biograficheskii ocherk*. 2d ed. Saint Petersburg: A. F. Marks, 1898.

Appendix 3
"My Experience
with the Russian Censor"
by Isabel F. Hapgood

[Isabel Hapgood (1850–1928) is known chiefly for her translations into English of works by Tolstoi, Turgenev, Gogol', Gor'kii, Leskov, and other prominent Russian writers. However, she was also a shrewd observer of the Russian scene and her reports on Russian literature and society before and after the Revolution make fascinating reading. Returning from her first trip to Russia, a two-year stay during which she traveled widely, Hapgood published a piece in the *Nation* (23 October 1890) entitled "My Experience with the Russian Censor." The article, reproduced below, describes her encounters with the Foreign Censorship Committee and is a most fitting conclusion to this book.]

In spite of the advantage which I enjoyed in a preliminary knowledge of the Russian language and literature, I was imbued with various false ideas, the origin of which it is not necessary to trace on this occasion. I freed myself from some of them; among others, from my theory as to the working of the censorship in the case of foreign literature. My theory was the one commonly held by Americans, and, as I found to my surprise, by not a few Russians, viz., that books and periodicals which have been wholly or in part condemned by the Censor are to be procured only in a mutilated condition, or by surreptitious means, or not at all. That this is not the case I acquired ample proof through my personal experience.

The first thing that an American does on his arrival in St. Petersburg is to scan the foreign newspapers in the hotels eagerly for traces of the Censor's blot—*le masque noir*, "caviare"—his idea being that at least one-half of the page will be thus veiled from sight. But specimens are not always or even very often to be procured with ease. In fact, the demand exceeds the supply sometimes, if I may judge from my own observations, and from the pressing applications for these curiosities which I received from disappointed seekers. The finest of these black diamonds may generally be found in the inventive news columns of the London dailies and in the flippant paragraphs of *Punch*.

Like the rest of the world, I was on the lookout for the Censor's work from the day of my arrival, but it was a long time before my search was rewarded by anything except a caricature of the Censor himself in *Kladderadatsch*. That it was left unmasked was my first proof that the gentleman, individually and collectively, was not deficient in a sense of humor. The sketch represented a dishevelled scribe seated three-quarters submerged in a bottle of ink, from the half-open cover of which his quill pen projected like a signal of distress. This was accompanied by an inscription to the effect that as the Russian Censor had blacked so many other people, he might now sit in the black for a while himself. Perhaps the Censor thought that remarks of that sort came with peculiar grace from martinet-ruled Berlin. About this time I received a copy of the *Century* containing—or rather, not containing—the first article in the prohibited series by Mr. Kennan. I made no remonstrance, but mentioned the fact, as an item of interest, to the sender who forthwith despatched the article in an envelope. The envelope being small, the plump package had the appearance of containing a couple of pairs of gloves or other dutiable merchandise. Probably that was the reason why the authorities cut open one end. Finding that it was merely innocent printed matter, they gave it to me on the very day of its arrival in Petersburg, and thirteen days from the date of posting in New York. I know that it was my duty to get excited over this incident, as did a foreign (that is, non-Russian) acquaintance of mine, when he received an envelope of similar plump aspect containing a bulky Christmas card, which was delivered decorated with five very frank and huge official seals, after having been opened for contraband goods. I did not feel aggrieved, however, and, being deficient in the Mother Eve quality which attributes vast importance to whatever is forbidden, I suggested that nothing more which was obnoxious to the Russian Government should be sent to me.

But when the foreigner offered the magazine to me, regularly, unmutilated, I did not refuse it. When a Russian volunteered to furnish me with it later on, I read it. When I saw summaries of the prohibited articles in the Russian press, I looked them over to see whether they were well done. When I saw another copy of the *Century*, with other American magazines, at the house of a second Russian, I did not shut my eyes to the fact, neither did I close my ears when I was told that divers instructors of youth in Petersburg, Moscow, and elsewhere were in regular receipt of it, on the principle which is said to govern clergymen away from home, viz., that in order to preach effectively against evil one must make personal acquaintance with it. I was also told at the English Bookstore that they had seven or eight copies of the magazine, which had been subscribed through them, lying at the Censor's office awaiting proper action on the part of the subscribers. What that action was I did not ask at the time, in my embarrassment of riches. It will be perceived that when we add the copies received by officials, and those given to the members of the Diplomatic Corps who desired it, there was no real dearth of the *Century* at any time.

About this time, also, I had occasion to hunt up a package of miscellaneous newspapers which had lingered as such parcels are apt to linger in all post-offices. In pursuance of my preconceived notions, I jumped to the conclusion that the Censor had them, regardless of the contingency that they might have been lost out of Russia. I called to ask for the papers. The official whom I found explained, with native Russian courtesy, that I had come to the wrong place, that office being devoted to foreign matter in book-form; but that, in all probability, the papers had become separated from their wrapper in the newspaper department (which was heedless) when they had been opened for examination, and hence it had been impossible to deliver them. Still, they might have been detained for some good reason, and he would endeavor to find some record of them.

While he was gone, my eyes fell upon his account book which lay open before me. It constituted a sort of literary book-keeping. The entries showed what books had been received, what had been forbidden, what was to be erased, whose property had been manipulated, and, most interesting of all, which forbidden books had been issued by permission, and to whom. Among these I read the titles of works by Stepniak, and of various works on Nihilism, all of which must certainly have come within the category of utterly proscribed literature, and not of that which is promptly forwarded to its address after a more or less liberal sprinkling of "caviare." As I am not in the habit of reading private records on the sly, even when thus tempted, I informed the official, on his return, of my action, and asked a question or two.

"Do you really let people have these forbidden books?" "Certainly," was his half-surprised, half-indignant reply. "And what can one have?" "Anything," said he, "only we must, of course, have some knowledge of the person. What should you like?"

I could only express my regret that I felt no craving for any prohibited literature at that moment, but I told him that I would endeavor to cultivate a taste in that direction to oblige him, and I suggested that, as his knowledge of me was confined to the last ten minutes, I did not quite understand how he could pass judgement as to what mental and moral food was suited to my constitution, and as to the use I might make of it. He laughed amiably, and said: "*Nitchevo*—that's all right; you may have whatever you please." I never had occasion to avail myself of the offer, but I know that many Russians who are well posted do so, although I also know that many Russians are not aware of their privileges in this direction. It is customary to require from Russians who receive literature of this sort a promise that they will let no other person see it—an engagement which is as religiously observed as might be expected, as the authorities are doubtless aware.

I did not pursue my search for the missing papers. I had allowed so much time to elapse that I perceived the uselessness of further action; they were evidently lost, and it mattered little as to the manner. Shortly afterwards I received the first of my only two specimens of Censorial caviare. It was on a political cartoon in a New York comic paper. I sent it back to America for identification of the picture, and it was lost between New York and Boston; which reconciled me to the possible carelessness of the Russian Post-office in the case of the newspapers just cited.

My next experience was with Count Lyeff N. Tolstoy's work entitled 'Life.' This was not allowed to be printed in book form, although nearly the whole of it subsequently appeared in instalments, as "extracts," in a weekly journal. I received the manuscript as a registered mail packet. The author was anxious that my translation should be submitted in the proof-sheets to a philosophical friend of his in Petersburg, who read English, in order that the latter might see if I had caught the sense of the somewhat abstract and complicated propositions. It became a problem how those proof-sheets were to reach me safely and promptly. The problem was solved by having them directed outright to the Censor's office, whence they were delivered to me; and, as there proved to be nothing to alter, they speedily returned to America as a registered parcel. My own opinion now is, that they would not have reached me a whit less safely or promptly had they been addressed straight to me. The bound volumes of my translation were so addressed later on, and I do not think that they were even opened at the office, the law to the contrary notwithstanding.

All this time I had been receiving a New York weekly paper with very little delay and no mutilation. But at this juncture an amiable friend subscribed in my name for the *Century*, and I determined to make a personal trial of the workings of the Censorship in as strong a case as I could have found had I deliberately desired to invent a test case. I may as well remark here that "The Censor" is not the hard-working omnivorous reader of mountains of print and manuscript which the words represent to the mind of the ordinary foreigner. The work of auditing literature, so to speak, is subdivided among such a host of men that office hours are brief, much of the foreign reading at least is done at home, and the lucky members of the committee keep themselves agreeably posted upon matters in general, while enjoying the fruits of office.

The Censor's waiting-room was well patronized on my arrival. An official who was holding a consultation with one of the visitors inquired my business. I stated it briefly, and shortly afterwards he retired into an adjoining room, which formed the beginning of a vista of apartments and officials. While I waited, a couple of men were attended to so near me that I heard their business. It consisted in obtaining official permission to print the bills and programmes of a musical and variety entertainment. To this end they had brought not only the list of performers and proposed selections, but also the pictures for the advertisement, and the music which was to be given. As the rare traveller who can read Russian is already aware, the programme of every public performance bears the printed authorization of the Censor, as a matter of course, quite as much as does a book. It is an easy way of controlling the character of assemblages, the value of which can hardly be disputed even by those prejudiced persons who insist upon seeing in this Russian proceeding something more arbitrary than the ordinary city license which is required for performances else-where. In Russia, as elsewhere, an ounce of prevention is worth fully a pound of cure. This, by the way, is the only form in which a foreigner is likely to come in contact with the domestic censure in Russia unless he should wish to insert an advertisement in a newspaper, or issue printed invitations to a gathering at his house, or send new [sic], telegrams. In these cases he may be obliged to submit to delay in the appearance of his advertisement, or requested to go to the elegance and expense of engraved invitations, or to detain his telegram for a day or two.

Just as these gentlemen had paid their fee, and resigned their documents to the official who had charge of their case, another official issued from the inner room, approached me, requested me to sign my name in a huge ledger, and, that being done, thrust into my hands a bulky manuscript, and departed. The manuscript had a taking title, but I did not pause to examine it. Penetrating the inner sanctum, I brought out the official and endeavored to return the packet. He refused to take it—it was legally mine. This contest lasted for several minutes until I saw a literary-looking man enter from the ante-room and look rather wildly at us. Evidently this was the owner, and, elevating the manuscript, I inquired if it was his. He hastened to my assistance and proved his rights. But, as erasures do not look well in account books, and as my name already occupied the space allotted to that particular parcel, he was not requested to sign for it, and I believe that I am still legally qualified to read, perform, or publish—whatever it was—that talented production.

A dapper little gentleman, with a dry, authoritative air, then emerged and assumed charge of me. I explained my desire to receive, uncensored, a journal which was prohibited.

"Certainly," said he, without inquiring how I knew the facts. "Just write down your application and sign it."

"I don't know the form," I answered.

He seemed surprised at my ignorance of such an every-day detail, but fetched paper and dictated a petition, which I wrote down and signed. When we reached the point where the name of the publication was to be inserted, he paused to ask: "How many should you like?"

"How many copies of the *Century*? Only one," said I.

"No, no; how many periodical publications should you like?"

"How many can I have on this petition?" I retorted in Yankee fashion.

"As many as you please. Do you want four—six—eight? Write in the names legibly."

I gasped, but told him that I was not grasping; I preferred to devote my time to Russian publications while in Russia, and that I would only add the name of the weekly which I was already receiving, merely with the object of expediting its delivery a little. The document was then furnished with the regulation eighty-kopek stamp (worth at that time about thirty-seven cents), and the business was concluded. As I was in summer quarters out of town, and it was not convenient for me to call in person and inquire whether permission had been granted, another stamp was added to insure the answer being sent to me. The license arrived in a few days, and the magazine began to come promptly, unopened. I was not even asked not to show it to other people. I may state here that, while I never circulated any of the numerous prohibited books and manuscripts which came into my possession during my stay in Russia, I never concealed them. I showed the *Century* occasionally to personal friends of the class who could have had it themselves had they taken any permanent interest in the matter; but it is certain that they kept their own counsel and mine in all respects.

Everything proceeded satisfactorily until I went to Moscow to stay for a time. It did not occur to me to inform the Censor of my move, and the result was that the first number of the magazine which I received there was as fine a "specimen" as heart could desire. The line on the title-page which referred to the obnoxious article had been scratched out; the body of the article had been cut out; the small concluding portion at the top of a page had been artistically "caviared." Of course, the article ending upon the back of the first page extracted had been spoiled. On this occasion I was angry, not at the mutilation as such, but at the breach of faith. I sat down, while my wrath was still hot, and indited a letter to the Head Censor in Petersburg. I do not recollect the exact terms of that letter, but I know I told him that he had no right to cut the book after granting me leave to receive it intact, without first sending me word that he had changed his mind, and giving valid reasoning therefor; that the course he had adopted was injudicious in the extreme, since it was calculated to arouse curiosity instead of allaying it, and that it would be much better policy to ignore the matter. I concluded requesting him to restore the missing article, if he had preserved it, and if he had not, to send at once to London (that being nearer than New York) and order me a fresh copy of the magazine at his expense.

A month elapsed, no answer came; but at the end of the month another mutilated *Century* arrived. This time I waited two or three days in the hope of inventing an epistle which should be more forcible—if such a thing were possible—than my last, and yet calm. The letter was half written when an official envelope made its appearance from Petersburg, containing cut pages and an apologetic explanation to the effect that the Moscow Censor, through an over-sight, had not been duly instructed in his duty towards me. A single glance showed me that the enclosed sheets belonged to the number just received, not to the preceding number. I drove immediately to the Moscow office and demanded the Censor. "You can tell me what you want with him," said the ante-room Cerberus. "Send me the Censor," said I. After further repetition, he retired and sent in a man who requested me to state my business. "You are not the Censor," I said, after a glance at him. "Send him out or I will go to him." Then they decided that I was a connoisseur in censors, and the proper official made his appearance, accompanied by an interpreter, on the strength of the foreign name upon my card. Convinced that the latter would not understand English well, like many Russians who can talk the language fluently enough, I declined his services, produced my documents from the Petersburg Censor, and demanded restitution of the other confiscated article. I obtained it, being allowed my pick from a neatly labelled package of contraband goods. That scratched, cut, caviared magazine is now in my possession, with the restored sheets and the Censor's apology appended. It is my proof to unbelievers that the Russian Censor is not so black as he is painted.

As we shook hands with this Moscow official, after a friendly chat, I asked him if he would be a little obtuse arithmetically as to the old and new style of reckoning, and let me have my January *Century* if it arrived before my departure for Petersburg, as my license expired January 1. He smilingly agreed to do so. I also called on the Moscow Book Censor, to find some books. The courtesy and readiness to oblige me on the part of the officials had been so great, that I felt aggrieved upon this occasion when this Censor requested me to return on the regular business day, and declined to overhaul his whole department for me on the spot. I did return on the proper day, and watched operations while due search was being made for my missing property. It reached me a few days later, unopened, the delay having occurred at my banker's, not in the post-office or Censor's department.

On my return to Petersburg, my first visit was to the Censor's office, where I copied my original petition, signed it, and dismissed the matter from my mind until my February *Century* reached me with one article missing and two articles spoiled. I paid another visit to the office, and was informed that my petition for a renewal of permission had not been granted.

"Why didn't you send me word earlier?" I asked.

"We were not bound to do so without the extra stamp," replied my dapper official.

"But why has my application been refused?"

"Too many people are seeing that journal; some one must be refused."

"Nonsense," said I. "And if it really is so, *I* am not the proper person to be rejected. It will hurt some of these Russian subscribers more than it will me, becaue it is only a question of *when* I shall read it, not of whether I shall read it at all. I wonder that so many demoralizing things do not affect the officials. However, that is not the point: pray keep for your own use anything which you regard as deleterious to me. I am obliged to you for your consideration. But you have no right to spoil three or four articles, and by a proper use of scissors and caviare that can easily be avoided. In any case, it will be much better to give me the book unmutilated."

The official and the occupants of the reception-room seemed to find my view very humorous; but he declared that he had no power in the matter.

"Very well," said I, taking a seat. "I will see the Censor."

"I am the Censor," he replied.

"Oh no. I happen to be aware that the Head Censor is expected in a few minutes, and I will wait."

My (apparently) intimate knowledge of the ways of censors again won the day. The chief actually was expected, and I was granted the first audience. I explained matters and repeated my arguments. He sent for the assistant.

"Why was not this application granted?" he asked impressively.

"We don't know, your Excellency," was the meek reply.

"You may go," said his Excellency. Then he turned graciously to me. "You will receive it."

"Uncut?"

"Yes."

"But will they let me have it?"

"Will—they—let—you—have—it—when—I—say—so?" he retorted with tremendous dignity.

Then I knew that I should have no further trouble; and I was right. I received no written permission, but the magazine was never interfered with again. Thus it will be seen that one practically registers periodicals wholesale, at a wonderfully favorable discount.

During the whole of my stay in Russia I received many books unread, apparently even unopened to see whether they belonged on the free list. In one case, at least, volumes which were posted before the official date of publication reached me by the next city delivery after the letter announcing their despatch. Books which were addressed to me at the Legation, to assure delivery when my exact address was unknown or when my movements were uncertain, were, in every case but one, sent to me direct from the post-office. I have no reason to suppose that I was unusually favored in any way. I used no "influence," I mentioned no names.

An incident which procured for me the pleasure of an interview with the Chief Censor for newspapers and so forth, will illustrate some of the erroneous ideas entertained by strangers. I desired to send some friends in Russia a year's subscription each of a certain American magazine, which sometimes justly receives a sprinkling of caviare, for its folly, but which is not on the black list, and is fairly well known in Petersburg. After some delay an answer came to the effect that the publishers had consulted the United States postal officials, and had been informed that "*no* periodical literature could be sent to Russia, this being strictly prohibited." I took this letter to the Newspaper Censor, who found it amusingly and amazingly stupid. He explained that the only thing which is absolutely prohibited is Russian text printed outside of Russia, which would never be delivered. He did not explain the reason, but I knew that he referred to the socialistic, nihilistic, and other proscribed works which are published in Geneva or Leipzig. Daily foreign newspapers can be received regularly only by persons who are duly authorized. Permission cannot be granted to receive occasional packages of miscellaneous contents, the reason for this regulation being very clear. And *all* books must be examined if new, or treated according to the place assigned them on the lists if they have already had a verdict pronounced upon them. I may add, in this connection, that I had the magazines I wished subscribed for under another name, to avoid the indelicacy of contradicting my fellow-countrymen. They were then forwarded direct to the Russian addresses, where they were duly and regularly recieved. Whether they were mutilated, I do not know. They certainly need not have been had the recipients taken the trouble to obtain permission as I did, if they were aware of the possibility. It is probable that I could have obtained permission for them had I not been pressed for time.

I once asked a member of the Censorship Committee on foreign books on what principle of selection he proceeded. He said that disrespect to the Emperor and the Greek Church was officially prohibited, that he admitted everything which did not err too grossly in that direction, and, in fact, *everything* except French novels of the modern realistic school. He drew the line at these, as pernicious to both men and women. He asked me if I had read a certain new book which was on the proscribed list. I said that I had, and in the course of the discussion which ensued, I rose to fetch the volume in question from the table behind him to verify a passage. (This occurred during a friendly call.) I recollected, however, that that copy had not entered the country by post, and that, consequently, the name of the owner therein inscribed would not be found on the list of authorized readers any more than my own. I am sure, however, that nothing would have happened if he had seen it, and he must have understood my movement. My business dealings were wholly with strangers.

It seems to be necessary, although it ought not to be so, to remind American readers that Russia is not the only land where the censorship exists, to a greater or less extent. Even in the United States, which is popularly regarded as the land of the unlicensed license in a literary sense—even in the Boston Public Library, which is admitted to be a model of good sense and wide liberality—all books are not bought or issued indiscriminately to all readers irrespective of age and so forth. The necessity for making special application may, in some cases, whet curiosity, but it also, undoubtedly, acts as a check upon unhealthy tastes, even when the book may be publicly purchased. I have heard Russians who did not wholly agree with their own censorship assert, nevertheless, that a strict censure was better than the total absence of it, apparently, in America, the utterances of whose press are regarded by foreigners in general as decidedly startling.

Notes

INTRODUCTION

1 C. Homburg, *Ein Winter in St. Petersburg* (Leipzig: Otto Wigand, 1860), pp. 100–101. The Bernard book must have been a German translation of *Les Ailes d'Icare* by Charles de Bernard.

2 M. I. Finley, "Censorship in Classical Antiquity," *Times Literary Supplement*, 29 July 1977, p. 924.

3 J. Laplanche and J.-B. Pontalis, *The Language of Psychoanalysis* (London: Hogarth Press, 1973), pp. 65–66.

4 Donald Thomas, *A Long Time Burning: The History of Literary Censorship in England* (New York: Praeger, 1969), p. 7.

5 Paul O'Higgins, *Censorship in Britain* (London: Nelson, 1972), p. 11.

6 Erik Barnouw, *The Sponsor: Notes on a Modern Potentate* (New York: Oxford University Press, 1978), p. 54.

7 Heinrich Heine, "Almansor," *Sämtliche Werke* (Munich: Winkler-Verlag, 1969), 2:859 (my translation).

8 Quoted in Friedrich Schulze, *Der deutsche Buchhandel und die geistigen Strömungen der letzten Hundert Jahre* (Leipzig: Börsenverein der deutschen Buchhändler, 1925), pp. 252–53.

9 Richard Pipes, *Russia under the Old Regime* (London: Weidenfeld and Nicholson, 1974), p. 314.

10 K. Bekker, "Materialy dlia statistiki gazetnogo i zhurnal'nogo dela v Rossii za 1869," *Zhurnal Ministerstva narodnogo prosveshcheniia* (September–October 1871): xxxv–xxxix; C. F. Müller Firm, Leipzig, *Addressbuch des deutschen Buchhandels und Verwandter Berufszweige* 13 (1908): 234–37.

11 Nicholas V. Riasanovsky, *A History of Russia* (New York: Oxford University Press, 1963), p. 423.

12   Anton Chekhov, *The Cherry Orchard*, in *The Portable Chekhov*, edited, and with an introduction, by Avrahm Yarmolinsky (New York: Viking Press, 1947), p. 568.

1   BUILDING THE FENCE

1   Mikhail Zetlin, *The Decembrists*, trans. George Panin (New York: International Universities Press, 1958), p. 14; P. V. Annenkov, *Literaturnye vospominaniia* (Leningrad: "Academia," 1928), pp. 301–2.

2   N. Ia. Novombergskii, *Osvobozhdenie pechati vo Frantsii, Germanii, Anglii, i Rossii* (Saint Petersburg: Tipo-lit. F. Vaisberga i P. Gershunina, 1906), pp. 214–16.

3   H. H. Houben, *Hier Zensur—Wer dort? Antworten von gestern auf Fragen von heute* (Leipzig: Brockhaus, 1918), pp. 34–38.

4   Ibid., pp. 39–46.

5   Julius Marx, *Die österreichische Zensur im Vormärz* (Munich: Oldenbourg, 1959), p. 4.

6   H. H. Houben, *Der gefesselte Biedermeier* (Leipzig: H. Haessel, 1924), pp. 75–76, 269.

7   Houben, *Hier Zensur*, pp. 17–19.

8   Ibid., p. 47.

9   Ibid., pp. 68–69.

10   A. G. Bolebrukh, *Peredovaia obshchestvenno-politicheskaia mysl' 2-i poloviny XVIII veka i tsarism (na materialakh deiatel'nosti tsenzurnykh organov)* (Dnepropetrovsk: DGU, 1979), pp. 14–16. Chapter 2 of Bolebrukh's interesting study is devoted to the organization of censorship in the second half of the eighteenth century; chapter 3 deals with the importation of foreign publications in the same period.

11   *Polnoe sobranie zakonov Rossiiskoi imperii* (Saint Petersburg: Tip. vtorogo otdeleniia Sobstvennoi E. I. V. Kantsiliarii, 1830–1916), no. 17508, 16 September 1796 (hereafter cited as *PSZ*).

12   *PSZ*, no. 17523, 22 October 1796.

13   Bolebrukh, *Peredovaia*, pp. 29, 31–33.

14   Bolebrukh, *Peredovaia*, p. 34.

15   See H. Reimer, *St. Petersburg am Ende seines ersten Jahrhunderts*, 2 vols. (Saint Petersburg: F. Dienemann, 1805), 2: 140.

16   *PSZ*, no. 18367, 11 February 1798.

17   *PSZ*, no. 18524, 17 May 1798.

18   Bolebrukh, *Peredovaia*, p. 37; see also V. V. Sipovskii, "Iz proshlogo russkoi tsenzury," *Russkaia starina* (April 1899): 167–70.

19   *PSZ*, no. 19010, 22 June 1799.

20   Bolebrukh, *Peredovaia*, p. 38; Houben, *Hier Zensur*, p. 9.

21   *PSZ*, no. 19387, 18 April 1800; Houben, *Hier Zensur*, pp. 107–8.

22   *PSZ*, no. 19807, 31 March 1801; no. 20139, 9 February 1802; no. 20210, 1 April 1802. This treaty is cited approvingly by Georgii Arbatov as an historical precedent of "law-enforced restrictions on what we today call foreign political propaganda" (G. A. Arbatov, *The War of Ideas in Contemporary International Relations* [Moscow: Progress Publishers, 1973], pp. 287–88). As director of the Institute for the Study of the U.S.A. and Canada, Arbatov is the man who often acts as the Soviet spokesman regarding relations with the West.

23   *PSZ*, no. 20741, 1 May 1803.

24 *PSZ*, no. 21388, 9 July 1804.

25 *PSZ*, no. 24687, 1811, articles 54, 84.

26 Houben, *Hier Zensur*, pp. 198, 180.

27 Houben, *Der gefesselte Biedermeier*, pp. 13, 215–16, 192.

28 *PSZ*, no. 28302, 1820, articles 222, 224. See also [N. Druzhinin], "K istorii russkoi tsenzury," *Russkaia starina* (December 1900): 652–54, on a Kharkov University professor's problems in obtaining foreign publications for personal use.

29 A. E. Egorov, *Stranitsy iz prozhitogo* (Odessa: Tip. E. Khrisogelosa, 1913), 2:29–30; *PSZ*, no. 38654, 10 September 1862; *PSZ*, no. 38984, 1 December 1862; *PSZ*, no. 38074, 17 March 1862; *PSZ*, no. 38133, 5 April 1862; Russia, Ministerstvo narodnogo prosveshcheniia, *Sbornik postanovlenii* (Saint Petersburg: Tip. V. S. Balasheva, 1877), 5:577; Egorov, *Stranitsy*, 2:180–81.

30 *PSZ*, no. 403, 10 June 1826.

31 A. M. Skabichevskii, *Ocherki istorii russkoi tsenzury (1700–1863 g)* (Saint Petersburg: Obshchestvennaia pol'za, 1892), p. 215.

32 See Sidney Monas, *The Third Section: Policy and Society in Russia under Nicholas I* (Cambridge: Harvard University Press, 1961), pp. 139–43.

33 Novombergskii, *Osvobozhdenie*, pp. 250–51; Houben, *Hier Zensur*, p. 135, Houben, *Der gefesselte Biedermeier*, p. 230.

34 Russia, Laws, Statutes, et al., *Svod zakonov Rossiiskoi Imperii*, 3d ed. (Saint Petersburg: Tip. vtorogo otdeleniia Sobstvennoi E. I. V. Kantsiliarii, 1857), vol. 14. The 1828 statute consists of an introduction (arts. 1–5) and seven chapters: internal censorship (arts. 6–97), censorship of foreign books (arts. 98–136), censorship in the Caucasian Educational District (arts. 137–59), the relationship of various places and people to the censorship (arts. 160–81), the ecclesiastical censorship (arts. 182–281), and property rights (arts. 282–356).

35 (V. V. Stasov), "Tsenzura v tsarstvovanie Imperatora Nikolaia I," *Russkaia starina* (August 1901): 395–404.

36 See L. I. Polianskaia, "Obzor Fonda Tsentral'nogo komiteta tsenzury inostrannoi," *Arkhivnoe delo*, no. 1 (1938): 64–65.

37 On the "black office," see S. Maiskii, "'Chernyi kabinet': Vospominaniia byvshego tsenzora," *Byloe* (July 1918): 185–97; "Nikolai II i samoderzhavie v 1903 g.," *Byloe* (February 1918): 190–222; M. E. Bakai, "O chernykh kabinetakh v Rossii," *Byloe* (July 1908): 119–33; R. Kantor, "K istorii 'chernykh kabinetov,'" *Katorga i ssylka* 37 (1927): 90–99. On the Soviet version of postal censorship, see Zhores A. Medvedev, *The Medvedev Papers* (London: Macmillan, 1971), pp. 295–471 ("Secrecy of Correspondence is Guaranteed by Law"), and an article by Leopol'd Avzeger, a former Soviet postal censor: "Ia vskryval Vashi pis'ma . . . Iz vospominanii byvshego tainogo tsenzora MGB," *Vremia i my*, no. 55 (1980): 224–53; no. 56 (1980): 254–78.

38 Novombergskii, *Osvobozhdenie*, p. 254.

39 Ibid., pp. 171–72.

40 Ibid., pp. 277, 270.

2 THE COMMITTEE AND THE BUREAUCRAT-CENSOR

1 Aleksei Ivanovich Ryzhov, "Aleksandr Ivanovich Krasovskii," *Russkaia starina* (January–April 1874): 107–40. The complete file of reports, including those of the branch committees, is housed in the Central State Historical Archives in Leningrad (*Fond* 779), described in the extensive article by L. I. Polianskaia, "Obzor Fonda Tsentral'nogo komiteta tsenzury inostrannoi," *Archivnoe delo*, no. 1 (1938). Polianskaia also quotes many censors' reports. The following three articles also include numerous reports: S. Reiser and A. Fedorov, "Gete v russkoi tsenzure," *Literaturnoe nasledstvo* 4–6 (1932): 915–34; A. Fedorov, "Genrikh Geine v tsarskoi tsenzure," *Literaturnoe nasledstvo* 22–24 (1935): 635–78; I. Aizenshtok and L. Polianskaia, "Frantsuzskie pisateli v otsenkakh tsarskoi tsenzury," *Literaturnoe nasledstvo* 33–34 (1939): 769–858. These four articles serve as my main source of reports written between 1828 and the Revolution.

2 Ryzhov, "Aleksandr Ivanovich Krasovskii," pp. 107–40.

3 M. L. Zlatkovskii, *Apollon Nikolaevich Maikov, 1821–1897 g.: Biograficheskii ocherk*, 2d ed. (Saint Petersburg: Tip. P. P. Soikina, 1898), pp. 33–39.

4 James H. Billington, *The Icon and the Axe: An Interpretive History of Russian Culture* (New York: Vintage Books, 1970), p. 296.

5 Ryzhov, "Aleksandr Ivanovich Krasovskii," pp. 108–9.

6 Ibid., p. 37.

7 Ibid., pp. 116, 133.

8 Ibid., p. 110.

9 F. I. Tiutchev, *Stikhotvoreniia, pisma* (Moscow: Gos. izd. khudozhestvennoi literatury, 1957), pp. 437, 571.

10 A. Fon-Tal, "Iz vospominanii Evgeniia Ivanovicha Lamanskago (1840–1890 gg.)" *Russkaia starina* (January 1915): 79; [V. V. Stasov], "Tsenzura v tsarstvovanie Imperatora Nikolaia I," *Russkaia starina* (June 1903): 669–71.

11 Ryzhov, "Aleksandr Ivanovich Krasovskii," pp. 116–17.

12 Ibid., p. 112.

13 Kh. Emmausskii, "Iz vospominanii varshavskogo tsenzora," *Novaia zhizn'* (January 1914): 130–31.

14 Ryzhov, "Aleksandr Ivanovich Krasovskii," pp. 122, 115.

15 Ibid., p. 121.

16 Ibid., p. 122.

17 Sidney Monas, "Šiškov, Bulgarin, and the Russian Censorship," in *Russian Thought and Politics*, Harvard Slavic Studies, 4 (Cambridge: Harvard University Press, 1957), p. 139.

18 Ryzhov, "Aleksandr Ivanovich Krasovskii," p. 122.

19 "Iz bumag kniazia V. F. Odoevskogo," *Russkii arkhiv* 12, no. 2 (1874): col. 25.

20 Aizenshtok, "Frantsuzskie pisateli," p. 796.

21 Ibid., p. 802; Fedorov, "Genrikh Geine," p. 658; Polianskaia, "Obzor fonda," p. 194; Fedorov, "Geinrikh Geine," p. 646. On Prussian censorship of Heine, Gutzkow, and other authors, see H. H. Houben, *Verbotene Literatur von der klassischen Zeit bis zur Gegenwart*, 2d ed., 2 vols. (Dessau: Karl Rauch Verlag, 1925; Bremen: Karl Schünemann Verlag, 1928).

22 Aizenshtok, "Frantsuzskie pisateli," p. 782. For discussion of Diderot and the Soviets,

see Maurice Friedberg, *A Decade of Euphoria: Western Literature in Post-Stalin Russia, 1954-64* (Bloomington: Indiana University Press, 1977), pp. 139-40.

23 Aizenshtok, "Frantsuzskie pisateli," p. 776.

24 Polianskaia, "Obzor fonda," p. 86; Aizenshtok, "Frantsuzskie pisateli," p. 821.

25 Fedorov, "Genrikh Geine," pp. 657, 656; Aizenshtok, "Frantsuzskie pisateli," p. 821.

26 Fedorov, "Genrikh Geine," p. 643.

27 Ibid., p. 659. On the plan for producing uniformity of thought, see Maurice Friedberg, *Russian Classics in Soviet Jackets* (New York: Columbia University Press, 1962), pp. 2-3.

28 Polianskaia, "Obzor fonda," p. 91.

29 Reiser, "Gete," p. 929.

30 Fedorov, "Genrikh Geine," p. 642.

31 Ibid., pp. 645, 649-50; Aizenshtok, "Frantsuzskie pisateli," p. 826.

32 Polianskaia, "Obzor fonda," pp. 76, 96; Fedorov, "Genrikh Geine," p. 639; Aizenshtok, "Frantsuzskie pisateli," p. 788.

33 Polianskaia, "Obzor fonda," pp. 87, 103; Aizenshtok, "Frantsuzskie pisateli," pp. 814-15.

34 Polianskaia, "Obzor fonda," pp. 105, 74, 75; Aizenshtok, "Frantsuzskie pisateli," p. 826.

35 Polianskaia, "Obzor fonda," p. 96.

36 Aizenshtok, "Frantsuzskie pisateli," pp. 813-14.

37 Ibid., p. 825; Reiser, "Gete," p. 929.

38 Polianskaia, "Obzor fonda," p. 78; Reiser, "Gete," pp. 932-34.

39 Polianskaia, "Obzor fonda," p. 88.

40 N. V. Zdobnov, "Novye tsenzurnye materialy o Lermontove (A. N. Maikov i I. A. Goncharov v roli tsenzorov sochinenii Lermontova)," *Krasnaia nov'*, nos. 10-11 (1939): 267-69. Lermontov's famous poem *Demon* is another interesting case: the internal censorship would not permit it, but the tsarist court had the poem published in Germany for import into Russia. I do not know whether this edition had to pass through the Foreign Censorship Committee on its way into the empire, or whether it was smuggled in.

41 Aizenshtok, "Frantsuzskie pisateli," pp. 826, 824.

42 Ibid., pp. 818-20, 826; Polianskaia, "Obzor fonda," pp. 98, 95.

43 Aizenshtok, "Frantsuzskie pisateli," p. 824.

3 THE COMMITTEE AND THE POET-CENSORS:
   THE TIUTCHEV YEARS

1 In addition to the sources cited for the earlier period, the following books and articles include censors' reports: K. V. Pigarev, *Zhizn' i tvorchestvo Tiutcheva* (Moscow: Izd. Akademii Nauk SSR, 1962); [L. I. Polianskaia], "Anatol Frans i tsarskaia tsenzura," *Krasnyi arkhiv* 6 (1934): 147-67; M. L. Lur'e and L. I. Polianskaia, "Kommunisticheskii manifest i tsarskaia tsenzura," *Istorik-Marksist* 66 (1938): 106-19.

2 Pigarev, *Zhizn' i tvorchestvo Tiutcheva*, pp. 158-59.

3 "Iz pisem F. I. Tiutcheva vo vremia Krymskoi voiny, 1854 god," *Russkii arkhiv* 37, no. 2 (1899): 274.

4 See Alfred Kerndl, "Studien über Heine in Russland, Teil II. Heine und Tjutcev," *Zeitschrift für slavische Philologie* 24 (1956): 284–337.

5 Jesse Zeldin, *Poems and Political Letters of F. I. Tyutchev* (Knoxville: University of Tennessee Press, 1973), pp. 196–214. The French original, "Lettre sur la censure en Russie," can be found in F. I. Tiutchev, *Polnoe sobranie sochinenii*, 6th ed. (Saint Petersburg: A. F. Marks, 1912), pp. 583–94.

6 Georgii Chulkov, *Letopis' zhizni i tvorchestva F. I. Tiutcheva* (Moscow: Academia, 1933), p. 126.

7 W. Bruce Lincoln, "Some Comments on the Cost of Living in Mid-Nineteenth Century St. Petersburg" (typewritten), p. 10.

8 Zlatkovskii, *Maikov*, 2d ed., p. 60.

9 "A. F. Aksakovoi," in F. I. Tiutchev, *Stikhotvoreniia, pis'ma* (Moscow: Gos. izd. khudozhestvennoi literatury, 1957), p. 486. Although Tiutchev himself attributed the translation to the writer Ivan Aksakov, his son-in-law, Chulkov and others claim that the translator was really F. I. Timiriazev (Chulkov, *Letopis'*, p. 231; Tiutchev, *Stikhotvoreniia, pis'ma*, p. 587).

10 A. V. Nikitenko, "F. I. Tiutchev," *Russkaia starina* (August 1873): unnumbered pages at end of issue; A. V. Nikitenko, *Dnevnik*, 3 vols. (Moscow: Gos. izd. khudozhestvennoi literatury, 1955), 2:27. Nikitenko's diary is a veritable goldmine of information about the operation of the imperial Russian censorship. An abridged translation of this diary is available in English: *The Diary of a Russian Censor: Aleksandr Nikitenko*, abridged, edited, and translated by Helen Saltz Jacobson (Amherst: University of Massachusetts Press, 1975).

11 Chulkov, *Letopis'*, p. 126.

12 See the Russian translation of Anna's diary: Anna Fedorovna Aksakova [Tiutcheva], *Pri dvore dvukh imperatorov*, 2 vols. (Moscow: Izd. M. i S. Sabashnikovyh, 1929), 2:178–81.

13 M. Briskman, "F. I. Tiutchev v komitete tsenzury inostrannoi," *Literaturnoe nasledstvo* 19–21 (1935): 565–78. Briskman maintains (page 566) that while Tiutchev did not personally write *all* of any single report, he certainly was the author of the concluding sections. Pigarev is not convinced of this, but concedes that whoever may actually have written the conclusions, they are immensely important because they characterize the work of the committee in this period (Pigarev, *Zhizn' i tvorchestvo Tiutcheva*, pp. 161–62). I shall assume that since the reports appear over Tiutchev's signature, they express his opinions, whether or not he actually wrote them. In addition to these four reports, a fragment of Tiutchev's 1871 report is included in an article by K. Pigarev, "F. I. Tiutchev o frantsuzskikh politicheskikh sobytiiakh 1870–1873 gg.," *Literaturnoe nasledstvo* 31–32 (1937): 774. The passage deals with anti-Russian sentiments in the German periodical press.

14 Pigarev, *Zhizn' i tvorchestvo Tiutcheva*, p. 164. For discussion of the transfer of censorship to the Ministry of Internal Affairs, see M. K. Lemke, *Epokha tsenzurnykh reform 1859–1865 gg.* (Saint Petersburg: "Gerol'd," 1904); and Charles Arthur Ruud, *Fighting Words: Imperial Censorship and the Russian Press, 1804–1906* (Toronto: University of Toronto Press, 1982).

15 For the 1858 report, see Briskman, "F. I. Tiutchev v komitete," pp. 568–69.

16 Pigarev, *Zhizn' i tvorchestvo Tiutcheva*, p. 162.

17 Briskman, "F. I. Tiutchev v komitete," p. 578.

18   Ibid., pp. 566–67.

19   Ibid., p. 568.

20   Zeldin, *Poems and Political Letters*, pp. 212, 213. For a history of Herzen's relations with the imperial government, see N. Ia. Eidel'man, *Gertsen protiv samoderzhaviia: Sekretnaia politicheskaia istoriia Rossii XVIII–XIX vekov i Vol'naia pechat'* (Moscow: Mysl', 1973). See also [I. Kovalev], "Gertsen i tsarskaia tsenzura (k 70-letiiu so dnia smerti)," *Krasnyi arkhiv* 98 (1940): 240–62, a selection of archival materials dealing with the imperial censorship's treatment of Herzen's publications dating from 1851 through 1911. Four documents reproduced in this article are of particular interest for this study: (1) instructions from Minister of Education Norov to Krasovskii in 1853 calling for special caution with regard to products of Herzen's London press (p. 244); (2) an April 1860 letter from Minister of Education Kovalevskii to V. A. Dolgorukov, chief of the Third Section, informing him that a box of books belonging to a Saint Petersburg bookseller and bearing the name of the Metropolitan of Saint Petersburg had just been examined at the Foreign Censorship Committee offices and had been found to contain issues of Herzen's journals *Kolokol* and *Poliarnaia zvezda* (North Star) (p. 246); (3) a report from Tiutchev dated March 1862 assuring his superiors that his staff was watching carefully for banned publications and would see that any unauthorized persons possessing such items were dealt with properly (p. 247); and (4) a 1907 report by Baron Kaul'bars, a junior censor at the committee in Saint Petersburg, on a German-language edition of Herzen's memoirs suggesting some excisions and comparing this edition with a 1906 Russian translation approved for circulation in the empire (p. 260).

21   "Lettres de Th. J. Tjutscheff à sa seconde epouse, nee baronne de Pfeffel," *Starina i novizna* 19 (1915): 182.

22   For the 1860 report, see Briskman, "F. I. Tiutchev v komitete," pp. 569–71.

23   Egorov, *Stranitsy*, 2:35.

24   For the 1863 report, see Briskman, "F. I. Tiutchev v komitete," pp. 571–74.

25   David Friedrich Strauss, *Das Leben Jesu, kritisch bearbeitet*, 2 vols. (Tübingen: Osiander, 1835–36); Ernest Renan, *La vie de Jésus* (Paris: Michel-Lévy Frères, 1863).

26   Briskman, "F. I. Tiutchev v komitete," p. 573.

27   For the 1865 report, see ibid., pp. 574–77.

28.   The particular book in question was Otto Flügel's *Der Materialismus vom Standpunkte der atomistisch-mechanischen Naturforschung* (Leipzig: Pernitzsch, 1865).

29   A. B. Dulk, *Jesus der Christ: Ein Stück für die Volksbühne* (Stuttgart: E. Ebner, 1865).

30   Nikitenko, *Dnevnik*, 2:554–55; 3:52.

31   Quoted in Chulkov, *Letopis'*, p. 179.

32   P. Kirillov, E. Pavlova, and I. Shakhovskoi, "Neizdannye pis'ma Tiutcheva i k Tiutchevu," *Literaturnoe nasledstvo* 19–21 (1935): 594–95.

33   *Muranovskii sbornik* (Muranovo: Izdanie Muzeia imeni poeta F. I. Tiutcheva v Muranove, 1928), p. 19; Tiutchev, *Stikhotvoreniia, pis'ma*, pp. 461–62.

34   Tiutchev, *Stikhotvoreniia, pis'ma*, p. 467; Pigarev, *Zhizn' i tvorchestvo Tiutcheva*, p. 168.

35   Chulkov, *Letopis'*, p. 198.

36   Pigarev, *Zhizn' i tvorchestvo Tiutcheva*, p. 161. Emphasis in original.

37   Ibid., pp. 167–68. Emphasis in original. The controversial biography was Arthur John Booth, *Robert Owen, the Founder of Socialism in England* (London: Trübner, 1869).

38   Egorov, *Stranitsy*, 2:59–60.

39 Pigarev, *Zhizn' i tvorchestvo Tiutcheva*, p. 161.
40 Chulkov, *Letopis'*, pp. 135–36.
41 Kirillov, "Neizdannye pis'ma," pp. 595–96.
42 "Lettres de Th. J. Tjutscheff," *Starina i novizna* 21 (1961): 175, 196.
43 Aizenshtok, "Frantsuzskie pisateli," pp. 844–45.
44 Ibid., pp. 798–99.
45 Pigarev, *Zhizn' i tvorchestvo Tiutcheva*, pp. 162–63.
46 See, for example, F. Fidler's comments on Maikov as a translator of German poetry into Russian (F. F. Fidler, "Literaturnye siluety IV. A. N. Maikov," *Novoe slovo* [June 1914]: 25). The literary influence of Heine and other German poets on Maikov is discussed briefly by N. Ammon in his article "Obshchii obzor poeticheskoi deiatel'nosti Maikova i evoliutsiia ego idealov," in V. Pokrovskii, *Apollon Nikolaevich Maikov: Ego zhizn' i sochineniia*, 2d ed. (Moscow: Tip. G. Lissnera i D. Sobko, 1911), pp. 59–60.
47 Fedorov, "Genrikh Geine," pp. 676–77.
48 Ibid., pp. 662–63.
49 Ibid., p. 664.
50 Ibid., p. 666.
51 Ibid., pp. 666–67.
52 Ibid., pp. 667–69.
53 Ibid., p. 670; Pigarev, *Zhizn' i tvorchestvo Tiutcheva*, p. 163.
54 Fedorov, "Genrikh Geine," pp. 670–71.
55 Polianskaia, "Obzor fonda," pp. 95–96.
56 Aizenshtok, "Frantsuzskie pisateli," pp. 788–89. Aizenshtok also devotes considerable attention to the handling of Russian translations and dramatizations of the novel by the internal censorship (ibid., pp. 790–91).
57 Alexander Vucinich, *Science in Russian Culture* (Stanford: Stanford University Press, 1970), 2:118–19. For a comprehensive discussion of Darwin and the Russian censorship, see L. R. Kharakhorkin, "Charl'z Darvin i tsarskaia tsenzury," *Trudy Instituta istorii estestvoznaniia i tekhniki* 31 (1960): 82–100.
58 Polianskaia, "Obzor fonda," pp. 89–90.
59 Lur'e, "'Kommunisticheskii manifest' i tsarskaia tsenzura," p. 106.

4 THE COMMITTEE AND THE POET-CENSORS
FROM TIUTCHEV TO MAIKOV

1 Zlatkovskii, *Maikov*, 2d ed., p. 84.
2 A. E. Egorov, *Stranitsy*, 1:102–3, 129–32.
3 Ibid., pp. 143–53.
4 Ibid., pp. 210–13.
5 Zlatkovskii, *Maikov*, 2d ed., pp. 20–21, 24.
6 According to the author of Maikov's obituary in *Pravitel'stvennyi vestnik*, the poet attained the rank of Full State Councillor in 1867 and the rank of Privy Councillor in 1888 (see V. Pokrovskii, *Apollon Nikolaevich Maikov. Ego zhizn' i sochineniia*, 2d ed. [Moscow: Tipografiia G. Lissnera i D. Sobko, 1911], p. 17). This author states that Maikov was named chairman of the committee in 1875, an event that Zlatkovskii maintains occurred on 26 July 1882 (Zlatkovskii, *Maikov*, 2d ed., p. 33). Since Zlatkovskii was a close associate of

Maikov's at the committee for many years, I am inclined to accept his date. Zlatkovskii also indicates that Maikov was appointed at the rank of collegial assessor (ibid., p. 38).

7   Zlatkovskii, *Maikov*, 2d ed., pp. 34–35, 17–18, 54–55; D. D. Iazykov, "Zhizn' i trudy A. N. Maikova," *Russkii vestnik* (December 1897): 249.

8   Zlatkovskii, *Maikov*, 2d ed., pp. 35–36, 38.

9   Ibid., pp. 82–83.

10   Egorov, *Stranitsy*, 1:146, 150–53.

11   A. Chumikov, "Moi tsenzurnye mytarstva. (Vospominaniia)," *Russkaia starina* (July–September 1899): 620–21.

12   Zlatkovskii, *Maikov*, 2d ed., p. 85, 87.

13   N. N. Beliavskii, "Stranichka iz vospominanii o A. N. Maikove i Ia. P. Polonskom," in *Sertum bibliologicum v chest' Prezidenta Russkogo bibliologicheskogo obshchestva Prof. A. I. Maleina* (Saint Petersburg: Gos. izd., 1922), pp. 264, 267; V. A. Alekseev, "A. N. Maikov (Iz dnevnika)," *Istoricheskii vestnik* (February 1914): 524.

14   N. Mardar'ev, "Nechto iz proshlogo (Iz vospominanii byvshego tsenzora)," *Golos minuvshego* (May–June 1916): 372.

15   Elena Andreevna Stackenschneider, *Dnevnik i zapiski (1854–1886)* (Moscow: Academia, 1934), pp. 314, 471–72.

16   Ibid., pp. 399, 435, 322, 23, 530; Egorov, *Stranitsy*, 2:63–64.

17   Mardar'ev, "Nechto iz proshlogo," p. 373. It is not clear exactly when Polonskii was appointed to the council, but it was sometime after 1895; see "Iakov Petrovich Polonskii [Nekrolog]," *Istoricheskii vestnik* 19, no. 11 (1898): 731.

18   Mardar'ev, "Nechto iz proshlogo," p. 372; Beliavskii, "Stranichka," pp. 266–67.

19   Beliavskii, "Stranichka," p. 266.

20   Ieronim Ieronimovich Iasinskii, *Roman moei zhizni* (Moscow: Gos. izd., 1926), pp. 209, 144–45.

21   V. S. Serova, *Serovy, Aleksandr Nikolaevich i Valentin Aleksandrovich. Vospominaniia* (Saint Petersburg: Shipovnik, 1914), p. 25; Egorov, *Stranitsy*, 1:117.

22   Egorov, *Stranitsy*, 1:148; Iasinskii, *Roman moei zhizni*, pp. 211–13. Pushkin is quoted in Friedberg, *A Decade of Euphoria*, p. 86. Regarding Polonskii's title of "general": although there was no rank of general in the Russian civil service, the government occasionally broke its own rules and gave a civil servant that rank. Sometimes a person of equivalent civil rank simply called himself a general. For a discussion of ranks and titles, see L. E. Shlepev, *Otmennye istorei chiny, zvaniia, i tituly v rossiiskoi imperii* (Leningrad: Nauka, 1977).

23   Polianskaia, "Obzor fonda," p. 93; Aizenshtok, "Frantsuzskie pisateli," pp. 779–80.

24   Polianskaia, "Obzor fonda," pp. 89, 96; Friedberg, *A Decade of Euphoria*, p. 165.

25   "Pisma K. P. Pobedonostseva k E. M. Feoktistovu," *Literaturnoe nasledstvo* 22–24 (1935): 518–19. See also Aizenshtok's discussion of *Germinal* (Aizenshtok, "Frantsuzskie pisateli," pp. 836–37).

26   Polianskaia, "Obzor fonda," pp. 83, 91, 74.

27   Ibid., p. 88.

28   See Edith W. Clowes's forthcoming book, *The Revolution of Moral Consciousness: The Impact of Friedrich Nietzsche upon Russian Literature and Society, 1890–1914* (in press), her dissertation ("A philosophy 'For all and None': The Early Reception of Friedrich Nietzsche's Thought in Russian Literature, 1892–1912," Yale University, 1981), and

her article, "Friedrich Nietzsche and Russian Censorship," *Germano-Slavica* 4, no. 3 (1983): 135–42; Ann M. Lane, "Nietzsche in Russia 1892–1917" (Ph.D. dissertation, University of Wisconsin, 1976); and a collection of essays edited by Bernice Glatzer Rosenthal on Nietzsche in Russia (forthcoming).

29 Polianskaia, "Obzor fonda," pp. 104, 90, 89.

30 Ibid., pp. 89, 91.

31 Aizenshtok, "Frantsuzskie pisateli," pp. 848–49; Polianskaia, "Obzor fonda," p. 88.

32 Aizenshtok, "Frantsuzskie pisateli," pp. 849–50.

33 Ibid., p. 830; [L. I. Polianskaia], "Anatol Frans i tsarskaia tsenzura," *Krasnyi arkhiv* 6 (1934): 151–54; Polianskaia, "Obzor fonda," p. 108.

34 Polianskaia, "Obzor fonda," pp. 78–79. For a comprehensive review of reports on various editions of Marx's works, see also pp. 80–82. For a discussion in English of the reception of *Kapital* in Russia, see Albert Resis, "*Das Kapital* Comes to Russia," *Slavic Review* 29 (1970): 219–37.

35 Zlatkovskii, *Maikov*, 2d ed., p. 61.

36 Egorov, *Stranitsy*, 1:116–17.

37 Zlatkovskii, *Maikov*, 2d ed., pp. 85–87.

38 S. Umanets, "Iz vospominanii ob A. N. Maikove," *Istoricheskii vestnik* (May 1897): 467–68.

39 Zlatkovskii, *Maikov*, 2d ed., p. 88.

40 Egorov, *Stranitsy*, 1:145–46.

41 Chulkov, *Letopis'*, pp. 157–58; Zlatkovskii, *Maikov*, 2d ed., pp. 88, 92–96; Tiutchev, *Stikhotvoreniia, pis'ma*, p. 448.

42 Zlatkovskii, *Maikov*, 2d ed., pp. 87–88, 100–102.

43 Count A. Golenishchev-Kutuzov, "Apollon Nikolaevich Maikov," *Zhurnal Ministerstva narodnogo prosveshcheniia* (April 1897): 50–51; Mardar'ev, "Nechto iz proshlogo," p. 373.

5 PATTERNS OF BANNING

1 Russia, Glavnoe upravlenie po delam pechati, *Alfavitnyi katalog sochineniiam na frantsuzskom, nemetskom i angliiskom iazykakh, zapreshchennym inostrannoiu tsenzuroiu ili dozvolennym k obrashcheniiu s iskliucheniem nekotorykh mest, s 1856 po 1 iiulia 1869 goda* (Saint Petersburg: Tip. Ministerstva vnutrennykh del, 1870); *Katalog rassmotrennykh inostrannoiu tsenzuroiu sochinenii, zapreshchennykh i dozvolennykh s iskliucheniiami, s 1-go iiulia 1871 g. po 1-e ianvaria 1897 g.* (Saint Petersburg: Tip. Ministerstva vnutrennykh del, 1898).

2 Polianskaia, "Obzor fonda," p. 67.

3 Russia, Tsentral'nyi komitet tsenzury inostrannoi, *Alfavitnyi spisok sochineniiam, rassmotrennykh inostrannoiu tsenzuroiu* (Saint Petersburg: n.p., for the years specified).

4 Imperatorskaia publichnaia biblioteka, *Katalog inostrannykh pechatnykh knig priobretennykh bibliotekoiu* (Saint Petersburg: Tip. V. A. Rogal'skogo, for the years specified).

5 In his annual reports Tiutchev included some statistics on imported and banned publications. Unfortunately I was unable to use these figures to supplement the monthly list because his method of counting was not clear to me. I preferred to use only the monthly list, where I could rely on my own counting.

6   Since different sampling fractions were used for the two samples, it was necessary to multiply ("weight") each by the inverse of its sampling fraction (permitted was multiplied by 50 and banned multiplied by 2.5). For example, in the category of belles lettres there were 309 items in the sample of permitted publications; mutliplying by 50, the estimated number of permitted publications in the category is 15,450. There were 526 items classified as belles lettres in the sample of banned publications; multiplying by 2.5, the estimated number of banned publications in the category is 1,315. Thus the combined estimated total for belles lettres is 16,765, approximately 23.7 percent of all imported publications.

7   [V. V. Stasov], "Tsenzura v tsarstvovanii Imperatora Nikolaia I," *Russkaia starina* (August 1903): 407–8, 412–13; Egorov, *Stranitsy*, 2:8.

8   One limitation of the data becomes apparent here. In order to determine the percentage of publications banned one must run tabulations across the two samples of banned and permitted publications and, as is evident from table 5-3, a few of the resulting figures are somewhat unreliable; the standard deviations indicated varying margins of error in the figures for different categories. Belles lettres, pure science, and arts have the widest margins of error. For instance, the estimate of percentage banned for belles lettres was 7.8, but after adding and subtracting the standard deviation of 3.6, the percentage can range from 4.2 to 11.4. All the other standard deviations in tables 5-3 and 5-4 are small and would not substantially affect the rank ordering of the categories.

9   In considering these figures, new problems are added to those mentioned above. Some degree of reliability is lost because when only those works published between 1856 and 1894 (the reigns of Alexander II and III) are considered, the number of cases is reduced, thus putting a greater burden on the samples. In fact, because no data on permitted publications was available prior to 1864, the first eight years of Alexander II's reign had to be eliminated from the comparison, thus reducing the number of cases in the samples still further.

10   Daniel Balmuth's statistics on the censorship of foreign works during the second half of the nineteenth century support this conclusion. They also confirm my finding that there was a dramatic increase in imported publications—from nearly 4 million volumes in 1866 to nearly 30 million in 1904—and that the censorship did not expand to keep up with this increase (Daniel Balmuth, *Censorship in Russia, 1865–1905* [Washington, D.C.: University Press of America, 1979], pp. 145–47).

6   APPLYING THE "CAVIAR": RESPECT
     FOR ROYALTY AND THE SOCIAL ORDER

1   Isaiah Berlin, "Introduction," in Marc Raeff, *Russian Intellectual History: An Anthology* (New York: Harcourt, Brace & World, 1966), p. 9.

2   The 40 percent sample of banned German works discussed in chapter 5 includes 791 entries permitted with excisions. Of these, 373 passages, or 47 percent, were obtained; this is 18.9 percent of the estimated total number of entries permitted with excisions.

3   D. S. Mirsky, *A History of Russian Literature From Its Beginnings to 1900*, ed. Francis J. Whitfield (New York: Vintage Books, 1958), p. 71.

4   Dmytro Chyzhevs'kyi, *Russian Intellectual History*, trans. John C. Osborne, ed. Martin P. Rice (Ann Arbor, Michigan: Ardis, 1978), pp. 141–42.

5   Mirsky, *History*, p. 46; Raeff, *Russian Intellectual History*, pp. 114, 157.

6   Nicholas V. Riasanovsky, *A History of Russia* (New York: Oxford University Press, 1963), pp. 316–17.

7   Chyzhevs'kyi, *Russian Intellectual History*, p. 185.

8   Nestor Kotliarevskii, "Inostrannaia kniga v rukakh molodogo cheloveka 1855–1861 godov," *Vestnik evropy* (April 1914): 173, 176.

9   Franco Venturi, *Roots of Revolution: A History of the Populist and Socialist Movements in Nineteenth Century Russia*, translated from the Italian by Francis Haskell (New York: Alfred A. Knopf, 1960), pp. 323–24.

10 Isaiah Berlin, *Russian Thinkers* (New York: Viking Press, 1978), p. 136.

11 Bolebrukh, *Peredovaia*, p. 38.

12 Mirsky, *History*, p. 224; see also pp. 88, 91, 99, 117, 118, 119, 121, 132–33, 146, 147, 178, 194, 197, 218.

13 Ernst Hellmuth, "Das russische Kaiserhaus," *Bibliothek der Unterhaltung und des Wissens*, no. 3 (1882): 235.

14 Ibid., pp. 236, 239, 241, 243.

15 Ibid., pp. 244–48.

16 An example is Karl Gottfried Naumann, *Genealogische Geschichte der europäischen Staaten als Hülfsmittel bei historischen Studien und zum Gebrauch höherer Lehranstalten* (Jena: Friedrich Mauke, 1855).

17 Ernst Hellmuth, *Kaiser Joseph II, Ein Buch für's Volk* (Prague: J. L. Kober, 1862), pp. 151–52; Wolfgang Menzel, *Allgemeine Weltgeschichte von Anfang bis jetzt*, 12 vols. (Stuttgart: Verlag von Adolph Krabbe, 1863), 9:154.

18 A. Oskar Klaussmann, *Die Hofdame der Kaiserin, Bibliothek der Unterhaltung und des Wissens*, no. 7 (1894): 32; Moritz Spiess and Bruno Berlet, eds., *Weltgeschichte in Biographien für höhere Schulen: Zweiter Kursus, für einen injährigen Unterricht in einer mittleren Klasse berechnet* (Bucholz: Verlag der Adlerschen Buchhandlung [Ludwig Nonne], 1857), p. 273.

19 C. G. Weisflog, *Fürstenbilder, historische Skizzen und Züge von Seelenadel, Hochherzigkeit, Grösse, Tapferkeit und Herzensgüte europäischer, besonders deutscher Fürsten und Fürstinnen: Zur Stärkung der Liebe und Treue jugendlicher Herzen für Fürstenhaus und Vaterland* (Weimar: B. F. Voight, 1858), pp. 611–12.

20 Ernst Wiehr, *Napoleon und Bernadotte im Herbstfeldzuge 1813* (Berlin: Siegfried Cronbach, 1893), first unnumbered page at back of book.

21 Carl Wernicke, *Die Geschichte der Welt*, 6th ed., 6 vols. (Berlin: Paetel, 1881), 5:118.

22 Gustav Felix, *Moskau 1812: Schauspiel in fünf Aufzügen* (Berlin: L. Steinthal's Buchhandlung, 1886), p. 82; "Das Attentat auf König Wilhelm I von Preussen," *Der neue Pitaval, Eine Sammlung der interessantesten Criminalgeschichten*, 3d ser., 32, no. 8 (1862): 14.

23 *Russkii biograficheskii slovar'*, s.v. "Pavel I," by Evgenii Shumigorskii; Heinrich von Sybel, "Die Ermordung des Kaisers Paul I von Russland am 23. März 1801," *Historische Zeitschrift* 13 (1860): 133.

24 Johannes Scherr, *Blücher: Seine Zeit und sein Leben*, 3 vols. (Leipzig: Otto Wigand, 1862), 1:64; Heinrich von Sybel, *Geschichte der Revolutionszeit von 1789 bis 1793*, 3 vols., 2d ed. (Düsseldorf: Julius Buddeus, 1859), 2:152.

25 Eduard Reich, *Politik der Bevölkerung und Gesellschaft* (Leipzig: August Dieckmann, 1896), p. 156.

26 Otto Henne am Rhyn, *Die Frau in der Kulturgeschichte* (Berlin: Allgemeiner Verein für Deutsche Literatur, 1892), p. 333; Oskar Jäger, *Weltgeschichte*, 4 vols. (Bielefeld: Velhagen & Klasing, 1887–89), 3:565; Christoph Hoffmann, *Fortschritt und Rückschritt in den zwei letzten Jahrhunderten geschichtlich nachgewiesen, oder Geschichte des Abfalls*, 3 vols. (Stuttgart: J. F. Steinkopf, 1864–68), 2:26.

27 Karl von Rotteck, *Allgemeine Geschichte vom Anfang der historischen Kenntniss bis auf unsere Zeiten: Für denkende Geschichtsfreunde bearbeitet*, 21st ed., 11 vols. (Braunschweig: George Westermann, 1861), 8:27; Sybel, *Geschichte der Revolutionszeit*, 2:152.

28 Ludwig Siegrist, *Leben, Wirken und Ende weiland Seiner Excellenz der Oberfürstlich Winkelkram'schen Generals der Infanterie Freiherrn Leberich vom Knopf: Aus dem Nachlass eines Offiziers . . .* , 2d ed. (Darmstadt: Eduard Zernin, 1877), p. 47; Wanda von Dunajew, *Der Roman einer tugendhaften Frau: Ein Gegenstück zur 'geschiedenen Frau' von Sacher-Masoch* (Prague: Aktien-Gesellschaft Bohemia, 1873), p. 52. For more information on Sacher-Masoch and Wanda von Dunajew, who wrote under this pseudonym but was in fact Sacher-Masoch's wife, see Marianna Tax Choldin, "German Writers and Tsarist Censorship," *Germano-Slavica* 4, no. 3 (1983): 13–31. Many of the German writers of belles-lettres mentioned in Chapters 6 and 7 are discussed in this article.

29 Johann Heinrich Schwicker, *Die Letzten Regierungsjahre der Kaiserin-Königin Maria Theresia (1763–1870)*, 2 vols. (Vienna: Karl Gronemeyer, 1871), 2:9; Johannes Scherr, *Allgemeine Geschichte der Literatur*, 3d ed., 2 vols. (Stuttgart: Carl Conradi, 1869), 2:391; Constantin Frantz, *Die Weltpolitik unter besonderer Bezugnahme auf Deutschland* (Chemnitz: Ernst Schmeitzner, 1882), p. 126.

30 Ludmilla Assing, *Briefwechsel zwischen Varnhagen von Ense und Oelsner nebst Briefen von Rahel*, 3 vols. (Stuttgart: A. Kröner, 1865), 1:95; Heinrich von Sybel, "Graf Joseph de Maistre," *Historische Zeitschrift* (1859): 175; Wolfgang Menzel, *Geschichte der Deutschen bis auf die neuesten Tage*, 6th ed., 3 vols. (Stuttgart: A. Kröner, 1872), 3:102; J. F. Neigebaur, *Die Heirath des Markgrafen Carl von Brandenburg mit der Markgräfin Catharina von Balbiano* (Breslau: Johann Urban Kern, 1856), p. 156.

31 *Schulthess' europäischer Geschichtskalender* 21 (1880): 468–69; F. A. Pischon, *Denkmäler der deutschen Sprache von Haller bis jetzt*, 6 vols. (Berlin: Duncker und Humblot, 1838–51), 3, pt. 1, 254.

32 *Brockhaus' Conversations-Lexikon*, 13th ed., s.v. "Nikolaus, Grossfurst von Russland"; "Kaiser Nikolaus und Kaiser Alexander," *Der Kulturkämpfer Zeitschrift für öffentliche Angelegenheiten* (15 June 1880): 21; Adolf Ebeling, *Napoleon III und sein Hof. Denkwürdigkeiten, Erlebnisse und Erinnerungen aus der Zeit des zweiten französischen Kaiserreiches 1851–1870*, 2d ed. (Cologne: Albert Ahn, 1892), pp. 315–16.

33 Ivan Holovackij, *Russisches Lesebuch: Poetischer Teil* (Vienna: n.p., 1850), pp. 165–70; Otto Fock, *Schleswig-Holsteinische Erinnerungen besonders aus den Jahren 1848–1851* (Leipzig: Veit, 1863), p. 50.

34 August, Graf von Platen-Hallermünde, *Platens Werke*, 2 vols. (Leipzig: Bibliographisches Institut, 1895), 1:254, 293–318; Karl von Rotteck, *Allgemeine Weltgeschichte für alle Stände von den frühesten Zeiten bis zum Jahr 1860*, 7th ed., 6 vols. (Stuttgart: Rieger, 1861), 6:635; Menzel, *Geschichte der Deutschen*, p. 609.

35 J. N. von Ringseis, *Erinnerungen des Dr. Johann Nepomuk v. Ringseis*, gesammelt . . . von Emilie Ringseis, 4 vols. (Regensburg: J. Habbel, 1891), 4:36; Maximilian Perty, *Der jetzige Spiritualismus und verwandte Erfahrungen der Vergangenheit und*

Gegenwart (Leipzig: Winter, 1877), pp. 212–19.

36 Hans Marschall, "Am Hofe des Kaisers Nikolaus: Nach den Denkwürdigkeiten eines Diplomaten," *Bibliothek der Unterhaltung und des Wissens*, no. 3 (1888): 198–99; Thomas Gaspey, *Englisches Conversations-Lesebuch für die mittleren und unteren Klassen* (Heidelberg: Julius Groos, 1856), p. 23.

37 Wiehr, *Napoleon*, back cover; Georg Büchmann, *Geflügelte Worte: Citatenschatz des deutschen Volkes*, 18th ed. (Berlin: Haude und Spener, 1895), p. 419.

38 Raeff, *Russian Intellectual History*, pp. 6, 9–10; Kotliarevskii, "Inostrannaia," p. 168.

39 Venturi, *Roots*, p. 475.

40 Ibid., p. 81; Kotliarevskii, "Inostrannaia," p. 162.

41 Venturi, *Roots*, p. 306.

42 Ibid., pp. 480, 328.

43 Ibid., p. 133; Kotliarevskii, "Inostrannaia," pp. 173, 181–83, 177.

44 Chyzhevs'kyi, *Russian Intellectual History*, p. 231; Venturi, *Roots*, pp. 356, 283. There is an extensive Soviet literature on the revolutionary movement, containing much information about the revolutionaries' use of forbidden Western works. Further examination of this literature is beyond the scope of this study, but one might use the following two excellent reference works as a starting point for research on this subject: *Deiateli revoliutsionnogo dvizheniia v Rossii; Bio-bibliograficheskii slovar'. Ot predshestvennikov dekabristov do padeniia tsarizma*, 5 vols. (Moscow: [Vsesoiuznoe obshchestvo politicheskikh katorzhan i ssyl'no-poselentsev], 1927–34); and *Istorria SSSR; Ukazatel' sovetskoi literatury za 1917–1952 gg.*, 2 vols. and 2 supplements (Moscow: Akademiia nauk SSSR, 1956–58).

45 Bolebrukh, *Peredovaia*, p. 11; Venturi, *Roots*, p. 344.

46 J. L. Hoffmann, *Lucian der Satiriker im Hinblick auf Glauben und Leben der Gegenwart* (Nuremberg: Bauer und Raspe, 1856), p. 2; Anton Philippe von Segesser, *Sammlung kleiner Schriften*, 3 vols. (Bern: K. J. Wyss, 1877), 1:76; J. Neumark, *Die Revolution in China in ihrer Entstehung, ihrer politischen und religiösen Bedeutung und ihrem bisherigen Verlauf, nebst Darstellung des auf christlicher Grundlage beruhenden Religions-systems der Insurgenten* (Berlin: Heinrich Schindler, 1857), p. 19.

47 Cajus Möller, *Geschichte Schleswig-Holsteins, von der ältesten Zeit bis auf die Gegenwart: Dem deutschen Volk erzählt* (Hannover: Carl Rümpler, 1865), p. 25; "Die Gründung des englischen Reichs in Indien," *Historisches Taschenbuch*, 3d ser., 7 (1856): 48; Karl Friedrich Neumann, *Geschichte des englischen Reiches in Asien*, 2 vols. (Leipzig: F. A. Brockhaus, 1857), 1:315.

48 *Schulthess' europäischer Geschichtskalender* 19 (1878): 451; Ludwig Stacke, *Erzählungen aus der neuesten Geschichte (1815–1881)*, 5th ed. (Oldenburg: Gerhard Stalling, 1886), p. 581; "Die Gründung des englischen Reichs in Indien," p. 5.

49 *Der Salon für Literatur, Kunst und Gesellschaft* 8 (n.d.): 237; Johannes Scherr, *Neues Historienbuch*, 2d ed. (Leipzig: Otto Wigand, 1884), pp. 9–60; Wilhelm Roscher, *Politik: Geschichtliche Naturlehre der Monarchie, Aristokratie und Demokratie* (Stuttgart: Cotta, 1892), p. 200.

50 The story is by A. Oskar Haussmann, published in *Bibliothek der Unterhaltung und des Wissens*, no. 7 (1892), p. 14.

51 *Vielliebchen: Historisch-romantisches Taschenbuch*, n.s. 7 (1856): 13.

52 "Nihilismus und Nihilisten," *Der Kulturkämpfer* (15 December 1880): 15;

Schulthess' europäischer Geschichtskalender 21 (1880): 593.

53 "Das unterirdische Russland," *Der Kulturkämpfer*, no. 6 (1882): 28; *Schulthess' europäischer Geschichtskalender* 23 (1882): 454; A. Krauss, *Die Psychologie des Verbrechens: Ein Beitrag zur Erfahrungsseelenkunde* (Tübingen: Laupp, 1884), p. 341.

54 Ludwig Stacke, *Erzählungen*, pp. 577–82; A. D. Klaussmann, "Politische Geheimpolizei," *Bibliothek der Unterhaltung und des Wissens*, no. 1 (1890): 220; Otto Funcke, *Der Wandel vor Gott: Dargelegt nach den Fusstapfen des Patriarchen Joseph* (Bremen: Müller, 1890), p. 256; Erwin Bauer, *Caveat populas! (Deutsches Volk, sei auf der Hut!) Wider den "neuen Kurs"* (Leipzig: Reinhold Werther, 1892), p. 55.

55 *Schulthess' europäischer Geschichtskalender*, n.s. 8 (1892): 377; Hans Scharwerker, "Aus der Werkstatt der Anarchisten: Kriminalistische Skizze." *Bibliothek der Unterhaltung und des Wissens*, no. 10 (1894): 175–200.

56 Carl Ludwig Michelet, *Eine italienische Reise in Briefen: Dem Freunde der Natur, der Kunst und des Alterthums gewidmet* (Berlin: Heinrich Schindler, 1856), p. 175; Johann Kaspar Bluntschli, *Bluntschli's Staatswörterbuch*, 2d ed., 3 vols. (Leipzig: Expedition des Staatswörterbuches, 1875–76), 3: 62–63.

57 Hermann Bahr, *Die neuen Menschen: Ein Schauspiel* (Zürich: Verlags-Magazin, 1887), p. 56; J. Retcliffe, *Von Berlin nach Königsgrätz, historischer Roman* (Leipzig: Julius Häfele, 1867), p. 68.

58 Georg Brandes, *Menschen und Werke: Essays* 2d ed. (Frankfurt am Main: Rütten & Loening, 1895), p. 329. See Georg Brandes, *Friedrich Nietzsche*, translated from the Danish by A. G. Chater (London: William Heinemann, 1914), p. 98; "Iakov Petrovich Polonskii (Nekrolog)," *Istoricheskii vestnik* 19, no. 11 (1898): 730.

59 Karl Gutzkow, *Säkularbilder*, in *Gesammelte Werke von Karl Gutzkow*, 12 vols. (Frankfurt am Main: Literarische Anstalt, 1846), 10:301, 303, 305.

60 Karl Gutzkow, *Wiener Eindrücke: 1845*, in *Gesammelte Werke von Karl Gutzkow*, 3:299, 319–20.

61 L. Mühlbach, *Kaiser Joseph und Maria Theresia*, 4 vols. (Berlin: Otto Janke, 1856), 3:90–132.

62 Heinrich Berghaus, *Was man von der Erde weiss: Ein Lesebuch zur Selbstbelehrung für die Gebildeten aller Stände*, 4 vols. (Berlin: Hasselberg, 1856–58), 2:225; Johannes Scherr, *Dichterkönige* (Leipzig: Verlag von Otto Wigand, 1855), pp. 469–70, 487–90, 513–15; Alexander von Reinholdt, *Geschichte der russischen Literatur von ihren Anfängen bis auf die neueste Zeit* (Leipzig: Wilhelm Friedrich, 1886), p. 672.

63 *Meyers Konversations-Lexikon*, 34th ed., s.v. "Herzen, Alexander"; Marschall, "Am Hofe des Kaisers Nikolaus," p. 195.

64 Karl Friedrich Neumann, *Geschichte des englisch-chinesischen Krieges*, 2d ed. (Leipzig: Teubner, 1855), p. 356.

7 APPLYING THE "CAVIAR": DEFENDING COUNTRY,
RELIGION AND MORALS

1 Chyzhevs'kyi, *Russian Intellectual History*, pp. 138–40.

2 Raeff, *Russian Intellectual History*, p. 258; Chyzhevs'kyi, *Russian Intellectual History*, p. 138.

3 Hans Rogger, *National Consciousness in Eighteenth-Century Russia* (Cambridge,

Mass.: Harvard University Press, 1960), pp. 196, 254.

4   Heinrich Berghaus, *Was man von der Erde weiss: Ein Lesebuch zur Selbstbelehrung für die Gebildeten aller Stände*, 4 vols. (Berlin: Hasselberg, 1856–58), 2:245; Hermann Adalbert Daniel, *Handbuch der Geographie*, 6th ed., 4 vols. (Leipzig: Reisland, 1895), 2:1005–7; Carl Endemann, *Staatslehre und Volkswirtschaft auf höheren Schulen: Praktische Anleitung zu politischen und wirtschaftlichen Belehrungen im historisch-geographischen Unterricht* (Bonn: Friedrich Cohen, 1895), pp. 151–52.

5   Gustav Zeiss, *Lehrbuch der allgemeinen Geschichte vom Standpunkte der Kultur für die oberen Klassen der Gymnasien*, 3 vols. (Weimar: Hermann Böhlau, 1856), 3:294.

6   Menzel, *Geschichte der Deutschen*, p. 102; Neigebaur, *Die Heirath*, p. 156.

7   *Historisches Taschenbuch*, 3d ser., 8 (1857): 460; Johann Gottlieb Kutzner, *Die Weltgeschichte in zusammenhängenden Einzelbildern nach schul- und volkspädagogischen Grundsätzen für Volkslehranstalten und zur Sebstbelehrung für Jedermann aus dem Volke*, 3 vols. (Berlin: Georg Reimer, 1859), 3:181; Ernst Moritz Arndt, *Meine Wanderungen und Wandelungen mit dem Reichsfreiherrn Heinrich Karl Friedrich vom Stein* (Leipzig: Philipp Reclam, 1896), pp. 24–25.

8   Georg Weber, *Lehrbuch der Weltgeschichte mit Rücksicht auf Cultur, Literatur und Religionswesen, und einem Abriss der deutschen Literaturgeschichte als Anhang*, 11th ed., 2 vols. (Leipzig: Wilhelm Engelmann, 1865), 2:591; Hellmuth, "Das russische Kaiserhaus," p. 246.

9   Alexandre Dumas, *Reise im Kaukasas, 1858–1859*, nach dem französischen Manuscripte von Dr. G. F. W. Rödiger, 4 vols. (Pest: Hartleben, 1859), 1:53–54.

10   Friedrich Wilhelm Ghillany, *Europäische Chronik von 1492 bis Ende Dezember 1876 . . . Ein Handbuch für Freunde der Politik und Geschichte*, 4 vols. (Leipzig: Otto Wigand, 1878), 4:76.

11   *Schulthess' europäischer Geschichtskalender*, n.s., 5 (1889): 394. The instructions for excision indicate lines 5–9 from the top of the page, but since those lines contain nothing of interest and lines 5–9 from the bottom consist of the remarks quoted, it is reasonable to assume an error. I have noted a few other similar errors, understandable in such a lengthy catalog that was probably copied at least once, by hand, from the monthly lists.

12   Paul Stettiner, *Aus der Geschichte der Albertina (1544–1894)* (Königsberg: Hartung, 1894), title page.

13   Robert Eduard Prutz, *Zehn Jahre: Geschichte der neuesten Zeit, 1840–1850*, 2 vols. (Leipzig: J. J. Weber, 1850–56), 1:88; Christian Ney, *Sammlung leicht ausführbarer Theater-stücke ernsten und launigen Inhalts, zum Gebrauche für katholische Gesellen-Vereine und andere gesellige Kreise* (Paderborn: Ferdinand Schöningh, 1886), p. 74; *Kladderadatsch in London: Humoristische Schilderungen über die Industrie-Ausstellung* (Berlin: A. Hofmann, 1851), p. 10.

14   Carl Scherzer, *Wanderungen durch die mittel-amerikanischen Freistaaten Nicaragua, Honduras und San Salvador: Mit Hinblick auf deutsche Emigration und deutschen Handel* (Braunschweig: George Westermann, 1857), p. 491; Louise von Gall, *Frauenleben: Novellen und Erzählungen*, 2 vols. (Leipzig: F. A. Brockhaus, 1856), 1:327; Emanuel Geibel, *Moderne Klassiker: Deutsche Literaturgeschichte der neuen Zeit in Biographien, Kritiken und Proben*, vol. 4 (Cassel: Ernst Balde, 1852), pp. 34–36.

15   Karl Eduard Poenitz, *Kriegerische und friedliche Träumereien über Vergangenes, Gegen-*

wärtiges und Zukünftiges (Leipzig: B. G. Teubner, 1857), p. 57; Otto Hartmann, *Der Antheil der Russen am Feldzug von 1799 in der Schweiz: Ein Beitrag zur Geschichte dieses Feldzugs und zur Kritik seiner Geschichtschreiber* (Zürich: A. Munk, 1892), p. 189; Julius von Wickede, *Vergleichende Characteristik der k.k. österreichischen, preussichen, englischen und französischen Landarmee* (Stuttgart: Eduard Hallberger, 1856), pp. 78, 161, 343.

16   von Rotteck, *Allgemeine Geschichte*, 9:197; Gustaf Björklund, *Friede und Abrüstung: Kritische Darstellung der aus allen civilisierten Ländern eingegangenen Antworten auf die schwedische Preisfrage* . . . (Berlin: Dümmler, 1895), p. 42.

17   Wilhelm Schulz-Bodmer, *Der Froschmäusekrieg zwischen den Pedanten des Glaubens und Unglaubens* (Leipzig: F. A. Brockhaus, 1856), p. 191; August Scheibe, "Ein russischer Apostel," *Bibliothek der Unterhaltung und des Wissens*, no. 7 (1893): 171–72.

18   Giacomo Margotti, *Die Siege der Kirche in dem ersten Jahrzehnte des Pontifikates Pius IX*, 2d ed. (Innsbruck: Wagner, 1860), p. 149; Alois Knöpfler, *Lehrbuch der Kirchengeschichte* (Freiburg im Breisgau: Herder, 1895), p. 675; Wolfgang Menzel, *Geschichte der Neuzeit*, 13 vols. (Stuttgart: Adolph Krabbe, 1866–71), 10, pt. 1, 401–2.

19   *Archiv für katholisches Kirchenrecht* 61 (1892): 200; Joseph Alexander, Freiherr von Helfert, *Aus Böhmen nach Italien, März 1848* (Frankfurt am Main: Hermann, 1862), p. 306; Helmina von Chezy, *Unvergessenes. Denkwürdigkeiten aus dem Leben von Helmina von Chezy, von ihr selbst erzählt*, 2 vols. (Leipzig: F. A. Brockhaus, 1858), 2: 201.

20   Menzel, *Geschichte der Neuzeit*, 1:405–6; *Deutscher Geschichtskalender: Sachlich geordnete Zusammenstellung der politisch wichtigsten Vorgänge im In- und Ausland* 8 (1892): 269–70.

21   Heinrich Zschokke, *Heinrich Zschokke's Aehrenlese* (Aarau: H. R. Sauerländer, 1844), p. 125; Isaac Baer Levinsohn, *Die Blutlüge (Efess Demim)*, translated from the Hebrew and with a preface and notes by Albert Katz (Berlin: Hugo Schildberger, 1892), p. 47.

22   Isaak da Costa, *Israel und die Völker: Eine Uebersicht der Juden bis auf unsere Zeit*, translated from Dutch by K. Mann (Frankfurt am Main: Heinrich Ludwig Brönner, 1855), pp. 419–20; Joseph Fiebermann, *Internationales Montefiore-Album* (Frankfurt am Main: Mahlau & Waldschmidt, 1888), p. 4; *Schulthess' europäischer Geschichtskalender* 23 (1882): 579.

23   H. Graetz, *Volkstümliche Geschichte der Juden*, 3 vols. (Leipzig: Oskar Leiner, 1888–89), 1:571–72; Michael Heller, "Anti-Semitism in Soviet Mythology," *Midstream* (January 1980): 11.

24   Eugen Schmitt, "Berühmte Kerker," *Bibliothek der Unterhaltung und des Wissens*, no. 12 (1888): 207; Kropotkin, *Memoirs*, pp. 143–44.

25   Wiehr, *Napoleon*, third unnumbered page at back of book.

26   Julius Vargha, *Die Abschaffung der Strafknechtschaft: Studien zur Strafrechtsreform*, 2 vols. (Graz: Leuschner & Lubensky, 1897), 2:378–82; M. Piehlmann, "Verbannt. Nach Berichten von Augenzeugen," *Bibliothek der Unterhaltung und des Wissens*, no. 3 (1891), p. 200.

27   Karl Emil Franzos, *Vom Don zur Donau: Neue Culturbilder aus "Halb-Asien"*, 2 vols. (Leipzig: Duncker & Humblot, 1878), 2:1–58; Karl Emil Franzos, *Vom Don zur Donau: Neue Culturbilder aus "Halb-Asien"*, 2d ed., 2 vols. (Stuttgart: Adolf Bonz, 1890), 2:54–55.

28   "Wo ist dein Schwur?" in A. Hungari, comp., *Katholischer Anekdoten-Schatz zur Unter-*

haltung und Belehrung für alle Stände, vol. 4: *Schule der Weisheit* (Frankfurt am Main: J. D. Sauerländer, 1857), pp. 503–6.

29 Franz Isodor Proschko, *Die Höllenmaschine: Historischer Roman aus der französischen Consular- und Kaiserzeit*, 2d ed., 2 vols. (Prague: J. L. Kober, 1858), 1:115.

30 *Kladderadatsch in London*, p. 36.

31 Kotliarevskii, "Inostrannaia," pp. 175, 178.

32 Moritz Müller, *Die Fortsetzung unseres Lebens im Jenseits* (Halle am Saale: Pfeffer, 1884), p. 96; Pischon, *Denkmäler der deutschen Sprache*, 3, pt. 2, 959–63; *Deutsche Warte: Umschau über das Leben und Schaffen der Gegenwart* 3 (1872): 449–61; N. G. Chernyshevskii, *Chto delat'?* (Moscow: Khudozhestvennaia literatura, 1969), p. 109.

33 J. G. Findel, *Die classische Periode der deutschen Nationalliteratur im achtzehnten Jahrhundert, in einer Reihe von Vorlesungen dargestellt* (Leipzig: Emil Graul, 1857), p. 121; Richard Gumprecht, *Modernes Seelenleben: Betrachtungen über die Tendenz des modernen Seelenlebens* (Leipzig: Wilhelm Friedrich, 1892), p. 85; *Deutsche Warte* 4 (1893): 148.

34 Karl Grün, *Fragmente aus Italien: Natur und Kunst* (Munich: Fleischmann, 1862), p. 123; A. Bastian, *Die Rechtsverhältnisse bei verschiedenen Völkern der Erde: Ein Beitrag zur vergleichenden Ethnologie* (Berlin: Georg Reimer, 1872), p. xlii.

35 Johannes Scherr, *Dämonen*, 2d ed. (Leipzig: Otto Wigand, 1878), pp. 151–52; Ferdinand Christian Baur, *Die christliche Kirche des Mittelalters in den Hauptmomenten ihrer Entwicklung* (Tübingen: Fues, 1861), pp. 396–97; Michelet, *Eine italienische Reise*, p. 224; Philipp Spiller, *Das Leben: Naturwissenschaftliche Entwickelung des organischen Seelen- und Geisteslebens* (Berlin: Stuhr, 1878), p. 153; Bastian, *Die Rechtsverhältnisse*, p. xlii.

36 Alfred Edmund Brehm, *Reiseskizzen aus Nord-Ost-Afrika oder den unter egyptischer Herrschaft stehenden Ländern Egypten, Nubien, Sennahr, Rosseeres und Korofahn, gesammelt auf seinen in den Jahren 1847 bis 1852 unternommenen Reisen*, 3 vols. (Jena: Friedrich Mauke, 1855), 2:2; Karl Gutzkow, *Fritz Ellrodt*, 3 vols. (Jena: Hermann Costenoble, 1872), 3:102; *Nach Constantinopel und Brussa: Ferien-Reise eines preussischen Juristen* (Berlin: F. Schneider, 1855), p. 363; Edgar Bauer, *Englische Freiheit* (Leipzig: Otto Wigand, 1857), p. 155.

37 Michelet, *Eine italienische Reise*, pp. 220–21; Friedrich Paulsen, *System der Ethik mit einem Umriss der Staats- und Gesellschaftslehre*, 2 pts. (Berlin: Wilhelm Hertz, 1889), 1:51–64; Johannes Scherr, *Allgemeine Geschichte der Literatur: Ein Handbuch*, 2d ed. (Stuttgart: Franck, 1861), p. 101.

38 Bastian, *Die Rechtsverhältnisse*, p. xlii; Wilhelm Kiesselbach, *Socialpolitische Studien* (Stuttgart: Cotta, 1862), p. 372; Ferdinand Siegmund, *Untergegangene Welten: Eine populäre Darstellung der Geschichte der Schöpfung und der Wunder der Vorwelt, nach den neuesten Forschungen der Wissenschaft bearbeitet* (Vienna: Hartleben, 1877), p. 76; Schulz-Bodmer, *Der Froschmäusekrieg*, p. 27.

39 Eduard Robinson, *Neuere Biblische Forschungen in Palästina und in den angränzenden Ländern: Tagebuch einer Reise im Jahre 1852* (Berlin: Georg Reimer, 1857), p. 340; David Friedrich Strauss, *Das Leben Jesu, kritisch bearbeitet*, 2 vols. (Tübingen: Osiander, 1835–36); Ernest Renan, *Vie de Jésus* (Paris: Michel-Lévy frères, 1863); C. Zeller, "Strauss und Renan," *Historische Zeitschrift* 12 (1864): 70–133; "Die Tübinger historische Schule," *Historische Zeitschrift* 4 (1860): 90–173; *Meyers Kleines Konversations-Lexikon*, 5th ed., s.v. "Jesus."

40   Hoffman, *Fortschritt*, p. 27; Karl von Hase, *Kirchengeschichte auf der Grundlage aka-demischer Vorlesungen*, 3 vols. (Leipzig: Breitkopf und Härtel, 1892), 3, pt. 2, 945; Lucian Herbert, *Erinnerungen an Leopold I. König der Belgier* (Leipzig: Friedr. Wilh. Grunow, 1866), p. 41.

41   Franz Hoffmann, *Franz von Baader, als Begründer der Philosophie der Zukunft: Sammlung der vom Jahre 1851 bis 1856 erschienenen Recensionen und literarischen Notizen über Franz von Baader's sämmtliche Werke* (Leipzig: Hermann Bethmann, 1856), p. 92; *Historisch-politische Blätter für das katholische Deutschland* 35 (1855): 924; Jean Baptiste Caussette, *Die Vernünftigkeit des Glaubens: Apologie des Christenthums und der katholischen Kirche* (Mainz: Franz Kirchheim, 1888), p. 453; Pischon, *Denkmäler der deutschen Sprachen*, p. 307.

42   Wilhelm Vischer, *Erinnerungen und Eindrücke aus Griechenland* (Basel: Schweighauser, 1857), p. 485; Ludwig Völter, *Das Heilige Land und das Land der israelitischen Wanderung: für Bibelfreunde geschildert* (Stuttgart: J. F. Steinkopf, 1855), p. 137; C. Sandreczki, *Reise von Smyrna bis Mosul: Mittheilungen aus dem Tagebuche von C. Sandreczki* (Stuttgart: J. F. Steinkopf, 1857), p. 103.

43   Ibid., p. 147; Caussette, *Die Vernünftigkeit*, pp. 502, 504, 506.

44   *Theologisches Handwörterbuch*, 2 vols. (Calw: Verlag der Vereinsbuchhandlung, 1891), 1:594; Johannes Hesse, *Die Missionsjahrhundert, Züge aus dem Missionsleben der Gegenwart, insbesondere zum Vorlesen in Missionsvereinen* (Calw: Verlag der Vereinsbuchhandlung, 1893), p. 11.

45   James Baker, *Die Türken in Europa*, authorized German edition, with an introduction, "Die orientalische Frage als Culturfrage," by Hermann Vanbery, 2d ed. (Stuttgart: Levy und Müller, 1879), p. xxxvi; *Astraea: Taschenbuch für Freimaurer* 20 (1859–60): 303; Egorov, *Stranitsy*, 2:21–22.

46   Sybel, *Graf Joseph de Maistre*, pp. 190, 189; Johannes Scherr, *Blätter im Winde* (Leipzig: Ernst Julius Günther, 1875), p. 39.

47   Oskar Ludwig Bernhard Wolff, *Poetischer Hausschatz des deutschen Volkes*, 16th ed. (Leipzig: Otto Wigand, 1853), p. 653; Hermann Joseph Aloys Körner, *Lebenskämpfe in der alten und neuen Welt: Eine Selbstbiographie* (New York: L. W. Schmidt, 1865), pp. 304–5.

48   Alexander Engel, *Das Recht auf Thorheit: Geschichten einer Schellenkappe* (Dresden: E. Pierson, 1894), pp. 237–38.

49   Julius von Wickede, *Die Rechte und Pflichten des Offiziers: Leitfaden für junge Männer, welche sich dem Offizierstande gewidmet haben oder noch widmen wollen* (Stuttgart: Eduard Hallberger, 1857), p. 211.

50   Carl Michael Bellman, *Der schwedische Anakreon. Auswahl aus C. M. Bellman's Poesien*, translated from Swedish by A. v. Winterfeld (Berlin: A. Hofmann, 1856), pp. 170–71.

51   Richard Dehmel, *Aber die Liebe: Ein Ehemanns- und Menschenbuch* (Munich: E. Albert, 1893), pp. 218–21; Moritz Gottlieb Saphir, ed., *Conversations-Lexikon für Geist, Witz und Humor*, 2d ed., 5 vols. (Dresden: Robert Schaefer, 1859–60), 2:412.

52   *Sommerfest: Ein moderner Musen-Almanach*, 1st ser., 1 (1891): 7; *Moderner Musen-Almanach: Ein Sammelbuch deutscher Kunst* 1 (1893): 83–95; Julius Vanselow, *Sonnenregen: Gedichte von Julius Vanselow* (Grossenhain: Baumert & Ronge, 1893), p. 143; Oskar Ludwig Bernhard Wolff, ed., *Encyclopaedie der deutschen Nationalliteratur oder biographisch-kritisches Lexikon der deutschen Dichter*, 6 vols.

(Leipzig: Otto Wigand, 1834–40), 4:18–19, 6.

53 Ludovic Halévy, *Der Traum* in *Madame und Monsieur Cardinal: Zwölf Novellen*, 2d ed. (Vienna: L. Rosner, 1875); Alphonse Daudet, *Port Tarascon: Letzte Abenteuer des berühmten Tartarin*, authorized translation from French by Natalie Rümelin (Stuttgart: J. Engelhorn, 1890), pp. 45–53.

54 Eduard von Bauernfeld, *Gedichte*, 2d ed. (Leipzig: F. A. Brockhaus, 1856), pp. 322, 341; L. Mühlbach, *Erzherzog Johann und Metternich*, 3 vols. (Berlin: Otto Janke, 1860), 2:223.

55 Scherr, *Blätter im Winde*, p. 148.

CONCLUSION

1 V. I. Mezhov, comp., *Sistematicheskii katalog russkim knigam, prodaiushchimsia v knizhnom magazine Aleksandra Fedorovicha Bazunova* . . . (Saint Petersburg: Izdanie knigoprodavtsa A. F. Bazunova, 1869), pp. 108–11, 696–853.

2 Zlatkovskii, *Maikov*, 2d ed., p. 90.

3 Raeff, *Russian Intellectual History*, p. 262.

4 Egorov, *Stranitsy*, 2:305–7.

5 V. Binshtok, "Materialy po istorii russkoi tsenzury," *Russkaia starina* (April 1897): 203.

6 Berlin, *Russian Thinkers*, p. 147.

Bibliography

Three categories of material are included here: works cited in the text, works consulted in the course of the study, and some suggested readings on the general topic of censorship and on Russian culture and society.

Archival materials such as the records of the Foreign Censorship Committee, though preserved in the Soviet Union, are in practice all but inaccessible, and especially so to foreign researchers, in part perhaps because of the undesirable associations these might suggest with present-day practices. Fortunately there is every reason to believe that the really important archival materials were published by the Soviets in the 1920s and 1930s, in *Literaturnoe nasledstvo* and other publications cited in the text. These items, together with the considerable number of published works available from the tsarist period, including official catalogs and lists, constitute the primary sources on which the study is based. I have concluded that while the archives might yield some additional interesting examples, it is most unlikely that such material would change the picture in any significant way.

BIBLIOGRAPHIES, BIBLIOGRAPHIC SURVEYS,
DESCRIPTIONS OF ARCHIVES, CATALOGS,
COLLECTIONS OF LAWS, OTHER OFFICIAL DOCUMENTS

Adres-Kalendar'. Obshchaia rospis' nachal'stvuiushchikh i prochikh dolzhnostnykh lits po vsem upravleniem v Rossiiskoi imperii. Saint Petersburg: n.p., 1765–1916.

Bernov, P. I., ed. *Spravochnyi ukazatel' knig i zhurnalov, arestovannykh s 17 okt. 1905 g. po 1. ianv. 1909 g.* Moscow: Sytin, 1909.

Brodovskii, M. M. *Spravochnaia knizhka dlia pisatelei, literatorov i izdatelei.* Saint Petersburg: Izd. K. Pentkovskago, 1890.

Deiateli revoliutsionnogo dvizheniia v Rossii; Bio-bibliograficheskii slovar'. Ot predshestvennikov dekabristov do padeniia tsarizma. 5 vols. Moscow: [Vsesoiuznoe obshchestvo politicheskikh katorzhan i ssyl'no-poselentsev], 1927–34.

Dobrovol'skii, L. M. "Bibliograficheskii obzor dorevoliutsionnoi i sovetskoi literatury po istorii russkoi tsenzury." *Trudy Biblioteki Akademii Nauk SSSR i Fundamental'noi biblioteki obshchestvennykh nauk AN SSSR* 5 (1961): 245–52.

———. *Zapreshchennaia kniga v Rossii 1825–1904.* Moscow: Izd. vsesoiuznoi knizhnoi palaty, 1962.

Imperatorskaia publichnaia biblioteka. *Katalog inostrannykh pechatnykh knig, priobretennykh bibliotekoi.* Saint Petersburg: Tip. V. A. Rogal'skogo, 18–.

Istoriia SSSR; Ukazatel' sovetskoi literatury za 1917–1952 gg. 2 vols. and 2 supps. Moscow: AN SSSR, 1956–58.

Izlozhenie postanovlenii o tsenzure i pechati. Saint Petersburg: Tip. Imperatorskoi Akademii Nauk, 1865.

Karamyshev, Ivan Petrovich, ed. *Sbornik tsirkuliarov i rasporiazhenii po delam pechati, ob'iavlennykh inspektorami tipografii soderzhateliam zavedenii pechati g. S.-Peterburga s 1882 po 1897 g.* Saint Petersburg: M. M. Gutsats, 1897.

Klevenskii, M. M.; Kusheva, E. M.; and Markova, O. P. *Russkaia podpol'naia i zarubezhnaia pechat' za 1831–1877 gg.* Moscow: Izd. Politkatorzhan, 1935.

"Komitet tsenzury inostrannoi." *Spisok chinov Ministerstva vnutrennykh del 1895* (1895): 365–69.

Kozlovskii, B. I. "Nelegal'nye i zapreshchennye izdaniia XIX v. v otdele redkikh knig gosudarstvennoi biblioteki SSSR im. V. I. Lenina." *Trudy Gosudarstvennoi biblioteki imeni V. I. Lenina* 8 (1965): 10–23.

Kusheva, E. N. "Bibliografiia russkoi nelegal'noi literatury 50-80-kh godov." *Katorga i ssylka* 89 (1932): 128–35.

Mez'er, A. V. "Tsenzory." In *Slovarnyi ukazatel' po knigovedeniiu.* 3 vols. Moscow: Sotsekgiz, 1934.

Mezhov, V. I., comp. *Sistematicheskii katalog russkim knigam, prodaiushchimsia v knizhnom magazine Aleksandra Fedorovicha Bazunova . . .* Saint Petersburg: Izdanie knigoprodavtsa A. F. Bazunova, 1869.

Mseriants, Z. M., comp. *Zakony o pechati. Nastol'naia spravochnaia kniga.* 3d ed. Moscow: Tip. T. Ris, 1873.

Nikolaev, A. S., and Oksman, Iu. G., eds. *Literaturnyi muzeum: tsenzurnye materialy I-go otd. IV sektsii gosudarstvennogo arkhivnogo fonda.* Saint Petersburg: 2-ia Gos. tip., [1921].

Pereselenkov, S. A. "Zakonodatel'stvo i tsenzurnaia praktika v Rossii v 1-iu chetvert' 19-go veka." *Opisanie del arkhiva Ministerstva narodnogo prosveshcheniia* 2 (1921): xi–xxxii.

Petrova, L. N. "Obzor nelegal'nykh i zapreschchennykh izdanii, postupivshikh v gos. biblioteki SSSR im. V. I. Lenina iz kollektsii V. A. Desnitskogo." *Trudy Gosudarstvennoi biblioteki SSSR im V. I. Lenina* 9 (1956): 95–107.

Polianskaia, L. I. "Arkhivnyi fond Glavnogo upravleniia po delam pechati." *Literaturnoe nasledstvo* 22–24 (1935): 603–34.

———. "Obzor fonda Tsentral'nogo komiteta tsenzury inostrannoi." *Arkhivnoe delo,* no. 1 (1938), pp. 62–116.

Russia. Glavnoe upravlenie po delam pechati. *Alfavitnyi katalog sochineniiam na frantsuzskom, nemetskom i angliiskom iazykakh, zapreshchennym inostrannoiu tsenzuroiu ili dozvolennym k obrashcheniiu s iskliucheniem nekotorykh mest, s 1856 po 1 iiulia 1869 goda.* Saint Petersburg: Tip. Ministerstva vnutrennykh del, 1870.

———. *Katalog razsmotrennykh inostrannoiu tsenzuroiu sochinenii, zapreshchennykh i dozvo-*

lennykh s iskliucheniiami, s 1-go iiulia 1871 g. po 1-e ianvaria 1897 g. Saint Petersburg: Tip. Ministerstva vnutrennykh del, 1898.

———. *Sobstvennoruchnie otmetki Ministra vnutrennykh del na zhurnalakh Soveta Glavnogo upravleniia po delam pechati.* Saint Petersburg: n.p., 1868.

Russia. Komitet tsenzury inostrannoi. *Obshchii alfavitnyi spisok knigam na angliiskom iazyke, pozvolennym inostrannoiu tsenzuroiu* . . . Saint Petersburg: Tip. E. Pratsa, 1856.

Russia. Laws, statutes, et al. *Polnoe sobranie zakonov Rossiiskoi Imperii.* 134 vols. Saint Petersburg: Tip. vtorogo otdeleniia Sobstvennoi E. I. V. Kantseliarii, 1830–1916.

———. *Sbornik postanovlenii i rasporiazhenii po tsenzure s 1720–1862 god.* Saint Petersburg: Tip. Morskogo ministerstva, 1862.

———. *Svod zakonov Rossiiskoi Imperii.* 3d ed. 16 vols. Saint Petersburg: Tip. vtorogo otdeleniia Sobstvennoi E. I. V. Kantseliarii, 1857.

Russia. Ministerstvo narodnogo prosveshcheniia. *Obzor deiatel'nosti Ministerstva narodnogo prosveshcheniia i podvedomstvennykh emu uchrezdenii v 1862, 63 i 64 godakh.* Saint Petersburg: Tip. F. S. Sushchinskogo, 1865.

———. *Sbornik postanovlenii.* Saint Petersburg: V. S. Balashev, 1877.

———. *Sbornik rasporiazhenii po delam pechati s 1863 po 1-e sent. 1865 g.* Saint Petersburg: n.p., 1865.

Russia. Osobaia komissiia dlia peresmotra deistvuiushchikh postanovlenii o tsenzure i pechati. *Materialy, sobrannye osoboiu komissieiu, vysoch. uchrezhdennoiu 2 noiabria 1869 g* . . . 5 vols. Saint Petersburg: Tip. vtorogo otdeleniia Sobstvennoi E. I. V. Kantseliarii, 1870.

Russia. Osoboe soveshchanie dlia sostavleniia novogo ustava o pechati, Saint Petersburg, 1905. *Proekt ustava o pechati (Materialy Vysochaishe utverzhdennogo Osobogo soveshchaniia dlia sostavleniia novogo ustava o pechati).* Saint Petersburg: n.p., 1905.

———. *Protokoly Vysochaishe uchrezhdennogo Osobogo soveshchaniia dlia sostavleniia novogo ustava o pechati.* Saint Petersburg: n.p., 1905.

Russia. Tsentral'nyi komitet tsenzury inostrannoi. *Alfavitnyi spisok sochineniiam, rassmotrennykh inostrannoiu tsenzuroiu.* Saint Petersburg: n.p., 18–.

———. *Obshchii alfavitnyi spisok knigam na frantsuzskom iazyke, zapreshchennym inostrannoiu tsenzuroiu bezuslovno i dlia publiki, s 1815 po 1853 g. vkliuchitel'no* . . . Saint Petersburg: Tip. F. Pratsa, 1855.

Smirnov, N. P. *Bibliograficheskie materialy.* Saint Petersburg: Tip. A. Porokhovshchikova, 1898.

Svodnyi katalog russkoi nelegal'noi i zarubezhnoi pechati XIX veka. 9 vols. Moscow: Rotaprint Gos. biblioteki SSSR imeni V. I. Lenina, 1971.

"Tsenzura." In Muratova, K. D., ed. *Istoriia russkoi literatury xix veka. Bibliograficheskii ukazatel'.* Moscow: Izd. Akademii Nauk SSSR, 1962.

"Tsenzura." In Muratova, K. D., ed. *Istoriia russkoi literatury kontsa xix-nachala xx veka.* Moscow: Izd. Akademii Nauk SSSR, 1963.

Ul'ianinskii, Dmitrii Vasil'evich. *Biblioteka D. V. Ul'ianinskogo; bibliograficheskoe opisanie.* 3 vols. Moscow: Vol'f, 1912–1915.

Zapiska predsedatelia Komiteta dlia peresmotra tsenzurnogo ustava, deistvitel'nogo sovetnika Berte, i chlena sego komiteta statskogo sovetnika Iankevicha. [Saint Petersburg]: n.p., 1862.

Zdobnov, Nikolai Vasil'evich. *Istoriia russkoi bibliografii do nachala XX veka.* 3d ed. Moscow: Gos. izd. kul'turno-prosvetitel'noi literatury, 1955.

WORKS DEALING WITH RUSSIAN
CENSORSHIP IN GENERAL

Aksakov, I. S. "K istorii tsenzury. Vypiski iz zhurnala Moskovskogo tsenzurnogo komiteta, 10 apr. 1831." *Russkii arkhiv* I, no. 14 (1910): 44.

Aleksandrov, Mikhail Stepanovich (Ol'minskii). *O pechati*. Leningrad: "Priboi," 1926.

Arsen'ev, K. K. "Russkie zakony o pechati." *Vestnik evropy*, April 1869: 794–811; June 1869: 732–90.

———. *Zakonodatel'stvo o pechati*. Saint Petersburg: Knigoizd. P. Gershunina, 1903.

Balmuth, Daniel. "Censorship in Russia, 1848–1855." Ph.D. dissertation, Cornell University, 1959.

———. *Censorship in Russia, 1865–1905*. Washington, D.C.: University Press of America, 1979.

Berezina, V. G. "Dopolnenie k stat'e 'Iz tsenzurnoi istorii zhurnala *Moskovskii telegraf.*'" *Russkaia literatura*, no. 4 (1983): 133–36.

———. "Iz tsenzurnoi istorii zhurnala *Moskovskii telegraf.*" *Russkaia Literatura*, no. 4 (1982): 164–73.

Berkov, P. N. *Bibliograficheskoe opisanie izdanii Vol'noi russkoi tipografii v Londone 1853–1865*. Moscow: n.p., 1935.

Berlin, Isaiah. "Russia in 1848." *Slavonic and East European Review* 26 (1948): 341–60.

Binshtok, V. "Materialy po istorii russkoi tsenzury." *Russkaia starina*, March 1897: 581–97; April 1897: 179–206; May 1897: 341–55.

Bolebrukh, A. G. *Peredovaia obshchestvenno-politicheskaia mysl' 2-i poloviny XVIII veka i tsarism (na materialakh deiatel'nosti tsenzurnykh organov)*. Dnepropetrovsk: DGU, 1979.

Censorship in the Slavic World: An Exhibition in the New York Public Library, June 1–October 15, 1984. Marianna Tax Choldin, guest curator. New York: New York Public Library, 1984.

Chirskova, I. M. "Tsenzura istoricheskoi literatury v tsarskoi Rossii (1881–1904 gg.)." In *Nekotorye voprosy istochnikovedeniia istorii SSSR. Sbornik statei*, edited by N. P. Eroshkina and V. I. Durnovtseva. Moscow: [Moskovskii gosudarstvennyi istoriko-arkhivnyi institut], 1977.

Dewhirst, Martin, and Farrell, Robert. *The Soviet Censorship*. Metuchin, N.J.: Scarecrow Press, 1973.

Doctorov, Gilbert Steven. "Reforma tsarskoi tsenzury." *Kontinent* 36 (1983): 177–218.

Drizen, N. V. *Dramaticheskaia tsenzura dvukh epokh 1825–1881 gg*. Saint Petersburg: "Prometei," 1917.

[Dubrovnin, N.]. "K istorii russkoi tsenzury (1814–1820 gg.)" *Russkaia starina* (December 1900): 643–64.

Dzhanshiev, G. A. *Epokha velikikh reform* . . . 10th ed. Saint Petersburg: Vol'f, 1907.

Edwards, D. W. "Russian Ecclesiastical Censorship During the Reign of Tsar Nicholas I." *Journal of Church and State* 19 (1977): 83–93.

Engel'gardt, N. A. "Dvukhsotletie pechati." *Istoricheskii vestnik* January 1903: 174–99; February 1903: 558–77.

———. *Ocherki istorii russkoi tsenzury v sviazi s razvitiem pechati (1703–1903)*. Saint Petersburg: A. Suvorin, 1904.

———. "Ocherki nikolaevskoi tsenzury." *Istoricheskii vestnik*, September 1901: 850–73;

October 1901: 156–79; November 1901: 582–606; December 1901: 970–1000.

Entsiklopedicheskii slovar' (Brockhaus-Efron). S.v. "Tsenzura," by V. Vodovozov.

Friedberg, Maurice. *Russian Classics in Soviet Jackets.* New York: Columbia University Press, 1962.

Gradovskii, G. K. "K istorii russkoi pechati." *Russkaia starina,* February 1882: 491–510; March 1882: 672–90.

Inikova, S. A. "Tovarishchestvo I.D. Sytina i tsenzura (1883–1914 gg.)." *Problemy istorii SSSR* 12 (1982): 157–69.

Istoricheskie svedeniia o tsenzure v Rossii. Saint Petersburg: Tip. F. Persona, 1862.

"Istoricheskii ocherk russkogo zakonodatel'stva o pechati." *Istoricheskii vestnik* (January 1881): 224–28.

"Iz zapisok barona (v posledstvie grafa) M. A. Korfa." *Russkaia starina,* May 1899: 371–95; June 1899: 511–42; July 1899: 3–30; August 1899: 271–95; September 1899: 481–515; October 1899: 25–58; November 1899: 267–99; December 1899: 481–521; January 1900: 25–56; February 1900: 317–54; March 1900: 545–88; April 1900: 27–50; May 1900: 261–92; June 1900: 505–27; July 1900: 33–55.

Kniazhevich, A. M. "K istorii russkoi tsenzury." *Russkaia starina* (May 1872): 784–86.

Kotovich, A. N. *Dukhovnaia tsenzura v Rossii (1799–1855).* Saint Petersburg: "Rodnik," 1909.

[Kovalev, I.] "Gertsen i tsarskaia tsenzura (k 70-letiiu so dnia smerti)." *Krasnyi arkhiv* 98 (1940): 240–62.

Kozyrev, Nikolai. "Iz proshlogo nashei tsenzury." *Nasha starina* (July 1914): 679–86.

Lemke, M. K. *Epokha tsenzurnykh reform 1859–65 gg.* Saint Petersburg: "Gerol'd," 1904.

———. *Nikolaevskie zhandarmy i literatura 1826–1855 gg.* 2d ed. Saint Petersburg: S. V. Bunin, 1909.

———. "Ocherki po istorii tsenzury." *Russkoe bogatstvo,* January 1903: 221–48; February 1903: 109–53.

———. *Ocherki po istorii russkoi tsenzury i zhurnalistiki XIX stoletiia.* Saint Petersburg: "Trud," 1904.

Lincoln, W. Bruce. "The Last Years of the Nicholas 'System': The Unpublished Diaries and Memoirs of Baron Korf and General Tsimmerman." *Oxford Slavonic Papers* n.s. 6 (1973): 12–27.

Mazon, A. "Goncharov kak tsenzor." *Russkaia starina* (March 1896): 543–65.

"Mnenie A. S. Shishkova o tsenzure i knigopechatanii v Rossii 1826 goda." *Russkaia starina* (July 1904): 201–11.

Monas, Sidney. "Šiškov, Bulgarin, and the Russian Censorship." In *Russian Thought and Politics.* Harvard Slavic Studies, vol. 4. Cambridge: Harvard University Press, 1961.

———. *The Third Section: Police and Society in Russia under Nicholas I.* Cambridge: Harvard University Press, 1961.

Nifontov, A. S. *1848 god v Rossii.* Moscow: Gos. uchebno-pedagog. izd., 1949.

Nikitenko, Aleksandr Vasil'evich. *The Diary of a Russian Censor: Aleksandr Nikitenko.* Abridged, edited, and translated by Helen Saltz Jacobson. Amherst: University of Massachusetts Press, 1975.

———. *Dnevnik.* 3 vols. Leningrad: Gos. Izd. khudozhestvennoi literatury, 1955–56.

Notovich, Osip Konstantinovich. *Istoricheskii ocherk nashego zakonodatel'stva o pechati.* Saint Petersburg: Tip. Tsederbaum i Gol'denbliuma, 1873.

"Obshchii otchet po Ministerstvu narodnogo prosveshchenii za 1848 g." *Zhurnal Ministerstva narodnogo prosveshcheniia* (April 1849, Otdel ofitsial'nyi): 124–125.

Orzhekovskii, I. V. *Administratsiia i pechat' mezhdu dvumia revoliutsionnymi situatsiiami 1866–1878.* Gorki: Gor'kovskii gosudarstvennyi universitet imeni N. I. Lobachevskogo, 1973.

Pavlov, N. M. "Sergei Timofeevich Aksakov kak tsenzor." *Russkii arkhiv* 36, no. 5 (1898): 81–96.

Piksanov, Nikolai Kir'iakovich. *Shestidestiatye gody.* Moscow: Izd. Akademii Nauk SSSR, 1940.

Ravitz, E. F. "An Era of Censorship Terror in Russia (1825–1855)." M.A. thesis, Columbia University, 1937.

Rigberg, Benjamin. "The Tsarist Press Law, 1894–1905." *Jahrbücher für Geschichte Osteuropas* 13 (1965): 331–43.

———. "The Efficacy of Tsarist Censorship Operations, 1894–1917." *Jahrbücher für Geschichte Osteuropas* 14 (1966): 327–46.

———. "Tsarist Censorship Performance, 1894–1905." *Jahrbücher für Geschichte Osteuropas* 17 (1969): 59–76.

Rosenberg, Vladimir Aleksandrovich. *Iz istorii russkoi pechati, 1863–1918.* Prague: Plamia, 1924.

———. *Letopis' russkoi pechati, 1907–1914.* Moscow: Izd. M. i S. Sabashnikovykh, 1914.

Rosenberg, Vladimir, and Iakushkin, V. *Russkaia pechat' i tsenzura v proshlom i nastoiashchem.* Moscow: Izd. M. i S. Sabashnikovykh, 1905.

Rozhdestvenskii, S. V., comp. *Istoricheskii obzor deiatel'nosti Ministerstva narodnogo prosveshcheniia, 1802–1902.* Saint Petersburg: Izd. Ministerstva narodnogo prosveshcheniia, 1902.

Rudakov, V. E. *Poslednie dni tsenzury v Ministerstve narodnogo prosvescheniia.* Saint Petersburg: Tip. A. S. Suvorina, 1911.

Russia. Ministerstvo vnutrennykh del. *Ministerstvo vnutrennykh del: istoricheskii ocherk.* 3 vols. Saint Petersburg: Tip. Ministerstva vnutrennykh del, 1901–2.

Ruud, Charles Arthur. "The Russian Censorship, 1855–1865: A Study in the Formation of Policy." Ph.D. dissertation, University of California at Berkeley, 1965.

———. *Fighting Words: Imperial Censorship and the Russian Press, 1804–1906.* Toronto: University of Toronto Press, 1982.

Semennikov, V. P. "K istoriiu tsenzury v ekaterinskuiu epokhu." *Russkii bibliofil* (January 1913): 52–71.

Semevskii, V. I. "Materialy po istorii tsenzury v Rossii." *Golos minuvshego* March 1913: 217–29; April 1913: 207–28.

———. "Iz zapisok moskovskogo tsenzora." *Golos minuvshego,* January–March 1918, pp. 93–114.

Sidorov, A. A. "V Kieve (Vospominaniia byvshego tsenzora)." *Golos minuvshego,* April–June 1918: 221–29; July–September 1918: 133–45.

Skabichevskii, A. M. *Ocherki istorii russkoi tsenzury (1700–1863 g.).* Saint Petersburg: F. Pavlenkov, 1892.

Smirnov, S. "Tsenzurnaia vedomost' 1786–1788 godov." In *Osmnadtsatyi vek: istoricheskii sbornik,* edited by P. I. Bartenev. 4 vols. Moscow: n.p., 1868–69.

Squire, P. S. *The Third Department: The Establishment and Practices of the Political Police in the Russia of Nicholas I.* Cambridge: Cambridge University Press, 1968.

[Stasov, V. V.]. "Tsenzura v tsarstvovanie Imperatora Nikolaia I." *Russkaia starina*, July 1902: 151–67; August 1901: 395–404; September 1901: 648–68; February 1903: 305–28; March 1903: 571–91; April 1903: 163–82; May 1903: 379–96; June 1903: 643–71; July 1903: 137–57; August 1903: 405–37; September 1903: 641–66; October 1903: 165–83; December 1903: 683–98; January 1904: 207–22; February 1904: 433–43.

Sukhomlinov, M. I. *Materialy dlia istorii obrazovaniia v Rossii v tsarstvovanie Imperatora Aleksandra I.* 2 vols. Saint Petersburg: Tip. F. S. Sushchinskogo, 1865–66.

Twarog, Leon I. "Literary Censorship in Russia and the Soviet Union." In *Essays on Russian Intellectual History.* Austin: University of Texas Press, 1971.

Val'denberg, V. "Iz istorii russkoi tsenzury." *Proshloe i nastoiashchee* 1 (1924): 55–59.

Vodovozov, V. V. *Materialy dlia kharakteristiki polozheniia russkoi pechati.* Geneva: "Soiuz russkikh demokratov," 1898.

Voronich, Kliment Ivanovich. *Predstavitel' pechati v Komissii.* Saint Petersburg: Tip. S. Dobrodeev, 1880.

Yarmolinsky, A. "Censorship in Russia: A Historical Study." *Russian Review* (July 1917): 93–103.

WORKS DEALING WITH RUSSIAN IMPORTATION AND
CENSORSHIP OF FOREIGN PUBLICATIONS

General Works and Works on Particular Writers and Censors

Aizenshtok, I., and Polianskaia, L. "Frantsuzskie pisateli v otsenkakh tsarskoi tsensury." *Literaturnoe nasledstvo* 33–34 (1939): 769–858.

Avzeger, Leopol'd. "Ia vskryval Vashi pis'ma . . . Iz vospominanii byvshego tainogo tsenzora MGB." *Vremia i my*, no. 55 (1980): 224–53; no. 56 (1980): 154–78.

Bakai, M. E. "Iz vospominanii M. E. Bakaia. O chernykh kabinetakh v Rossii." *Byloe* (July 1908): 119–33.

Baryshnikov, N. P. "F. O. Tumanskii. Tsenzurnaia ego deiatel'nost' v 1800–1801 gg." *Russkaia starina* (October 1873): 589–93.

Choldin, Marianna Tax. "A Fence Around the Empire: The Censorship of Foreign Books in Nineteenth-century Russia." Ph.D. dissertation, University of Chicago, 1979.

———. "German Writers and Tsarist Censorship." *Germano-Slavica* 4 (1983): 125–34.

Clowes, Edith W. "A Philosophy 'For All and None': The Early Reception of Friedrich Nietzsche's Thought in Russian Literature, 1892–1912." Ph.D. dissertation, Yale University, 1981.

———. "Friedrich Nietzsche and Russian Censorship." *Germano-Slavica* 4 (1983): 135–42.

———. *The Revolution of Moral Consciousness: The Impact of Friedrich Nietzsche upon Russian Literature and Society, 1890–1914.* Forthcoming.

Egorov, Anatolii Evgen'evich. *Stranitsy iz prozhitogo.* 2 vols. Odessa: Tip. E. Krisogelosa, 1913.

Emmausskii, Kh. "Iz vospominanii varshavskogo tsenzora." *Novaia zhizn'*, January 1914: 124–40; February 1914: 136–51.

Fedorov, A. "Genrikh Geine v tsarskoi tsenzure." *Literaturnoe nasledstvo*, 22–24 (1935): 635–78.

Friedberg, Maurice. *A Decade of Euphoria: Western Literature in Post-Stalin Russia, 1954–64.*

Bloomington: Indiana University Press, 1977.

Grech, N. I. *Zapiski o moei zhizni.* Moscow: Academia, 1930.

Grigor'ev, V. V. *Zhizn' i trudy P.S. Savel'eva preimushchestvenno po vospominaniiam i perepiske s nim.* Saint Petersburg: Tip. Imp. Akademii Nauk, 1861.

Hapgood, Isabel. "My Experience with the Russian Censor." *The Nation* 51 (23 October 1890): 318–21.

"Iz bumag kniazia V. F. Odoevskogo." *Russkii arkhiv* 12, no. 2 (1874): 11–54.

Kantor, R. "K istorii 'chernykh kabinetov.'" *Katorga i ssylka* 37 (1927): 90–99.

"Karl Marks i tsarskaia tsenzura." *Krasnyi arkhiv* 56 (1933): 3–32.

Kerndel, A. "Studien über Heine in Russland, II. Heine und Tjutčev." *Zeitschrift für slavische Philologie* 24 (1956): 284–337.

Kharakhorkin, L. R. "Charl'z Darvin i tsarskaia tsenzura." *Trudy Instituta istorii estestvoznaniia i tekhniki* 31 (1960): 82–100.

Kotliarevskii, Nestor. "Ocherki iz istorii obshchestvennogo nastroeniia shestidesiatykh godov. Inostrannaia kniga v rukakh molodogo cheloveka 1855–1861 godov." *Vestnik evropy* (April 1914): 161–86.

Kuniskii, S. D. *Russkoe obshchestvo i Parizhskaia Kommuna; otkliki v Rossii na franko-prusskuiu voinu i Parizhskuiu Kommunu.* Moscow: n.p., 1962.

Lane, Ann M. "Nietzsche in Russia 1892–1917." Ph.D. dissertation, University of Wisconsin, 1976.

Lur'e, M. L., and Polianskaia, L. I., comps. "Kommunisticheskii manifest' i tsarskaia tsenzura." *Istorik-Marksist* 66 (1938): 106–19.

Mardar'ev, N. "Nechto iz proshlogo (Iz vospominanii byvshego tsenzora)." *Golos minuvshego* (May–June 1916): 372–91.

Oksman, Iulian. "Mery nikolaevskoi tsenzury protiv fur'erizma i kommunizma." *Golos minuvshego* (May–June 1917): 69–72.

Opochinin, E. *Pamiati kniazia Pavla Petrovicha Viazemskogo.* Saint Petersburg: n.p., 1888.

"Pis'ma K. P. Pobedonostseva k E. M. Feoktistovu." *Literaturnoe nasledstvo* 22–24 (1935): 497–560.

[Polianskaia, L. I.]. "Anatol' Frans i tsarskaia tsenzura." *Krasnyi arkhiv* 6 (1934): 147–67.

Resis, Albert. "*Das Kapital* Comes to Russia." *Slavic Review* 29 (1970): 219–37.

Ryzhov, Aleksei Ivanovich. "Aleksandr Ivanovich Krasovskii." *Russkaia starina* (January–April 1874): 107–40.

Serova, V. S. *Serovy, Aleksandr Nikolaevich i Valentin Aleksandrovich. Vospominaniia.* Saint Petersburg: Shipovnik, 1914.

Sipovskii, V. V. "Iz proshlogo russkoi tsenzury." *Russkaia starina*, April 1899: 161–75; May 1899: 435–53.

Yarmolinsky, A. "Note on the Censorship of Foreign Books in Russia under Nicholas I." *Bulletin of the New York Public Library* 38 (1934): 907–10.

The German and Russian Booktrades: Importation

Bekker, K. "Materialy dlia statistiki gazetnogo i zhurnal'nogo dela v Rossii za 1869 god." *Zhurnal Ministerstva narodnogo prosveshcheniia,* (September–October 1871): i–xlvi, 160–74.

Bondi, Gerhard. *Deutschlands Aussenhandel 1815–1870.* Schriften des Instituts für Ge-

258 Bibliography

schichte, ser. 1: Allgemeine und deutsche Geschichte, vol. 5. Berlin: Akademie-Verlag, 1958.

Goldfriedrich, Johann. *Geschichte des deutschen Buchhandels vom Beginn der Fremdherrschaft bis zur Reform des Börsenvereins im neuen deutschen Reiche (1805–1889)*. Leipzig: Börsenverein der deutschen Buchhändler, 1913.

———. *Geschichte des deutschen Buchhandels vom Beginn der klassischen Literaturperiod bis zum Beginn der Fremdherrschaft (1740–1804)*. Berlin: Börsenverein der deutschen Buchhändler, 1909.

Govorov, A. A. *Istoriia knizhnoi torgovli*. Moscow: "Kniga," 1966.

Hiller, Helmut, ed. *Der deutsche Buchhandel: Wesen, Gestalt, Aufgabe*. Gutersloh: C. Bertelsmann, 1961.

"Izvlechenie iz otcheta Ministerstva narodnogo prosveshcheniia za 1857 god." *Zhurnal Ministerstva narodnogo prosveshcheniia* (April 1858): 2–146.

Kuczynski, Jürgen. *Die deutsch-russischen Handelsbeziehungen in den letzten 150 Jahren*. Berlin: Verlag Die Wirtschaft, 1947.

Kufaev, M. N. *Istoriia russkoi knigi v XIX veke*. Leningrad: "Nachatki znanii," 1927.

Lisenkov, I. T. "Vospominaniia v proshedshem vremeni o knigoprodavtsakh i avtorakh." In *Materialy dlia istorii russkoi knizhnoi torgovli*. Saint Petersburg: Tip. I. I. Glazunova, 1879.

Lohrer, Liselotte (Bäuerle). *Cotta: Geschichte eines Verlags, 1659–1959*. [Stuttgart: n.p., 1959].

Martynov, I. F. "Peterburgskii knigotorgovets i knigoizdatel' XVIII veka Iogann Iakob Veitbrekht." In *Knigopechatanie i knizhnye sobraniia v Rossii do serediny XIX veka. Sbornik nauchnykh trudov*. Leningrad: Akademiia Nauk SSSR, 1979.

Martynova-Poniatovskaia, N. G. "Materialy k istorii frantsuzskoi knizhnoi torgovli v Moskve." *Sbornik Publichnoi biblioteki SSSR imeni V. I. Lenina* 1 (1928): 113–31; 2 (1929): 153–80.

Materialy dlia istorii russkoi knizhnoi torgovli. Saint Petersburg: Tip. I. I. Glazunova, 1879.

Meyer, F. H. "Der Aussenhandel deutscher Buchhändler im 18. Jahrhundert." *Archiv für Geschichte des deutschen Buchhandels* 14 (1891): 183–95.

———. "Die Leipziger Büchermesse von 1780 bis 1837." *Archiv für Geschichte des deutschen Buchhandels* 14 (1891): 288–316.

Müller, C. F. (Leipzig firm). *Adressbuch des deutschen Buchhandels und verwandter Berufszweige* 13 (1908): 234–37.

Muratov, M. N., ed. *Knizhnaia torgovlia*. Moscow: Gos. Izd., 1925.

Muratov, M. V. *Knizhnoe delo v Rossii XIX i XX vekakh*. Moscow: Gos. sotsial'no-ekonomicheskoe izd., 1931.

Schulze, Friedrich. *Der deutsche Buchhandel und die geistigen Strömungen der letzten hundert Jahre*. Leipzig: Börsenverein der deutschen Buchhändler, 1925.

Simoni, P. K. *Knizhnaia torgovlia v Moskve XVIII–XIX stoletii: Moskovskie knigoprodavtsy Kol'chuginy v ikh knigotorgovoi deiatel'nosti i v bytovoi obstanovke*. Leningrad: Izd. Leningradskogo obshchestva bibliofilov, 1927.

Stolpianskii, P. N. "Kniga v starom Peterburge." *Russkoe proshloe*, no. 1 (1923): 109–20; no. 4 (1923): 123–34.

———. "Materialy dlia istorii knizhnoi torgovli v Rossii." *Russkii bibliofil* (February 1911): 18–30.

Tiutchev, Maikov, and Polonskii as Censors

Tiutchev

Aksakov, Ivan S. *Biografiia Fedora Ivanovicha Tiutcheva*. Moscow: Tip. M. G. Volchaninova, 1886.

———. "Fedor Ivanovich Tiutchev. Biograficheskii ocherk." *Russkii archiv* 12, no. 2 (1874): 5–496.

Aksakova, Anna Fedorovna [Tiutcheva]. *Pri dvore dvukh imperatorov. Vospominaniia, dnevnik, 1855–1882*. Perevod E. V. Ger'e. 2 vols. Moscow: Izd. M. i S. Sabashnikovykh, 1928–29.

Briskman, M. "F. I. Tiutchev v komitete tsenzury inostrannoi." *Literaturnoe nasledstvo* 19–21 (1935): 565–78.

Briusov, V. Ia. "F. I. Tiutchev. Kritiko-biograficheskii ocherk." In *Polnoe sobranie sochinenii*, by F. I. Tiutchev. 6th ed. Saint Petersburg: A. F. Marks, 1912.

Chulkov, Georgii. *Letopis' zhizni i tvorchestva F. I. Tiutcheva*. Moscow: Academia, 1933.

———. "Tiutchev i Aksakov v bor'be s tsenzuroiu." In *Muranovskii sbornik*. Muranovo: Izd. Muzeia imeni poeta F. I. Tiutcheva, 1928.

Conant, Roger. "The Political Poetry and Ideology of Fedor Tiutchev: A Study in Compensatory Nationalism." *Slavic and Soviet Series* 2 (1977): 61–94.

Gregg, Richard A. *Fedor Tiutchev: The Evolution of a Poet*. New York: Columbia University Press, 1965.

"Iz pisem F. I. Tiutcheva vo vremia Krymskoi voiny, 1854 god." *Russkii arkhiv* 37, no. 2 (1899): 269–80.

Kazanovich, E. P., ed. *Uraniia. Tiutchevskii al'manakh 1803–1828*. Leningrad: Priboi, 1928.

Kirillov, P., Pavlova, E., and Shakhovskoi, I. "Neizdannye pis'ma Tiutcheva i k Tiutchevu." *Literaturnoe nasledstvo* 19–21 (1935): 579–602.

Koplan-Shakhmatova, S. "Pis'ma F. I. Tiutcheva k Ia. P. Polonskomu." In *Uraniia. Tiutchevskii al'manakh 1803–1828*, edited by E. P. Kazanovich. Leningrad: Priboi, 1928.

———. "Pis'mo F. I. Tiutcheva k A. N. Maikovu." In *Uraniia. Tiutchevskii al'manakh 1803–1828*, edited by E. P. Kazanovich. Leningrad: Priboi, 1928.

"Lettres de Th. J. Tjutscheff à sa seconde épouse, née baronne de Pfeffel." *Starina i novizna* 19 (1915): 104–276; 21 (1916): 155–232.

Muranovskii sbornik. Muranovo: Izd. Muzeia imeni poeta F. I. Tiutcheva, 1928.

Nikitenko, A. V. "F. I. Tiutchev." *Russkaia starina* (August 1873): unnumbered pages at end of issue.

Pigarev, K. V. "F. I. Tiutchev o frantsuzskikh politicheskikh sobytiiakh 1870–1873 gg." *Literaturnoe nasledstvo* 31–32 (1937): 753–76.

———. *Zhizn' i tvorchestvo Tiutcheva*. Moscow: Izd. Akademii Nauk, 1962.

Stremooukhoff, D. *La Poésie et l'idéologie de Tiouttchev*. Paris: Les Belles Lettres, 1937.

Tiutchev, F. I. "Lettre sur la censure en Russie." In *Polnoe sobranie sochinenii* by F. I. Tiutchev. 6th ed. Saint Petersburg: A. F. Marks, 1912.

———. *Polnoe sobranie sochinenii*. 6th ed. Saint Petersburg: A. F. Marks, 1912.

———. *Stikhotvoreniia, pis'ma*. Moscow: Gos. izd. khudozhestvennoi literatury, 1957.

Zeldin, Jesse. *Poems and Political Letters of F. I. Tyutchev*. Knoxville: University of Tennessee Press, 1973.

Maikov

Alekseev, V. A. "A. N. Maikov (Iz dnevnika)." *Istoricheskii vestnik* (February 1914): 522–29.

Ammon, N. "Obshchii obzor poeticheskoi deiatel'nosti Maikova i evoliutsiia ego idealov." In *Apollon Nikolaevich Maikov. Ego zhizn' i sochineniia*, by V. Pokrovskii. 2d ed. Moscow: Tip. G. Lissnera i D. Sobko, 1911.

Beliavskii, N. N. "Stranichka iz vospominanii o A. N. Maikove i Ia. P. Polonskom." In *Sertum bibliologicum v chest' Prezidenta Russkogo bibliologicheskogo obshchestva Prof. A. I. Maleina*. Saint Petersburg: Gos. izd., 1922.

Chumikov, A. "Moi tsenzurnye mytarstva. (Vospominaniia)." *Russkaia starina* (July–September 1899): 617–27.

Feoktistov, E. M. "Pis'mo A. N. Maikovu. 26 Apr. 1886." *Literaturnoe nasledstvo* 33–34 (1939): 857–58.

Fidler, F. F. "Literaturnye siluety. IV. A. N. Maikov." *Novoe slovo* (June 1914): 23–29.

Golenishchev-Kutuzov, A., Count. "Apollon Nikolaevich Maikov." *Zhurnal Ministerstva narodnogo prosveshcheniia* (April 1897): 46–53.

Iazykov, D. D. "Zhizn' i trudy A. N. Maikova." *Russkii vestnik*, May 1897: 122–36; July 1897: 43–55; November 1897: 291–98; December 1897: 235–55.

Pokrovskii, V. *Apollon Nikolaevich Maikov. Ego zhizn' i sochineniia*. 2d ed. Moscow: Tip. G. Lissnera i D. Sobko, 1911.

Umanets, S. "Iz vospominanii ob A. N. Maikove." *Istoricheskii vestnik* (May 1897): 460–70.

Zdobnov, N. "Novye tsenzurnye materialy o Lermontove (A. N. Maikov i I. A. Goncharov v roli tsenzorov sochinenii Lermontova)." *Krasnaia nov'* (October–November 1939): 259–69.

Zlatkovskii, Mikhail Leont'evich. *Apollon Nikolaevich Maikov. Biograficheskii ocherk*. Saint Petersburg: Tip. P. P. Soikina, 1888.

———. *Apollon Nikolaevich Maikov. Biograficheskii ocherk*. Saint Petersburg: A. F. Marks, 1898.

Polonskii

"Ia. P. Polonskii v Baden-Baden 1857 g." *Golos minuvshego* (January–April 1919): 119–30.

"Iakov Petrovich Polonskii (Nekrolog)." *Istoricheskii vestnik* (November 1898): 722–33.

Iasinskii, Ieronim Ieronimovich. *Roman moei zhizni*. Moscow: Gos. izd., 1926.

"Iz dnevnika Ia. P. Polonskogo." *Golos minuvshego* (January–April 1919): 101–19.

Stackenschneider, Elena Andreevna. *Dnevnik i zapiski (1854–1886)*. Moscow: Academia, 1934.

SELECTED WORKS ON CENSORSHIP IN
GENERAL AND IN SPECIFIC COUNTRIES

Bachman, Albert. *Censorship in France from 1715 to 1750: Voltaire's Opposition*. New York: Publications of the Institute of French Studies, 1934.

Barrier, Norman Gerald. *Banned: Controversial Literature and Political Control in British India 1907–1947*. Columbia: University of Missouri Press, 1974.

Bodi, Leslie. *Tauwetter in Wien: Zur Prosa der österreichischen Aufklärung 1781–1795*. Frankfurt am Main: S. Fischer Verlag, 1977.

Busch, Rüdiger. *Die Aufsicht über das Bücher-und Pressewesen in den Rheinbundstaaten Berg, Westfalen und Frankfurt.* Studien und Quellen zur Geschichte des deutschen Verfassungsrechts, ser. A: Studien, vol. 7. Karlsruhe: C. F. Müller, 1970.

Censorship: 500 Years of Conflict. Published for the Exhibition, "Censorship: 500 Years of Conflict," New York Public Library, June 1–October 15, 1984. New York: Oxford University Press, 1984.

Craig, Alec. *Suppressed Books: A History of the Conception of Literary Obscenity.* Cleveland and New York: World Publishing Co., 1963.

Dowden, W. S. "Byron and the Austrian Censorship." *Keats-Shelley Journal* (Winter 1955): 67–75.

Emerson, Donald E. *Metternich and the Political Police: Security and Subversion in the Hapsburg Monarchy (1815–1930).* The Hague: Martinus Nijhoff, 1968.

Finley, M. I. "Censorship in Classical Antiquity." *Times Literary Supplement,* 29 July 1977, 923–25.

Fisher, John Robert. *The Law of the Press: A Digest of the Law Affecting Newspapers in England, India, and the Colonies.* 2d ed. London: n.p., 1898.

Haight, Anne Lyon. *Banned Books: Informal Notes on Some Books Banned for Various Reasons at Various Times and in Various Places.* 3d ed. New York: R. R. Bowker Co., 1970.

Herrman-Mascard, Nicole. *La censure des livres a Paris à la fin de l'ancien régime (1750–1789).* Travaux et recherches de la faculté de droit et des sciences economiques de Paris, ser. "Sciences historiques," no. 13. Paris: Presses Universitaires de France, 1968.

Houben, H. H. *Der gefesselte Biedermeier.* Leipzig: H. Haessel, 1924.

———. *Hier Zensur—Wer dort? Antworten von gestern auf Fragen von heute.* Leipzig: Brockhaus, 1918.

———. *Der Polizeiwidrige Goethe.* Berlin: G. Grote, 1932.

———. *Verbotene Literatur von der klassischen Zeit bis zur Gegenwart.* 2d ed. 2 vols. Dessau: Karl Rauch Verlag, 1925; Bremen: Karl Schünemann Verlag, 1928.

Klawitter, Willy. *Geschichte der Zensur in Schlesien* Deutschkundliche Arbeiten, B. Schlesische series, vol. 2. Breslau: Maruschke und Berendt, 1934.

Klingenstein, Grete. *Staatsverwaltung und kirchliche Autorität im 18. Jahrhundert: Das Problem der theresianischen Reform.* Vienna: Verlag für Geschichte und Politik: 1970.

Kramer, Margarete. *Die Zensur in Hamburg 1819 bis 1848: Ein Beitrag zur Frage staatlicher Lenkung der Öffentlichkeit während des deutschen Vormärz.* Hamburger Historische Studien, no. 5. Hamburg: Helmut Buske Verlag, 1975.

Lin, Yutang. *A History of the Press and Public Opinion in China.* Chicago: University of Chicago Press, 1936.

Ma, Tai-loi. "Censorship of Fiction in Ming and Ch'ing China, ca. 1368–ca. 1900." M.A. thesis, University of Chicago, 1972.

McCormick, John, and MacInnes, Mairi, eds. *Versions of Censorship.* Garden City, N.Y.: Anchor Books, 1962.

McCoy, Ralph E. *Freedom of the Press: An Annotated Bibliography.* Carbondale: Southern Illinois University Press, 1968.

———. *Freedom of the Press: A Bibliocyclopedia.* Ten-year Supplement (1967–77). Carbondale: Southern Illinois University Press, 1979.

MacPherson, Harriet Dorothea. *Censorship Under Louis XIV 1661–1715: Some Aspects of its Influence.* New York: Publications of the Institute of French Studies, 1929.

Marx, Julius. "Die amtlichen Verbotslisten." *Mitteilungen des österreichischen Staatsarchives* 9 (1956): 150–85; 11 (1958): 412–66.

————. "Dolliners Manuskript: Ein Beitrag zur Geschichte der Zensur im Vormärz." *Jahrbuch des Vereines für Geschichte der Stadt Wien* 7 (1948): 42–51.

————. "Metternich als Zensur." *Jahrbuch des Vereines für Geschichte der Stadt Wien* 11 (1954): 112–35.

————. *Die österreichische Zensur im Vormärz.* Munich: Oldenbourg, 1959.

————. *Österreichs Kampf gegen die liberalen, radikalen und kommunistischen Schriften, 1835–1848. Archiv für Österreichische Geschichte,* vol. 128, no. 1. Vienna: Böhlau, 1969.

————. "Schiller und Österreich." *Wiener Geschichtsblätter,* no. 4 (1955), pp. 77–81.

————. "Vormärzliche österreichische Zensur." *Wiener Geschichtsblätter,* no. 4 (1954): 77–83; no. 1 (1956): 20.

————. "Die Zensur der Kanzlei Metternichs." *Österreichische Zeitschrift für öffentliches Recht,* no. 2 (1951): 170–237.

Matrosov, E. N. "Istoriia i sovremennoe sostoianie literaturnoi tsenzury v S. Shtatakh Severnoi Ameriki (Sotsiologicheskii ocherk)." *Istoricheskii vestnik,* August 1908: 650–74; September 1908: 1024–66.

Moreno, Roberto. *Un Caso de Censura de Libros en el Siglo XVIII Novohispano: Jorge Mas Theóphoro.* Supplementos al Boletin del Instituto de Investigaciones Bibliograficas, 4. Mexico: Universidad Nacional Autónoma de México, 1978.

Novombergskii, N. *Osvobozhdenie pechati vo Frantsii, Germanii, Anglii i Rossii: Lektsii, chitannye v Russkoi vysshei shkole obshchestvennykh nauk v Parizhe.* Saint Petersburg: Tipo-lit. F. Vaisberga i P. Gershunina, 1906.

O'Higgins, Paul. *Censorship in Britain.* London: Nelson, 1972.

Otto, Ulla. *Die literarische Zensur als Problem der Soziologie der Politik.* Bonner Beiträge zur Soziologie; Institut für Soziologie der Universität Bonn, no. 3. Stuttgart: Enke, 1968.

Popper, William. *The Censorship of Hebrew Books.* New York: Knickerbocker Press, 1899.

Prussia. Laws, Statutes, et al. 1861–88 (William I). *Gesetz über die Presse vom 7. Mai 1874* . . . Berlin: Hempel, 1874.

Radlik, Ute. "Heine in der Zensur der Restaurationsepoche." In *Zur Literatur der Restaurationsepoche 1815–1848; Forschungsreferate und Aufsätze,* edited by Jost Hermand and Manfred Windfuhr. Stuttgart: J. B. Metzler, 1970.

Reisner, Hanns-Peter. *Literatur unter der Zensur: die politische Lyrik des Vormärz.* Stuttgart: Ernst Klett, 1975.

Rose, Margaret A. *Reading the Young Marx and Engels: Poetry, Parody, and the Censor.* London: Croom Helm; Totowa, N.J.: Rowman and Littlefield, 1978.

Ruud, Charles A. "Limits on the 'Freed' Press of 18th- and 19th-Century Europe." *Journalism Quarterly* 56, no. 3 (1979): 521–30, 693.

Sashegyi, Oskar. *Zensur und Geistesfreiheit unter Joseph II: Beitrag zur Kulturgeschichte der Habsburgischen Länder.* Studia Historica Academiae Scientiarum Hungaricae, vol. 16. Budapest: Akademiai Kiado, 1958.

Sierra Corella, Antonio. *La Censura de Libros y Papeles en España y los Indices y Catalogos españoles de los prohibidos y expurgados.* Madrid: Cuerpo Facultativo de Archiveros, Bibliotecarios y Arqueologos, 1947.

Strothmann, Dietrich. *Nationalsozialistische Literaturpolitik.* 2d ed. Abhandlungen zur Kunst-, Musik- und Literaturwissenschaft, vol. 13. Bonn: Bouvier, 1960.

Thilo, Gustav, ed. *Das preussische Gesetz über die Presse vom 12. Mai 1851* . . . Berlin: Verlag von Carl Heymann, 1862.

Thomas, Donald. *A Long Time Burning: The History of Literary Censorship in England.* New York: Praeger, 1969.

Welschinger, Henri. *La Censure sous le Premier Empire.* Paris: Charavay frères, 1882.

Wiesner, Adolf Carl. *Denkwürdigkeiten der österreichischen Zensur vom Zeitalter der Reformazion bis auf die Gegenwart.* Stuttgart: A. Krabbe, 1847.

Wyatt, Sibyl White. *The English Romantic Novel and Austrian Reaction.* New York: Exposition Press, 1967.

OTHER WORKS CONSULTED

Annenkov, P. V. *Literaturnye vospominaniia.* Leningrad: "Academia," 1928.

Arbatov, G. A. *The War of Ideas in Contemporary International Relations.* Moscow: Progress Publishers, 1973.

Bank, B. V. *Izuchenie chitatelei v Rossii (XIX v.).* Moscow: Izd. "Kniga," 1969.

Barnouw, Erik. *The Sponsor: Notes on a Modern Potentate.* New York: Oxford University Press, 1978.

Beaumarchais, Pierre Augustin Caron de. *Le Mariage de Figaro.* Paris: A. Quantin, 1884.

Billington, James H. *The Icon and the Axe: An Interpretive History of Russian Culture.* New York: Vintage Books, 1970.

Berlin, Isaiah. *Russian Thinkers.* Edited by Henry Hardy and Aileen Kelly. New York: Viking, 1978.

Brooks, Jeffrey. "Popular Literature and its Enemies in Imperial Russia." Paper presented at the Tenth Annual Convention of the American Association for the Advancement of Slavic Studies, Columbus, Ohio, 13 October 1978.

————. "Readers and Reading at the End of the Tsarist Era." In *Literature and Society in Imperial Russia, 1800–1914.* Stanford: Stanford University Press, 1978.

————. "The Response of Educated Russians to Mass Literacy: Literature for the Common People." Paper presented at the History of Education Workshop, University of Chicago, 1 June 1979.

Chyzhev'kyi, Dmytro. *Russian Intellectual History.* Translated by John C. Osborne, edited by Martin P. Rice. Ann Arbor, Mich.: Ardis, 1978.

Dubnow, S. M. *History of the Jews in Russia and Poland from the Earliest Times Until the Present Day.* Translated from the Russian by I. Friedlaender. 3 vols. Philadelphia: Jewish Publication Society of America, 1916–20.

Eidel'man, N. Ia. *Gertsen protiv samoderzhaviia: Sekretnaia politicheskaia istoriia Rossii XVIII– XIX vekov i Vol'naia pechat'.* Moscow: Mysl', 1973.

Florinsky, Michael T. *Russia: A History and an Interpretation.* 2 vols. New York: Macmillan, 1953.

Fon-Tal, A. "Iz vospominanii Evgeniia Ivanovicha Lamanskago. (1840–1890 gg.)" *Russkaia starina* (January 1915): 73–87.

Heine, Heinrich. *Sämtliche Werke.* Munich: Winkler-Verlag, 1969. 2 vols.

Kropotkin, Peter. *Memoirs of a Revolutionist.* Edited by James Allen Rogers. New York: Anchor Books, 1962.

Laplanche, J., and Portalis, J.-B. *The Language of Psychoanalysis.* London: Hogarth Press, 1973.

Leikina-Svirskaia, V. R. *Intelligentsiia v Rossii vo vtoroi polovine XIX veka*. Moscow: Mysl', 1971.

Lincoln, W. Bruce. *Nicholas I*. Bloomington: Indiana University Press, 1978.

————. "A Profile of the Russian Bureaucracy on the Eve of the Great Reforms." *Jahrbücher für Geschichte Osteuropas* 27 (1979): 181–96.

————. "Some Comments on the Cost of Living in Mid-Nineteenth Century St. Petersburg." Typewritten.

Martini, Fritz. *Deutsche Literaturgeschichte von den Anfangen bis zur Gegenwart*. 6th ed. Stuttgart: Alfred Kroner Verlag, 1955.

Mirsky, D. S. *A History of Russian Literature from the Beginnings to 1900*. Edited by Frances J. Whitfield. New York: Vintage, 1958.

Mosse, Werner Eugen. *The European Powers and the German Question 1848–1871, with Special Reference to England and Russia*. Cambridge: Cambridge University Press, 1956.

Oliva, L. Jay. *Russia and the West from Peter to Krushchev*. Boston: D. D. Heath, 1965.

Pipes, Richard. *Russia under The Old Regime*. London: Weidenfeld and Nicholson, 1974.

Raeff, Marc. *Russian Intellectual History: An Anthology*. New York: Harcourt, Brace and World, 1966.

Reimers, H. *St. Petersburg am Ende seines ersten Jahrhunderts*. 2 vols. Saint Petersburg: F. Dienemann, 1805.

Riasanovsky, Nicholas V. *A History of Russia*. New York: Oxford University Press, 1963.

Rogger, Hans. *National Consciousness in Eighteenth-Century Russia*. Cambridge: Harvard University Press, 1969.

Shlepov, L. E. *Otmennye istoriei chiny, zvaniia, i tituly v rossiiskoi imperii*. Leningrad: Nauka, 1977.

Venturi, Franco. *Roots of Revolution: A History of the Populist and Socialist Movements in Nineteenth Century Russia*. Translated from the Italian by Francis Haskell. New York: Alfred A. Knopf, 1960.

Vucinich, Alexander S. *Science in Russian Culture*. 2 vols. Stanford: Stanford University Press, 1963–70.

————. *Social Thought in Tsarist Russia: The Quest for a General Science of Society, 1861–1917*. Chicago: University of Chicago Press, 1976.

Zaionchkovskii, P. A. *Rossiiskoe samoderzhavie v kontse XIX stoletiia*. Moscow: Mysl', 1970.

Zetlin, Mikhail. *The Decembrists*. Translated by George Panin. New York: International Universities Press, 1958.

WORKS ON RUSSIAN CULTURE AND SOCIETY

Ambler, Effie. *Russian Journalism and Politics, 1861–1881: The Career of A. S. Suvorin*. Detroit: Wayne State University Press, 1972.

Black, Cyril E., ed. *The Transformation of Russian Society: Aspects of Social Change Since 1861*. Cambridge: Harvard University Press, 1960.

Blackwell, William L. *The Beginnings of Russian Industrialization, 1800–1860*. Princeton: Princeton University Press, 1968.

Bonnell, Victoria E., ed. *The Russian Worker: Life and Labor under the Tsarist Regime*. Berkeley: University of California Press, 1983.

Brower, Daniel R. *Training the Nihilist: Education and Radicalism in Tsarist Russia*.

Ithaca: Cornell University Press, 1975.

Byrnes, Robert Francis. *Pobedonostsev: His Life and Thought*. Bloomington: Indiana University Press, 1968.

Carr, Edward Hallett. *Mikhail Bakunin*. New York: Vintage Books, 1961.

The Memoirs of Catherine the Great. Edited by Dominique Maroger, with an introduction by G. P. Gooch; translated from the French by Moura Budberg. New York: Colliers, 1961.

Curtiss, John Shelton. *The Russian Army under Nicholas I, 1825–1855*. Durham: Duke University Press, 1965.

Edelman, Robert. *Gentry Politics on the Eve of the Russian Revolution: The Nationalist Party, 1907–1917*. New Brunswick: Rutgers University Press, 1980.

Emmons, Terence. *The Emancipation of the Russian Serfs*. New York: Holt, Rinehart and Winston, 1970.

Freeze, Gregory L. *The Parish Clergy in Nineteenth-Century Russia*. Princeton: Princeton University Press, 1983.

Frieden, Nancy Mandelker. *Russian Physicians in an Era of Reform and Revolution, 1856–1905*. Princeton: Princeton University Press, 1981.

Garrard, John Gordon, ed. *The Eighteenth Century in Russia*. Oxford: Clarendon Press, 1973.

Gerschenkron, Alexander. *Economic Backwardness in Historical Perspective*. Cambridge: Belknap Press of Harvard University, 1962.

Gleason, Abbott. *Young Russia: The Genesis of Russian Radicalism in the 1860s*. New York: Viking Press, 1980.

Glickman, Rose. *Russian Factory Women: Workplace and Society 1880–1914*. Berkeley: University of California Press, 1984.

Hamm, Michael, ed. *The City in Russian History*. Lexington: University Press of Kentucky, 1976.

Hare, Richard. *Pioneers of Russian Social Thought: Studies of Non-Marxian Formation in Nineteenth-Century Russia and of its Partial Revival in the Soviet Union*. London, New York: Oxford University Press, 1951.

Johnson, Robert Eugene. *Peasant and Proletarian: The Working Class of Moscow in the Late Nineteenth Century*. New Brunswick: Rutgers University Press, 1979.

Kohn, Hans, ed. *Pan-Slavism: Its History and Ideology*. New York: Vintage Press, 1960.

Kucherov, Samuel. *Courts, Lawyers and Trials under the Last Three Tsars*. Praeger Publications in Russian History and World Communism, no. 7. New York: Praeger, 1953.

Lincoln, W. Bruce. *In War's Dark Shadow: The Russians Before the Great War*. New York: Dial Press, 1983.

———. *The Romanovs, Autocrats of All the Russias*. New York: Dial Press, 1981.

Madariaga, Isabel de. *Russia in the Age of Catherine the Great*. New Haven: Yale University Press, 1981.

Malia, Martin. *Alexander Herzen and the Birth of Russian Socialism, 1812–1855*. Russian Research Studies, no. 39. Cambridge: Harvard University Press, 1961.

Manning, Roberta Thompson. *The Crisis of the Old Order in Russia: Gentry and Government*. Princeton: Princeton University Press, 1982.

McConnell, Allen. *A Russian Philosophe: Alexander Radishchev*. The Hague: M. Nijhoff, 1964.

Mosse, Werner Eugen. *Alexander II and the Modernization of Russia*. New York: Macmillan, 1958.

Orlovsky, Daniel T. *The Limits of Reform: The Ministry of Internal Affairs in Imperial Russia, 1802–1881*. Russian Research Center Studies, no. 81. Cambridge: Harvard University Press, 1981.

Papmehl, K. A. *Freedom of Expression in Eighteenth Century Russia*. The Hague: Nijhoff, 1971.

Pintner, Walter McKenzie, and Rowney, Don Karl, eds. *Russian Officialdom: The Bureaucratization of Russian Society from the Seventeenth to the Twentieth Century*. Chapel Hill: University of North Carolina Press, 1980.

Pipes, Richard R., ed. *The Russian Intelligentsia*. New York: Columbia University Press, 1961.

Pomper, Philip. *The Russian Revolutionary Intelligentsia*. New York: Crowell, 1970.

Radishchev, Aleksander Nikolaevich. *A Journey from St. Petersburg to Moscow*. Edited by R. Thaler. Translated by Leo Wiener. Cambridge: Harvard University Press, 1958.

Raeff, Marc. *Origins of the Russian Intelligentsia: The Eighteenth Century Nobility*. New York: Harcourt Brace Jovanovich, 1966.

Raeff, Marc, ed. *The Decembrist Movement*. Englewood Cliffs, N.J.: Prentice-Hall, 1966.

Ransel, David L. *The Politics of Catherinian Russia: The Panin Party*. New Haven: Yale University Press, 1975.

Ransel, David L., ed. *The Family in Imperial Russia—New Lines of Historical Research*. Urbana: University of Illinois Press, 1978.

Robinson, Geroid Tanquary. *Rural Russia Under the Old Regime: A History of the Landlord-Peasant World and a Prologue to the Peasant Revolution of 1917*. Reprint of 1932 ed. New York: Macmillan, 1967.

Schapiro, Leonard Bertram. *Rationalism and Nationalism in Russian Nineteenth-Century Political Thought*. Yale Russian and East European Studies, vol. 4. New Haven: Yale University Press, 1967.

Troyat, Henri. *Daily Life in Russia Under the Last Tsar*. Translated by Malcolm Barnes. Stanford: Stanford University Press, 1962.

Valkenier, Elizabeth K. *Russian Realist Art: The State and Society: The Peredvizhniki and Their Tradition*. Ann Arbor, Mich.: Ardis, 1977.

Weissman, Neil B. *Reform in Tsarist Russia: The State Bureaucracy and Local Government, 1900–1914*. New Brunswick: Rutgers University Press, 1981.

Whelan, Heide W. *Alexander III and the State Council—Bureaucracy and Counter-Reform in Late Imperial Russia*. New Brunswick: Rutgers University Press, 1981.

Wortman, Richard S. *The Crisis of Russian Populism*. London: Cambridge University Press, 1967.

———. *The Development of a Russian Legal Consciousness*. Chicago: University of Chicago Press, 1976.

Yaney, George L. *The Systematization of Russian Government*. Urbana: University of Illinois Press, 1973.

Index

Note: It is difficult, if not impossible, to be certain of the identities of some of the Western authors named in various sources used for this book. The author apologizes for any errors that may have been made.

Marianna Tax Choldin is Assistant
Director of General Services and
Head of the Slavic and East
European Library, and Research
Director of the Russian and East
European Center, at the University
of Illinois at Urbana-Champaign.